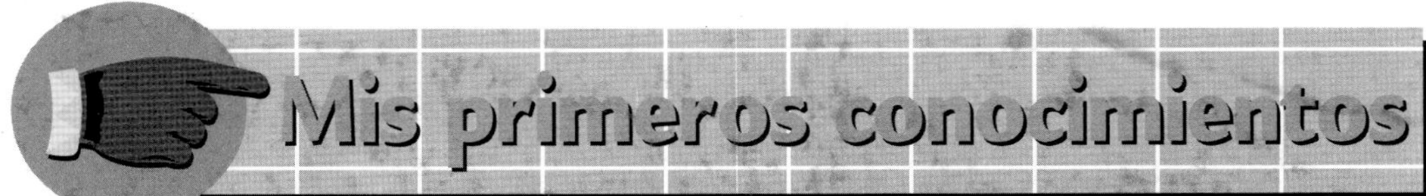

ATLAS

MEL PICKERING

PRINCETON ■ LONDON

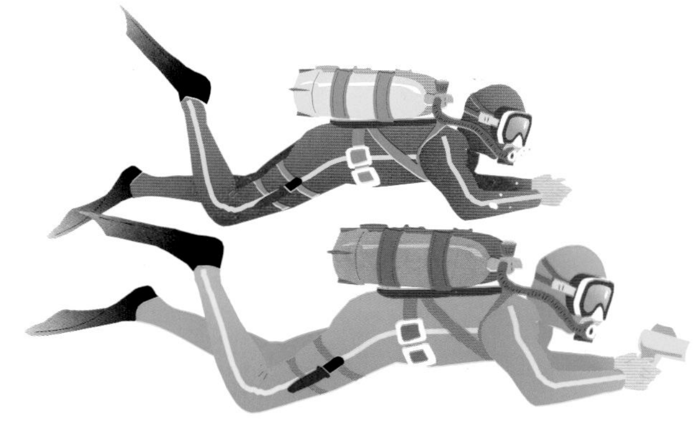

Texto Andrew Solway
Asesor Steve Watts
Ilustraciones Mel Pickering, Jacqueline Land
Editores Deborah Kespert, Kate Asser
Apoyo editorial Claire Llewellyn, Julia Hillyard, Claire Yude
Dirección artística Belinda Webster
Diseño Helen Holmes

Published in the United States and Canada by
Two-Can Publishing LLC
234 Nassau Street
Princeton, NJ 08542

Para más información sobre libros y multimedia de Two-Can,
tel 1-609-921-6700, fax 1-609-921-3349, o ver nuestro Web site
http://www.two-canpublishing.com

ISBN: 1-58728-656-4
LC: 96-60464

Impreso en España

1 2 3 4 5 6 7 8 9 10 02 01 00

Contenido

¿Qué es un atlas?

Un atlas es un libro de mapas que te enseña diferentes partes del mundo. Los mapas son dibujos de grandes lugares hechos a escala. Te muestran lugares tan pequeños como un pueblo o tan grandes como el mundo. Puedes utilizar los atlas y mapas de muchas maneras. Te enseñan cómo orientarte y te dicen cómo es un lugar.

1 Uno de los mapas más difíciles de dibujar es el del mundo. Esto se debe a que el mundo es redondo como una gran pelota, pero los mapas son planos. Imagina que pintas el mundo sobre la cáscara de una naranja.

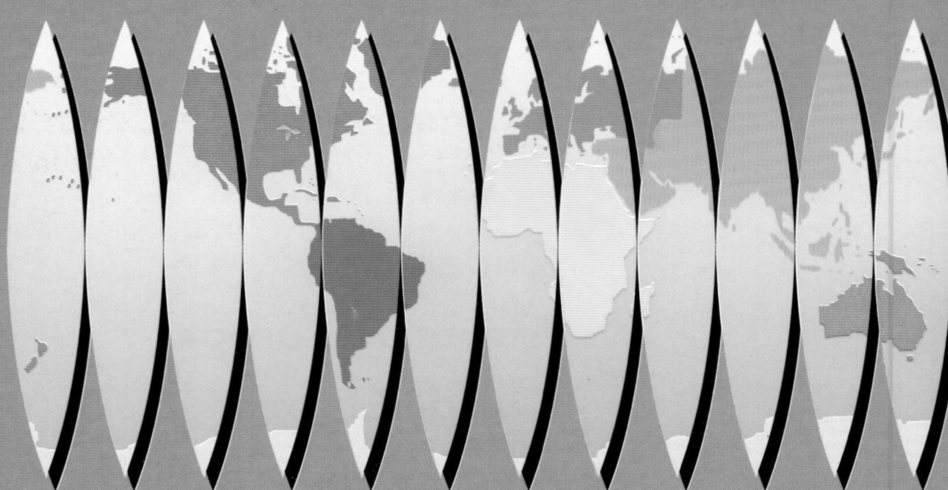

2 Podrías pelar con cuidado la cáscara en segmentos

3 Después podrías extenderla sobre algo plano para hacer un mapa del mundo.

OCÉANO ÁRTICO
Círculo Polar Ártico
EUROPA
ASIA
NORTEAMÉRICA
OCÉANO PACÍFICO
OCÉANO ATLÁNTICO
ÁFRICA
Ecuador
OCÉANO ÍNDICO
SUDAMÉRICA
AUSTRALIA
Círculo Polar Antártico
ANTÁRTIDA

4 Los cartógrafos rellenan los huecos extendiendo algunas partes del mapa y comprimiendo otras. En este mapa puedes observar que más de la mitad de la Tierra está cubierta por cuatro grandes océanos. El resto se divide en siete grandes zonas de superficie terrestre llamadas continentes. Hay además tres líneas imaginarias en el mapa. El Ecuador rodea a la Tierra por la mitad, el Círculo Polar Ártico –en la parte superior– y el Antártico –en la inferior.

Diferentes tipos de mapas muestran distintos detalles, pero en todos aparecen los lugares más pequeños de lo que realmente son.

1 Este es un dibujo de una casa en la esquina de la Calle del Parque, la cual pertenece a un pueblo costero. Se puede ver la esquina que rodea la casa, el árbol y un poco de la calle, pero no se puede ver el pueblo entero, ya que el dibujo no es suficientemente grande para mostrar todos los detalles.

2 En este mapa aparece la Calle del Parque como si hubiera sido dibujada desde arriba. Muestra menos detalles que el dibujo anterior, pero vemos un área mayor. ¿Puedes encontrar la casa de la esquina? En este mapa la Calle del Parque mide 10 cm pero en realidad tiene 1 km de largo. Esto significa que 10 cm en el mapa equivalen a 1 km real. A esto se le llama escala.

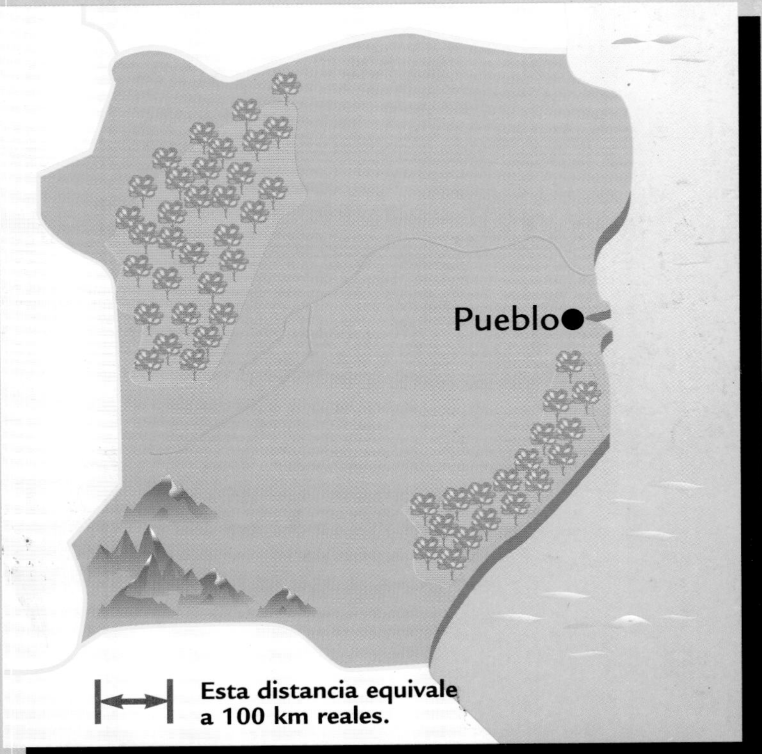

3 En este mapa se ve un área mayor que en el mapa anterior, ya que está hecho a escala más pequeña. Nos muestra el pueblo entero. No se pueden ver las casas ni todas las calles, pero sí se ve la Calle del Parque. En este mapa la Calle del Parque mide 5 cm. Esto significa que 5 cm en el mapa equivalen a 1 km.

4 En este mapa se ve el país donde se halla el pueblo. Ahora el pueblo es sólo un punto negro. La barra de la escala nos dice que 1 cm en el mapa equivale a 100 km reales. En este atlas cada mapa tiene una escala diferente. En las páginas 10 y 11 se pueden ver todos los países del mundo a la misma escala.

Calor y frío

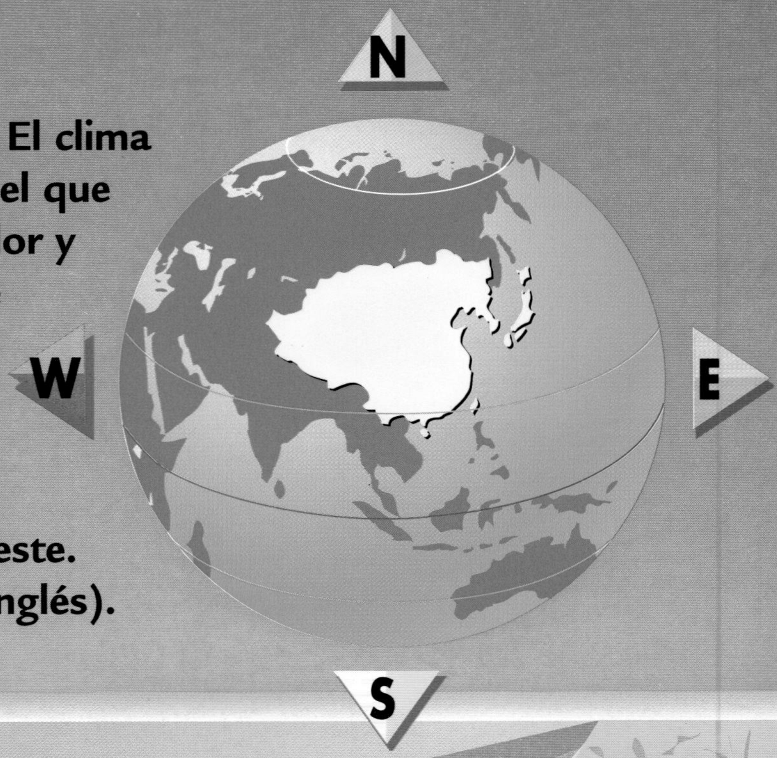

En el mundo hay diferentes tipos de climas. El clima de un país depende del lugar del mundo en el que se halle. Cerca del Ecuador hace siempre calor y cerca de los Polos Norte y Sur hace siempre frío. En todos los mapas de este atlas encontrarás un dibujo localizador que te dice dónde se sitúan los países y continentes en el mundo. El dibujo tiene 4 flechas que te indican el norte, sur, este y oeste. El oeste se representa con una W (*west* en inglés).

N
W
E
S

El Sol calienta toda la Tierra, pero brilla más intensamente en unos países que en otros. Estos países tienen un clima más cálido. El clima también varía según la estación del año: primavera, verano, otoño o invierno.

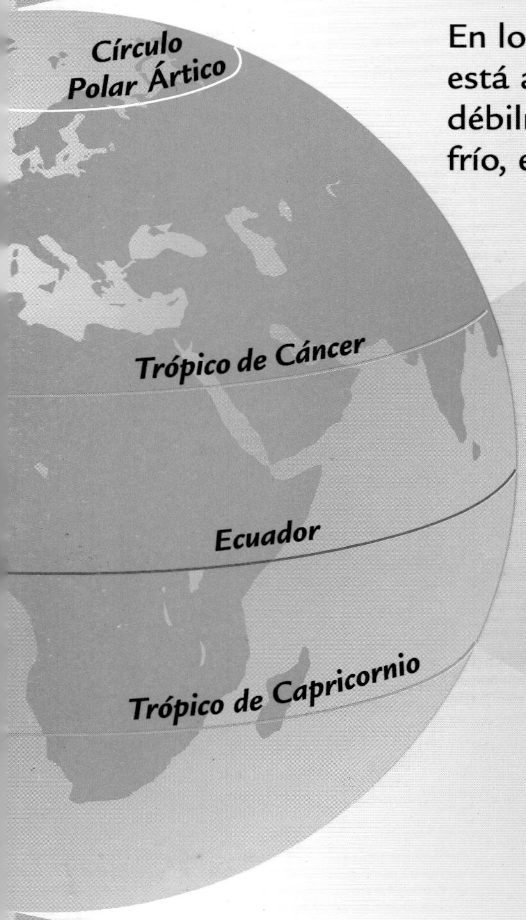

Círculo Polar Ártico
Trópico de Cáncer
Ecuador
Trópico de Capricornio

En los Polos Norte y Sur el Sol nunca está alto en el cielo y brilla débilmente, por eso siempre hace frío, especialmente en invierno.

Cerca del Ecuador el Sol brilla con más intensidad y directamente desde arriba. Aquí el clima es más cálido, con estaciones lluviosas y secas.

Por encima y por debajo del Ecuador hay dos líneas imaginarias llamadas Trópico de Cáncer y Trópico de Capricornio. Los países situados entre esas líneas y los Polos tienen veranos templados e inviernos fríos.

A cada clima se adapta un particular tipo de plantas, animales y personas. Si un lugar tiene un clima lluvioso, crecen muchas plantas, pero si el lugar tiene un clima seco sólo crecen algunas plantas.

En el mapa inferior y en los mapas de este atlas se representan los diferentes tipos de vegetación con pequeños dibujos llamados símbolos y con colores. Estas fotos te enseñan cómo son estos tipos de vegetación.

Normalmente los Polos están congelados. En verano sólo unas cuantas plantas crecen en el Ártico.

Los bosques de hoja caduca crecen en áreas frías. Los árboles pierden sus hojas en otoño.

Los bosques de hoja perenne están verdes todo el año. Estos bosques crecen en lugares fríos.

Las praderas incluyen la sabana tropical (ver foto), tierras de cultivo y extensas llanuras llamadas pampas.

Únicamente los animales y las plantas más resistentes pueden sobrevivir en los desiertos.

Las frondosas y verdes selvas tropicales se encuentran donde el clima es cálido y húmedo todo el año.

En las montañas rocosas crecen pocas plantas, ya que suelen estar cubiertas de nieve.

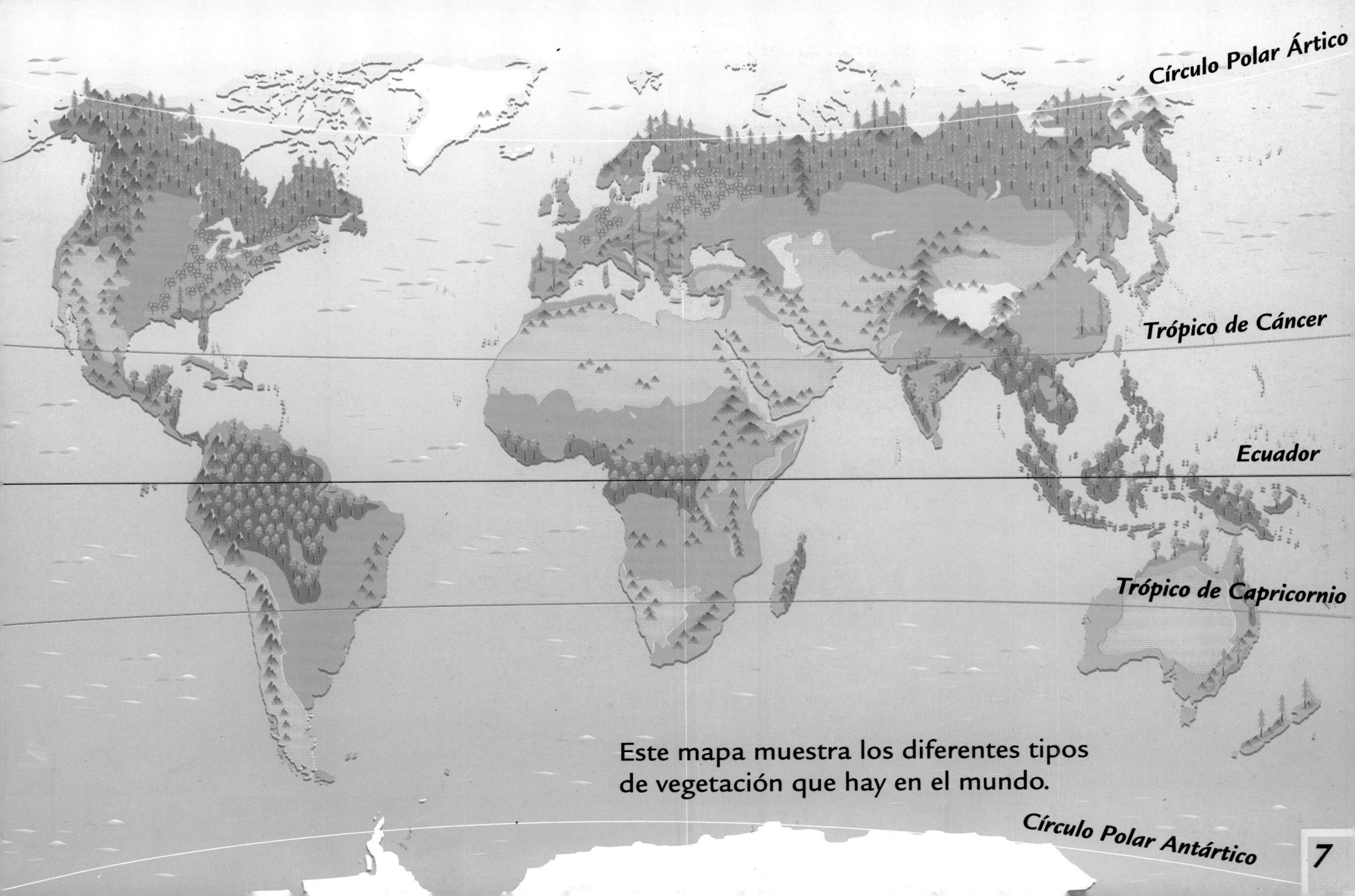

Círculo Polar Ártico

Trópico de Cáncer

Ecuador

Trópico de Capricornio

Este mapa muestra los diferentes tipos de vegetación que hay en el mundo.

Círculo Polar Antártico

Acerca de este atlas

Los mapas de este atlas te dicen muchas cosas sobre los lugares que aparecen en él. Mira atentamente los dibujos para averiguar más cosas.

Las capitales de cada país están indicadas con la bandera del país y una estrella.

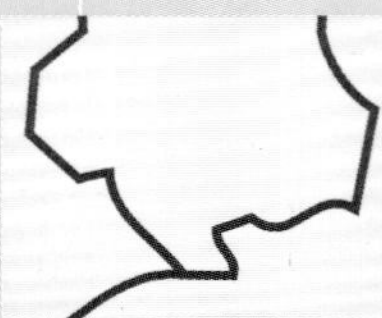

La frontera del país está marcada con una línea gris. Cuando los países están en conflicto por sus fronteras o no están seguros de cuál es, esta línea es de puntos.

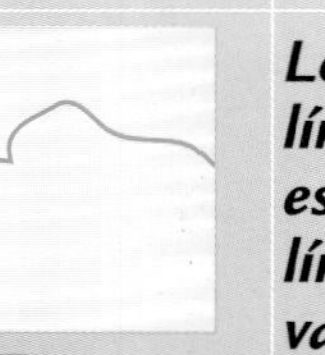

Los ríos están marcados con líneas azules. El nombre está escrito a lo largo de estas líneas. Un río puede atravesar varios países.

Hay diferentes tipos de cultivos en todo el mundo. Busca en los mapas trigo, maíz, arroz, frutas, hortalizas, café, té y caña de azúcar.

En los mapas también aparecen edificios, como monumentos famosos, ruinas de edificaciones antiguas o tipos de viviendas.

Este dibujo indica el lugar, en la tierra o en el mar, donde se perfora para sacar petróleo, el cual se usa para producir energía.

Diferentes tipos de animales viven en distintas zonas del mundo. Busca animales que vivan en el mar, en la tierra o en el aire.

Este dibujo indica donde hay minas. De las minas se extraen diamantes, carbón, plata, piedras preciosas, oro, cobre, estaño o hierro.

Diferentes tipos de personas viven en el mundo. Busca gente que esté practicando un deporte o bailando una danza tradicional.

Gramma loreto
Petróleo
VENEZUELA
Arroz
Arroz
Georgetown
GUYANA
Paramaribo
SURINÁM
Cayena
GUYANA FRANCESA (Francia)
Diamantes
Oro
Cataratas del Ángel
Oro
Ecuador
Cocodrilo
Boa esmeralda
Canoas
Piraña
Río Amazonas
BRASIL
Petróleo
Tucán
Oro
Tabaco
Barcos de carga
Caña de azúcar
Algodón
Recife
Diamantes
Palafito
Pájaro paraguas
Perezoso
Oro
Tala de la selva
Río San Francisco
Camarón
Petróleo
Murciélago vampiro
Jaguar
Algodón
Caña de azúcar
Oro
Maíz
Hierro
Brasilia
Turismo
Langosta
BOLIVIA
Petróleo
Oro
Arroz
Naranjas
La Paz
Algodón
Gas
Trigo
Algodón
Hierro
CORDILLERA DE LOS ANDES
Papas
Ganadería
Carnaval

1 2 3 4 5 6 7 8
E F G H I J K L M

Sobre los datos

En cada página encontrarás datos e información sobre los lugares que aparecen en el mapa. Así, averiguarás cosas sobre un animal o planta que vive en determinada zona del mundo. Mira el dibujo que corresponde a cada dato y después localízalo en el mapa. Estos datos pertenecen al mapa de Sudamérica de la página anterior. ¿Puedes localizar todos estos dibujos en ese mapa?

En la página 42 encontrarás una sección llamada Asombroso, que contiene muchos datos sobre los diferentes países del mundo.

Datos

En Sudamérica habita casi un cuarto de todas las especies de animales conocidas y alrededor de 2,500 clases de árboles diferentes.

La cordillera más larga del mundo es la de los Andes, en Sudamérica.

La mitad de la población de Sudamérica vive en Brasil.

EXPLORADOR

Cada mapa tiene un fondo cuadriculado que lo divide. Las columnas van de arriba a abajo y tienen letras. Las filas van de izquierda a derecha y tienen números. Así, cada cuadrito tiene un nombre o coordenada formado por una letra y un número.

El Explorador contiene preguntas sobre lugares en el mapa. Podrás encontrar las respuestas buscando en el mapa las coordenadas indicadas.

Aquí tienes una pregunta sobre el mapa de Sudamérica.

▶ ¿Cómo se llama la catarata más alta del mundo? (Ver coordenadas E4.)

Para encontrar la coordenada E4, coloca una regla al lado de la columna E y pon tu dedo en la fila 4. Mueve el dedo en línea recta hasta la regla y ahí está la coordenada E4.

En E4 encontrarás las Cataratas del Ángel, que están en Venezuela.

▼ Esta niña está contestando una pregunta del Explorador. Utiliza una regla y el dedo para encontrar las coordenadas correctas.

Mapamundi

El mundo está dividido en casi 200 países. Este mapa nos muestra casi todos. Están iluminados con diferentes colores para que los puedas distinguir mejor. Algunos países poseen territorios en otras zonas del mundo; en este atlas estos sitios se reconocen porque además de su nombre tienen entre paréntesis las iniciales del país al que pertenecen.

ALASKA (EEUU)
CANADÁ
GROENLANDIA (Dinamarca)
OCÉANO ÁRTICO
FINLANDIA
NORUEGA
ISLANDIA
HOLANDA
SUECIA
ESTONIA
LETONIA
GRAN BRETAÑA
REPÚBLICA DE IRLANDA
BÉLGICA
Estos países de Europa se muestran con detalle en el círculo de la página 11.
FRANCIA
ANDORRA
ESPAÑA
PORTUGAL
OCÉANO ATLÁNTICO
ESTADOS UNIDOS DE AMÉRICA
AZORES (Portugal)
ISLAS MADEIRA (Portugal)
ISLAS BALEARES (España)
MALTA
CRETA (Grecia)
TÚNEZ
MARRUECOS
ISLAS CANARIAS (España)
ARGELIA
LIBIA
BERMUDAS (GB)
REPÚBLICA DOMINICANA
PUERTO RICO (EEUU)
ISLAS VÍRGENES (EEUU Y GB)
ANGUILLA (GB)
SAN CRISTÓBAL Y NEVIS
ANTIGUA Y BARBUDA
GUADALUPE (Francia)
DOMINICA
MARTINICA (Francia)
SANTA LUCÍA
BARBADOS
GRANADA
TRINIDAD Y TOBAGO
MÉXICO
BAHAMAS
CUBA
BELICE
JAMAICA
HONDURAS
HAITÍ
GUATEMALA
MONTSERRAT (GB)
SAN VICENTE Y LAS GRANADINAS
EL SALVADOR
NICARAGUA
COSTA RICA
PANAMÁ
VENEZUELA
GUYANA
SURINAM
GUYANA FRANCESA (Francia)
COLOMBIA
ISLAS GALÁPAGOS (Ecuador)
ECUADOR
PERÚ
BRASIL
OCÉANO PACÍFICO
BOLIVIA
PARAGUAY
CHILE
URUGUAY
ARGENTINA
ISLAS MALVINAS (GB)
ISLAS GEORGIAS DEL SUR (GB)
SAHARA OCCIDENTAL
ISLAS CABO VERDE
MAURITANIA
MALI
NÍGER
SENEGAL
GAMBIA
GUINEA-BISSAU
GUINEA
BURKINA FASO
CHAD
NIGERIA
GHANA
BENIN
SIERRA LEONA
COSTA DE MARFIL
LIBERIA
TOGO
REPÚBLICA CENTRO-AFRICANA
CAMERÚN
SANTO TOMÉ Y PRÍNCIPE
GABÓN
GUINEA ECUATORIAL
CONGO
ZAIRE
CABINDA (Angola)
ANGOLA
ZAMBIA
NAMIBIA
BOTSWANA
REPÚBLICA DE SUDÁFRICA
LESOTHO
OCÉANO ATLÁNTICO
ANTÁRTIDA

RUSIA
KAZAJASTÁN
MONGOLIA
AZERBAIJÁN
ARMENIA
UZBEKISTÁN
KYRGUIZSTÁN
TURKMENISTÁN
TAJIKISTÁN
SIRIA
LÍBANO
IRÁN
AFGANISTÁN
IRAK
JORDANIA
KUWAIT
BAHREIN
PAQUISTÁN
QATAR
EMIRATOS ÁRABES UNIDOS
ARABIA SAUDITA
OMÁN
YEMEN
ERITREA
DJIBOUTI
SOCOTRA (Yemen)
ETIOPÍA
SOMALIA
KENIA
RUANDA
BURUNDI
MALAWI
COMORES
MAYOTTE (Francia)
SEYCHELLES
MADAGASCAR
ZIMBABWE
CHINA
NEPAL
BUTÁN
INDIA
BANGLADESH
MYANMAR
COREA DEL NORTE
COREA DEL SUR
JAPÓN
MACAO (Portugal)
TAIWÁN (China)
HONG KONG
LAOS
TAILANDIA
VIETNAM
CAMBOYA
FILIPINAS
BRUNEI
MALASIA
SINGAPUR
ISLAS ADAMÁN (India)
ISLAS NICOBAR (India)
ISLAS MALDIVAS
SRI LANKA
OCÉANO ÍNDICO
OCÉANO PACÍFICO
INDONESIA
IRIAN JAYA (Indonesia)
PAPUA NUEVA GUINEA
ISLAS SALOMÓN
ISLAS MARIANAS (EEUU)
GUAM (EEUU)
ISLAS MARSHALL
PALAU (EEUU)
ESTADOS DE MICRONESIA
NAURU
KIRIBATI
TUVALU
VANUATU
FIJI
NUEVA CALEDONIA (Francia)
AUSTRALIA
TASMANIA (Australia)
NUEVA ZELANDA
SUECIA
LETONIA
LITUANIA (Rusia)
DINAMARCA
POLONIA
BIELORRUSIA
ALEMANIA
LUXEMBURGO
REPÚBLICA CHECA
ESLOVAQUIA
UCRANIA
MOLDAVIA
LIECHTENSTEIN
AUSTRIA
HUNGRÍA
SUIZA
ESLOVENIA
RUMANIA
CROACIA
REPÚBLICA FEDERAL DE YUGOSLAVIA
SAN MARINO
BOSNIA-HERZEGOVINA
MÓNACO
BULGARIA
ITALIA
MACEDONIA
CÓRCEGA (Francia)
TURQUÍA
CERDEÑA (Italia)
ALBANIA
CIUDAD DEL VATICANO
GRECIA
SICILIA (Italia)

En esta parte de Europa hay muchos países. En el círculo están dibujados a una escala mayor para que los puedas ver.

A B C D E F G H

El Ártico

El Ártico es la parte del mundo que está más cerca del Polo Norte. Alrededor, el Océano Ártico está congelado casi todo el año, aunque en verano el hielo y la nieve se derriten. En invierno apenas brilla el Sol, por lo que el Ártico es muy frío. Casi no crece vegetación, excepto pequeñas plantas como líquenes y musgos.

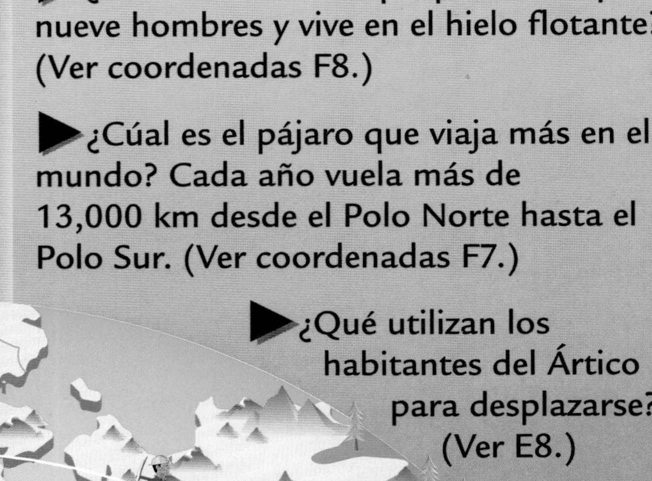

EXPLORADOR

▶¿Cuál es el animal que pesa más que nueve hombres y vive en el hielo flotante? (Ver coordenadas F8.)

▶¿Cúal es el pájaro que viaja más en el mundo? Cada año vuela más de 13,000 km desde el Polo Norte hasta el Polo Sur. (Ver coordenadas F7.)

▶¿Qué utilizan los habitantes del Ártico para desplazarse? (Ver E8.)

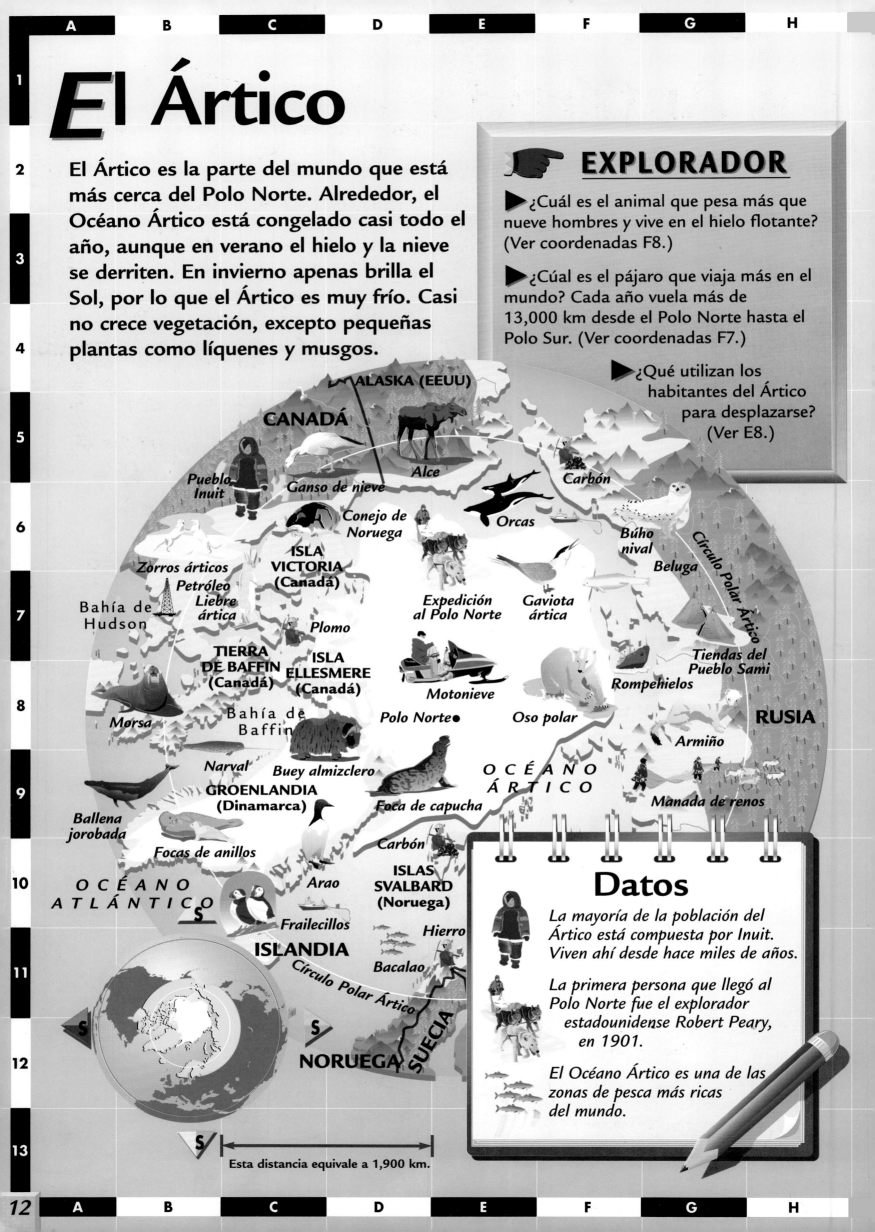

Esta distancia equivale a 1,900 km.

Datos

La mayoría de la población del Ártico está compuesta por Inuit. Viven ahí desde hace miles de años.

La primera persona que llegó al Polo Norte fue el explorador estadounidense Robert Peary, en 1901.

El Océano Ártico es una de las zonas de pesca más ricas del mundo.

La Antártida

La Antártida es un enorme continente cubierto de hielo situado cerca del Polo Sur. Es el lugar más frío y con más viento en toda la Tierra. Pocos animales viven en el Polo, pero en las costas hay focas y pájaros, y peces en el mar. Las únicas personas que viven en la Antártida son científicos, dedicados a estudiar la fauna.

Datos

En 1911, Roald Amundsen, un explorador noruego, fue el primero en llegar al Polo Sur.

Cada año casi 30,000 turistas navegan por las aguas de la Antártida para ver la vida silvestre.

En la Antártida hay muchos icebergs. El más grande que se ha encontrado medía el triple que Chipre.

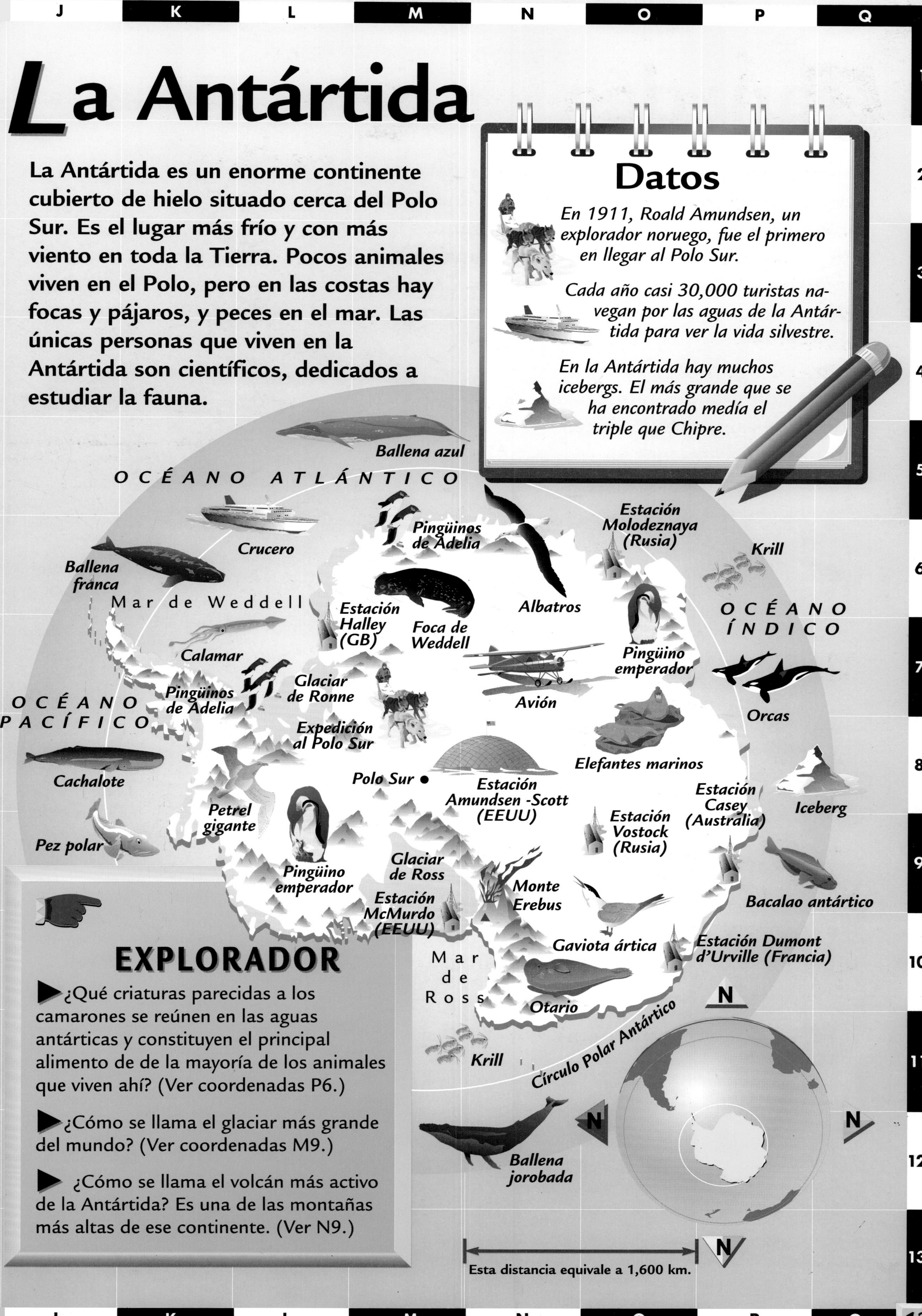

EXPLORADOR

▶ ¿Qué criaturas parecidas a los camarones se reúnen en las aguas antárticas y constituyen el principal alimento de de la mayoría de los animales que viven ahí? (Ver coordenadas P6.)

▶ ¿Cómo se llama el glaciar más grande del mundo? (Ver coordenadas M9.)

▶ ¿Cómo se llama el volcán más activo de la Antártida? Es una de las montañas más altas de ese continente. (Ver N9.)

Canadá

Canadá es el segundo país más grande del mundo después de Rusia. Algunas zonas de Canadá son frías y están deshabitadas. En el norte hay grandes bosques de pinos y el clima suele ser muy frío. La mayoría de la gente vive en el sur, que es más cálido. Canadá tiene petróleo y minas de carbón, plata, oro y cobre. Posee buenas tierras de cultivo donde los agricultores plantan trigo. Cuenta con grandes fábricas, sobre todo en el este, que producen automóviles, camiones y trenes.

EXPLORADOR

- ¿Cuál es el deporte más popular del país; se juega en una pista de hielo con un disco y un bastón? (Ver coordenadas F9.)
- ¿Qué gran animal recorría en manadas las praderas de Canadá y hoy vive en parques nacionales? (Ver coordenadas H10.)
- Canadá tiene dos lenguas oficiales: inglés y francés. ¿En qué provincia o distrito vive la mayoría de los francófonos? (Ver coordenadas N9.)

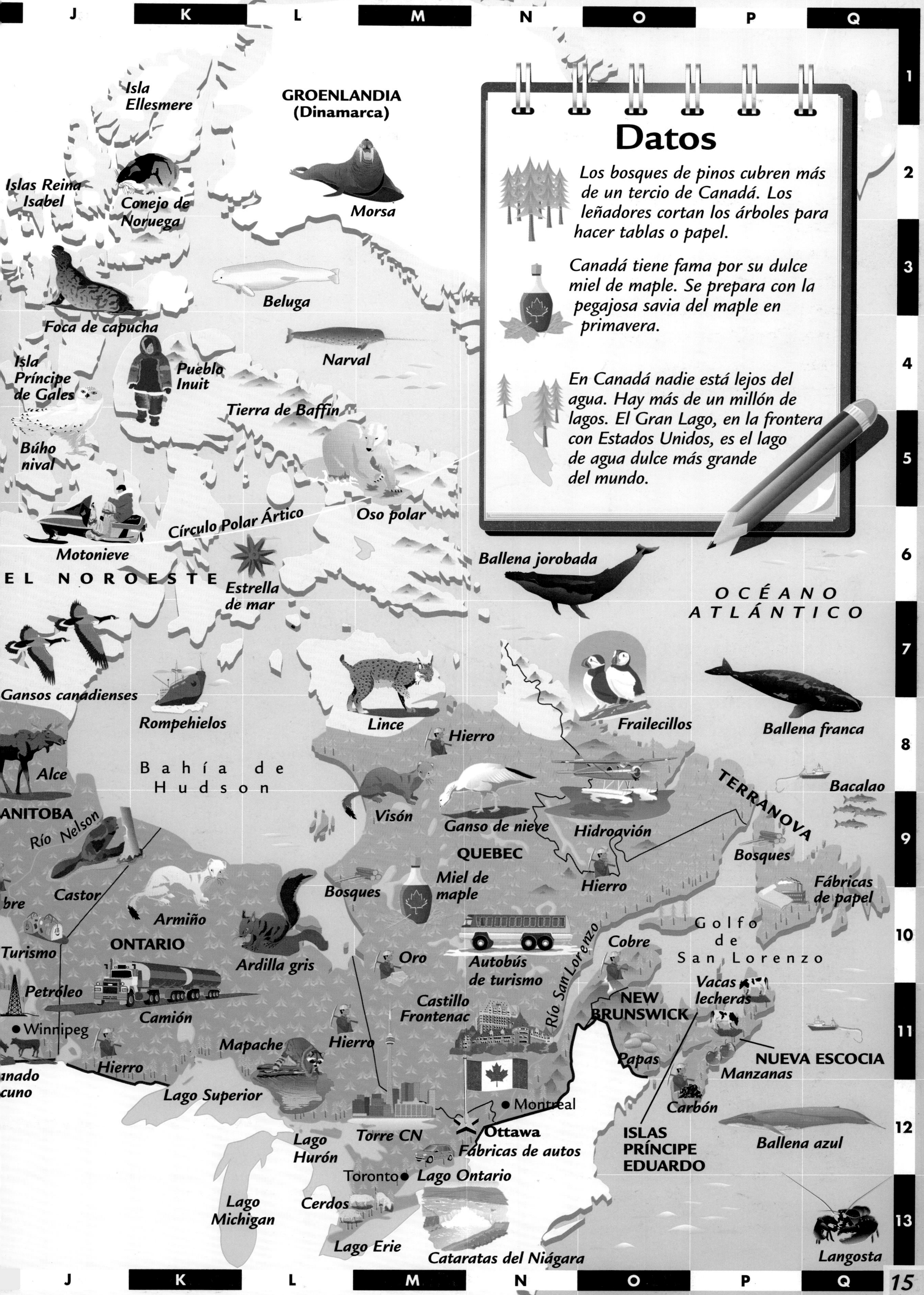

Datos

Los bosques de pinos cubren más de un tercio de Canadá. Los leñadores cortan los árboles para hacer tablas o papel.

Canadá tiene fama por su dulce miel de maple. Se prepara con la pegajosa savia del maple en primavera.

En Canadá nadie está lejos del agua. Hay más de un millón de lagos. El Gran Lago, en la frontera con Estados Unidos, es el lago de agua dulce más grande del mundo.

Estados Unidos

Estados Unidos es un enorme territorio dividido en 50 estados, incluyendo Alaska y Hawai. Tanto sus paisajes como sus habitantes son muy variados. En el oeste hay montañas altas y bosques. El centro es una gran llanura donde se cultiva trigo y maíz. Al noreste hay montañas más pequeñas, minas de carbón y fábricas de automóviles. Cuenta con ciudades con grandes rascacielos como Nueva York. En los últimos 500 años, millones de personas han ido a vivir a Estados Unidos.

Datos

El águila pescadora es el ave nacional de Estados Unidos. Vive sobre todo en Alaska, donde hay muchos peces, su alimento favorito.

Casi la mitad de la producción mundial de maíz se cultiva en Estados Unidos.

La bandera de Estados Unidos tiene una estrella por cada estado.

EXPLORADOR

▶ ¿Dónde se encuentra un famoso géiser que lanza un chorro de agua caliente de 30 m de altura cada hora? (Ver coordenadas H3.)

▶ ¿Qué montaña de Dakota del Sur tiene esculpidas las caras de cuatro presidentes de Estados Unidos? (Ver coordenadas J4.)

▶ ¿Cómo se llama la torre de Chicago que mide 443 m de altura, tiene 110 pisos y es uno de los edificios más altos del mundo? (Ver M5.)

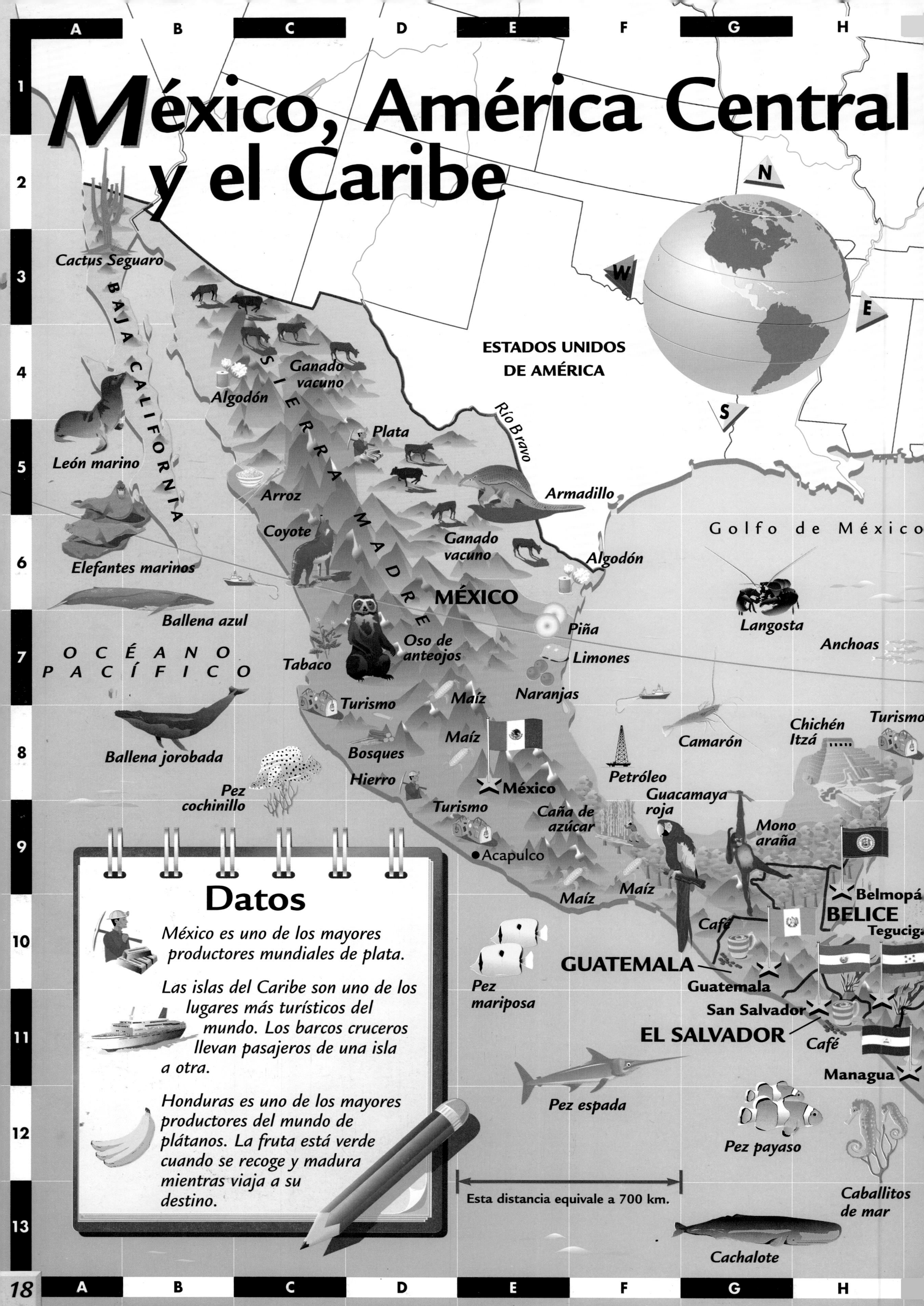

México, América Central y el Caribe
A B C D E F G H
1 2 3 4 5 6 7 8 9 10 11 12 13
N
W
E
S
ESTADOS UNIDOS DE AMÉRICA
Cactus Seguaro
BAJA CALIFORNIA
León marino
Elefantes marinos
Ballena azul
OCÉANO PACÍFICO
Ballena jorobada
Pez cochinillo
SIERRA MADRE
Ganado vacuno
Algodón
Plata
Arroz
Coyote
Tabaco
Oso de anteojos
Turismo
Maíz
Bosques
Hierro
Maíz
Turismo
MÉXICO
Río Bravo
Armadillo
Ganado vacuno
Algodón
Piña
Limones
Naranjas
México
Caña de azúcar
Acapulco
Maíz
Maíz
Petróleo
Golfo de México
Langosta
Anchoas
Camarón
Chichén Itzá
Turismo
Guacamaya roja
Mono araña
Belmopá
BELICE
Tegucig
Café
GUATEMALA
Guatemala
San Salvador
EL SALVADOR
Café
Managua
Pez mariposa
Pez espada
Pez payaso
Caballitos de mar
Esta distancia equivale a 700 km.
Cachalote
Datos
México es uno de los mayores productores mundiales de plata.
Las islas del Caribe son uno de los lugares más turísticos del mundo. Los barcos cruceros llevan pasajeros de una isla a otra.
Honduras es uno de los mayores productores del mundo de plátanos. La fruta está verde cuando se recoge y madura mientras viaja a su destino.

América Central es una estrecha franja de tierra que une Norteamérica y Sudamérica.
México es un país grande, populoso y con una larga historia. Al sur hay siete países más pequeños. Muchos de los habitantes se dedican a la agricultura de subsistencia o trabajan en plantaciones de caña de azúcar, café y plátanos. Al este, en el cálido Mar Caribe, hay cientos de islas soleadas, famosas por sus arrecifes de coral y por sus playas paradisiacas.

EXPLORADOR

- ¿Qué antigua ciudad de México fue construida por los mayas hace más de mil años y cuyas pirámides y edificios en ruinas se visitan actualmente? (Ver H8.)
- ¿Qué canal utilizan los barcos de carga para pasar del Océano Atlántico al Pacífico y viceversa? Tiene unos 82 km de longitud y alrededor de 34 barcos pasan por él diariamente. (Ver K12.)
- ¿Cuál es la única especie de oso que vive en México? Su nombre viene de los círculos blancos que tiene alrededor de los ojos. (Ver coordenadas D7.)
- ¿Cuál es una de las ciudades más pobladas del mundo? En ella vive más gente que en toda Australia. (Ver E8.)

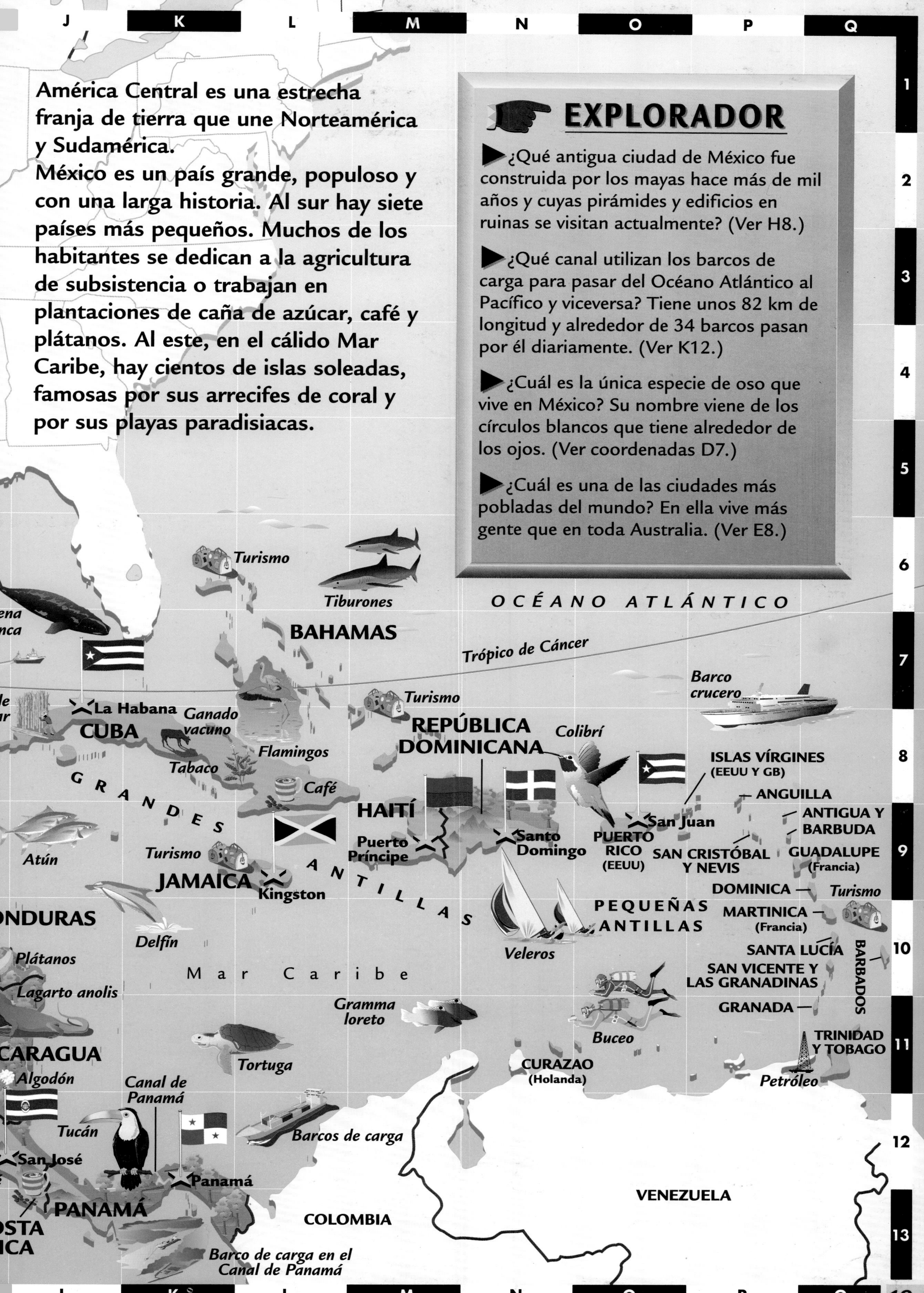

Sudamérica

Sudamérica se extiende desde el cálido Mar Caribe hasta las tormentosas aguas del Cabo de Hornos. En Sudamérica hace calor todo el año, excepto en el extremo sur y en la cordillera de los Andes. En el norte, el gran río Amazonas atraviesa la selva tropical. Algo más al sur hay extensas llanuras donde pasta el ganado. La mayoría de los sudamericanos vive en ciudades costeras. En el campo, los agricultores cultivan plátanos, café, frijoles y maíz.

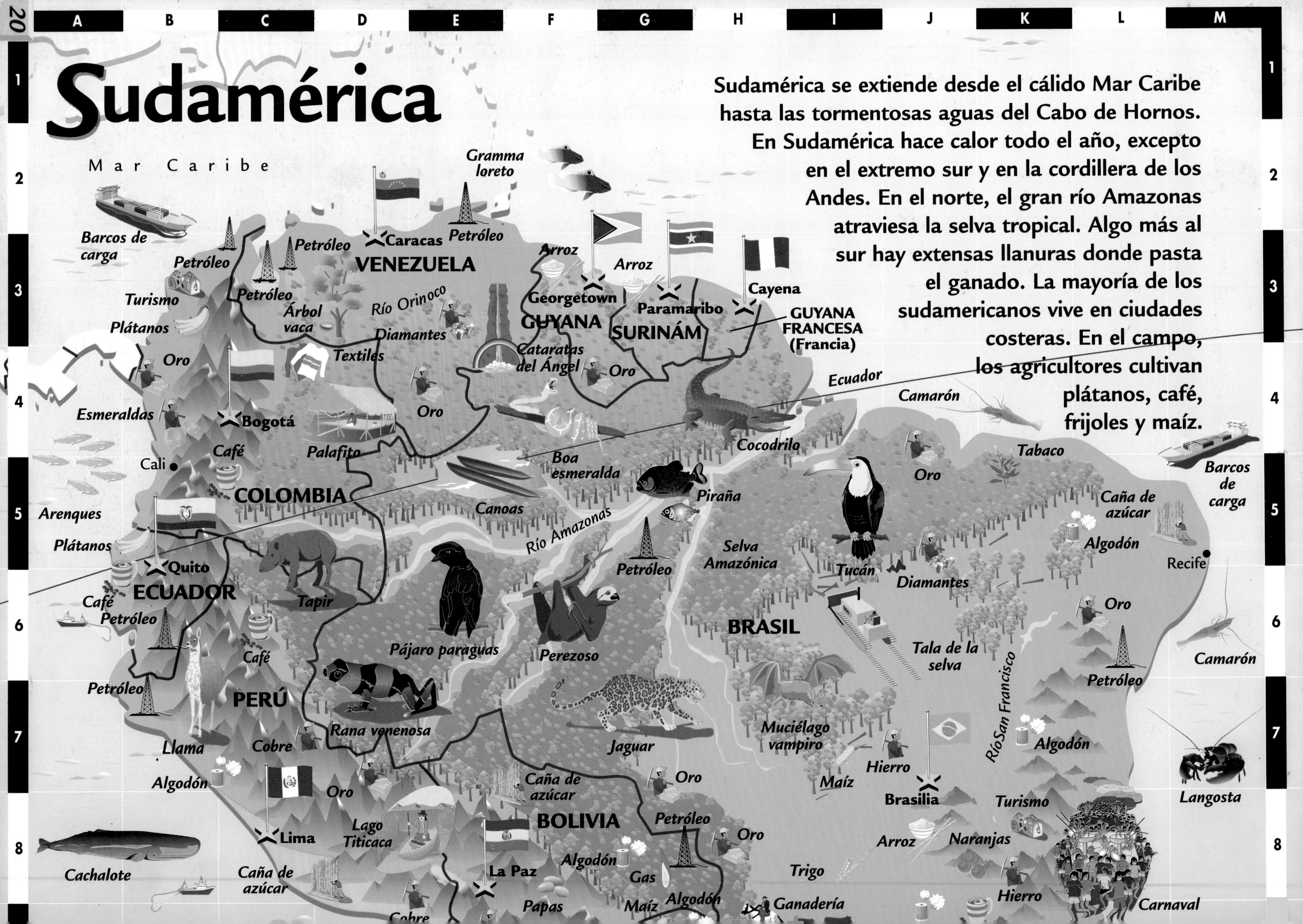

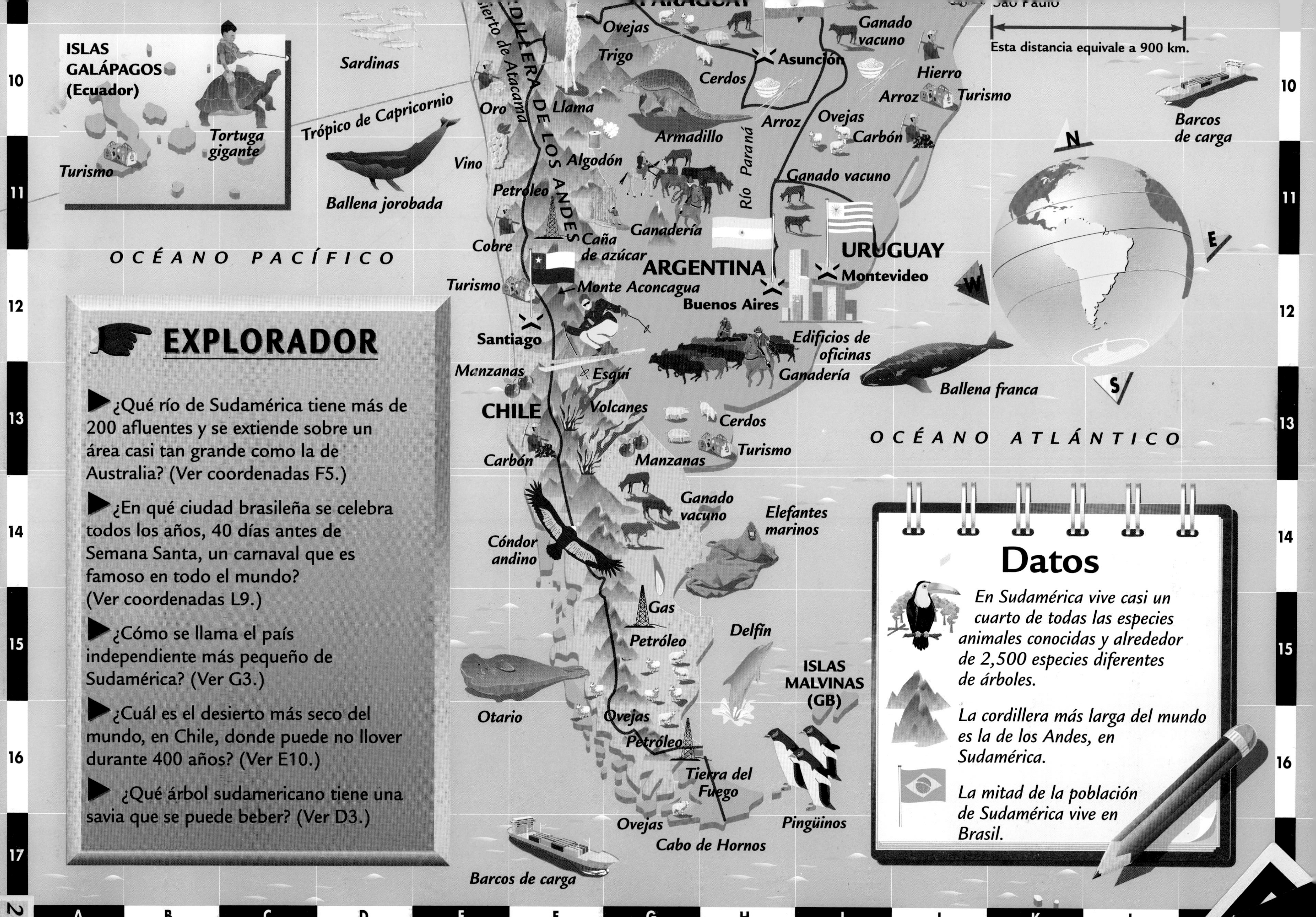

EXPLORADOR

- ¿Qué río de Sudamérica tiene más de 200 afluentes y se extiende sobre un área casi tan grande como la de Australia? (Ver coordenadas F5.)
- ¿En qué ciudad brasileña se celebra todos los años, 40 días antes de Semana Santa, un carnaval que es famoso en todo el mundo? (Ver coordenadas L9.)
- ¿Cómo se llama el país independiente más pequeño de Sudamérica? (Ver G3.)
- ¿Cuál es el desierto más seco del mundo, en Chile, donde puede no llover durante 400 años? (Ver E10.)
- ¿Qué árbol sudamericano tiene una savia que se puede beber? (Ver D3.)

Datos

En Sudamérica vive casi un cuarto de todas las especies animales conocidas y alrededor de 2,500 especies diferentes de árboles.

La cordillera más larga del mundo es la de los Andes, en Sudamérica.

La mitad de la población de Sudamérica vive en Brasil.

Norte de Europa

El norte de Europa es una zona bastante fría y en la que puede llover durante todo el año. Hay montañas y bosques de pinos en el extremo norte y en el sur se encuentran las montañas más altas. El centro es una extensa llanura que alguna vez estuvo cubierta de bosques. Durante cientos de años los árboles fueron talados para construir granjas, pueblos y ciudades. La mayoría de los noreuropeos trabajan en fábricas, tiendas y oficinas.

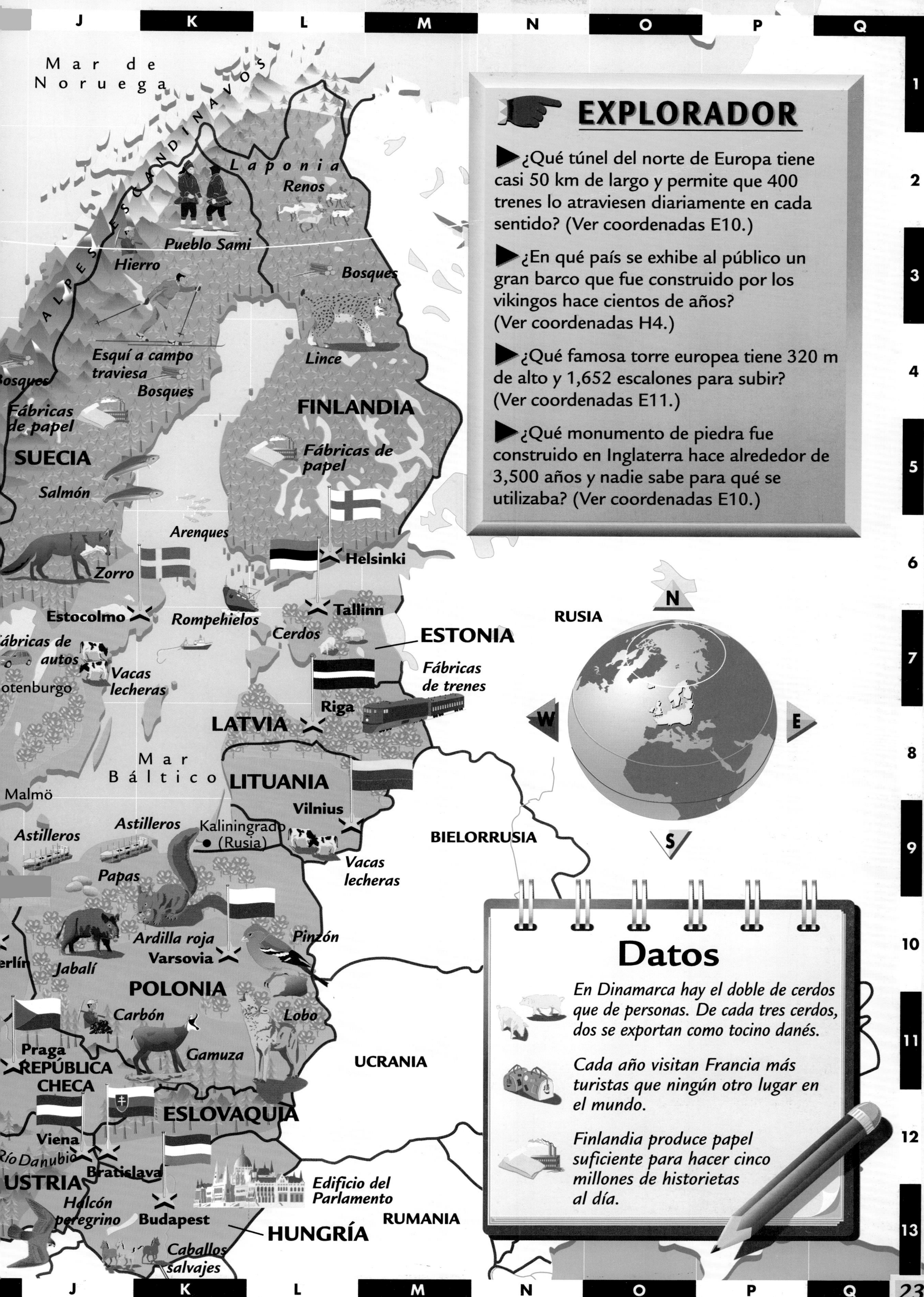
J K L M N O P Q
1 2 3 4 5 6 7 8 9 10 11 12 13
Mar de Noruega
ALPES ESCANDINAVOS
Laponia
Renos
Pueblo Sami
Hierro
Bosques
Esquí a campo traviesa
Lince
Bosques
Fábricas de papel
FINLANDIA
SUECIA
Fábricas de papel
Salmón
Arenques
Helsinki
Zorro
Estocolmo
Rompehielos
Tallinn
Cerdos
ESTONIA
Fábricas de autos
Vacas lecheras
otenburgo
Fábricas de trenes
Riga
LATVIA
Mar Báltico
LITUANIA
Malmö
Vilnius
Astilleros
Astilleros
Kaliningrado (Rusia)
Vacas lecheras
Papas
BIELORRUSIA
RUSIA
N
W
E
S
EXPLORADOR
¿Qué túnel del norte de Europa tiene casi 50 km de largo y permite que 400 trenes lo atraviesen diariamente en cada sentido? (Ver coordenadas E10.)
¿En qué país se exhibe al público un gran barco que fue construido por los vikingos hace cientos de años? (Ver coordenadas H4.)
¿Qué famosa torre europea tiene 320 m de alto y 1,652 escalones para subir? (Ver coordenadas E11.)
¿Qué monumento de piedra fue construido en Inglaterra hace alrededor de 3,500 años y nadie sabe para qué se utilizaba? (Ver coordenadas E10.)
Ardilla roja
Pinzón
Varsovia
erlín
Jabalí
POLONIA
Carbón
Lobo
Gamuza
Praga
REPÚBLICA CHECA
UCRANIA
ESLOVAQUIA
Viena
Río Danubio
Bratislava
USTRIA
Edificio del Parlamento
Halcón peregrino
Budapest
RUMANIA
HUNGRÍA
Caballos salvajes
Datos
En Dinamarca hay el doble de cerdos que de personas. De cada tres cerdos, dos se exportan como tocino danés.
Cada año visitan Francia más turistas que ningún otro lugar en el mundo.
Finlandia produce papel suficiente para hacer cinco millones de historietas al día.

Sur de Europa

El sur de Europa es cálido, soleado y seco en su mayor parte. Grandes zonas son montañosas, pero hay también muchas tierras de cultivo. En el sur de Europa mucha gente se dedica a la agricultura y produce cereales, frutas y hortalizas. Además, el sur de Europa cuenta con muchos edificios antiguos y obras de arte, por lo que cada año millones de turistas visitan sus ciudades y museos.

EXPLORADOR

- ¿Qué torre italiana construida hace más de 300 años empezó a inclinarse incluso antes de que fuera terminada? (Ver coordenadas I6.)
- ¿Cómo se llama el antiguo estadio romano donde los gladiadores luchaban con espadas y redes? (Ver J7.)
- ¿Qué antiguo templo griego fue construido para adorar a la diosa Atenea, protectora de Atenas? (Ver N8.)

Datos

El Monte Etna en Sicilia es el volcán más grande de Europa. Su última erupción fue en 1995.

España es el mayor productor mundial de aceite de oliva. Con ese aceite se podrían llenar, cada año, 160 albercas olímpicas.

Rusia y sus vecinos

EXPLORADOR

▶ ¿Qué centro espacial lanzó al espacio, en 1961, al primer astronauta del mundo Yuri Gagarin? (Ver coordenadas G8.)

▶ ¿Qué línea de ferrocarril rusa es la más larga del mundo? Se necesitan ocho días para recorrerla desde el principio hasta el final. (Ver coordenadas J8.)

Rusia se extiende por Europa y Asia y es el país más grande del mundo. Rusia y sus vecinos se llamaban antes Unión Soviética, pero en 1991 se separaron. La mayoría de los rusos vive en la parte europea de Rusia, donde se ubican las principales ciudades y hay buenas tierras de cultivo. En los extremos norte y este hay un enorme bosque llamado taiga, donde viven lobos y osos.

Datos

Rusia usó por primera vez esta bandera en 1699, pero cuando se creó la Unión Soviética la bandera fue sustituida por otra. En 1991 la Unión Soviética se desmembró y Rusia volvió a usar la antigua bandera.

En Rusia y los países que la rodean hay más petróleo que en ninguna otra parte del mundo.

Suroeste asiático

El suroeste de Asia también se llama Medio Oriente. Aquí, hace miles de años, la gente se dedicaba a la agricultura y más tarde se fundaron las primeras ciudades. Esta parte del mundo está constituida por un desierto seco y ardiente, por lo que cultivar es difícil. Hace 50 años se encontró petróleo debajo del desierto y la mejoría económica que esto produjo sirvió para realizar un sistema de regadío para poder cultivar territorios mayores.

Datos

Hace más de 5,000 años aparecieron en Medio Oriente, a lo largo de los ríos Tigris y Éufrates, las primeras ciudades del mundo.

Tres de las religiones más importantes del mundo aparecieron en Medio Oriente: judaísmo, cristianismo y el Islam.

En Medio Oriente se hacen a mano las alfombras más caras del mundo. Los que tejen y anudan la lana siguen diferentes diseños, que indican de qué zona procede cada alfombra.

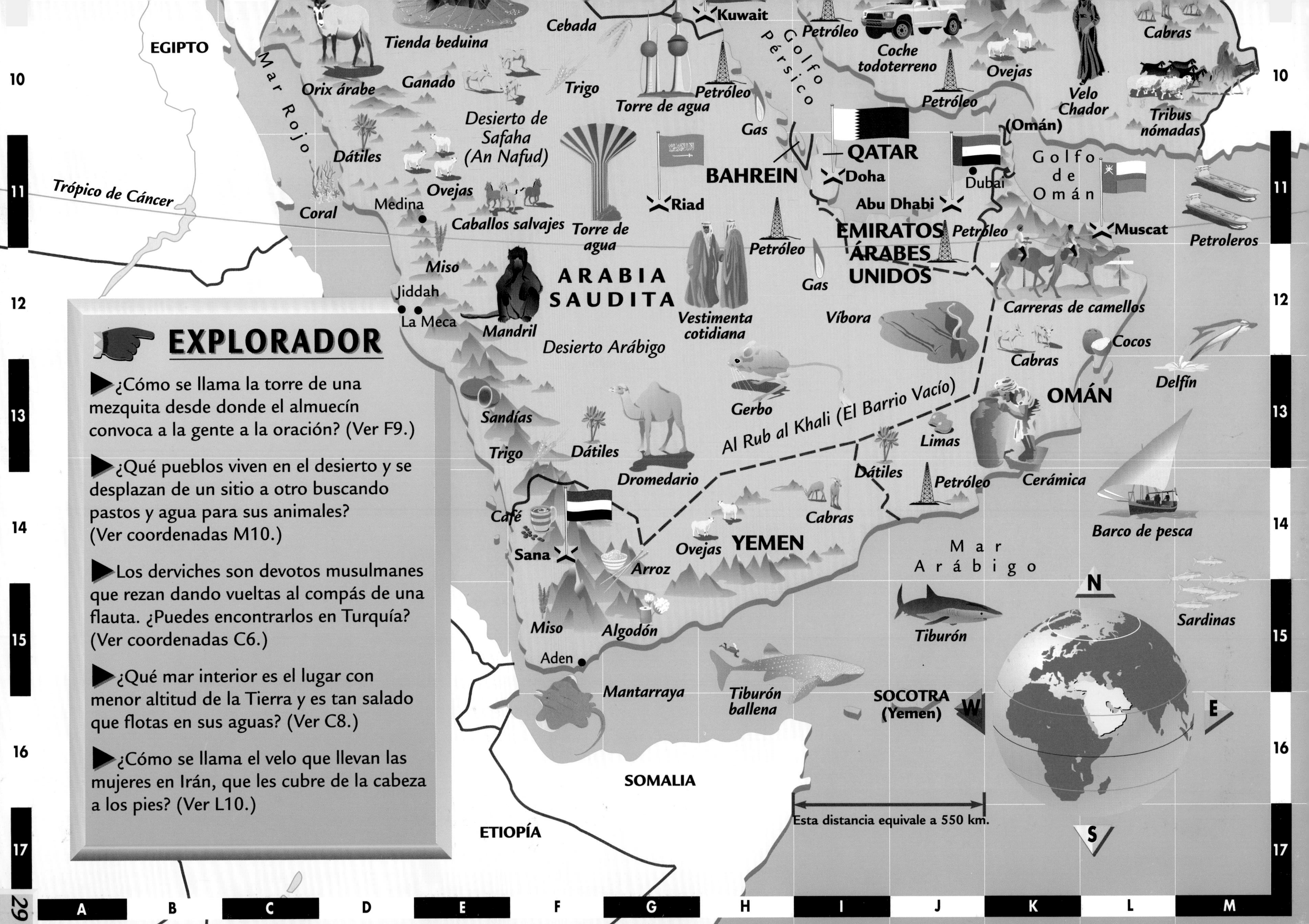

EXPLORADOR

- ¿Cómo se llama la torre de una mezquita desde donde el almuecín convoca a la gente a la oración? (Ver F9.)
- ¿Qué pueblos viven en el desierto y se desplazan de un sitio a otro buscando pastos y agua para sus animales? (Ver coordenadas M10.)
- Los derviches son devotos musulmanes que rezan dando vueltas al compás de una flauta. ¿Puedes encontrarlos en Turquía? (Ver coordenadas C6.)
- ¿Qué mar interior es el lugar con menor altitud de la Tierra y es tan salado que flotas en sus aguas? (Ver C8.)
- ¿Cómo se llama el velo que llevan las mujeres en Irán, que les cubre de la cabeza a los pies? (Ver L10.)

Norte de África

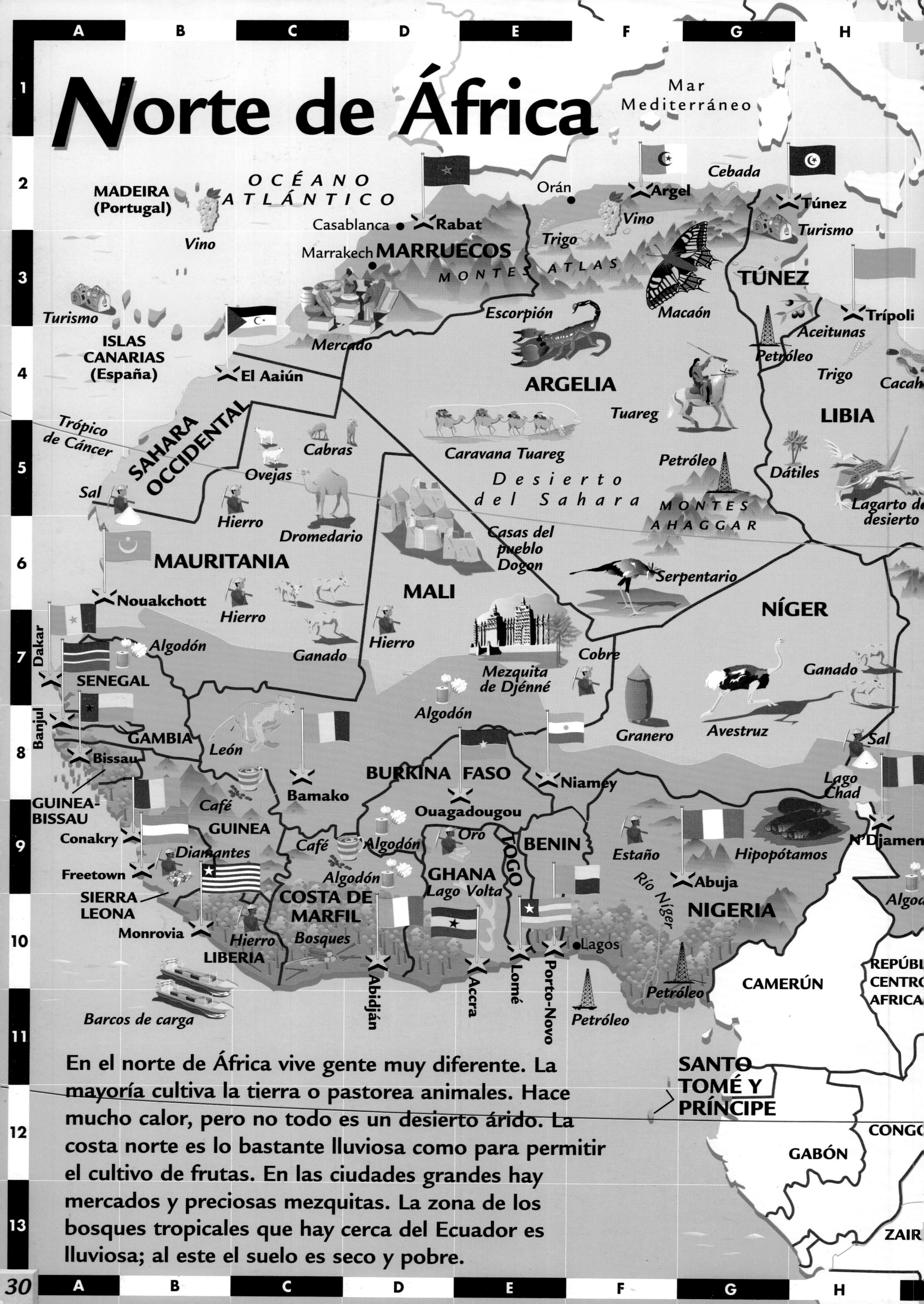

En el norte de África vive gente muy diferente. La mayoría cultiva la tierra o pastorea animales. Hace mucho calor, pero no todo es un desierto árido. La costa norte es lo bastante lluviosa como para permitir el cultivo de frutas. En las ciudades grandes hay mercados y preciosas mezquitas. La zona de los bosques tropicales que hay cerca del Ecuador es lluviosa; al este el suelo es seco y pobre.

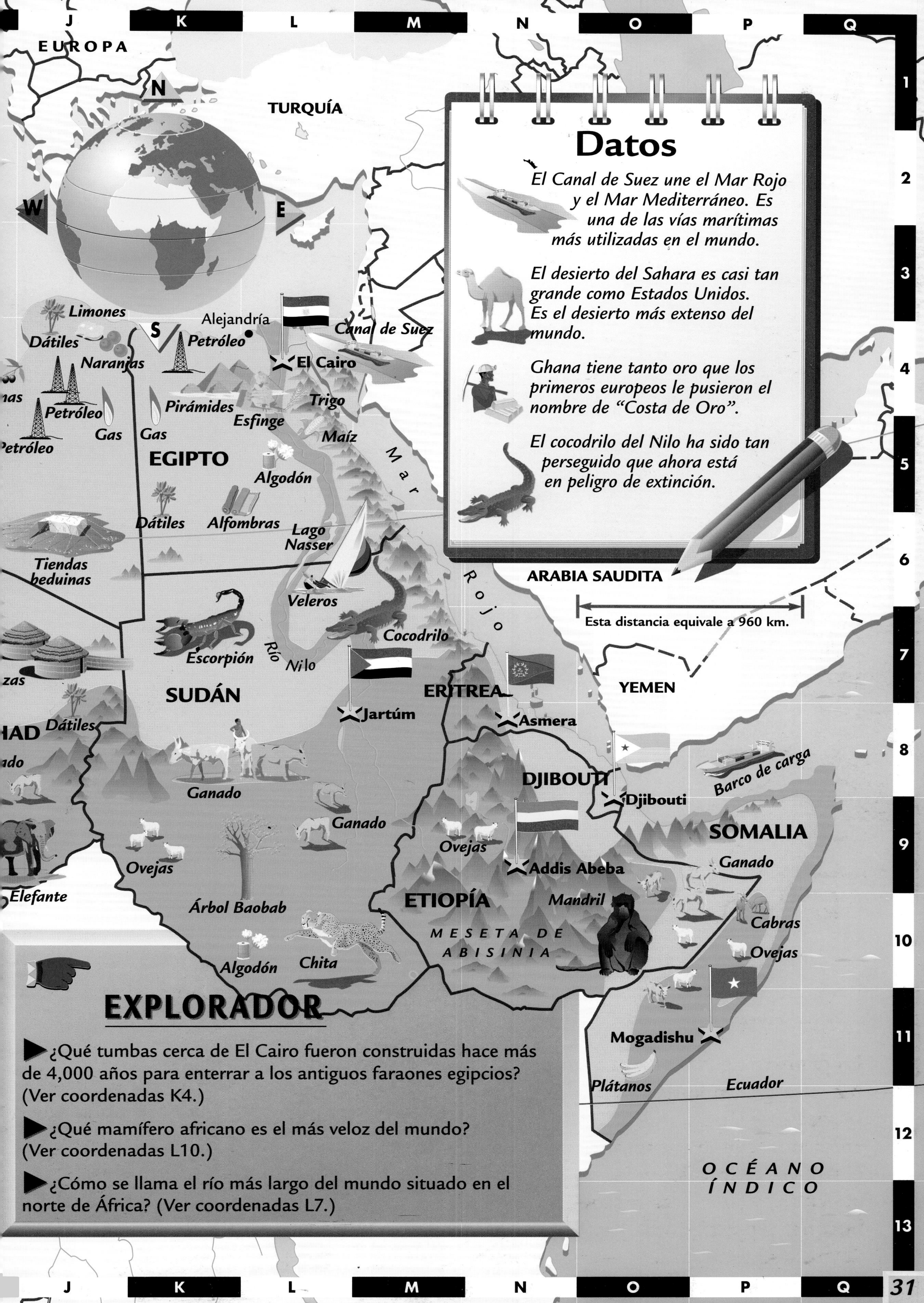

Datos

El Canal de Suez une el Mar Rojo y el Mar Mediterráneo. Es una de las vías marítimas más utilizadas en el mundo.

El desierto del Sahara es casi tan grande como Estados Unidos. Es el desierto más extenso del mundo.

Ghana tiene tanto oro que los primeros europeos le pusieron el nombre de "Costa de Oro".

El cocodrilo del Nilo ha sido tan perseguido que ahora está en peligro de extinción.

EXPLORADOR

- ¿Qué tumbas cerca de El Cairo fueron construidas hace más de 4,000 años para enterrar a los antiguos faraones egipcios? (Ver coordenadas K4.)
- ¿Qué mamífero africano es el más veloz del mundo? (Ver coordenadas L10.)
- ¿Cómo se llama el río más largo del mundo situado en el norte de África? (Ver coordenadas L7.)

Sur de África

El sur de África es una vasta tierra de praderas, bosques tropicales, montañas y desiertos. Las llanuras de Kenia y Tanzania son famosas por sus enormes manadas de animales. Más al oeste, en los bosques tropicales, hay gorilas, monos y pájaros tropicales. Gente muy variada vive en África; la mayoría cultiva la tierra y vive en poblados, pero las ciudades están creciendo. Muchos países tienen minas de cobre y oro y algunos también de diamantes.

Datos

En el sur de África viven el rinoceronte blanco y el gorila, dos animales en peligro de extinción.

El sur de África tiene grandes regiones de bosques tropicales. Casi un cuarto de todos los bosques del mundo están aquí.

Sudáfrica es el mayor productor mundial de oro.

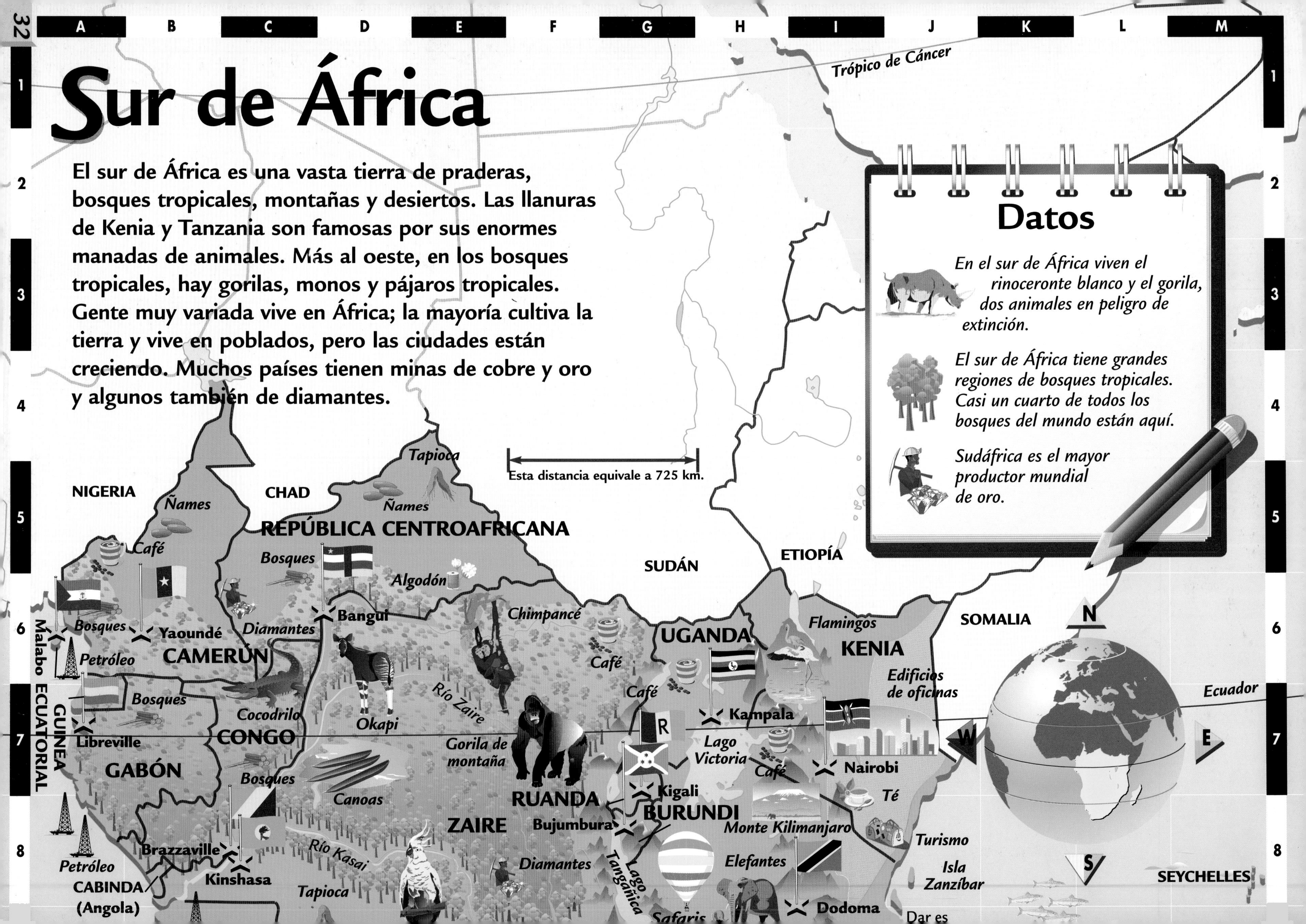

EXPLORADOR

▶ ¿Cómo se llama el lago más grande de África, que es el segundo más grande del mundo? (Ver coordenadas H7.)

▶ ¿Qué montaña africana cerca del Ecuador es tan alta que está siempre cubierta de nieve? (Ver coordenadas H8.)

▶ ¿Qué árbol africano es tan ancho que podría almacenar en su tronco más de 500 tinas de baño? (Ver coordenadas K14.)

Sur de Asia

El sur de Asia se extiende desde la Cordillera del Himalaya, al norte de la India, hasta la isla de Sri Lanka, al sur. El clima en general es cálido y seco, aunque durante algunos meses las lluvias son muy intensas. Casi mil millones de personas pueblan el sur de Asia; la mayoría vive en aldeas y cultiva la tierra, pero la migración hacia las ciudades es grande. Las ciudades mezclan modernos edificios y antiguos templos y palacios, las calles están llenas de coches y camiones, pero también de carros tirados por bueyes y elefantes.

EXPLORADOR

▶ ¿Qué templo de mármol blanco decorado con piedras preciosas fue construido en el siglo XVII por un marajá indio para sepultar a su esposa? (Ver coordenadas G8.)

▶ ¿Qué animal se emplea en India para hacer trabajos pesados tales como transportar troncos? (Ver F11.)

▶ ¿Qué se teje en Paquistán, Afganistán e India que ha dado fama a esos países? (Ver C6, C9 y F7.)

▶ ¿Qué vehículo de tres ruedas y parecido a una bicicleta se usa en India como medio de transporte en las ciudades? (Ver coordenadas I10.)

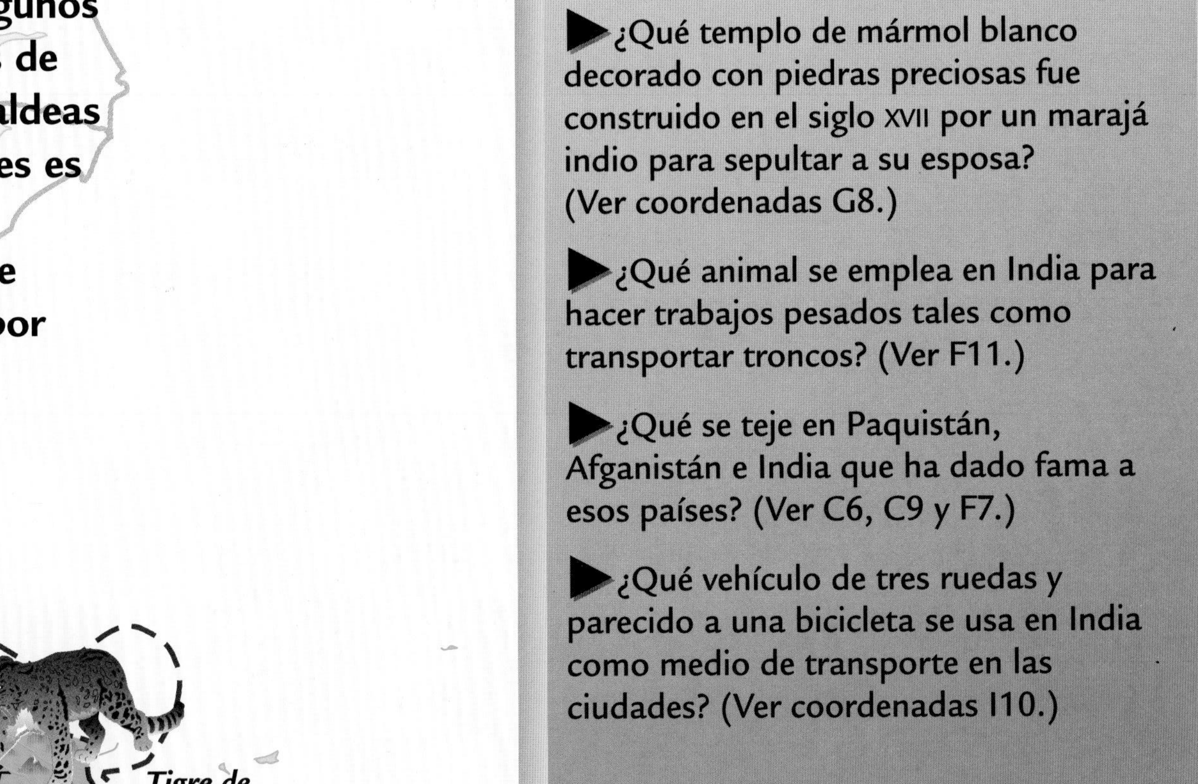

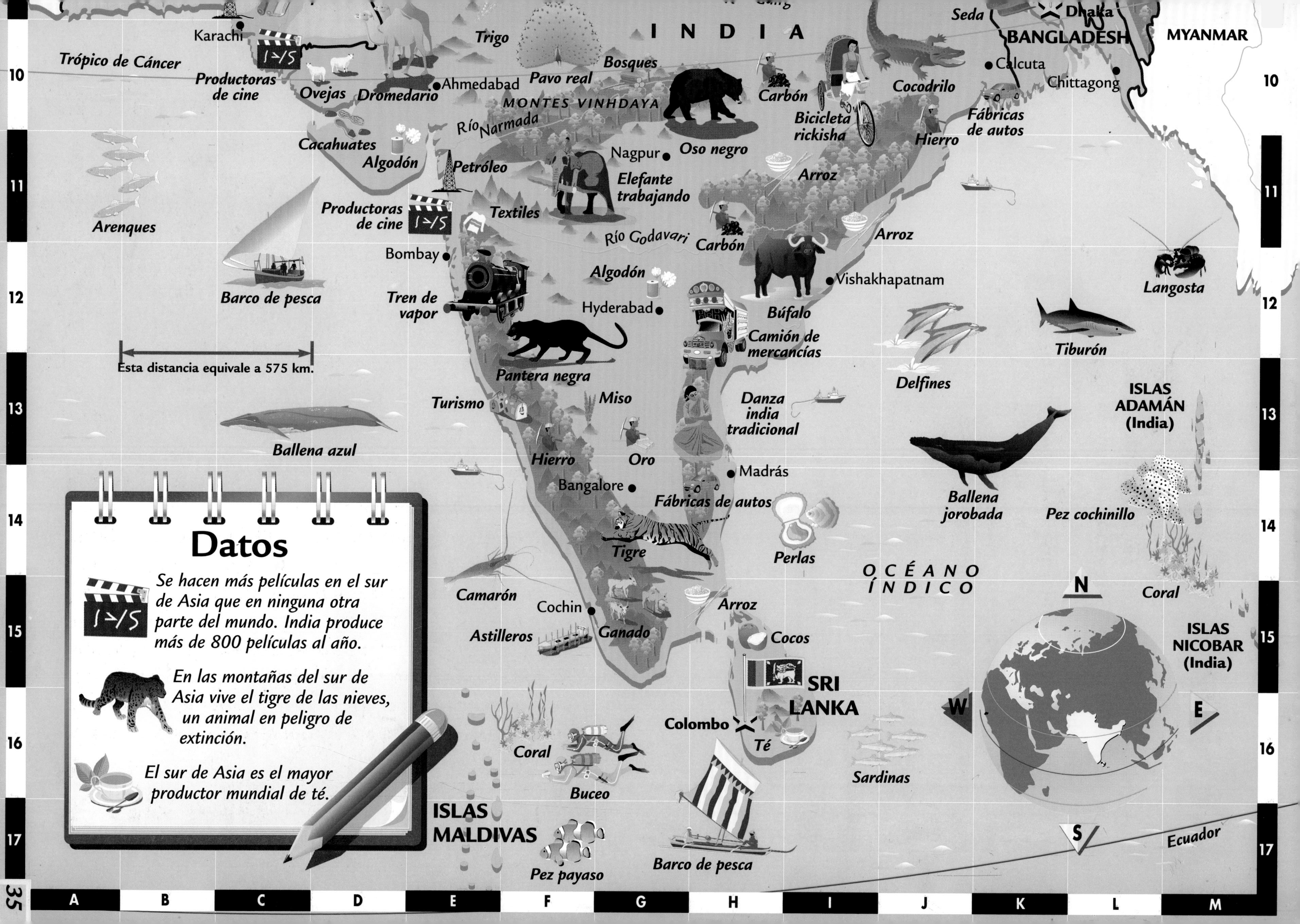
INDIA
MYANMAR
BANGLADESH
Dhaka
Calcuta
Chittagong
Seda
Karachi
Trópico de Cáncer
Productoras de cine
Ovejas
Dromedario
Ahmedabad
Trigo
Pavo real
Bosques
MONTES VINHDAYA
Río Narmada
Carbón
Bicicleta rickisha
Cocodrilo
Fábricas de autos
Hierro
Cacahuates
Algodón
Petróleo
Nagpur
Oso negro
Elefante trabajando
Arroz
Arenques
Productoras de cine
Textiles
Río Godavari
Carbón
Arroz
Bombay
Barco de pesca
Algodón
Vishakhapatnam
Langosta
Tren de vapor
Hyderabad
Búfalo
Camión de mercancías
Tiburón
Esta distancia equivale a 575 km.
Pantera negra
Delfines
Turismo
Miso
Danza india tradicional
ISLAS ADAMÁN (India)
Ballena azul
Hierro
Oro
Madrás
Bangalore
Fábricas de autos
Ballena jorobada
Pez cochinillo
Tigre
Perlas
OCÉANO ÍNDICO
Camarón
Cochin
Arroz
Coral
Astilleros
Ganado
Cocos
ISLAS NICOBAR (India)
SRI LANKA
Colombo
Té
Coral
Buceo
Sardinas
ISLAS MALDIVAS
Pez payaso
Barco de pesca
Ecuador
N
S
E
W
A B C D E F G H I J K L M
10 11 12 13 14 15 16 17
Datos
Se hacen más películas en el sur de Asia que en ninguna otra parte del mundo. India produce más de 800 películas al año.
En las montañas del sur de Asia vive el tigre de las nieves, un animal en peligro de extinción.
El sur de Asia es el mayor productor mundial de té.

Este de Asia

El este de Asia está formado por China, Mongolia, Japón, Corea del Norte, Corea del Sur, Taiwán y Hong Kong. Es una zona con montañas y desiertos en el norte y el oeste. La mayoría de la gente vive en el este, donde llueve y las tierras son aptas para los cultivos. China es un país enorme y la mayor parte de sus habitantes viven en el campo dedicados a la agricultura. En Japón casi todos viven en ciudades y trabajan en fábricas y oficinas.

EXPLORADOR

▶¿Qué antiguo ejercicio hacen los chinos para mantenerse en forma? (Ver coordenadas E7.)

▶¿Qué muralla mide más de 6,400 km y fue construida hace más de 500 años para proteger China de los invasores del norte? (Ver H6.)

▶¿Cómo se llaman las tiendas en las que viven las tribus nómadas de Mongolia? Protegen tanto del calor como del frío de las llanuras. (Ver coordendas G3.)

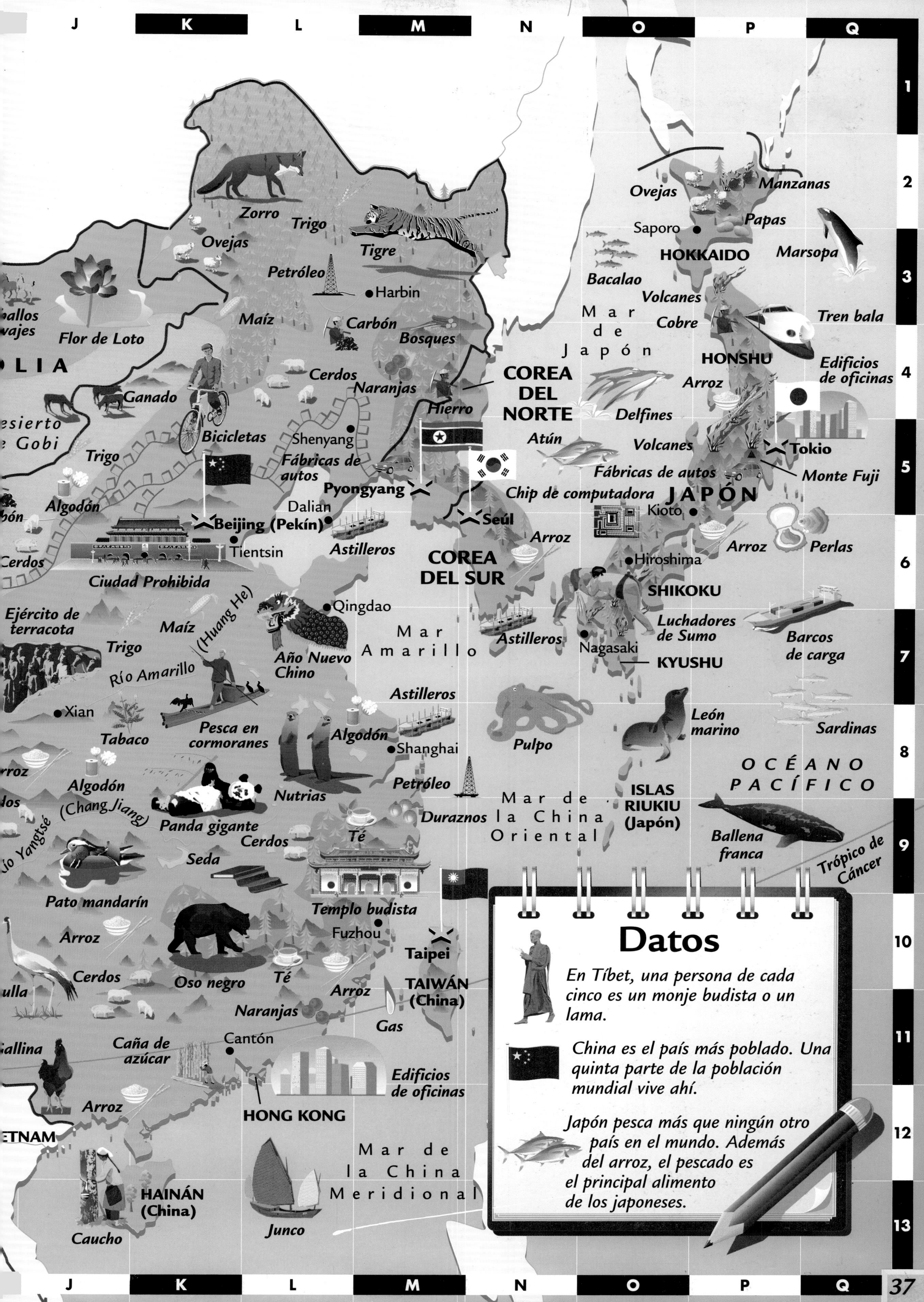
J
K
L
M
N
O
P
Q
1
2
3
4
5
6
7
8
9
10
11
12
13
Zorro
Trigo
Tigre
Ovejas
Petróleo
Harbin
Flor de Loto
Maíz
Carbón
Bosques
Cerdos
Naranjas
Ganado
Bicicletas
Hierro
Shenyang
Fábricas de autos
Trigo
Algodón
Pyongyang
Dalian
Beijing (Pekín)
Tientsin
Astilleros
Ciudad Prohibida
Ejército de terracota
Maíz
Trigo
(Huang He)
Río Amarillo
Qingdao
Año Nuevo Chino
Xian
Tabaco
Pesca en cormoranes
Algodón
Shanghai
Astilleros
Nutrias
Petróleo
Algodón
(Chang Jiang)
Panda gigante
Cerdos
Té
Duraznos
Seda
Pato mandarín
Templo budista
Fuzhou
Arroz
Cerdos
Oso negro
Té
Arroz
Taipei
TAIWÁN (China)
Naranjas
Gas
Caña de azúcar
Cantón
Edificios de oficinas
Arroz
HONG KONG
HAINÁN (China)
Caucho
Junco
Mar de la China Meridional
COREA DEL NORTE
COREA DEL SUR
Seúl
Arroz
Mar Amarillo
Astilleros
Mar de Japón
Delfines
Atún
Ovejas
Manzanas
Saporo
Papas
HOKKAIDO
Marsopa
Bacalao
Volcanes
Cobre
Tren bala
HONSHU
Edificios de oficinas
Arroz
Volcanes
Tokio
Fábricas de autos
Monte Fuji
Chip de computadora
JAPÓN
Kioto
Arroz
Perlas
Hiroshima
SHIKOKU
Luchadores de Sumo
Barcos de carga
Nagasaki
KYUSHU
León marino
Sardinas
Pulpo
OCÉANO PACÍFICO
ISLAS RIUKIU (Japón)
Mar de la China Oriental
Ballena franca
Trópico de Cáncer
Datos
En Tíbet, una persona de cada cinco es un monje budista o un lama.
China es el país más poblado. Una quinta parte de la población mundial vive ahí.
Japón pesca más que ningún otro país en el mundo. Además del arroz, el pescado es el principal alimento de los japoneses.

Sureste Asiático
CHINA
Trópico de Cáncer
TAIWÁN
Buceo
Coral
Pez payaso
Palafito
Mar de la China Meridional
Coral
LUZÓN
Cobre
Manila
Barcos de carga
Carbón
Hanoi
Jasbalí
MYANMAR
Búfalo
Elefante trabajando
LAOS
Tigre
Arroz
Río Irrawaddy
Vientiane
TAILANDIA
Río Mekong
VIETNAM
FILIP
Coral
Seda
Arenques
Tapioca
Plata
Marcado flotante
Arroz
Anchoas
Sardinas
Oro
Rangún
Bangkok
Maíz
OCÉANO ÍNDICO
Monasterio deAngkor
Phnom Penh
Ciudad Ho Chi Minh
Perlas
Petróleo
CAMBOYA
Arroz
Atún
Petróleo
Bandar Seri Begawan
BRUNEI
Tiburones
Langosta
Turismo
Gas
Caucho
Tortuga
Arroz
MALASIA
Pez cochinillo
Tapir malayo
Hierro
Bosques
Orangután
Edificios de oficinas
Coral
Turismo
Kuala Lumpur
SINGAPUR
BORNEO
Petróleo
Volcanes
Petróleo
SUMATRA
Barcos de carga
Bosques
Volcanes
Gas
IND
Orquí
EXPLORADOR
¿Cómo se llama el lagarto más grande del mundo? Llega a medir tres metros de largo y come de todo, incluso cerdos y ciervos. Sólo vive en Indonesia. (Ver coordenadas J11.)
¿Qué templo de Camboya es el edificio sagrado más grande del mundo? Fue construido hace más de 500 años en honor de Vishnú, un dios hindú. (Ver coordenadas D7.)
Flor Rafflesia
Jakarta
JAVA
Volcanes
Té
Caballitos de mar
Pez maripos
Coral
A B C D E F G H
1 2 3 4 5 6 7 8 9 10 11 12 13

J K L M N O P Q
1 2 3 4 5 6 7 8 9 10 11 12 13
El sureste asiático está formado por una estrecha franja de tierra y miles de pequeñas islas. La región tiene montañas altas, selvas tropicales y valles. El clima es cálido y húmedo todo el año. Muchas personas se dedican a al agricultura y cultivan arroz y maíz para alimentarse y caucho y café para exportar. Las ciudades están creciendo y mucha gente trabaja en fábricas y oficinas.
Esta distancia equivale a 800 km.
Datos
El caucho se obtiene de la savia de un árbol. El sureste asiático aporta más de tres cuartas partes a la producción mundial de caucho.
Hay más volcanes activos en el sureste asiático que en ninguna otra región del mundo. Las cenizas que dejan las erupciones volcánicas contribuyen a que el suelo sea fértil.
Indonesia está formada por más de 13,600 islas. Es la mayor cadena de islas del mundo y su población es la cuarta mayor del mundo.
Bicicleta rikisha
NAS
OCÉANO PACÍFICO
Cocos
MINDANAO
Barco de pesca
Ecuador
Atún
Ave del paraíso
Cocos
Esponja
Gas
Petróleo
IRIAN JAYA (Indonesia)
PAPUA NUEVA GUINEA
Cocos
MALUKU
Camarón
Plátanos
Puerto Moresby
Clavo
Canguro de árbol
Equidna
SULAWESI
Lagarto volador
Cangrejo
Ballena jorobada
Café
Mantarraya
E S I A
N
TIMOR
ragón de modo
FLORES
ALI
SUMBA
E
Camarón
Turismo
W
AUSTRALIA
Delfines
S
Trópico de Capricornio
J K L M N O P Q

Australia, Nueva Zelanda y las Islas del Pacífico

El Océano Pacífico está salpicado de miles de islas. Casi todos sus habitantes viven en pueblos y se dedican a cazar o a pescar. Australia es también una isla, pero tan grande que es un continente. La mayoría de los australianos vive en ciudades o en granjas. Gran parte de Australia es cálida y árida, pero también tiene montañas y selvas tropicales; además tiene animales y plantas que no hay en ninguna otra parte.

EXPLORADOR

▶ ¿Qué lago en el sur de Australia está seco la mayor parte del año y cubierto por una capa de sal de casi 4 metros de espesor? (Ver coordenadas H8.)

▶ ¿Qué animal tiene un cuerpo peludo, pico de pato, pone huevos y alimenta a sus crías con leche? Este extraño mamífero sólo vive en Australia. (Ver coordenadas J9.)

▶ Australia cuenta con rocas muy antiguas. ¿Puedes encontrar una con forma de ola y más de 3,000 millones de años de antigüedad? (Ver D9.)

Datos

La Barrera de Arrecifes de la costa este de Australia es el mayor arrecife de coral del mundo.

En el mundo existen 3,000 lenguas diferentes. Casi la mitad se hablan en las islas del Pacífico.

Australia es el continente más plano de la Tierra.

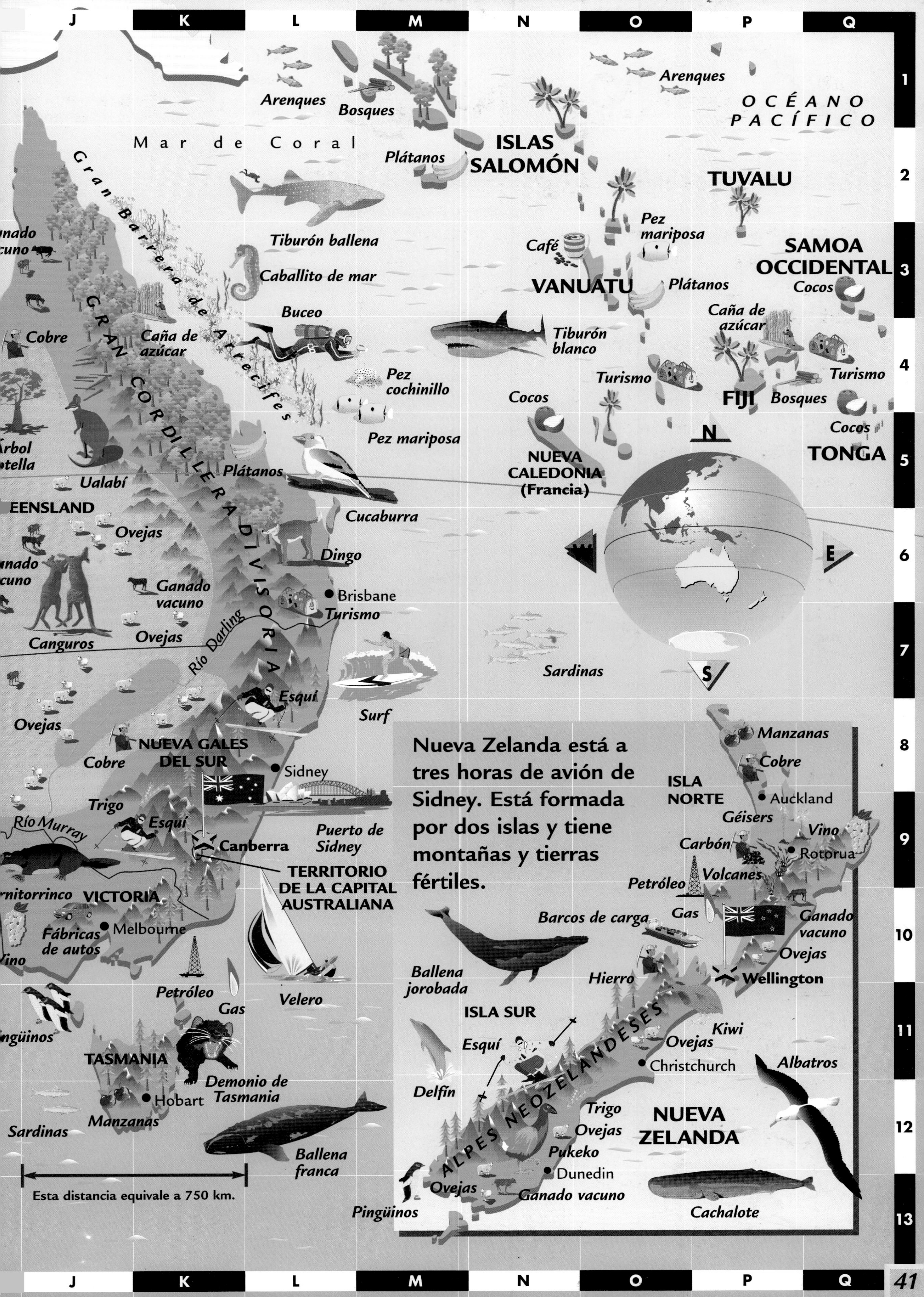

J K L M N O P Q
1 2 3 4 5 6 7 8 9 10 11 12 13
Mar de Coral
OCÉANO PACÍFICO
Gran Barrera de Arrecifes
GRAN CORDILLERA DIVISORIA
Arenques
Bosques
Arenques
Plátanos
ISLAS SALOMÓN
TUVALU
Tiburón ballena
Caballito de mar
Café
Pez mariposa
SAMOA OCCIDENTAL
Cocos
VANUATU
Plátanos
Buceo
Caña de azúcar
Cobre
Caña de azúcar
Tiburón blanco
Turismo
Turismo
Pez cochinillo
Cocos
FIJI
Bosques
Cocos
Pez mariposa
Árbol botella
N
NUEVA CALEDONIA (Francia)
TONGA
Plátanos
Ualabí
QUEENSLAND
Cucaburra
Ovejas
Dingo
W
E
Ganado vacuno
Ganado vacuno
Brisbane
Turismo
Río Darling
Canguros
Ovejas
Sardinas
S
Esquí
Ovejas
Surf
Cobre
NUEVA GALES DEL SUR
Sidney
Nueva Zelanda está a tres horas de avión de Sidney. Está formada por dos islas y tiene montañas y tierras fértiles.
Manzanas
Cobre
ISLA NORTE
Auckland
Géisers
Trigo
Esquí
Río Murray
Canberra
Puerto de Sidney
Carbón
Vino
Rotorua
TERRITORIO DE LA CAPITAL AUSTRALIANA
Volcanes
Petróleo
Ornitorrinco
VICTORIA
Fábricas de autos
Melbourne
Vino
Barcos de carga
Gas
Ganado vacuno
Ovejas
Ballena jorobada
Hierro
Wellington
Petróleo
Gas
Velero
Pingüinos
ISLA SUR
ALPES NEOZELANDESES
Kiwi
Ovejas
Esquí
Christchurch
Albatros
TASMANIA
Demonio de Tasmania
Hobart
Delfín
Trigo
Ovejas
NUEVA ZELANDA
Sardinas
Manzanas
Pukeko
Ballena franca
Dunedin
Ovejas
Ganado vacuno
Esta distancia equivale a 750 km.
Pingüinos
Cachalote

Asombroso

En estas páginas puedes descubrir cosas muy interesantes sobre el mundo. Busca los nombres de los lugares en el índice toponímico y averigua dónde se sitúan en los mapas.

¿Dónde se encuentra...

...el lugar más cálido?
Al Aziziyah en Libia. La temperatura más elevada ha sido 58°C.

En Al Aziziyah, podrías freír un huevo en una piedra a pleno sol.

...el lugar más frío?
Vostock en la Antártida. La temperatura más baja jamás registrada fue de -89°C. Tres veces más frío que un congelador.

...el lugar más húmedo?
Mawsynram, en la India, donde caen casi 12 metros de lluvia cada año.

...el lugar más seco?
el desierto de Atacama, en Chile, donde en los últimos 400 años ha llovido muy pocas veces.

¿Qué país es el...

...más grande?
Rusia. Tiene 17,075,400 km^2 de superficie.

...más pequeño?
Ciudad del Vaticano. Su superficie es de 0.44 km^2.

Si Rusia fuera del tamaño de una cancha de futbol, Ciudad del Vaticano sería como un sello postal.

...menos habitado?
Mongolia, que tiene un enorme desierto y altas montañas. Hay muy pocas ciudades y están muy alejadas unas de otras.

...más poblado?
Monaco, que es un país europeo muy pequeño. La orquesta de Mónaco está compuesta por más personas que su ejército.

¿Dónde está...

...la montaña más alta del mundo?
El Monte Everest en la Cordillera del Himalaya, en Nepal. Mide 8,848 m sobre el nivel del mar –es más de nueve veces más alta que la catarata más alta del mundo.

8,848 m

...la catarata más alta del mundo?
Las Cataratas del Ángel en Venezuela. Tiene una caída de 979 m, más del doble que el edifico más alto de Norteamérica.

979 m

...el edificio más alto de Norteamérica?
La Torre Sears en EEUU mide 443 metros de altura, casi cuatro veces más que el géiser más alto del mundo.

443 m

...el géiser más alto del mundo?
El géiser Steamboat en EEUU. Ha llegado a alcanzar 115 metros de altura, un poco más que el árbol más alto del mundo.

115 m

...el árbol más alto del mundo?
Una secuoya de California, EEUU. Mide 112 m de alto –más de 40 veces más alta que el hombre más alto del mundo.

112 m

¿Quién ha sido el hombre más alto del mundo?
Un estadounidense llamado Robert Pershing Wadlow, quien medía 2.70 metros.

EXPLORADOR

Busca estos lugares en el atlas.

- La montaña más alta (página 34, J8).
- La catarata más alta (página 20, E4).
- El río más largo (página 31, L7).
- El lugar más seco (página 21, E9).

¿Qué hora es?

En el mundo los relojes marcan en el mismo momento diferentes horas. Esto se debe a que el mundo está dividido en zonas horarias. El tiempo se mide desde Greenwich, en Londres, GB. Cuando cruzas una zona horaria en dirección este, debes adelantar el reloj una hora; si la cruzas en dirección oeste, debes atrasarlo una hora

Las letras am significan antes meridiano, es decir las horas comprendidas entre medianoche y mediodía. Las letras pm significan pasado meridiano, es decir las horas comprendidas entre mediodía y medianoche.

Si son las 12 pm en Londres, ¿qué hora es en Nueva York y en Tokio?

Mar y tierra

Imagina el mundo como si fuera un pastel. La mayor parte sería de océanos y mares y sólo una pequeña porción sería de tierra. En ese pedazo tendrías desiertos, selvas, montañas, hielos y praderas. Menos de la mitad del trozo correspondería a lugares habitados y tierras cultivadas. En este atlas encontrarás la selva más grande en la página 20, coordenadas H5, y el desierto más grande en la página 30, coordenadas E5.

¿Cuáles son los tres ríos más largos?

El río Nilo, en el norte de África, mide 6,671 km de largo. Recorrerlo a pie de un extremo a otro te tomaría más de 4 meses.

El río Amazonas, en Sudamérica, mide 6,437 km de longitud. Tendrías que correr durante más de 2 meses para recorrerlo.

El río Yangtsé, en China, mide 6,300 km de largo. Tardarías más de un mes en recorrerlo de principio a fin en bicicleta.

Índice toponímico

Este índice contiene todos los nombres de los lugares que aparecen en este atlas. El número de página te indica qué mapa debes consultar y las coordenadas te dicen dónde se localiza en el mapa. En la página 9 encontrarás una explicación sobre cómo se emplean las coordenadas.

D

E

F

G

H

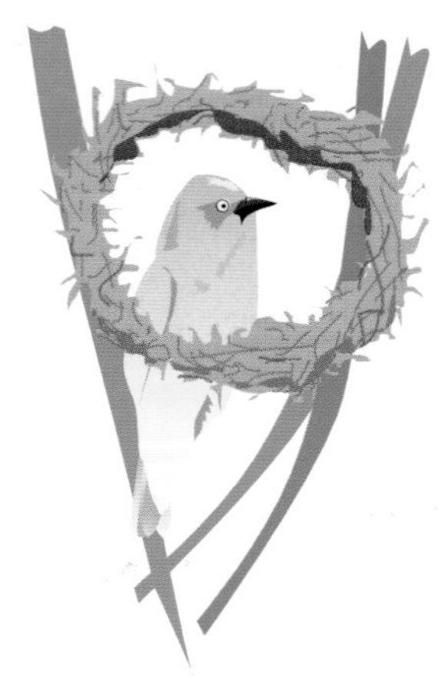

Algebra I Workbook

3rd Edition with Online Practice

by Mary Jane Sterling

Algebra I Workbook For Dummies®, 3rd Edition with Online Practice

Published by: **John Wiley & Sons, Inc.,** 111 River Street, Hoboken, NJ 07030-5774, www.wiley.com

For general information on our other products and services, please contact our Customer Care Department within the U.S. at 877-762-2974, outside the U.S. at 317-572-3993, or fax 317-572-4002. For technical support, please visit https://hub.wiley.com/community/support/dummies.

Wiley publishes in a variety of print and electronic formats and by print-on-demand. Some material included with standard print versions of this book may not be included in e-books or in print-on-demand. If this book refers to media such as a CD or DVD that is not included in the version you purchased, you may download this material at http://booksupport.wiley.com. For more information about Wiley products, visit www.wiley.com.

Library of Congress Control Number: 2017931102

ISBN 978-1-119-34895-5 (pbk); ISBN 978-1-119-34896-2 (ebk); ISBN 978-1-119-34898-6 (ebk)

Manufactured in the United States of America

C10012314_071719

order of operations
Proportional Statements
Powers & Roots
Mult & Div
Add & Subt
Left to Right

Contents at a Glance

Table of Contents

Introduction

Some of my earliest grade-school memories include receiving brand-new workbooks at the beginning of the school year. The pages of these workbooks were crisp, pristine, beautiful — and intimidating at the same time. But it didn't take long for those workbooks to become well-used and worn. My goal with *Algebra I Workbook For Dummies with Online Practice* is to give you that same workbook experience — without the intimidation, of course.

Remember, mathematics is a subject that has to be *handled.* You can read English literature and understand it without having to actually write it. You can read about biological phenomena and understand them, too, without taking part in an experiment. Mathematics is different. You really do have to do it, practice it, play with it, and use it. Only then does the mathematics become a part of your knowledge and skills. And what better way to get your fingers wet than by jumping into this workbook? Remember only practice, practice, and some more practice can help you master algebra! Have at it!

About This Book

This book is filled with algebra problems you can study, solve, and learn from. As you proceed through this book, you'll see plenty of road signs that clearly mark the way. You'll find explanations, examples, and other bits of info to make this journey as smooth an experience as possible. You also get to do your own grading with the solutions I provide at the end of each chapter. You can even go back and change your answers to the correct ones, if you made an error. No, you're not cheating. You're figuring out how to correctly work algebra problems. (Actually, changing answers to the correct ones is a great way to learn from your mistakes.)

I've organized this book very much like the way I organized *Algebra I For Dummies* (Wiley), which you may already have: I introduce basic concepts and properties first and then move on to the more complex ones. That way, if you're pretty unsteady on your feet, algebra-wise, you can begin at the beginning and build your skills and your confidence as you progress through the different chapters.

But maybe you don't need practice problems from beginning to end. Maybe you just need a bit of extra practice with specific types of algebra problems. One nice thing about this workbook is that you can start wherever you want. If your nemesis is graphing, for example, you can go straight to the chapters that focus on graphing. Formulas your problem area? Then go to the chapters that deal with formulas.

Bottom line: You do need to understand and know how to use the basic algebra concepts to start anywhere in this workbook. But, after you have those down, you can pick and choose where you want to work. You can jump in wherever you want and work from there.

I've also used the following conventions in this book to make things consistent and easy to understand, regardless which practice problems you're tackling:

- New terms are *italicized* and are closely followed by a clear definition.
- I **bold** the answers to the examples and the practice questions for easy identification. However, I don't bold the punctuation that follows the answer because I want to prevent any confusion with periods and decimal points that could be considered part of the answer.
- Algebra uses a lot of letters to represent numbers. In general, I use letters at the beginning of the alphabet (a, b, c, k) to represent *constants* — numbers that don't change all the time but may be special to a particular situation. The letters at the end of the alphabet usually represent *variables* — what you're solving for. I use the most commonly used letters (x, y, and z) for variables. And all constants and variables are *italicized.* And if, for any reason, I don't follow this convention, I let you know so that you aren't left guessing. (You may see breaks from the convention in some old, traditional formulas, for example, or when you want a particular letter to stand for someone's age, which just may happen to start with the letter A.)
- I use the corresponding symbols to represent the math operations of addition, subtraction, multiplication, and division: +, –, ×, and ÷. But keep the following special rules in mind when using them in algebra and in this book:
  - Subtraction (–) is an operation, but that symbol also represents *opposite of, minus*, and *negative*. When you get to the different situations, you can figure out how to interpret the wording, based on the context.
  - Multiplication (×) is usually indicated with a dot (·) or parentheses ( ) in algebra. In this book, I use parentheses most often, but you may occasionally see a × symbol. Don't confuse the × symbol with the italicized variable, x.
  - Division (÷) is sometimes indicated with a slash (/) or fraction line. I use these interchangeably in the problems throughout this book.

Foolish Assumptions

When writing this book, I made the following assumptions about you, my dear reader:

- You already have reasonable experience with basic algebra concepts and want an opportunity to practice those skills.
- You took or currently are taking Algebra I, but you need to brush up on certain areas.
- Your son, daughter, grandson, granddaughter, niece, nephew, or special someone is taking Algebra I. You haven't looked at an equation for years, and you want to help him or her.
- You love math, and your idea of a good time is solving equations on a rainy afternoon while listening to your iPod.

Icons Used in This Book

In this book, I include icons that help you find key ideas and information. Of course, because this entire workbook is chock-full of important nuggets of information, I highlight only the crème-de-la-crème information with these icons:

You find this icon throughout the book, highlighting the examples that cover the techniques needed to do the practice problems. Before you attempt the problems, look over an example or two, which can help you get started.

This icon highlights hints or suggestions that can save you time and energy, help you ease your way through the problems, and cut down on any potential frustration.

This icon highlights the important algebraic rules or processes that you want to remember, both for the algebra discussed in that particular location as well as for general reference later.

Although this icon isn't in red, it does call attention to particularly troublesome points. When I use this icon, I identify the tricky elements and tell you how to avoid trouble — or what to do to get out of it.

Beyond the Book

Be sure to check out the free Cheat Sheet for a handy guide of algebra fundamentals, such as the order of operations, rules for exponents, and more. To get this Cheat Sheet, simply go to `www.dummies.com` and search for "Algebra I Workbook" in the Search box.

The online practice that comes free with this book contains extra practice questions that correspond with each chapter in the book. To gain access to the online practice, all you have to do is register. Just follow these simple steps:

1. **Find your PIN access code located on the inside front cover of this book.**
2. **Go to Dummies.com and click** Activate Now.
3. **Find your product *(Algebra I Workbook For Dummies with Online Practice)* and then follow the on-screen prompts to activate your PIN.**

Now you're ready to go! You can go back to the program at `http://testbanks.wiley.com` as often as you want — simply log on with the username and password you created during your initial login. No need to enter the access code a second time.

Tip: If you have trouble with your PIN or can't find it, contact Wiley Product Technical Support at 877-762-2974 or go to `http://support.wiley.com`.

Where to Go from Here

Ready to start? All psyched and ready to go? Then it's time to take this excursion in algebra. Yes, this workbook is a grand adventure just waiting for you to take the first step. Before you begin your journey, however, I have a couple of recommendations:

- That you have a guidebook handy to help you with the trouble spots. One such guide is my book, *Algebra I For Dummies* (Wiley), which, as a companion to this book, mirrors most of the topics presented here. You can use it — or any well-written introductory algebra book — to fill in the gaps.
- That you pack a pencil with an eraser. It's the teacher and mathematician in me who realizes that mistakes can be made, and they erase easier when in pencil. That scratched-out blobby stuff is just not pretty.

When you're equipped with the preceding items, you need to decide where to start. No, you don't have to follow any particular path. You can venture out on your own, making your own decisions, taking your time, moving from topic to topic. You can do what you want. Or you can always stay with the security of the grand plan and start with the first chapter and carefully proceed through to the end. It's your decision, and any choice is correct.

1

Getting Down to the Nitty-Gritty on Basic Operations

IN THIS PART . . .

Brush up on the basics of deciphering signs in numbers.

Get a handle on algebraic properties.

Work with decimals and fractions.

Understand how to use exponents.

Rein in radicals.

Practice simplifying algebraic expressions.

» **Getting absolute value absolutely right**

» **Operating on signed numbers: Adding, subtracting, multiplying, and dividing**

Chapter 1
Deciphering Signs in Numbers

In this chapter, you practice the operations on signed numbers and figure out how to make these numbers behave the way you want them to. The behaving part involves using some well-established rules that are *good for you*. Heard that one before? But these rules (or *properties*, as they're called in math-speak) are very helpful in making math expressions easier to read and to handle when you're solving equations in algebra.

Assigning Numbers Their Place

You may think that identifying that 16 is bigger than 10 is an easy concept. But what about −1.6 and −1.04? Which of these numbers is bigger?

REMEMBER

The easiest way to compare numbers and to tell which is bigger or has a greater value is to find each number's position on the number line. The number line goes from negatives on the left to positives on the right (see Figure 1-1). Whichever number is farther to the right has the greater value, meaning it's bigger.

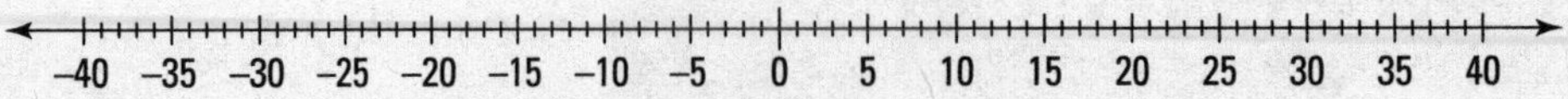

FIGURE 1-1: A number line.

–40 –35 –30 –25 –20 –15 –10 –5 0 5 10 15 20 25 30 35 40

EXAMPLE

Q. Using the number line in Figure 1-1, determine which is larger, –16 or –10.

A. **–10**. The number –10 is to the right of –16, so it's the bigger of the two numbers. You write that as $-10 > -16$ (read this as "negative 10 is greater than negative 16"). Or you can write it as $-16 < -10$ (negative 16 is less than negative 10).

Q. Which is larger, –1.6 or –1.04?

A. **–1.04**. The number –1.04 is to the right of –1.6, so it's larger.

1 Which is larger, –2 or –8?

-8 (crossed out)

-2

2 Which has the greater value, –13 or 2?

2

3 Which is bigger, –0.003 or –0.03?

-0.003

4 Which is larger, $-\frac{1}{6}$ or $-\frac{2}{3}$?

-1/6

Reading and Writing Absolute Value

The *absolute value* of a number, written as $|a|$, is an operation that evaluates whatever is between the vertical bars and then outputs a positive number. Another way of looking at this operation is that it can tell you how far a number is from 0 on the number line — with no reference to which side.

REMEMBER

The absolute value of a:

$|a| = a$, if a is a positive number ($a > 0$) or if $a = 0$.

$|a| = -a$, if a is a negative number ($a < 0$). Read this as "The absolute value of a is equal to the *opposite* of a."

EXAMPLE

Q. $|4| =$

A. 4

Q. $|-3| =$

A. 3

5 $|8| =$

8

6 $|-6| =$

6

7 $-|-6| =$

-6

8 $-|8| =$

-8

Adding Signed Numbers

Adding signed numbers involves two different rules, both depending on whether the two numbers being added have the same sign or different signs. After you determine whether the signs are the same or different, you use the absolute values of the numbers in the computation.

REMEMBER

To add signed numbers (assuming that a and b are positive numbers):

- **If the signs are the same:** Add the absolute values of the two numbers together and let their common sign be the sign of the answer.

  $(+a)+(+b)=+(a+b)$ **and** $(-a)+(-b)=-(a+b)$

- **If the signs are different:** Find the difference between the absolute values of the two numbers (subtract the smaller absolute value from the larger) and let the answer have the sign of the number with the larger absolute value. Assume that $|a|>|b|$.

  $(+a)+(-b)=+(a-b)$ **and** $(-a)+(+b)=-(a-b)$

EXAMPLE

Q. $(-6)+(-4)=-(6+4)=$

The signs are the same, so you find the sum and apply the common sign.

A. **−10**

Q. $(+8)+(-15)=-(15-8)=$

The signs are different, so you find the difference and use the sign of the number with the larger absolute value.

A. **−7**

9 $4+(-3)=$ 1

10 $5+(-11)=$ −6

11 $(-18)+(-5)=$ −23

12 $47+(-33)=$ 14

13 $(-3)+5+(-2)=$

14 $(-4)+(-6)+(-10)=$

15 $5+(-18)+(10)=$

16 $(-4)+4+(-5)+5+(-6)=$

Making a Difference with Signed Numbers

You really don't need a new set of rules when subtracting signed numbers. You just change the subtraction problem to an addition problem and use the rules for addition of signed numbers. To ensure that the answer to this new addition problem is the answer to the original subtraction problem, you change the operation from subtraction to addition, and you change the sign of the second number — the one that's being subtracted.

REMEMBER

To subtract two signed numbers:

$$a-(+b)=a+(-b) \quad \textbf{and} \quad a-(-b)=a+(+b)$$

EXAMPLE

Q. $(-8)-(-5)=$

Change the problem to $(-8)+(+5)=$

A. –3

Q. $6-(+11)=$

Change the problem to $6+(-11)=$

A. –5

17. $5-(-2)=$

18. $-6-(-8)=$

19. $4-87=$

20. $0-(-15)=$

21. $2.4-(-6.8)=$

22. $-15-(-11)=$

Multiplying Signed Numbers

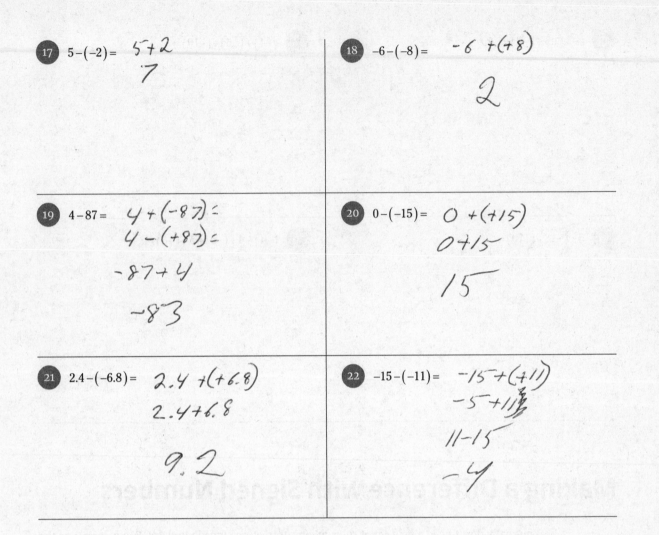

When you multiply two or more numbers, you just multiply them without worrying about the sign of the answer until the end. Then to assign the sign, just count the number of negative signs in the problem. If the number of negative signs is an even number, the answer is positive. If the number of negative signs is odd, the answer is negative.

REMEMBER

The product of two signed numbers:

$(+)(+)=+$ **and** $(-)(-)=+$

$(+)(-)=-$ **and** $(-)(+)=-$

The product of more than two signed numbers:

> (+)(+)(+)(−)(−)(−)(−) has a *positive* answer because there are an *even* number of negative factors.
>
> (+)(+)(+)(−)(−)(−) has a *negative* answer because there are an *odd* number of negative factors.

EXAMPLE

Q. (−2)(−3) =

There are two negative signs in the problem.

A. +6

Q. (−2)(+3)(−1)(+1)(−4) =

There are three negative signs in the problem.

A. −24

23 (−6)(3) =

24 (14)(−1) =

25 (−6)(−3) =

26 (6)(−3)(4)(−2) =

27 (−1)(−1)(−1)(−1)(−1)(2) =

28 (−10)(2)(3)(1)(−1) =

Dividing Signed Numbers

The rules for dividing signed numbers are exactly the same as those for multiplying signed numbers — as far as the sign goes. (See "Multiplying Signed Numbers" earlier in this chapter.) The rules do differ, though, because you have to divide, of course.

REMEMBER

When you divide signed numbers, just count the number of negative signs in the problem — in the numerator, in the denominator, and perhaps in front of the problem. If you have an even number of negative signs, the answer is positive. If you have an odd number of negative signs, the answer is negative.

EXAMPLE

Q. $\frac{-36}{-9} =$

A. **+4**. There are two negative signs in the problem, which is even, so the answer is positive.

Q. $\frac{-(-3)(-12)}{4} =$

A. **–9**. There are three negative signs in the problem, which is odd, so the answer is negative.

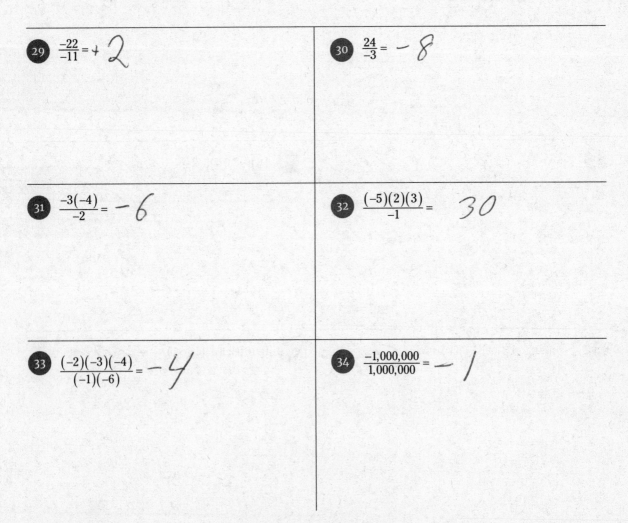

29 $\frac{-22}{-11} =$

30 $\frac{24}{-3} =$

31 $\frac{-3(-4)}{-2} =$

32 $\frac{(-5)(2)(3)}{-1} =$

33 $\frac{(-2)(-3)(-4)}{(-1)(-6)} =$

34 $\frac{-1{,}000{,}000}{1{,}000{,}000} =$

Answers to Problems on Signed Numbers

This section provides the answers (in bold) to the practice problems in this chapter.

1. Which is larger, –2 or –8? The answer is **–2 is larger.** The following number line shows that the number –2 is to the right of –8. So –2 is bigger than –8 (or $-2 > -8$).

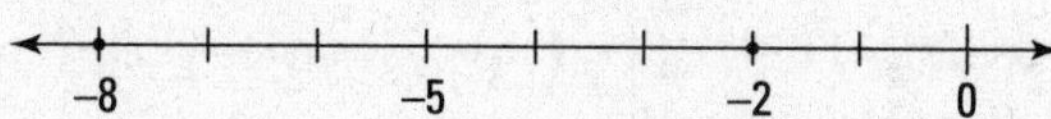

2. Which has the greater value, –13 or 2? **2 is greater**. The number 2 is to the right of –13. So 2 has a greater value than –13 (or $2 > -13$).

3. Which is bigger, –0.003 or –0.03? **–0.003 is bigger**. The following number line shows that the number –0.003 is to the right of –0.03, which means –0.003 is bigger than –0.03 (or $-0.003 > -0.03$).

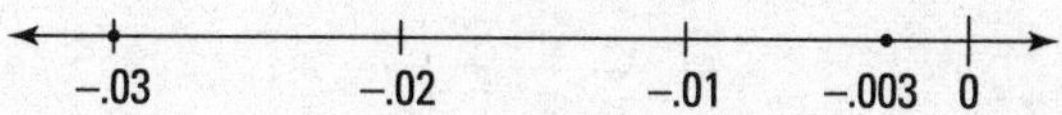

4. Which is larger, $-\frac{1}{6}$ or $-\frac{2}{3}$? $-\frac{1}{6}$ **is larger**. The number= $-\frac{2}{3} = -\frac{4}{6}$, and $-\frac{4}{6}$ is to the left of $-\frac{1}{6}$ on the following number line. So $-\frac{1}{6}$ is larger than $-\frac{2}{3}$ (or $-\frac{1}{6} > -\frac{2}{3}$).

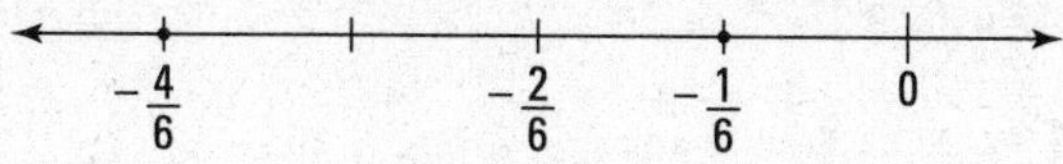

5. $|8| = \mathbf{8}$ because $8 > 0$.

6. $|-6| = \mathbf{6}$ because $-6 < 0$ and 6 is the opposite of –6.

7. $-|-6| = \mathbf{-6}$ because $|-6| = 6$ as in the previous problem.

8. $-|8| = \mathbf{-8}$ because $|8| = 8$.

9. $4+(-3) = \mathbf{1}$ because 4 is the greater absolute value.
$4+(-3) = +(4-3) = 1$

10. $5+(-11) = \mathbf{-6}$ because –11 has the greater absolute value.
$5+(-11) = -(11-5) = -6$

11. $(-18)+(-5) = \mathbf{-23}$ because both of the numbers have negative signs; when the signs are the same, find the sum of their absolute values. $(-18)+(-5) = -(18+5) = -23$

12. $47+(-33) = \mathbf{14}$ because 47 has the greater absolute value.
$47+(-33) = +(47-33) = 14$

13. $(-3)+5+(-2) = \mathbf{0}$
$(-3)+5+(-2) = [(-3)+5]+(-2) = (2)+(-2) = 0$

14. $(-4)+(-6)+(-10) = \mathbf{-20}$
$(-4)+(-6)+(-10) = -(4+6)+(-10) = (-10)+(-10) = -(10+10) = -20$

15. $5+(-18)+(10)=\mathbf{-3}$

    $5+(-18)+(10)=-(18-5)+10=-(13)+10=-(13-10)=-3$

    Or you may prefer to add the two numbers with the same sign first, like this:

    $5+(-18)+(10)=(5+10)+(-18)=15+(-18)=-(18-15)=-3$

    You can do this because order and grouping (association) don't matter in addition.

16. $(-4)+4+(-5)+5+(-6)=\mathbf{-6}$

    $(-4)+4+(-5)+5+(-6)=[(-4)+4]+[(-5)+5]+(-6)=0+0+(-6)=-6$

17. $5-(-2)=\mathbf{7}$

    $5-(-2)=5+(+2)=7$

18. $-6-(-8)=\mathbf{2}$

    $-6-(-8)=-6+(+8)=8-6=2$

19. $4-87=\mathbf{-83}$

    $4-87=4+(-87)=-(87-4)=-83$

20. $0-(-15)=\mathbf{15}$

    $0-(-15)=0+15=15$

21. $2.4-(-6.8)=\mathbf{9.2}$

    $2.4-(-6.8)=2.4+6.8=9.2$

22. $-15-(-11)=\mathbf{-4}$

    $-15-(-11)=-15+11=-(15-11)=-4$

23. $(-6)(3)=\mathbf{-18}$ because the multiplication problem has one negative, and 1 is an odd number.

24. $(14)(-1)=\mathbf{-14}$ because the multiplication problem has one negative, and 1 is an odd number.

25. $(-6)(-3)=\mathbf{18}$ because the multiplication problem has two negatives, and 2 is an even number.

26. $(6)(-3)(4)(-2)=\mathbf{144}$ because the multiplication problem has two negatives.

27. $(-1)(-1)(-1)(-1)(-1)(2)=\mathbf{-2}$ because the multiplication problem has five negatives.

28. $(-10)(2)(3)(1)(-1)=\mathbf{60}$ because the multiplication problem has two negatives.

29. $-22/_{-11}=\mathbf{2}$ because the division problem has two negatives.

30. $24/_{-3}=\mathbf{-8}$ because the division problem has one negative.

31. $\frac{-3(-4)}{-2}=\mathbf{-6}$ because three negatives result in a negative.

32. $\frac{(-5)(2)(3)}{-1}=\mathbf{30}$ because the division problem has two negatives.

33. $\frac{(-2)(-3)(-4)}{(-1)(-6)}=\mathbf{-4}$ because the division problem has five negatives.

34. $\frac{-1{,}000{,}000}{1{,}000{,}000}=\mathbf{-1}$ because the division problem has one negative.

- Distributing over addition and subtraction
- Utilizing the associative and commutative rules

Chapter 2

Incorporating Algebraic Properties

Algebra has rules for everything, including a sort of shorthand notation to save time and space. The notation that comes with particular properties cuts down on misinterpretation because it's very specific and universally known. (I give the guidelines for doing operations like addition, subtraction, multiplication, and division in Chapter 1.) In this chapter, you see the specific rules that apply when you use grouping symbols and rearrange terms.

Getting a Grip on Grouping Symbols

The most commonly used *grouping symbols* in algebra are (in order from most to least common):

- Parentheses ( )
- Brackets [ ]
- Braces { }
- Fraction lines /

- Radicals $\sqrt{\ }$
- Absolute value symbols | |

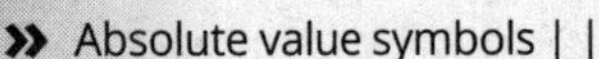

Here's what you need to know about grouping symbols: You must compute whatever is inside them (or under or over, in the case of the fraction line) first, before you can use that result to solve the rest of the problem. If what's inside isn't or can't be simplified into one term, then anything outside the grouping symbol that multiplies one of the terms has to multiply them all — that's the *distributive property,* which I cover in the very next section.

EXAMPLE

Q. $16-(4+2)=$

A. **10**. Add the 4 and 2; then subtract the result from the 16: $16-(4+2)=16-6=10$

Q. Simplify $2[6-(3-7)]$.

A. **20**. First subtract the 7 from the 3; then subtract the −4 from the 6 by changing it to an addition problem. You can then multiply the 2 by the 10: $2[6-(3-7)]=2[6-(-4)]$
$=2[6+4]=2[10]=20$

EXAMPLE

Q. $1-|-8+19|+3(4+2)=$

A. **8**. Combine what's in the absolute value and parentheses first, before combining the results:

$$1-|-8+19|+3(4+2)=1-|11|+3(6)$$
$$=1-11+18=-10+18=8$$

When you get to the three terms with subtract and add, $1-11+18$, you always perform the operations in order, reading from left to right. See Chapter 6 for more on this process, called *the order of operations.*

Q. $\frac{32}{30-2(3+4)}=$

A. **2**. You have to complete the work in the denominator first before dividing the 32 by that result:

$$\frac{32}{30-2(3+4)}=\frac{32}{30-2(7)}=\frac{32}{30-14}$$
$$=\frac{32}{16}=2$$

1. $3(2-5)+14=$

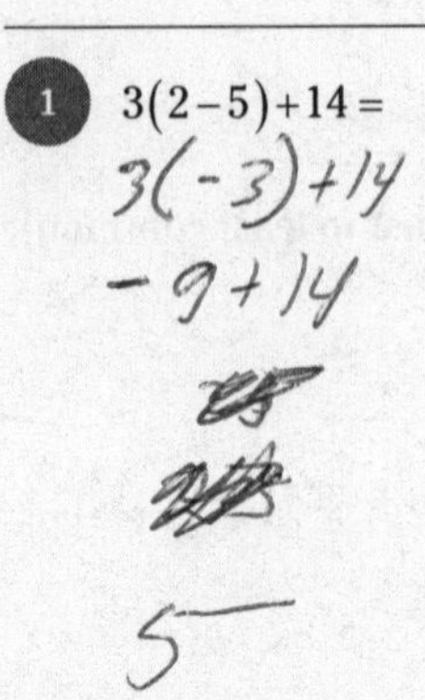

2. $4[3(6-8)+2(5+9)]-11=$

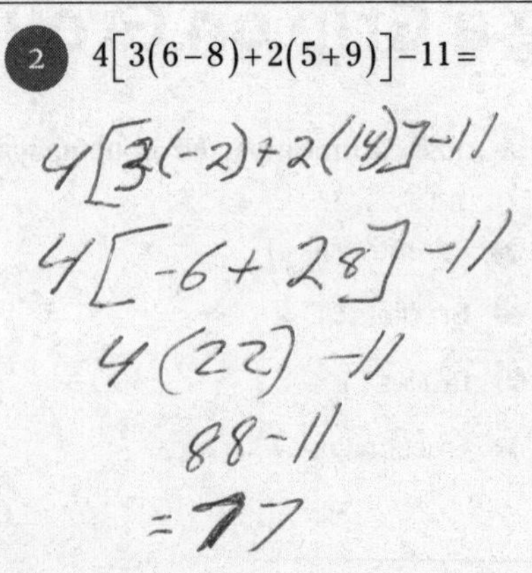

3 $5\{8[2+(6-3)]-4\}=$

4 $\dfrac{\sqrt{19-3(6-8)}}{6[8-4(5-2)]-1}=$

5 $4-5|6-3(8-2)|=$

6 $\dfrac{(9-1)5-4(6)}{\sqrt{11-2}-\sqrt{4-\sqrt{2+7}}}=$

Distributing the Wealth

The *distributive property* is used to perform an operation on each of the terms within a grouping symbol. The following rules show distributing multiplication over addition and distributing multiplication over subtraction:

$a(b+c)=a\times b+a\times c$ **and** $a(b-c)=a\times b-a\times c$

EXAMPLE

Q. $3(6-4)=$

A. **6**. First, distribute the 3 over the $6-4$: $3(6-4)=3\times6-3\times4=18-12=6$. Another (simpler) way to get the correct answer is just to subtract the 4 from the 6 and then multiply: $3(2)=6$. However, when you can't or don't want to combine what's in the grouping symbols, you use the distributive property.

Q. $5\left(a-\frac{1}{5}\right)=$

A. $\mathbf{5a-1}$

$5\times a-5\times\frac{1}{5}=5a-1$

7. $4(7+y)=$

8. $-3(x-11)=$

9. $\frac{2}{3}(6+15y)=$

10. $-8\left(\frac{1}{2}-\frac{1}{4}+\frac{3}{8}\right)=$

11. $4a(\pi-2)=$

12. $5\left(z+\frac{4}{5}-2\right)=$

Making Associations Work

The *associative rule* in math says that in addition and multiplication problems, you can change the *association*, or groupings, of three or more numbers and not change the final result. The associative rule looks like the following:

$$a+(b+c)=(a+b)+c \quad \textbf{and} \quad a\times(b\times c)=(a\times b)\times c$$

REMEMBER

This rule is special to addition and multiplication. It doesn't work for subtraction or division. You're probably wondering why even use this rule? Because it can sometimes make the computation easier.

- Instead of doing $5+(-5+17)$, change it to $\left[5+(-5)\right]+17=0+17=17$.
- Instead of $6\left(\frac{1}{6}\times 19\right)$, do $\left(6\times\frac{1}{6}\right)19=(1)19=19$.

EXAMPLE

Q. $-14+(14+23)=$

A. **23**. Reassociate the terms and then add the first two together: $-14+(14+23)=(-14+14)+23=0+23=23$.

Q. $4(5\times 6)=$

A. **120**. You can either multiply the way the problem is written, $4(5\times 6)=4(30)=120$, or you can reassociate and multiply the first two factors first: $(4\times 5)6=(20)6=120$.

13 $16+(-16+47)=$

14 $(5-13)+13=$

15 $18\left(\frac{5}{9}\times 7\right)=$

16 $(110\times 8)\frac{1}{8}=$

Computing by Commuting

The *commutative property* of addition and multiplication says that the order that you add or multiply numbers doesn't matter. Be careful, though, because the order of subtraction and division *does* matter. You get the same answer whether you 3×4 or 4×3. The rule looks like the following:

$$a+b=b+a \quad \textbf{and} \quad a\times b=b\times a$$

You can use this rule to your advantage when doing math computations. In the following two examples, the associative rule finishes off the problems after changing the order.

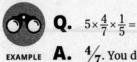

EXAMPLE

Q. $5\times\frac{4}{7}\times\frac{1}{5}=$

A. $^4/_7$. You don't really want to multiply fractions unless necessary. Notice that the first and last factors are multiplicative inverses of one another: $5\times\frac{4}{7}\times\frac{1}{5}=$ $5\times\frac{1}{5}\times\frac{4}{7}=\left(5\times\frac{1}{5}\right)\times\frac{4}{7}=(1)\frac{4}{7}=\frac{4}{7}$. The second and last factors were reversed.

Q. $-3+16+303=$

A. **316**. The second and last terms are reversed, and then the first two terms are grouped.

$$-3+16+303=-3+303+16=$$
$$(-3+303)+16=300+16=316.$$

17 $8+5+(-8)=$

$[8+(-8)]+5$

5

or

$(-8+8)+5$

5

18 $5\times47\times2=$

$(2\times5)\times47$

10×47

470

19 $\frac{3}{5}\times13\times10=$

$(3/5\times10)\times13$

6×13

78

20 $-23+47+23-47+8=$

$(-23+23)+(47-47)+8$

8

Answers to Problems on Algebraic Properties

This section provides the answers (in bold) to the practice problems in this chapter.

1. $3(2-5)+14=\mathbf{5}$

   $3(2-5)+14=3(-3)+14=(-9)+14=5$

2. $4\left[3(6-8)+2(5+9)\right]-11=\mathbf{77}$

   $$\begin{aligned}4\left[3(6-8)+2(5+9)\right]-11&=4\left[3(-2)+2(14)\right]-11\\&=4[-6+28]-11\\&=4[22]-11=88-11=77\end{aligned}$$

3. $5\left\{8\left[2+(6-3)\right]-4\right\}=\mathbf{180}$

   $$\begin{aligned}5\left\{8\left[2+(6-3)\right]-4\right\}&=5\{8[2+3]-4\}\\&=5\{8[5]-4\}=5\{40-4\}=5\{36\}=180\end{aligned}$$

4. $\dfrac{\sqrt{19-3(6-8)}}{6\left[8-4(5-2)\right]-1}=-\mathbf{\dfrac{1}{5}}$

   $$\frac{\sqrt{19-3(6-8)}}{6\left[8-4(5-2)\right]-1}=\frac{\sqrt{19-3(-2)}}{6\left[8-4(3)\right]-1}=\frac{\sqrt{19+6}}{6[8-12]-1}=\frac{\sqrt{25}}{6[-4]-1}=\frac{5}{-24-1}=\frac{5}{-25}=-\frac{1}{5}$$

5. $4-5|6-3(8-2)|=\mathbf{-56}$

   $$\begin{aligned}4-5|6-3(8-2)|&=4-5|6-3(6)|=4-5|6-18|\\&=4-5|-12|=4-5(12)\\&=4-60=-56\end{aligned}$$

6. $\dfrac{(9-1)5-4(6)}{\sqrt{11-2}-\sqrt{4-\sqrt{2+7}}}=\mathbf{8}$

   $$\frac{(9-1)5-4(6)}{\sqrt{11-2}-\sqrt{4-\sqrt{2+7}}}=\frac{(8)5-24}{\sqrt{9}-\sqrt{4-\sqrt{9}}}=\frac{40-24}{3-\sqrt{4-3}}=\frac{16}{3-\sqrt{1}}=\frac{16}{3-1}=\frac{16}{2}=8$$

7. $4(7+y)=\mathbf{28+4y}$

   $4(7+y)=4\times7+4\times y=28+4y$

8. $-3(x-11)=\mathbf{-3x+33}$

   $-3(x-11)=(-3)x-(-3)(11)=-3x+33$

9. $\frac{2}{3}(6+15y)=\mathbf{4+10y}$

   $\frac{2}{3}(6+15y)=\frac{2}{3}\times6+\frac{2}{3}(15y)=\frac{2\times6}{3}+\frac{2\times15}{3}y=4+10y$

10 $-8\left(\frac{1}{2}-\frac{1}{4}+\frac{3}{8}\right)=\mathbf{-5}$

$$-8\left(\frac{1}{2}-\frac{1}{4}+\frac{3}{8}\right)=(-8)\left(\frac{1}{2}\right)-(-8)\left(\frac{1}{4}\right)+(-8)\left(\frac{3}{8}\right)=-\frac{8}{2}+\frac{8}{4}-\frac{8\times 3}{8}$$
$$=-4+2-3$$
$$=(-4+2)-3=-2-3=-5$$

11 $4a(\pi-2)=\mathbf{4a\pi-8a}$

$$4a(\pi-2)=(4a\times\pi)-(4a\times 2)=4a\pi-8a$$

12 $5\left(z+\frac{4}{5}-2\right)=\mathbf{5z-6}$

$$5\left(z+\frac{4}{5}-2\right)=5\times z+5\left(\frac{4}{5}\right)-5(2)=5z+\frac{5\times 4}{5}-10$$
$$=5z+4-10=5z-6$$

13 $16+(-16+47)=\mathbf{47}$

$$16+(-16+47)=[16+(-16)]+47=0+47=47$$

14 $(5-13)+13=\mathbf{5}$

$$(5-13)+13=[5+(-13)]+13=5+[(-13)+13]=5+0=5$$

15 $18\left(\frac{5}{9}\times 7\right)=\mathbf{70}$

$$18\left(\frac{5}{9}\times 7\right)=\left(18\times\frac{5}{9}\right)7=\left(\frac{18\times 5}{9}\right)7=(10)7=70$$

16 $(110\times 8)\frac{1}{8}=\mathbf{110}$

$$(110\times 8)\frac{1}{8}=110\left(8\times\frac{1}{8}\right)=110(1)=110$$

17 $8+5+(-8)=\mathbf{5}$

$$8+5+(-8)=5+8+(-8)=5+[8+(-8)]=5+0=5$$

18 $5\times 47\times 2=\mathbf{470}$

$$5\times 47\times 2=5\times 2\times 47=(5\times 2)47=10\times 47=470$$

19 $\frac{3}{5}\times 13\times 10=\mathbf{78}$

$$\frac{3}{5}\times 13\times 10=\frac{3}{5}\times 10\times 13=\left(\frac{3}{5}\times 10\right)13=\left(\frac{3\times 10}{5}\right)13=6\times 13=78$$

20 $-23+47+23-47+8=\mathbf{8}$

$$-23+47+23-47+8=-23+23+47-47+8$$
$$=(-23+23)+(47-47)+8$$
$$=0+0+8=8$$

» Making proportions work for you

» Operating on fractions

Chapter 3

Making Fractions and Decimals Behave

You can try to run and hide, but you may as well face it. Fractions are here to stay. People don't usually eat a whole pizza, buy furniture that's exactly 5 feet long, or grow to be an even number of inches tall. Fractions are not only useful, but they're also an essential part of everyday life.

Fractions are equally as important in algebra. Many times, to complete a problem, you have to switch from one form of a fraction to another. This chapter provides you plenty of opportunities to work out all your fractional frustration.

Converting Improper and Mixed Fractions

REMEMBER

An *improper fraction* is one where the *numerator* (the number on the top of the fraction) has a value greater than or equal to the *denominator* (the number on the bottom of the fraction) — the fraction is top heavy. Improper fractions can be written as *mixed numbers* or whole numbers — and vice versa. For example, $^{14}/_{3}$ is an improper fraction, and $4\,^{2}/_{3}$ is a mixed number.

- **To change an improper fraction to a mixed number,** divide the numerator by the denominator and write the remainder in the numerator of the new fraction.
- **To change a mixed number to an improper fraction,** multiply the whole number times the denominator and add the numerator. This result goes in the numerator of a fraction that has the original denominator still in the denominator.

EXAMPLE

Q. Change $29/8$ to a mixed number.

A. $3\,5/8$. First, divide the 29 by 8:

$$\begin{array}{r} 3 \\ 8\overline{)29} \\ \underline{24} \\ 5 \end{array}$$

Then write the mixed number with the *quotient* (the number of times the denominator divides into the numerator) as the whole number and the remainder as the numerator of the fraction in the mixed number: $3\,5/8$.

Q. Change $6\,5/7$ to an improper fraction:

A. $47/7$. Multiply the 6 and 7 and then add the 5, which equals 47. Then write the fraction with this result in the numerator and the 7 in the denominator: $47/7$.

1 Change the mixed number $4\,7/8$ to an improper fraction.

$\frac{39}{8}$

2 Change the mixed number $2\,1/13$ to an improper fraction.

$\frac{27}{13}$

3 Change the improper fraction $16/5$ to a mixed number.

$3\frac{1}{5}$

4 Change the improper fraction $-19/7$ to a mixed number.

$-2\frac{5}{7}$

Finding Fraction Equivalences

In algebra, all sorts of computations and manipulations use fractions. In many problems, you have to change the fractions so that they have the same denominator or so that their form is compatible with what you need to solve the problem. Two fractions are *equivalent* if they have the same value, such as $\frac{1}{2}$ and $\frac{3}{6}$. To create an equivalent fraction from a given fraction, you multiply or divide the numerator and denominator by the same number. This technique is basically the same one you use to reduce a fraction.

EXAMPLE

Q. Find a fraction equivalent to $\frac{7}{8}$ with a denominator of 40.

A. $\frac{35}{40}$. Because 5 times 8 is 40, you multiply both the numerator and denominator by 5. In reality, you're just multiplying by 1, which doesn't change the real value of anything.

$$\frac{7}{8}\times\frac{5}{5}=\frac{7\times5}{8\times5}=\frac{35}{40}$$

Q. Reduce $\frac{15}{36}$ by multiplying the numerator and denominator by $\frac{1}{3}$. The same thing is accomplished if you divide both numerator and denomina-tor by 3.

A. $\frac{5}{12}$

$$\frac{15}{36}\times\frac{1/3}{1/3}=\frac{15\times1/3}{36\times1/3}=\frac{15/3}{36/3}=\frac{5}{12} \text{ or}$$

$$\frac{15\div3}{36\div3}=\frac{5}{12}$$

5 Find an equivalent fraction with a denominator of 28 for $\frac{3}{7}$.

$\frac{3}{7}\times\frac{4}{4}=\frac{12}{28}$

6 Find an equivalent fraction with a denominator of 30 for $\frac{x}{6}$.

$\frac{x}{6}\times\frac{5}{5}=\frac{5x}{30}$

7 Reduce this fraction: $\frac{16}{60}$.

$\frac{16}{60}=\frac{8}{30}=\frac{4}{15}$

8 Reduce this fraction: $\frac{63}{84}$.

$\frac{63}{84}=\frac{21}{28}=\frac{3}{4}$

28
3)84
6
24

Making Proportional Statements

REMEMBER

A *proportion* is an equation with two fractions equal to one another. Proportions have some wonderful properties that make them useful for solving problems — especially when you're comparing one quantity to another or one percentage to another.

Given the proportion $\frac{a}{b} = \frac{c}{d}$, then the following are also true:

- $a \times d = c \times b$ (The cross products form an equation.)
- $\frac{b}{a} = \frac{d}{c}$ (The "flip" is an equation.)
- $\frac{a}{b} = \frac{c \cdot \cancel{k}}{d \cdot \cancel{k}}$ (You can reduce either fraction vertically.)
- $\frac{a}{b \cdot \cancel{k}} = \frac{c}{d \cdot \cancel{k}}$ (You can reduce the numerator or denominator horizontally.)

EXAMPLE

Q. Find the missing value in the following proportion: $\frac{42}{66} = \frac{28}{d}$

A. **44.** The numerator and denominator in the fraction on the left have a common factor of 6. Multiply each by $\frac{1}{6}$. Flip the proportion to get the unknown in the numerator of the right-hand fraction. Then you see that the two bottom numbers each have a common factor of 7. Divide each by 7. Finally, cross-multiply to get your answer:

$$\frac{42}{66} \times \frac{1/6}{1/6} = \frac{7}{11} = \frac{28}{d}$$

$$\frac{11}{7} = \frac{d}{28}$$

$$\frac{11}{{}_{1}\cancel{7}} = \frac{d}{\cancel{28}_{4}}$$

$$\frac{11}{1} = \frac{d}{4}$$

$$11 \times 4 = 1 \times d$$

$$44 = d$$

Q. If Agnes can type 60 words per minute, then how long will it take her to type a manuscript containing 4,020 words (if she can keep typing at the same rate)?

A. **67 minutes (1 hour and 7 minutes).** Set up a proportion with words in the two numerators and the corresponding number of minutes in the denominators:

$$\frac{60 \text{ words}}{1 \text{ minute}} = \frac{4020 \text{ words}}{x \text{ minutes}}$$

Divide both numerators by 60 and then cross-multiply to solve for x.

$$\frac{{}^{1}\cancel{60}}{1} = \frac{\cancel{4020}^{67}}{x}$$

$$1 \times x = 1 \times 67$$

$$x = 67$$

9 Solve for x: $\frac{7}{21} = \frac{x}{24}$

10 Solve for x: $\frac{45}{x} = \frac{60}{200}$

11 Solve for x: $\frac{x}{90} = \frac{60}{108}$

12 Solve for x: $\frac{26}{16} = \frac{65}{x}$

13 A recipe calls for 2 teaspoons of cinnamon and 4 cups of flour. You need to increase the flour to 6 cups. To keep the ingredients proportional, how many teaspoons of cinnamon should you use?

14 A factory produces two faulty iPods for every 500 iPods it produces. How many faulty iPods would you expect to find in a shipment of 1,250?

Finding Common Denominators

Before you can add or subtract fractions, you need to find a common denominator for them. Ideally that common denominator is the *least common multiple* — the smallest number that each of the denominators can divide into without a remainder. A method of last resort, though, is to multiply the denominators together. Doing so gives you a number that the denominators divide evenly. You may have to work with larger numbers using this method, but you can always reduce the fractions at the end.

EXAMPLE

Q. How would you write the fractions $^1/_3$ and $^3/_4$ with the same denominator?

A. **$^4/_{12}$ and $^9/_{12}$.** The fractions $^1/_3$ and $^3/_4$ have denominators with no factors in common, so the least common denominator is 12, the product of the two numbers. Now you can write them both as fractions with a denominator of 12:

$$\frac{1}{3}\times\frac{4}{4}=\frac{4}{12} \text{ and } \frac{3}{4}\times\frac{3}{3}=\frac{9}{12}$$

Q. What is the least common denominator for the fractions $^7/_{20}$ and $^5/_{24}$?

A. **120.** The fractions $^7/_{20}$ and $^5/_{24}$ have denominators with a greatest common factor of 4. So multiplying the two denominators together gives you 480, and then dividing 480 by that common factor gives you $480 \div 4 = 120$. The least common denominator is 120.

15 Rewrite the fractions $^2/_7$ and $^3/_8$ with a common denominator.

16 Rewrite the fractions $^5/_{12}$ and $^7/_{18}$ with a common denominator.

17 Rewrite the fractions $^9/_x$ and $^5/_6$ with a common denominator.

18 Rewrite the fractions $\frac{5}{x}$ and $\frac{1}{x+6}$ with a common denominator.

19 Rewrite the fractions $\frac{1}{2}$, $\frac{1}{3}$, and $\frac{1}{5}$ with a common denominator.

20 Rewrite the fractions $\frac{2}{3}$, $\frac{5}{x}$, and $\frac{3}{2x}$ with a common denominator.

Adding and Subtracting Fractions

You can add fractions together or subtract one from another if they have a common denominator. After you find the common denominator and change the fractions to their equivalents, then you can add the numerators together or subtract them (keeping the denominators the same).

EXAMPLE

Q. $\frac{5}{6}+\frac{7}{8}=$

A. $1\frac{17}{24}$. First find the common denominator, 24, and then complete the addition:

$$\left(\frac{5}{6}\times\frac{4}{4}\right)+\left(\frac{7}{8}\times\frac{3}{3}\right)=\frac{20}{24}+\frac{21}{24}$$
$$=\frac{41}{24}=1\frac{17}{24}$$

Q. $2\frac{1}{2}+\left(-1\frac{1}{3}\right)+5\frac{3}{10}=$

A. $6\frac{7}{15}$. You need a common denominator of 30:

$$2\frac{1}{2}+\left(-1\frac{1}{3}\right)+5\frac{3}{10}$$
$$=2+\left(\frac{1}{2}\times\frac{15}{15}\right)-1-\left(\frac{1}{3}\times\frac{10}{10}\right)+5+\left(\frac{3}{10}\times\frac{3}{3}\right)$$

The whole number parts are separated from the fractional parts to keep the numbers in the computations smaller.

$$=2+\left(\frac{15}{30}\right)-1-\left(\frac{10}{30}\right)+5+\left(\frac{9}{30}\right)$$
$$=2-1+5+\left(\frac{15-10+9}{30}\right)=6+\frac{14}{30}=6\frac{7}{15}$$

EXAMPLE

Q. $2\frac{1}{8}-1\frac{1}{7}=$

A. $\frac{55}{56}$. In this problem, change both mixed numbers to improper fractions. The common denominator is 56:

$$\frac{17}{8}-\frac{8}{7}=\left(\frac{17}{8}\times\frac{7}{7}\right)-\left(\frac{8}{7}\times\frac{8}{8}\right)$$
$$=\frac{119}{56}-\frac{64}{56}=\frac{55}{56}$$

Q. $1-\frac{11}{13}=$

A. $\frac{2}{13}$. Even though the 1 isn't a fraction, you need to write it as a fraction with a denominator of 13. The subtraction problem becomes $\frac{13}{13}-\frac{11}{13}$.

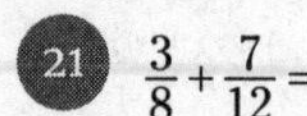

21 $\frac{3}{8}+\frac{7}{12}=$

22 $3\frac{1}{3}+4\frac{3}{5}+\frac{7}{15}=$

23 $1\frac{5}{12}-\frac{7}{9}=$

24 $3\frac{2}{3}-\left(-6\frac{1}{2}\right)=$

Multiplying and Dividing Fractions

Multiplying fractions is really a much easier process than adding or subtracting fractions, because you don't have to find a common denominator. Furthermore, you can take some creative steps and reduce the fractions before you even multiply them.

TIP

When multiplying fractions, you can pair up the numerator of any fraction in the problem with the denominator of any other fraction; then divide each by the same number (reduce). Doing so saves your having large numbers to multiply and then to reduce later.

When you start with mixed numbers, you have to change them to improper fractions before starting the reduction and multiplication process.

REMEMBER

Algebra really doesn't have a way to divide fractions. If you want to divide fractions, you just have to change them to multiplication problems. Sounds easy, right? Just change the division to multiplication and use the *reciprocal* — where the numerator and denominator switch places — of the second fraction in that new problem. The answer to this multiplication problem is the same as the answer to the original division problem.

EXAMPLE

Q. $\frac{25}{14}\times\frac{49}{30}\times\frac{27}{10}=$

A. $7\frac{7}{8}$. First, reduce: The 25 and 30 have a common factor of 5, the 14 and 49 have a common factor of 7, the 6 and 27 have a common factor of 3, and the 5 and 10 have a common factor of 5.

$$\frac{\overset{5}{\cancel{25}}}{14}\times\frac{49}{\underset{6}{\cancel{30}}}\times\frac{27}{10}=\frac{5}{\underset{2}{\cancel{14}}}\times\frac{\overset{7}{\cancel{49}}}{6}\times\frac{27}{10}=$$
$$=\frac{5}{2}\times\frac{7}{\underset{2}{\cancel{6}}}\times\frac{\overset{9}{\cancel{27}}}{10}$$
$$=\frac{5}{2}\times\frac{7}{2}\times\frac{9}{10}$$

Reduce the 5 and 10 by dividing by 5. And then, to multiply the fractions, multiply all the numerators together and all the denominators together to make the new fraction:

$$\frac{\overset{1}{\cancel{5}}}{2}\times\frac{7}{2}\times\frac{9}{\underset{2}{\cancel{10}}}=\frac{1}{2}\times\frac{7}{2}\times\frac{9}{2}=\frac{63}{8}=7\frac{7}{8}$$

Q. $-2\frac{2}{9}\times1\frac{1}{8}=$

A. $-2\frac{1}{2}$.

First, write the mixed numbers as improper fractions. Then reduce where possible and multiply.

$$-2\frac{2}{9}\times1\frac{1}{8}=-\frac{20}{9}\times\frac{9}{8}$$
$$=-\frac{\overset{5}{\cancel{20}}}{\underset{1}{\cancel{9}}}\times\frac{\overset{1}{\cancel{9}}}{\underset{2}{\cancel{8}}}$$
$$=-\frac{5}{1}\times\frac{1}{2}=-\frac{5}{2}=-2\frac{1}{2}$$

EXAMPLE

Q. $6\frac{1}{8}\div5\frac{1}{4}=$

A. $1\frac{1}{6}$. First change the mixed numbers to improper fractions. Then change the *divide* to *multiply* and the second (right) fraction to its reciprocal. Finally, do the multiplication problem to get the answer:

$$\frac{49}{8}\div\frac{21}{4}=\frac{49}{8}\times\frac{4}{21}$$
$$=\frac{\overset{7}{\cancel{49}}}{\underset{2}{\cancel{8}}}\times\frac{\overset{1}{\cancel{4}}}{\underset{3}{\cancel{21}}}$$
$$=\frac{7}{2}\times\frac{1}{3}=\frac{7}{6}$$
$$=1\frac{1}{6}$$

Q. $2\div\frac{3}{5}=$

A. $3\frac{1}{3}$. First change the 2 to a fraction: $\frac{2}{1}$. Then change the divide to multiply and the second (right) fraction to its reciprocal. Then do the multiplication problem to get the answer $\frac{10}{3}$, which can be changed to the mixed number.

$$2\div\frac{3}{5}=\frac{2}{1}\times\frac{5}{3}=\frac{10}{3}=3\frac{1}{3}$$

25 $\frac{6}{11}\times\left(-\frac{10}{21}\right)\times\frac{77}{25}=$

26 $4\frac{1}{5}\times\frac{25}{49}=$

27 $\left(-\frac{7}{27}\right)\times\frac{18}{25}\times\left(-\frac{15}{28}\right)=$

28 $-\frac{15}{14}\div\left(-\frac{20}{21}\right)=$

29 $2\frac{1}{2}\div\frac{3}{4}=$

30 $7\frac{1}{7}\div 3\frac{3}{14}=$

Simplifying Complex Fractions

A *complex fraction* is a fraction within a fraction. If a fraction has another fraction in its numerator or denominator (or both), then it's called *complex*. Fractions with this structure are awkward to deal with and need to be simplified. To simplify a complex fraction, you first work at creating improper fractions or integers in the numerator and denominator, independently, and then you divide the numerator by the denominator.

EXAMPLE

Q. $\dfrac{4\frac{1}{2}}{\frac{6}{7}} =$

A. $5\frac{1}{4}$. First, change the mixed number in the numerator to an improper fraction. Then divide the two fractions by multiplying the numerator by the reciprocal of the denominator.

$$\frac{4\frac{1}{2}}{\frac{6}{7}} = \frac{\frac{9}{2}}{\frac{6}{7}} = \frac{9}{2} \div \frac{6}{7} = \frac{9}{2} \times \frac{7}{6}$$

$$= \frac{{}^{3}\cancel{9}}{2} \times \frac{7}{\cancel{6}_{2}} = \frac{21}{4} = 5\frac{1}{4}$$

Q. $\dfrac{1\frac{9}{25} - \frac{4}{5}}{\frac{1}{2} + \frac{1}{3} + \frac{4}{5}} =$

A. $\frac{12}{35}$. First, find a common denominator for the fractions in the numerator separate from those in the denominator. Then subtract the fractions in the numerator and add the fractions in the denominator. Finally divide the two fractions by multiplying the numerator by the reciprocal of the denominator.

$$\frac{1\frac{9}{25} - \frac{4}{5}}{\frac{1}{2} + \frac{1}{3} + \frac{4}{5}} = \frac{\frac{34}{25} - \frac{4}{5}}{\frac{1}{2} + \frac{1}{3} + \frac{4}{5}}$$

$$= \frac{\frac{34}{25} - \frac{20}{25}}{\frac{15}{30} + \frac{10}{30} + \frac{24}{30}} =$$

$$= \frac{\frac{14}{25}}{\frac{49}{30}} = \frac{14}{25} \div \frac{49}{30} = \frac{14}{25} \times \frac{30}{49}$$

$$= \frac{{}^{2}\cancel{14}}{{}_{5}\cancel{25}} \times \frac{\cancel{30}^{6}}{\cancel{49}_{7}} = \frac{12}{35}$$

31 $\dfrac{\frac{16}{21}}{\frac{4}{7}} =$

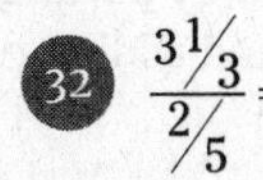

32 $\dfrac{3\frac{1}{3}}{\frac{2}{5}} =$

33 $\dfrac{4\frac{2}{7}}{1\frac{1}{14}} =$

34 $\dfrac{2\frac{1}{3}+4\frac{1}{5}}{10-1\frac{5}{6}} =$

Changing Fractions to Decimals and Vice Versa

Every fraction with an integer in the numerator and denominator has a decimal equivalent. Sometimes these decimals end (terminate); sometimes the decimals go on forever, repeating a pattern of digits over and over.

To change a fraction to a decimal, divide the denominator into the numerator, adding zeros after the decimal point until the division problem either ends or shows a repeating pattern. To indicate a pattern repeating over and over, draw a line across the top of the digits that repeat (for example, $0.2\overline{345}$) or just write a few sets of repeating digits (such as, 0.2345345345. . .) and put dots at the end.

To change a decimal to a fraction, place the digits of a terminating decimal over a power of 10 with as many zeros as there are decimal values. Then reduce the fraction. To change a repeating decimal to a fraction (this tip works only for those repeating decimals where the same digits repeat over and over from the beginning — with no other digits appearing), place the repeating digits in the numerator of a fraction that has 9's in the denominator. It should have as many 9's as digits that repeat. For instance, in the repeating decimal .123123123 . . . you'd put 123 over 999 and then reduce the fraction.

EXAMPLE

Q. Change $\frac{1}{25}$ to a decimal.

A. **0.04**. Divide 25 into 1 by putting a decimal after the 1 and adding two zeros.

Q. Change $\frac{5}{11}$ to a decimal.

A. $\mathbf{0.\overline{45}}$ **or 0.454545. . .** Divide 11 into 5, adding zeros after the decimal, until you see the pattern.

Q. Change 0.452 to a fraction.

A. $\mathbf{\frac{113}{250}}$. Put 452 over 1,000 and reduce.

Q. Change $0.\overline{285714}$ to a fraction.

A. $\mathbf{\frac{2}{7}}$. Put 285,714 over 999,999 and reduce. The divisors used to reduce the fractions are, in order, 9, 3, 11, 13, and 37. Whew!

$$\frac{285714}{999999} = \frac{\cancel{285714}^{31746}}{\cancel{999999}_{111111}} = \frac{\cancel{31746}^{10582}}{\cancel{111111}_{37037}}$$

$$= \frac{\cancel{10582}^{962}}{\cancel{37037}_{3367}} = \frac{\cancel{962}^{74}}{\cancel{3367}_{259}} = \frac{\cancel{74}^{2}}{\cancel{259}_{7}} = \frac{2}{7}$$

35 Change $\frac{3}{5}$ to a decimal.

36 Change $\frac{40}{9}$ to a decimal.

37 Change $\frac{2}{11}$ to a decimal.

38 Change 0.45 to a fraction.

39 Change $0.\overline{36}$ to a fraction.

40 Change $0.\overline{405}$ to a fraction.

Performing Operations with Decimals

Decimals are essentially fractions whose denominators are powers of 10. This property makes for much easier work when adding, subtracting, multiplying, or dividing.

- When adding or subtracting decimal numbers, just line up the decimal points and fill in zeros, if necessary.
- When multiplying decimals, just ignore the decimal points until you're almost finished. Count the number of digits to the right of the decimal point in each multiplier, and the total number of digits is how many decimal places you should have in your answer.
- Dividing has you place the decimal point *first*, not last. Make your divisor a whole number by moving the decimal point to the right. Then adjust the number you're dividing into by moving the decimal point the same number of places. Put the decimal point in your answer directly above the decimal point in the number you're dividing into (the dividend).

EXAMPLE

Q. $14.536 + 0.000004 - 2.3 =$

A. **12.236004**. Line up the decimal points in the first two numbers and add. Put in zeros to help you line up the digits. Then subtract the last number from the result.

$$\begin{array}{r} 14.536000 \\ +0.000004 \\ \hline 14.536004 \end{array} \qquad \begin{array}{r} 14.536004 \\ -2.300000 \\ \hline 12.236004 \end{array}$$

Q. $5.6 \times 0.123 \div 3.6 =$

A. **0.191333. . . .** Multiply the first two numbers together, creating an answer with four decimal places to the right of the decimal point. Then divide the result by 36, after moving the decimal point one place to the right in both divisor and dividend.

$$\begin{array}{r} 0.123 \\ \times\ 5.6 \\ \hline 738 \\ 615 \\ \hline .6888 \end{array} \qquad \begin{array}{r} .19133333 \\ 3.6_{\wedge}\overline{)0.6_{\wedge}888} \\ 3\ 6 \\ \hline 328 \\ 324 \\ \hline 40 \\ \vdots \end{array}$$

41 $(35.42 - 3.02) \div 0.0009 =$

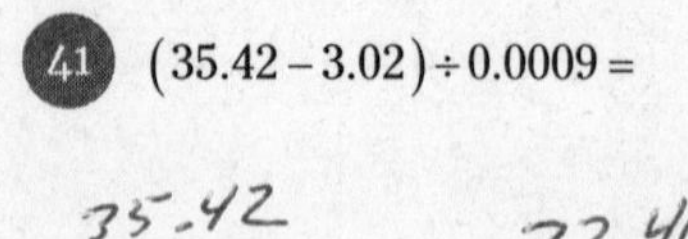

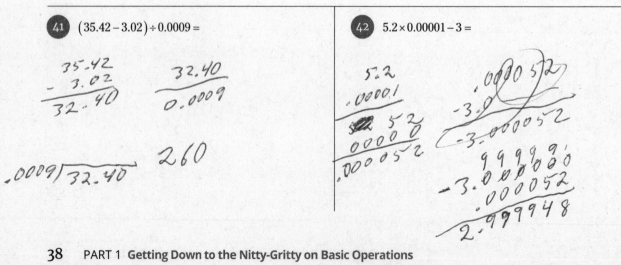

42 $5.2 \times 0.00001 - 3 =$

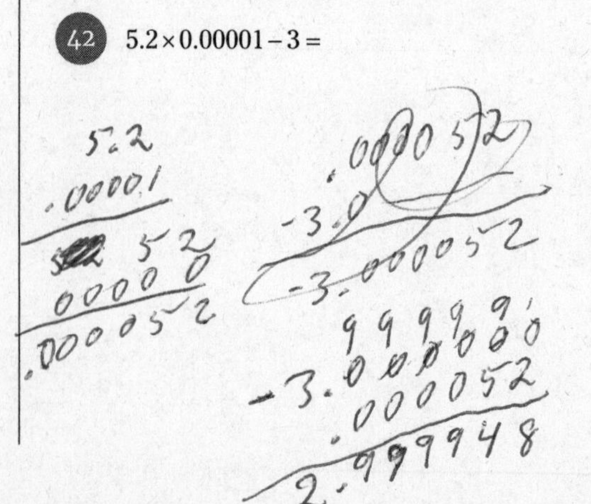

Answers to Problems on Fractions

This section provides the answers (in bold) to the practice problems in this chapter.

1. Change the mixed number $4\frac{7}{8}$ to an improper fraction. The answer is $\mathbf{\frac{39}{8}}$.

   $4 \times 8 + 7 = 32 + 7 = 39$ so the improper fraction is $\frac{39}{8}$.

2. Change the mixed number $2\frac{1}{13}$ to an improper fraction. The answer is $\mathbf{\frac{27}{13}}$.

   $2 \times 13 + 1 = 26 + 1 = 27$, so the improper fraction is $\frac{27}{13}$.

3. Change the improper fraction $\frac{16}{5}$ to a mixed number. The answer is $\mathbf{3\frac{1}{5}}$.

$$\begin{array}{r} 3 \\ 5\overline{)16} \\ \underline{15} \\ 1 \end{array}$$

   Think of breaking up the fraction into two pieces: One piece is the whole number 3, and the other is the remainder as a fraction, $\frac{1}{5}$.

4. Change the improper fraction $-\frac{19}{7}$ to a mixed number. The answer is $\mathbf{-2\frac{5}{7}}$.

   The negative part of the fraction comes in at the beginning and at the end. $-\frac{19}{7} = -\left(\frac{19}{7}\right)$. Do the division, using just the positive fraction:

$$\begin{array}{r} 2 \\ 7\overline{)19} \\ \underline{14} \\ 5 \end{array}$$

5. Find an equivalent fraction with a denominator of 28 for $\frac{3}{7}$. The answer is $\mathbf{\frac{12}{28}}$. To get 28 in the denominator, multiply 7 by 4: $\frac{3}{7} = \frac{3}{7} \times \frac{4}{4} = \frac{12}{28}$

6. Find an equivalent fraction with a denominator of 30 for $\frac{x}{6}$. The answer is $\mathbf{\frac{5x}{30}}$. $\frac{x}{6} = \frac{x}{6} \times \frac{5}{5} = \frac{5x}{30}$

7. Reduce this fraction: $\frac{16}{60}$. The answer is $\mathbf{\frac{4}{15}}$. 4 is the greatest common divisor of 16 and 60 because $16 = 4 \times 4$ and $60 = 15 \times 4$. So multiply $\frac{16}{60}$ by $\frac{\frac{1}{4}}{\frac{1}{4}}$. You get

$$\frac{16}{60} = \frac{16}{60} \times \frac{\frac{1}{4}}{\frac{1}{4}} = \frac{16 \times \frac{1}{4}}{60 \times \frac{1}{4}} = \frac{4}{15}$$

8. Reduce this fraction: $\frac{63}{84}$. The answer is $\mathbf{\frac{3}{4}}$. 21 is the largest common divisor of 63 and 84 because $63 = 3 \times 21$ and $84 = 4 \times 21$. So

$$\frac{63}{84} = \frac{63}{84} \times \frac{\frac{1}{21}}{\frac{1}{21}} = \frac{63 \times \frac{1}{21}}{84 \times \frac{1}{21}} = \frac{3}{4}$$

9. Solve for x: $\frac{7}{21} = \frac{x}{24}$. The answer is $\boldsymbol{x = 8}$.

$$\frac{7}{21} = \frac{x}{24} \rightarrow \frac{7 \div 7}{21 \div 7} = \frac{x}{24} \rightarrow \frac{1}{{}_1\cancel{3}} = \frac{x}{{}_8\cancel{24}} \rightarrow 1 \times 8 = x \times 1 \rightarrow x = 8$$

(10) Solve for x: $\frac{45}{x}=\frac{60}{200}$. The answer is $\boldsymbol{x}$ **= 150.**

$$\frac{45}{x}=\frac{60}{200}\rightarrow\frac{45}{x}=\frac{60\div20}{200\div20}\rightarrow\frac{{}^{15}\cancel{45}}{x}=\frac{{}^{1}\cancel{3}}{10}\rightarrow15\times10=1\times x\rightarrow x=150$$

(11) Solve for x: $\frac{x}{90}=\frac{60}{108}$. The answer is $\boldsymbol{x}$ **= 50.**

$$\frac{x}{90}=\frac{60}{108}\rightarrow\frac{x}{90}=\frac{60\div12}{108\div12}\rightarrow\frac{x}{{}^{10}\cancel{90}}=\frac{5}{{}^{1}\cancel{9}}\rightarrow1\times x=5\times10\rightarrow x=50$$

(12) Solve for x: $\frac{26}{16}=\frac{65}{x}$. The answer is $\boldsymbol{x}$ **= 40.**

$$\frac{26}{16}=\frac{65}{x}\rightarrow\frac{26\div2}{16\div2}=\frac{65}{x}\rightarrow\frac{{}^{1}\cancel{13}}{8}=\frac{{}^{5}\cancel{65}}{x}\rightarrow1\times x=5\times8\rightarrow x=40$$

(13) A recipe calls for 2 teaspoons of cinnamon and 4 cups of flour. You need to increase the flour to 6 cups. To keep the ingredients proportional, how many teaspoons of cinnamon should you use? Hint:

Fill in the proportion. $\frac{\text{original cinnamon}}{\text{original flour}}=\frac{\text{new cinnamon}}{\text{new flour}}$ and let x represent the new cinnamon. The answer is $\boldsymbol{x}$ **= 3.**

$$\frac{2}{4}=\frac{x}{6}\rightarrow\frac{2\div2}{4\div2}=\frac{x}{6}\rightarrow\frac{1}{{}^{1}\cancel{2}}=\frac{x}{{}^{3}\cancel{6}}\rightarrow1\times x=1\times3\rightarrow x=3$$

(14) A factory produces two faulty iPods for every 500 iPods it produces. How many faulty iPods would you expect to find in a shipment of 1,250? The answer is $\boldsymbol{x}$ **= 5.**

$$\frac{2\text{ faulty iPods}}{500\text{ iPods}}=\frac{x\text{ faulty iPods}}{1{,}250\text{ iPods}}\rightarrow\frac{2}{500}=\frac{x}{1{,}250}\rightarrow\frac{\cancel{2}^{1}}{\cancel{500}_{250}}=\frac{x}{1{,}250}$$

$$\rightarrow\frac{1}{250}=\frac{x}{1{,}250}=\frac{1}{{}_{1}\cancel{250}}=\frac{x}{{}_{5}\cancel{1{,}250}}\rightarrow1\times x=1\times5\rightarrow x=5$$

(15) Rewrite the fractions $^2/_7$ and $^3/_8$ with a common denominator. The answers are $\mathbf{^{16}/_{56}}$ **and** $\mathbf{^{21}/_{56}}$.

The largest common factor of 7 and 8 is 1. So the least common denominator is 56: $\left(\frac{7\times8}{1}=56\right)$. Here are the details:

$$\frac{2}{7}=\frac{2}{7}\times\frac{8}{8}=\frac{16}{56}\text{ and }\frac{3}{8}=\frac{3}{8}\times\frac{7}{7}=\frac{21}{56}$$

(16) Rewrite the fractions $^5/_{12}$ and $^7/_{18}$ with a common denominator. The answers are $\mathbf{^{15}/_{36}}$ **and** $\mathbf{^{14}/_{36}}$. The largest common factor of 12 and 18 is 6. The least common denominator is 36 $\left(\frac{12\times18}{6}=36\right)$. Here are the details:

$$\frac{5}{12}=\frac{5}{12}\times\frac{3}{3}=\frac{15}{36}\text{ and }\frac{7}{18}=\frac{7}{18}\times\frac{2}{2}=\frac{14}{36}$$

(17) Rewrite the fractions $^9/_x$ and $^5/_6$ with a common denominator. The answers are $\mathbf{^{54}/_{6x}}$ **and** $\mathbf{^{5x}/_{6x}}$. The largest common factor of x and 6 is 1. The least common denominator is their product: 6x. Break it down: $\frac{9}{x}=\frac{9}{x}\times\frac{6}{6}=\frac{54}{6x}$ and $\frac{5}{6}=\frac{5}{6}\times\frac{x}{x}=\frac{5x}{6x}$.

(18) Rewrite the fractions $5/x$ and $\frac{1}{x+6}$ with a common denominator. The answers are $\boldsymbol{\frac{5x+30}{x(x+6)}}$ **and** $\boldsymbol{\frac{x}{x(x+6)}}$. The largest common factor of x and $x+6$ is 1. Their least common denominator is their product: $x(x+6)$. Here's the long of it: $\frac{5}{x}=\frac{5}{x}\times\frac{x+6}{x+6}=\frac{5x+30}{x(x+6)}$ and $\frac{1}{x+6}=\frac{1}{x+6}\times\frac{x}{x}=\frac{x}{x(x+6)}$.

(19) Rewrite the fractions $1/2$, $1/3$, and $1/5$ with a common denominator. The answers are $\boldsymbol{15/30}$, $\boldsymbol{10/30}$, **and** $\boldsymbol{6/30}$. The least common denominator of fractions with denominators of 2, 3, and 5 is 30. Write it out:

$$\frac{1}{2}=\frac{1}{2}\times\frac{15}{15}=\frac{15}{30}, \frac{1}{3}=\frac{1}{3}\times\frac{10}{10}=\frac{10}{30}, \text{ and } \frac{1}{5}=\frac{1}{5}\times\frac{6}{6}=\frac{6}{30}$$

(20) Rewrite the fractions $2/3$, $5/x$, and $3/2x$ with a common denominator. The answers are $\boldsymbol{4x/6x}$, $\boldsymbol{30/6x}$, **and** $\boldsymbol{9/6x}$. The last two denominators, $5/x$ and $3/2x$, have a common factor of x. And the product of all three denominators is $6x^2$. Divide the product by x and you get $6x$. In long hand:

$$\frac{2}{3}=\frac{2}{3}\times\frac{2x}{2x}=\frac{4x}{6x}, \frac{5}{x}=\frac{5}{x}\times\frac{6}{6}=\frac{30}{6x}, \text{ and } \frac{3}{2x}=\frac{3}{2x}\times\frac{3}{3}=\frac{9}{6x}$$

(21) $\frac{3}{8}+\frac{7}{12}=\boldsymbol{23/24}$ because the least common denominator is 24.

$$\frac{3}{8}+\frac{7}{12}=\left(\frac{3}{8}\times\frac{3}{3}\right)+\left(\frac{7}{12}\times\frac{2}{2}\right)=\frac{9}{24}+\frac{14}{24}=\frac{23}{24}$$

(22) $3\,1/3+4\,3/5+7/15=\boldsymbol{8\,2/5}$ because the least common denominator is 15.

$$3\frac{1}{3}+4\frac{3}{5}+\frac{7}{15}=\frac{10}{3}+\frac{23}{5}+\frac{7}{15}=\left(\frac{10}{3}\times\frac{5}{5}\right)+\left(\frac{23}{5}\times\frac{3}{3}\right)+\frac{7}{15}$$

$$=\frac{50}{15}+\frac{69}{15}+\frac{7}{15}=\frac{126}{15}\times\frac{\frac{1}{3}}{\frac{1}{3}}=\frac{42}{5}=8\frac{2}{5}$$

Or, leaving the whole number parts separate:

$$3\frac{1}{3}+4\frac{3}{5}+\frac{7}{15}=3+\left(\frac{1}{3}\times\frac{5}{5}\right)+4+\left(\frac{3}{5}\times\frac{3}{3}\right)+\frac{7}{15}$$

$$=3+4+\left(\frac{5}{15}+\frac{9}{15}+\frac{7}{15}\right)=7+\frac{21}{15}=7+1+\frac{6}{15}=8\frac{6}{15}=8\frac{2}{5}$$

(23) $1\,5/12-7/9=\boldsymbol{23/36}$

$$1\frac{5}{12}-\frac{7}{9}=\frac{17}{12}-\frac{7}{9}=\left(\frac{17}{12}\times\frac{3}{3}\right)-\left(\frac{7}{9}\times\frac{4}{4}\right)=\frac{51}{36}-\frac{28}{36}=\frac{23}{36}$$

(24) $3\,2/3-\left(-6\,1/2\right)=\boldsymbol{10\,1/6}$

$$3\frac{2}{3}-\left(-6\frac{1}{2}\right)=3\frac{2}{3}+6\frac{1}{2}=\frac{11}{3}+\frac{13}{2}=\left(\frac{11}{3}\times\frac{2}{2}\right)+\left(\frac{13}{2}\times\frac{3}{3}\right)=\frac{22}{6}+\frac{39}{6}=\frac{61}{6}=10\frac{1}{6}$$

(25) $\frac{6}{11}\times\left(-\frac{10}{21}\right)\times\frac{77}{25}=\mathbf{-\frac{4}{5}}$

$$\frac{6}{11}\times\left(-\frac{10}{21}\right)\times\frac{77}{25}=-\frac{{}^{2}\cancel{6}\times10\times77}{11\times\underset{7}{\cancel{21}}\times25}=-\frac{2\times\overset{2}{\cancel{10}}\times77}{11\times7\times\cancel{25}_{5}}$$

$$=-\frac{2\times2\times\cancel{77}^{7}}{{}_{1}\cancel{11}\times7\times5}=-\frac{2\times2\times\cancel{7}^{1}}{1\times\cancel{7}_{1}\times5}=-\frac{2\times2\times1}{1\times1\times5}=-\frac{2\times2}{5}=-\frac{4}{5}$$

(26) $4\frac{1}{5}\times\frac{25}{49}=\mathbf{2\frac{1}{7}}$

$$4\frac{1}{5}\times\frac{25}{49}=\frac{21}{5}\times\frac{25}{49}=\frac{{}^{3}\cancel{21}\times25}{5\times\cancel{49}_{7}}=\frac{3\times\cancel{25}^{5}}{{}_{1}\cancel{5}\times7}=\frac{3\times5}{1\times7}=\frac{15}{7}=2\frac{1}{7}$$

(27) $\left(-\frac{7}{27}\right)\times\frac{18}{25}\times\left(-\frac{15}{28}\right)=\mathbf{\frac{1}{10}}$

$$\left(-\frac{7}{27}\right)\times\frac{18}{25}\times\left(-\frac{15}{28}\right)=+\frac{{}^{1}\cancel{7}\times18\times15}{27\times25\times\cancel{28}_{4}}=\frac{1\times\overset{2}{\cancel{18}}\times15}{{}_{3}\cancel{27}\times25\times4}$$

$$=\frac{1\times2\times\cancel{15}^{3}}{3\times\underset{5}{\cancel{25}}\times4}=\frac{1\times2\times3}{3\times5\times4}=\frac{1\times2\times\cancel{3}^{1}}{{}_{1}\cancel{3}\times5\times4}=\frac{1\times\cancel{2}^{1}\times1}{1\times5\times\cancel{4}_{2}}=\frac{1\times1\times1}{1\times5\times2}=\frac{1}{10}$$

(28) $-\frac{15}{14}\div\left(-\frac{20}{21}\right)=\mathbf{1\frac{1}{8}}$

$$-\frac{15}{14}\div\left(-\frac{20}{21}\right)=-\frac{15}{14}\times\left(-\frac{21}{20}\right)=\frac{15}{14}\times\frac{21}{20}=\frac{{}^{3}\cancel{15}\times21}{14\times\cancel{20}_{4}}$$

$$=\frac{3\times\cancel{21}^{3}}{{}_{2}\cancel{14}\times4}=\frac{3\times3}{2\times4}=\frac{9}{8}=1\frac{1}{8}$$

(29) $2\frac{1}{2}\div\frac{3}{4}=\mathbf{3\frac{1}{3}}$

$$2\frac{1}{2}\div\frac{3}{4}=\frac{5}{2}\div\frac{3}{4}=\frac{5}{2}\times\frac{4}{3}=\frac{5\times4}{2\times3}=\frac{5\times\cancel{4}^{2}}{{}_{1}\cancel{2}\times3}=\frac{5\times2}{1\times3}=\frac{10}{3}=3\frac{1}{3}$$

(30) $7{}^{1}\!/_{7}\div3{}^{3}\!/_{14}=\mathbf{2{}^{2}\!/_{9}}$

$$7\frac{1}{7}\div3\frac{3}{14}=\frac{50}{7}\div\frac{45}{14}=\frac{50}{7}\times\frac{14}{45}=\frac{{}^{10}\cancel{50}\times14}{7\times\cancel{45}_{9}}=\frac{10\times\cancel{14}^{2}}{{}_{1}\cancel{7}\times9}$$

$$=\frac{10\times2}{1\times9}=\frac{20}{9}=2\frac{2}{9}$$

(31) $$\frac{{}^{16}\!/_{21}}{{}^{4}\!/_{7}}=\frac{16}{21}\times\frac{7}{4}=\frac{{}^{4}\cancel{16}}{21}\times\frac{7}{\cancel{4}_{1}}=\frac{4}{{}_{3}\cancel{21}}\times\frac{\cancel{7}^{1}}{1}=\frac{4}{3}=\mathbf{1{}^{1}\!/_{3}}$$

(32) $$\frac{3{}^{1}\!/_{3}}{{}^{2}\!/_{5}}=\frac{{}^{10}\!/_{3}}{{}^{2}\!/_{5}}=\frac{10}{3}\times\frac{5}{2}=\frac{{}^{5}\cancel{10}}{3}\times\frac{5}{\cancel{2}_{1}}=\frac{25}{3}=\mathbf{8{}^{1}\!/_{3}}$$

(33) $$\frac{4{}^{2}\!/_{7}}{1{}^{1}\!/_{14}}=\frac{{}^{30}\!/_{7}}{{}^{15}\!/_{14}}=\frac{30}{7}\times\frac{14}{15}=\frac{{}^{2}\cancel{30}}{7}\times\frac{14}{\cancel{15}_{1}}=\frac{2}{{}_{1}\cancel{7}}\times\frac{\cancel{14}^{2}}{1}=\frac{4}{1}=\mathbf{4}$$

(34) $\dfrac{2\frac{1}{3}+4\frac{1}{5}}{10-1\frac{5}{6}}=\dfrac{\frac{7}{3}+\frac{21}{5}}{10-\frac{11}{6}}=\dfrac{\frac{35}{15}+\frac{63}{15}}{\frac{60}{6}-\frac{11}{6}}=\dfrac{\frac{98}{15}}{\frac{49}{6}}=\dfrac{98}{15}\times\dfrac{6}{49}=\dfrac{{}^{2}\cancel{98}}{{}_{5}\cancel{15}}\times\dfrac{\cancel{6}^{2}}{\cancel{49}_{1}}=\mathbf{\dfrac{4}{5}}$

(35) Change $^3/_5$ to a decimal. The answer is **0.6**. Dividing, you have $5\overset{\displaystyle 0.6}{\overline{)3.0}}$.

(36) Change $^{40}/_9$ to a decimal. The answer is **$4.\bar{4}$**.

$\frac{40}{9}=4\frac{4}{9}=4.\bar{4}$ because

$$
\begin{array}{r}
0.44 \\
9\overline{)4.00} \\
\underline{36} \\
40 \\
\underline{36} \\
4 \\
\vdots
\end{array}
$$

(37) Change $^2/_{11}$ to a decimal. The answer is **$0.\overline{18}$**.

$\frac{2}{11}=0.\overline{18}$ because

$$
\begin{array}{r}
0.1818 \\
11\overline{)2.0000} \\
\underline{1\,1} \\
90 \\
\underline{88} \\
20 \\
\vdots
\end{array}
$$

(38) Change 0.45 to a fraction. The answer is $\mathbf{^9/_{20}}$ because $0.45=\frac{45}{100}=\frac{\cancel{45}^{9}}{\cancel{100}_{20}}=\frac{9}{20}$.

(39) Change $0.\overline{36}$ to a fraction. The answer is $\mathbf{^4/_{11}}$.

$0.\overline{36}=\frac{36}{99}$ because two digits repeat $=\frac{\cancel{36}^{4}}{\cancel{99}_{11}}=\frac{4}{11}$.

(40) Change $0.\overline{405}$ to a fraction. The answer is $\mathbf{^{15}/_{37}}$.

$0.\overline{405}=\frac{405}{999}$ because three digits repeat: $\frac{\cancel{405}^{45}}{\cancel{999}_{111}}=\frac{\cancel{45}^{15}}{\cancel{111}_{37}}=\frac{15}{37}$.

(41) $(35.42-3.02)\div 0.0009=\mathbf{36{,}000}$. Simplify inside the parentheses first.

$$
\begin{array}{r}
35.42 \\
\underline{-3.02} \\
32.4
\end{array}
\qquad
\begin{array}{r}
36{,}000. \\
0.0009\overline{)32.4000}
\end{array}
$$

(42) $5.2\times 0.00001-3=\mathbf{-2.999948}$. By the order of operations, you multiply first and then subtract 3 from the result.

$$
\begin{array}{r}
5.2 \\
\underline{\times 0.00001} \\
0.000052
\end{array}
\qquad
\begin{array}{r}
0.000052-3= \\
-3.000000 \\
\underline{0.000052} \\
-2.999948
\end{array}
$$

» Recognizing the power of powers

» Operating on exponents

» Investigating scientific notation

Chapter 4
Exploring Exponents

In the big picture of mathematics, exponents are a fairly new discovery. The principle behind exponents has always been there, but mathematicians had to first agree to use algebraic symbols such as *x* and *y* for values, before they could agree to the added shorthand of superscripts to indicate how many times the value was to be used. As a result, instead of writing $x \cdot x \cdot x \cdot x \cdot x$, you get to write the *x* with an exponent of 5: x^5. In any case, be grateful. Exponents make life a lot easier.

This chapter introduces to you how exponents can be used (and abused), how to recognize scientific notation on a calculator, and how eeeeeasy it is to use *e*. What's this "*e*" business? The letter *e* was named for the mathematician Leonhard Euler; the Euler number, *e*, is approximately 2.71828 and is used in business and scientific calculations.

Multiplying and Dividing Exponentials

The number 16 can be written as 2^4, and the number 64 can be written as 2^6. When multiplying these two numbers together, you can either write $16 \times 64 = 1{,}024$ or you can multiply their two exponential forms together to get $2^4 \times 2^6 = 2^{10}$, which is equal to 1,024. The computation is easier — the numbers are smaller — when you use the exponential forms. Exponential forms are also better for writing very large or very small numbers.

REMEMBER

To multiply numbers with the same base (b), you add their exponents. The bases must be the same, or this rule doesn't work.

$$b^m \times b^n = b^{m+n}$$

When numbers appear in exponential form, you can divide them simply by subtracting their exponents. As with multiplication, the bases have to be the same in order to perform this operation.

REMEMBER

When the bases are the same and two factors are divided, subtract their exponents:

$$\frac{b^m}{b^n} = b^{m-n}$$

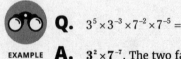

EXAMPLE

Q. $3^5 \times 3^{-3} \times 7^{-2} \times 7^{-5} =$

A. $3^2 \times 7^{-7}$. The two factors with bases of 3 multiply as do the two with bases of 7, but they don't mix together. The negative exponents probably look intriguing. You can find an explanation of what they're all about in the "Using Negative Exponents" section later in this chapter.

$$3^5 \times 3^{-3} \times 7^{-2} \times 7^{-5} = 3^{5+(-3)} \times 7^{-2+(-5)}$$
$$= 3^2 \times 7^{-7}$$

Q. $5^6 \times 5^{-7} \times 5 =$

A. **1**. In this case, the multiplier 5 is actually 5^1 because the exponent 1 usually isn't shown. Also, 5^0, or any non-zero number raised to the zero power, is equal to 1.

So $5^6 \times 5^{-7} \times 5 = 5^{6+(-7)+1} = 5^0 = 1$

Q. $\frac{3^4}{3^3} =$

A. **3**.

$$\frac{3^4}{3^3} = 3^{4-3} = 3^1 = 3$$

Q. $\frac{8^2 \times 3^5}{8^{-1} \times 3} =$

A. **41,472**. The bases of 8 and 3 are different, so you have to simplify the separate bases before multiplying the results together.

$$\frac{8^2 \times 3^5}{8^{-1} \times 3} = \frac{8^2}{8^{-1}} \times \frac{3^5}{3^1} = 8^{2-(-1)} \times 3^{5-1}$$
$$= 8^{2+1} \times 3^4 = 8^3 \times 3^4$$
$$= 512 \times 81 = 41{,}472$$

1. $2^3 \times 2^4 =$

2. $3^6 \times 3^{-4} =$

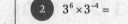

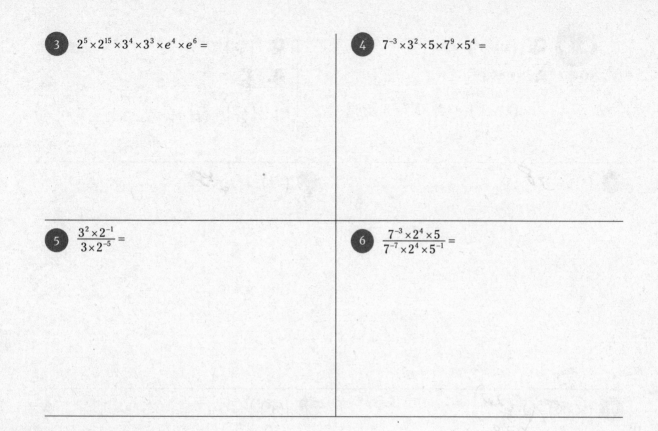

3. $2^5 \times 2^{15} \times 3^4 \times 3^3 \times e^4 \times e^6 =$

4. $7^{-3} \times 3^2 \times 5 \times 7^9 \times 5^4 =$

5. $\dfrac{3^2 \times 2^{-1}}{3 \times 2^{-5}} =$

6. $\dfrac{7^{-3} \times 2^4 \times 5}{7^{-7} \times 2^4 \times 5^{-1}} =$

Raising Powers to Powers

Raising a power to a power means that you take a number in exponential form and raise it to some power. For instance, raising 3^6 to the fourth power means to multiply the sixth power of 3 by itself four times: $3^6 \times 3^6 \times 3^6 \times 3^6$. As a power of a power, it looks like this: $\left(3^6\right)^4$. Raising something to a power tells you how many times it's multiplied by itself. The rule for performing this operation is simple multiplication.

REMEMBER

When raising a power to a power, don't forget these rules:

- $\left(b^m\right)^n = b^{m \times n}$. So to raise 3^6 to the fourth power, write $\left(3^6\right)^4 = 3^{6\times4} = 3^{24}$.
- $(a \times b)^m = a^m \times b^m$ and $\left(a^p \times b^q\right)^m = a^{p\times m} \times b^{q\times m}$.
- $\left(\dfrac{a}{b}\right)^m = \dfrac{a^m}{b^m}$ and $\left(\dfrac{a^p}{b^q}\right)^m = \dfrac{a^{p\times m}}{b^{q\times m}}$.

These rules say that if you multiply or divide two numbers and are raising the product or quotient to a power, then each factor gets raised to that power. (Remember, a *product* is the result of multiplying, and a *quotient* is the result of dividing.)

EXAMPLE

Q. $\left(3^{-4}\times5^{6}\right)^{7}=$

A. $\mathbf{3^{-28}\times5^{42}}$

$$\left(3^{-4}\times5^{6}\right)^{7}=3^{-4\times7}\times5^{6\times7}=3^{-28}\times5^{42}$$

Q. $\left(\frac{2^{5}}{5^{2}}\right)^{3}=$

A. $\mathbf{\frac{2^{15}}{5^{6}}}$

$$\left(\frac{2^{5}}{5^{2}}\right)^{3}=\frac{2^{5\times3}}{5^{2\times3}}=\frac{2^{15}}{5^{6}}$$

7 $\left(3^{2}\right)^{4}=$

8 $\left(2^{-6}\right)^{-8}=$

9 $\left(2^{3}\times3^{2}\right)^{4}=$

10 $\left(\left(3^{5}\right)^{2}\right)^{6}=$

11 $\left(\frac{2^{2}\times3^{4}}{5^{2}\times3}\right)^{3}=$

12 $\left(\frac{2^{3}}{e^{5}}\right)^{2}=$

Using Negative Exponents

Negative exponents are very useful in algebra because they allow you to do computations on numbers with the same base without having to deal with pesky fractions.

When you use the negative exponent b^{-n}, you are saying $b^{-n} = \frac{1}{b^n}$ and also $\frac{1}{b^{-n}} = b^n$.

So if you did problems in the sections earlier in this chapter and didn't like leaving all those negative exponents in your answers, now you have the option of writing the answers using fractions instead.

Another nice feature of negative exponents is how they affect fractions. Look at this rule:

$$\left(\frac{a^p}{b^q}\right)^{-n} = \left(\frac{b^q}{a^p}\right)^n = \frac{b^{qn}}{a^{pn}}$$

REMEMBER

A quick, easy way of explaining the preceding rule is to just say that a negative exponent flips the fraction and then applies a positive power to the factors.

EXAMPLE

Q. $4^3 \times 3^{-1} \times 6 \times 8^{-2} =$

A. **2.** Move the factors with the negative exponents to the bottom, and their exponents then become positive. Then you can reduce the fraction.

$$4^3 \times 3^{-1} \times 6 \times 8^{-2} = \frac{4^3 \times 6}{3^1 \times 8^2} = \frac{64 \times 6}{3 \times 64} = \frac{6}{3} = 2$$

Q. $\left(\frac{3^4 \times 2^3}{3^7 \times 2^2}\right)^{-2} =$

A. $\mathbf{\frac{729}{4}}$. First flip and then simplify the common bases before raising each factor to the second power.

$$\left(\frac{3^4 \times 2^3}{3^7 \times 2^2}\right)^{-2} = \left(\frac{3^7 \times 2^2}{3^4 \times 2^3}\right)^2$$

$$= \left(\frac{3^{7^3} \times 2^{2}}{3^{4} \times 2^{3^1}}\right)^2 = \left(\frac{3^3}{2^1}\right)^2 = \frac{3^6}{2^2} = \frac{729}{4}$$

13 Rewrite $\frac{1}{3^6}$, using a negative exponent.

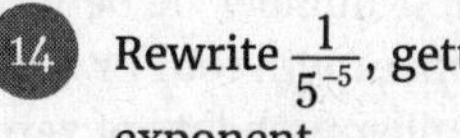

14 Rewrite $\frac{1}{5^{-5}}$, getting rid of the negative exponent.

15 Simplify $\left(\frac{3^{-4}}{2^{3}}\right)^{-2}$, leaving no negative exponent.

16 Simplify $\frac{\left(2^{3}\times 3^{2}\right)^{4}}{\left(2^{5}\times 3^{-1}\right)^{5}}$, leaving no negative exponent.

Writing Numbers with Scientific Notation

Scientific notation is a standard way of writing in a more compact and useful way numbers that are very small or very large. When a scientist wants to talk about the distance to a star being 45,600,000,000,000,000,000,000,000 light years away, having it written as 4.56×10^{25} makes any comparisons or computations easier.

REMEMBER

A number written in scientific notation is the product of a number between 1 and 10 and a power of 10. The power tells how many decimal places the original decimal point was moved in order to make that first number be between 1 and 10. The power is negative when you're writing a very small number (with four or more zeros after the decimal point) and positive when writing a very large number with lots of zeros in front of the decimal point.

EXAMPLE

Q. 32,000,000,000 =

A. $\mathbf{3.2\times 10^{10}}$. Many modern scientific calculators show numbers in scientific notation with the letter E. So if you see 3.2 E 10, it means 3.2×10^{10} or 32,000,000,000.

Q. 0.00000000032 =

A. $\mathbf{3.2\times 10^{-10}}$. (In a graphing calculator, this looks like 3.2 E − 10.)

17 Write 4.03×10^{14} without scientific notation.

18 Write 3.71×10^{-13} without scientific notation.

19 Write 4,500,000,000,000,000,000 using scientific notation.

20 Write 0.00000000000000003267 using scientific notation.

326.7x10'8

Answers to Problems on Discovering Exponents

This section provides the answers (in bold) to the practice problems in this chapter.

1. $2^3 \times 2^4 = \mathbf{2^7 \text{ or } 128}$

   $2^3 \times 2^4 = 2^{3+4} = 2^7$

2. $3^6 \times 3^{-4} = \mathbf{3^2 \text{ or } 9}$

   $3^6 \times 3^{-4} = 3^{6+(-4)} = \mathbf{3^2}$

3. $2^5 \times 2^{15} \times 3^4 \times 3^3 \times e^4 \times e^6 = \mathbf{2^{20} \times 3^7 \times e^{10}}$

   $2^5 \times 2^{15} \times 3^4 \times 3^3 \times e^4 \times e^6 = 2^{5+15} \times 3^{4+3} \times e^{4+6} = 2^{20} \times 3^7 \times e^{10}$

4. $7^{-3} \times 3^2 \times 5 \times 7^9 \times 5^4 = \mathbf{7^6 \times 3^2 \times 5^5}$

   $7^{-3} \times 3^2 \times 5 \times 7^9 \times 5^4 = 7^{-3} \times 7^9 \times 3^2 \times 5^1 \times 5^4 = 7^{-3+9} \times 3^2 \times 5^{1+4} = 7^6 \times 3^2 \times 5^5$

5. $\dfrac{3^2 \times 2^{-1}}{3 \times 2^{-5}} = \mathbf{3 \times 2^4 \text{ or } 48}$

   $\dfrac{3^2 \times 2^{-1}}{3 \times 2^{-5}} = 3^{2-1} \times 2^{-1-(-5)} = 3^1 \times 2^4 = 3 \times 2^4 \text{ or } 48$

6. $\dfrac{7^{-3} \times 2^4 \times 5}{7^{-7} \times 2^4 \times 5^{-1}} = \mathbf{7^4 \times 5^2}$

   $\dfrac{7^{-3} \times 2^4 \times 5}{7^{-7} \times 2^4 \times 5^{-1}} = 7^{-3-(-7)} \times 2^{4-4} \times 5^{1-(-1)} = 7^4 \times 2^0 \times 5^2 = 7^4 \times 1 \times 5^2 = 7^4 \times 5^2$

7. $\left(3^2\right)^4 = \mathbf{3^8}$

   $\left(3^2\right)^4 = 3^{2\times4} = 3^8$

8. $\left(2^{-6}\right)^{-8} = \mathbf{2^{48}}$

   $\left(2^{-6}\right)^{-8} = 2^{(-6)\times(-8)} = 2^{48}$

9. $\left(2^3 \times 3^2\right)^4 = \mathbf{2^{12} \times 3^8}$

   $\left(2^3 \times 3^2\right)^4 = 2^{3\times4} \times 3^{2\times4} = 2^{12} \times 3^8$

10. $\left[\left(3^5\right)^2\right]^6 = \mathbf{3^{60}}$

    $\left[\left(3^5\right)^2\right]^6 = \left(3^{5\times2}\right)^6 = 3^{(5\times2)6} = 3^{60}$

11. $\left(\dfrac{2^2 \times 3^4}{5^2 \times 3}\right)^3 = \mathbf{\dfrac{2^6 \times 3^9}{5^6}}$

    $\left(\dfrac{2^2 \times 3^4}{5^2 \times 3}\right)^3 = \left(\dfrac{2^2 \times 3^{4-1}}{5^2}\right)^3 = \left(\dfrac{2^2 \times 3^3}{5^2}\right)^3 = \dfrac{2^{2\times3} \times 3^{3\times3}}{5^{2\times3}} = \dfrac{2^6 \times 3^9}{5^6}$

12 $\left(\frac{2^3}{e^5}\right)^2 = \mathbf{\frac{2^6}{e^{10}}}$

$$\left(\frac{2^3}{e^5}\right)^2 = \frac{2^{3(2)}}{e^{5(2)}} = \frac{2^6}{e^{10}}$$

13 Rewrite $\frac{1}{3^6}$, using a negative exponent. The answer is $\mathbf{3^{-6}}$.

14 Rewrite $\frac{1}{5^{-5}}$, getting rid of the negative exponent. The answer is $\mathbf{5^5}$.

15 Simplify $\left(\frac{3^{-4}}{2^3}\right)^{-2}$, leaving no negative exponent. The answer is $\mathbf{2^6 \times 3^8}$.

$$\left(\frac{3^{-4}}{2^3}\right)^{-2} = \left(\frac{2^3}{3^{-4}}\right)^2 = \frac{2^{3\times2}}{3^{-4\times2}} = \frac{2^6}{3^{-8}} = 2^6 \times 3^8 \text{ because } \frac{1}{3^{-8}} = 3^8$$

16 Simplify $\frac{\left(2^3 \times 3^2\right)^4}{\left(2^5 \times 3^{-1}\right)^5}$, leaving no negative exponent. The answer is $\mathbf{\frac{3^{13}}{2^{13}}}$.

$$\frac{\left(2^3 \times 3^2\right)^4}{\left(2^5 \times 3^{-1}\right)^5} = \frac{2^{3\times4} \times 3^{2\times4}}{2^{5\times5} \times 3^{(-1)\times5}} = \frac{2^{12} \times 3^8}{2^{25} \times 3^{-5}} = 2^{12-25} \times 3^{8-(-5)} = 2^{-13} \times 3^{13} = \frac{3^{13}}{2^{13}}$$

17 Write 4.03×10^{14} without scientific notation. The answer is **403,000,000,000,000**. Move the decimal point 14 places to the right.

18 Write 3.71×10^{-13} without scientific notation. The answer is **0.000000000000371**. Move the decimal point 13 places to the left.

19 Write 4,500,000,000,000,000,000 using scientific notation. The answer is $\mathbf{4.5 \times 10^{18}}$.

20 Write 0.0000000000000003267 using scientific notation. The answer is $\mathbf{3.267 \times 10^{-16}}$.

- Trimming down radical fractions
- Working in fractional exponents
- Performing operations using fractional exponents

Chapter 5 Taming Rampaging Radicals

The operation of taking a square root, cube root, or any other root is an important one in algebra (as well as in science and other areas of mathematics). The radical symbol ($\sqrt{\ }$) indicates that you want to take a *root* (what multiplies itself to give you the number or value) of an expression. A more convenient notation, though, is to use a superscript, or power. This *superscript*, or exponent, is easily incorporated into algebraic work and makes computations easier to perform and results easier to report.

Simplifying Radical Expressions

Simplifying a radical expression means rewriting it as something equivalent using the smallest possible numbers under the radical symbol. If the number under the radical isn't a perfect square or cube or whichever power for the particular root, then you want to see whether that number has a factor that's a perfect square or cube (and so on) and factor it out.

REMEMBER

The root of a product is equal to the product of two roots containing the factors. The rule is $\sqrt{a \times b} = \sqrt{a} \times \sqrt{b}$ or, more generally, $\sqrt[n]{a \times b} = \sqrt[n]{a} \times \sqrt[n]{b}$.

In the following two examples, the numbers under the radicals aren't perfect squares, so the numbers are written as the product of two factors — one of them is a perfect square factor. Apply the rule for roots of products and write the expression in simplified form.

EXAMPLE

Q. $\sqrt{40} =$

A. $2\sqrt{10}$. The number 40 can be written as the product of 2 and 20 or 5 and 8, but none of those numbers are perfect squares. Instead, you use 4 and 10 because 4 is a perfect square.

$$\sqrt{40} = \sqrt{4 \times 10} = \sqrt{4} \times \sqrt{10} = 2\sqrt{10}$$

Q. $\sqrt{8} + \sqrt{18} =$

A. $5\sqrt{2}$. In this example, you can't add the two radicals together the way they are, but after you simplify them, the two terms have the same radical factor, and you can add them together.

$$\begin{aligned}\sqrt{8} + \sqrt{18} &= \sqrt{4 \times 2} + \sqrt{9 \times 2} \\ &= \sqrt{4} \times \sqrt{2} + \sqrt{9} \times \sqrt{2} \\ &= 2\sqrt{2} + 3\sqrt{2} = 5\sqrt{2}\end{aligned}$$

1 Simplify $\sqrt{12}$. $= \sqrt{4 \times 3} = \sqrt{4} \times \sqrt{3} =$ $2\sqrt{3}$

2 Simplify $\sqrt{200}$. $= \sqrt{100 \times 2} = \sqrt{100} \times \sqrt{2} =$ $10\sqrt{2}$

3 Simplify $\sqrt{63}$. $= \sqrt{9 \times 7} = \sqrt{9} \times \sqrt{7} =$ $3\sqrt{7}$

4 Simplify $\sqrt{75}$.

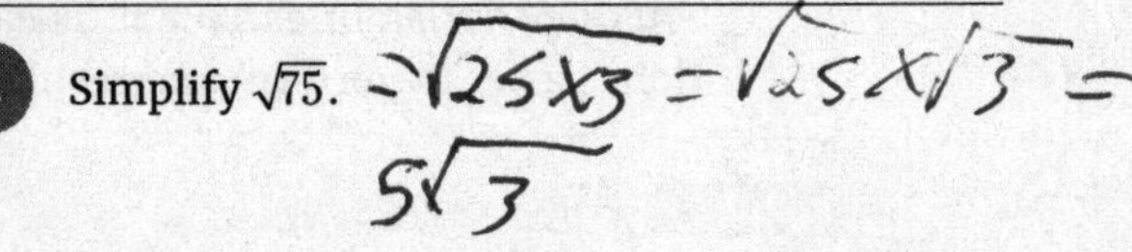

5 Simplify the radicals in $\sqrt{24} + \sqrt{54}$ before adding.

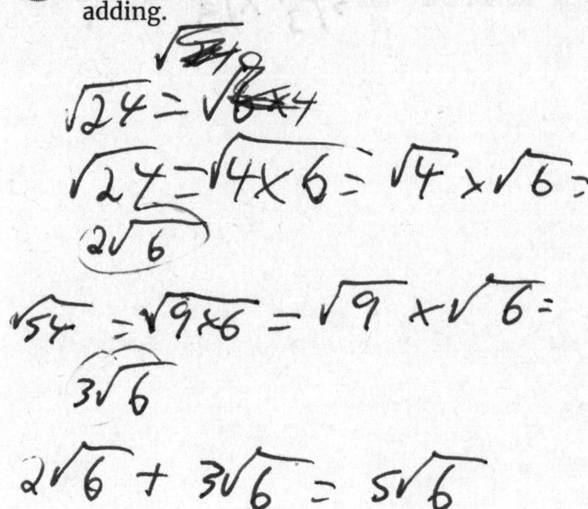

6 Simplify $\sqrt{72} - \sqrt{50}$ before subtracting.

$\sqrt{72} = \sqrt{36 \times 2} = \sqrt{6} \times \sqrt{2} = 6\sqrt{2}$

$\sqrt{50} = \sqrt{25 \times 2} = \sqrt{25} \times \sqrt{2} = 5\sqrt{2}$

$6\sqrt{2} - 5\sqrt{2} = 1\sqrt{2} = \sqrt{2}$

Rationalizing Fractions

You rationalize a fraction with a radical in its denominator (bottom) by changing the original fraction to an equivalent fraction that has a multiple of that radical in the numerator (top). Usually, you want to remove radicals from the denominator. The square root of a number that isn't a perfect square is *irrational.* Dividing with an irrational number is difficult because, when expressed as decimals, those numbers never end and never have a repeating pattern.

TIP

To rationalize a fraction with a square root in the denominator, multiply both the numerator and denominator by that square root.

EXAMPLE

Q. $\frac{10}{\sqrt{5}}$

A. $2\sqrt{5}$. Recall the property that $\sqrt{a \times b} = \sqrt{a} \times \sqrt{b}$. It works both ways: $\sqrt{a} \times \sqrt{b} = \sqrt{a \times b}$

Multiplying the denominator by itself creates a perfect square (so there'll be no radical). Simplify and reduce the fraction.

$$\frac{10}{\sqrt{5}} = \frac{10}{\sqrt{5}} \times \frac{\sqrt{5}}{\sqrt{5}} = \frac{10\sqrt{5}}{\sqrt{25}}$$
$$= \frac{10\sqrt{5}}{5} = \frac{{}^{2}\cancel{10}\sqrt{5}}{\cancel{5}_{1}} = 2\sqrt{5}$$

Q. $\frac{\sqrt{6}}{\sqrt{10}}$

A. $\frac{\sqrt{15}}{5}$. In this problem, you multiply both of the radicals by the radical in the denominator. The products lead to results that can be simplified nicely.

$$\frac{\sqrt{6}}{\sqrt{10}} = \frac{\sqrt{6}}{\sqrt{10}} \times \frac{\sqrt{10}}{\sqrt{10}} = \frac{\sqrt{60}}{\sqrt{100}}$$
$$= \frac{\sqrt{4}\sqrt{15}}{10} = \frac{2\sqrt{15}}{10} = \frac{{}^{1}\cancel{2}\sqrt{15}}{\cancel{10}_{5}} = \frac{\sqrt{15}}{5}$$

$\frac{12}{\sqrt{6}} = \frac{12}{\sqrt{6}} \times \frac{\sqrt{6}}{\sqrt{6}} = \frac{12\sqrt{6}}{\sqrt{36}} = \frac{12\sqrt{6}}{6} = 2\sqrt{6}$

7 Rationalize $\frac{1}{\sqrt{2}}$.

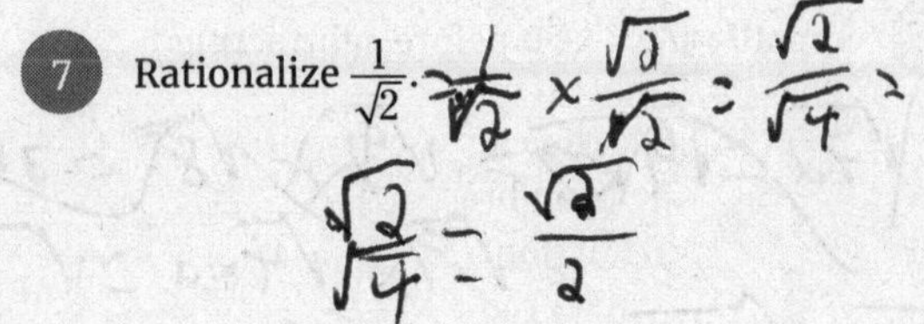

8 Rationalize $\frac{4}{\sqrt{3}}$.

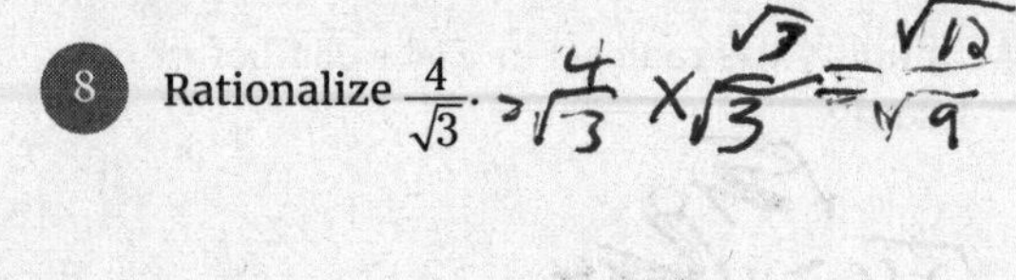

9 Rationalize $\frac{3}{\sqrt{6}}$.

10 Rationalize $\frac{\sqrt{21}}{\sqrt{15}}$.

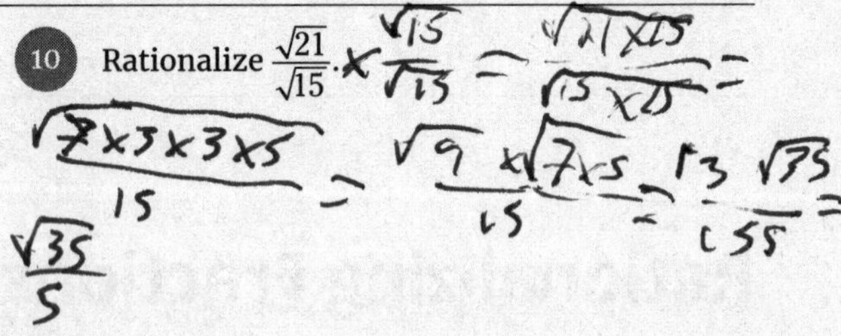

Arranging Radicals as Exponential Terms

The radical symbol indicates that you're to do the operation of taking a root — or figuring out what number multiplied itself to give you the value under the radical. An alternate notation, a *fractional exponent*, also indicates that you're to take a root, but fractional exponents are much more efficient when you perform operations involving powers of the same number.

The equivalence between the square root of a and the fractional power notation is $\sqrt{a} = a^{1/2}$. The 2 in the bottom of the fractional exponent indicates a square root. The general equivalence between all roots, powers, and fractional exponents is $\sqrt[n]{a^m} = a^{m/n}$.

EXAMPLE

Q. $\sqrt[3]{x^7} =$

A. $x^{7/3}$. The root is 3; you're taking a cube root. The 3 goes in the fraction's denominator. The 7 goes in the fraction's numerator.

Q. $\frac{1}{\sqrt{x^3}} =$

A. $x^{-3/2}$. The exponent becomes negative when you bring up the factor from the fraction's denominator. Also, when no root is showing on the radical, it's assumed that a 2 goes there because it's a square root.

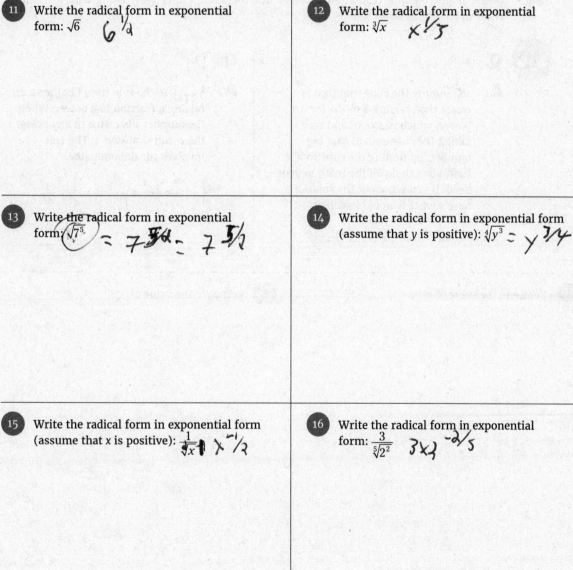

11 Write the radical form in exponential form: $\sqrt{6}$

12 Write the radical form in exponential form: $\sqrt[3]{x}$

13 Write the radical form in exponential form: $\sqrt{7^5}$

14 Write the radical form in exponential form (assume that y is positive): $\sqrt[4]{y^3}$

15 Write the radical form in exponential form (assume that x is positive): $\frac{1}{\sqrt[4]{x}}$

16 Write the radical form in exponential form: $\frac{3}{\sqrt[5]{2^2}}$

Using Fractional Exponents

Fractional exponents by themselves are fine and dandy. They're a nice, compact way of writing an operation to be performed on the power of a number. What's even nicer is when you can simplify or evaluate an expression, and its result is an integer. You want to take advantage of these simplification situations.

TIP

If a value is written $a^{m/n}$, the easiest way to evaluate it is to take the root first and then raise the result to the power. Doing so keeps the numbers relatively small — or at least smaller than the power might become. The answer comes out the same either way. Being able to compute these in your head saves time.

EXAMPLE

Q. $8^{4/3} =$

A. **16**. Finding the cube root first is easier than raising 8 to the fourth power, which is 4,096, and then taking the cube root of that big number. By finding the cube root first, you can do all the math in your head. If you write out the solution, here's what it would look like:

$$8^{4/3} = \left(8^{1/3}\right)^4 = \left(\sqrt[3]{8}\right)^4 = (2)^4 = 16$$

Q. $\left(\frac{1}{9}\right)^{3/2} =$

A. **$^1/_{27}$**. Use the rule from Chapter 4 on raising a fraction to a power. When the number 1 is raised to any power, the result is always 1. The rest involves the denominator.

$$\left(\frac{1}{9}\right)^{3/2} = \frac{1^{3/2}}{9^{3/2}} = \frac{1}{\left(9^{1/2}\right)^3} = \frac{1}{3^3} = \frac{1}{27}$$

17 Compute the value of $4^{5/2}$.

18 Compute the value of $27^{2/3}$.

19 Compute the value of $\left(\frac{1}{4}\right)^{3/2}$.

20 Compute the value of $\left(\frac{8}{27}\right)^{4/3}$.

Simplifying Expressions with Exponents

Writing expressions using fractional exponents is better than writing them as radicals because fractional exponents are easier to work with in situations where something complicated or messy needs to be simplified into something neater. The simplifying is done when you multiply and/or divide factors with the same base. When the bases are the same, you use the rules for multiplying (add exponents), dividing (subtract exponents), and raising to powers (multiply exponents). Refer to Chapter 4 if you need a reminder on these concepts. Here are some examples:

EXAMPLE

Q. $2^{4/3} \times 2^{5/3} =$

A. **8**. Remember, when numbers with the same base are multiplied together, you add the exponents.

$$2^{4/3} \times 2^{5/3} = 2^{4/3+5/3} = 2^{9/3} = 2^3 = 8$$

Q. $\frac{5^{9/2}}{25^{1/4}} =$

A. **625**. Notice that the numbers don't have the same base! But 25 is a power of 5, so you can rewrite it and then apply the fourth root.

$$\frac{5^{9/2}}{25^{1/4}} = \frac{5^{9/2}}{\left(5^2\right)^{1/4}} = \frac{5^{9/2}}{5^{1/2}} = 5^{9/2-1/2} = 5^4 = 625$$

21 Simplify $2^{1/4} \times 2^{3/4}$.

22 Simplify $\frac{6^{14/5}}{6^{4/5}}$.

23 Simplify $\frac{4^{7/4}}{8^{1/6}}$.

24 Simplify $\frac{9^{3/4} \times 3^{7/2}}{27^{3/2}}$.

Estimating Answers

Radicals appear in many mathematical applications. You need to simplify radical expressions, but it's also important to have an approximate answer in mind before you start. Doing so lets you evaluate whether the answer makes sense, based on your estimate. If you just keep in mind that $\sqrt{2}$ is about 1.4, $\sqrt{3}$ is about 1.7, and $\sqrt{5}$ is about 2.2, you can estimate many radical values. Here are some examples:

EXAMPLE

Q. Estimate the value of $\sqrt{200}$.

A. **About 14**. Simplifying the radical, you get $\sqrt{200} = \sqrt{100 \times 2} = \sqrt{100} \times \sqrt{2} = 10\sqrt{2}$. If $\sqrt{2}$ is about 1.4, then 10(1.4) is 14.

Q. Estimate the value of $\sqrt{20} + \sqrt{27}$.

A. **About 9.5**. Simplifying the radicals, you get $\sqrt{20} + \sqrt{27} = \sqrt{4 \times 5} + \sqrt{9 \times 3} = 2\sqrt{5} + 3\sqrt{3}$. If $\sqrt{5}$ is about 2.2, then 2(2.2) is 4.4. Multiplying 3(1.7) for 3 times root three, you get 5.1. The sum of 4.4 and 5.1 is 9.5.

25 Estimate $\sqrt{32}$.

26 Estimate $\sqrt{125}$.

27 Estimate $\sqrt{12} + \sqrt{18}$.

28 Estimate $\sqrt{160}$.

Answers to Problems on Radicals

This section provides the answers (in bold) to the practice problems in this chapter.

1. Simplify $\sqrt{12}$. The answer is $\mathbf{2\sqrt{3}}$.

   $\sqrt{12} = \sqrt{4 \times 3} = \sqrt{4}\sqrt{3} = 2\sqrt{3}$

2. Simplify $\sqrt{200}$. The answer is $\mathbf{10\sqrt{2}}$.

   $\sqrt{200} = \sqrt{100 \times 2} = \sqrt{100}\sqrt{2} = 10\sqrt{2}$

3. Simplify $\sqrt{63}$. The answer is $\mathbf{3\sqrt{7}}$.

   $\sqrt{63} = \sqrt{9 \times 7} = \sqrt{9}\sqrt{7} = 3\sqrt{7}$

4. Simplify $\sqrt{75}$. The answer is $\mathbf{5\sqrt{3}}$.

   $\sqrt{75} = \sqrt{25 \times 3} = \sqrt{25}\sqrt{3} = 5\sqrt{3}$

5. Simplify the radicals in $\sqrt{24} + \sqrt{54}$ before adding. The answer is $\mathbf{5\sqrt{6}}$.

   $\sqrt{24} + \sqrt{54} = \sqrt{4 \times 6} + \sqrt{9 \times 6} = \sqrt{4}\sqrt{6} + \sqrt{9}\sqrt{6} = 2\sqrt{6} + 3\sqrt{6} = 5\sqrt{6}$

6. Simplify $\sqrt{72} - \sqrt{50}$ before subtracting. The answer is $\mathbf{\sqrt{2}}$.

   $\sqrt{72} - \sqrt{50} = \sqrt{36 \times 2} - \sqrt{25 \times 2} = \sqrt{36}\sqrt{2} - \sqrt{25}\sqrt{2} = 6\sqrt{2} - 5\sqrt{2} = \sqrt{2}$

7. Rationalize $\frac{1}{\sqrt{2}}$. The answer is $\mathbf{\frac{\sqrt{2}}{2}}$.

   $\frac{1}{\sqrt{2}} = \frac{1}{\sqrt{2}} \times \frac{\sqrt{2}}{\sqrt{2}} = \frac{\sqrt{2}}{\sqrt{4}} = \frac{\sqrt{2}}{2}$

8. Rationalize $\frac{4}{\sqrt{3}}$. The answer is $\mathbf{\frac{4\sqrt{3}}{3}}$.

   $\frac{4}{\sqrt{3}} = \frac{4}{\sqrt{3}} \times \frac{\sqrt{3}}{\sqrt{3}} = \frac{4\sqrt{3}}{\sqrt{9}} = \frac{4\sqrt{3}}{3}$

9. Rationalize $\frac{3}{\sqrt{6}}$. The answer is $\mathbf{\frac{\sqrt{6}}{2}}$.

   $\frac{3}{\sqrt{6}} = \frac{3}{\sqrt{6}} \times \frac{\sqrt{6}}{\sqrt{6}} = \frac{3\sqrt{6}}{\sqrt{36}} = \frac{{}^{1}\cancel{3}\sqrt{6}}{\cancel{6}_{2}} = \frac{\sqrt{6}}{2}$

10. Rationalize $\frac{\sqrt{21}}{\sqrt{15}}$. The answer is $\mathbf{\frac{\sqrt{35}}{5}}$.

    $\frac{\sqrt{21}}{\sqrt{15}} = \frac{\sqrt{21}}{\sqrt{15}} \times \frac{\sqrt{15}}{\sqrt{15}} = \frac{\sqrt{21 \times 15}}{\sqrt{15 \times 15}} = \frac{\sqrt{7 \times 3 \times 3 \times 5}}{15} = \frac{\sqrt{9}\sqrt{7 \times 5}}{15} = \frac{{}^{1}\cancel{3}\sqrt{35}}{\cancel{15}_{5}} = \frac{\sqrt{35}}{5}$

11. Write the radical form in exponential form: $\sqrt{6}$. The answer is $\mathbf{6^{1/2}}$.

12. Write the radical form in exponential form: $\sqrt[3]{x}$. The answer is $\mathbf{x^{1/3}}$.

13. Write the radical form in exponential form: $\sqrt{7^5}$. The answer is $\mathbf{7^{5/2}}$.

(14) Write the radical form in exponential form: $\sqrt[4]{y^3}$. The answer is $\mathbf{y^{3/4}}$.

(15) Write the radical form in exponential form: $\frac{1}{\sqrt{x}}$. The answer is $\mathbf{x^{-1/2}}$.

(16) Write the radical form in exponential form: $\frac{3}{\sqrt[5]{2^2}}$. The answer is $\mathbf{3 \times 2^{-2/5}}$.

(17) Compute the value of $4^{5/2}$. The answer is **32**.

$$4^{5/2} = \left(4^{1/2}\right)^5 = \left(\sqrt{4}\right)^5 = 2^5 = 32$$

(18) Compute the value of $27^{2/3}$. The answer is **9**.

$$27^{2/3} = \left(27^{1/3}\right)^2 = \left(\sqrt[3]{27}\right)^2 = 3^2 = 9$$

(19) Compute the value of $\left(\frac{1}{4}\right)^{3/2}$. The answer is $\mathbf{1/8}$.

$$\left(\frac{1}{4}\right)^{3/2} = \frac{1^{3/2}}{4^{3/2}} = \frac{1}{\left(4^{1/2}\right)^3} = \frac{1}{2^3} = \frac{1}{8}$$

(20) Compute the value of $\left(\frac{8}{27}\right)^{4/3}$. The answer is $\mathbf{16/81}$.

$$\left(\frac{8}{27}\right)^{4/3} = \frac{8^{4/3}}{27^{4/3}} = \frac{\left(8^{1/3}\right)^4}{\left(27^{1/3}\right)^4} = \frac{2^4}{3^4} = \frac{16}{81}$$

(21) Simplify $2^{1/4} \times 2^{3/4}$. The answer is **2**.

$$2^{1/4} \times 2^{3/4} = 2^{1/4+3/4} = 2^{4/4} = 2^1 = 2$$

(22) Simplify $\frac{6^{14/5}}{6^{4/5}}$. The answer is **36**.

$$\frac{6^{14/5}}{6^{4/5}} = 6^{14/5-4/5} = 6^{10/5} = 6^2 = 36$$

(23) Simplify $\frac{4^{7/4}}{8^{1/6}}$. The answer is **8**.

$$\frac{4^{7/4}}{8^{1/6}} = \frac{\left(2^2\right)^{7/4}}{\left(2^3\right)^{1/6}} = \frac{2^{7/2}}{2^{1/2}} = 2^{7/2-1/2} = 2^{6/2} = 2^3 = 8$$

(24) Simplify $\frac{9^{3/4} \times 3^{7/2}}{27^{3/2}}$. The answer is $\mathbf{\sqrt{3}}$.

$$\frac{9^{3/4} \times 3^{7/2}}{27^{3/2}} = \frac{\left(3^2\right)^{3/4} \times 3^{7/2}}{\left(3^3\right)^{3/2}} = \frac{3^{3/2} \times 3^{7/2}}{3^{9/2}} = \frac{3^{3/2+7/2}}{3^{9/2}} = \frac{3^{10/2}}{3^{9/2}} = 3^{10/2-9/2} = 3^{1/2} = \sqrt{3}$$

(25) Estimate $\sqrt{32}$. The answer is **about 5.6**.

$$\sqrt{32} = \sqrt{16} \times \sqrt{2} = 4\sqrt{2} \approx 4(1.4) = 5.6$$

26 Estimate $\sqrt{125}$. The answer is **about 11.**

$\sqrt{125}=\sqrt{25}\times\sqrt{5}=5\sqrt{5}\approx 5(2.2)=11$

27 Estimate $\sqrt{12}+\sqrt{18}$. The answer is **about 7.6.**

$\sqrt{12}+\sqrt{18}=\left(\sqrt{4}\times\sqrt{3}\right)+\left(\sqrt{9}\times\sqrt{2}\right)=2\sqrt{3}+3\sqrt{2}\approx 2(1.7)+3(1.4)=7.6$

28 Estimate $\sqrt{160}$. The answer is **about 12.32.**

$\sqrt{160}=\sqrt{16}\times\sqrt{10}=\sqrt{16}\times\sqrt{2}\times\sqrt{5}=4\sqrt{2}\sqrt{5}\approx 4(1.4)(2.2)=12.32$

» Maintaining order with the order of operations

» Combining all the rules for simpler computing

Chapter 6
Simplifying Algebraic Expressions

The operations of addition, subtraction, multiplication, and division are familiar to every grade school student. Fortunately, these operations work the same, no matter what level or what kind of math you do. As I explain in this chapter, though, algebra and its properties introduce some new twists to those elementary rules. The good news is that you can apply all these basic rules to the letters, which stand for variables, in algebra. However, because you usually don't know what values the variables represent, you have to be careful when doing the operations and reporting the results. This chapter offers you multitudes of problems to make sure you keep everything in order.

REMEMBER

The most commonly used variable in algebra is *x*. Because the variable *x* looks so much like the times sign, ×, other multiplication symbols are used in algebra problems. The following are all equivalent multiplications:

$$x \times y = x \cdot y = (x)(y) = x(y) = (x)y = xy$$

In spreadsheets and on calculators, the * sign indicates multiplication.

Adding and Subtracting Like Terms

In algebra, the expression *like terms* refers to a common structure for the terms under consideration. *Like terms* have exactly the same variables in them, and each variable is "powered" the same (if x is squared and y cubed in one term, then x squared and y cubed occur in a *like term*). When adding and subtracting algebraic terms, the terms must be *alike*, with the same variables raised to exactly the same power, but the numerical coefficients can be different. For example, two terms that are *alike* are $2a^3b$ and $5a^3b$. Two terms that aren't *alike* are $3xyz$ and $4x^2yz$, where the power on the x term is different in the two terms.

EXAMPLE

Q. $6a+2b-4ab+7b+5ab-a+7=$

A. $\mathbf{5a+9b+ab+7}$. First, change the order and group the like terms together; then compute:

$$6a+2b-4ab+7b+5ab-a+7$$
$$=(6a-a)+(2b+7b)+(-4ab+5ab)+7$$

The parentheses aren't necessary, but they help to keep track of what you can combine.

Q. $8x^2-3x+4xy-9x^2-5x-20xy=$

A. $\mathbf{-x^2-8x-16xy}$. Again, combine like terms and compute:

$$8x^2-3x+4xy-9x^2-5x-20xy$$
$$=(8x^2-9x^2)+(-3x-5x)+(4xy-20xy)$$
$$=-x^2-8x-16xy$$

1 Combine the like terms in $4a+3ab-2ab+6a$.

4a + 3ab − 2ab + 6a
4a + 6a = 10a
3ab − 2ab = ab
10a + ab

2 Combine the like terms in $3x^2y-2xy^2+4x^3-8x^2y$.

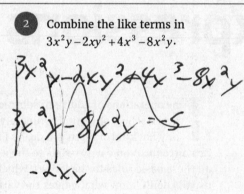

3x²y − 2xy² + 4x³ − 8x²y
3x²y − 8x²y = −5
−2xy

3 Combine the like terms in $2a^2+3a-4+7a^2-6a+5$.

2a² + 3a − 4 + 7a² − 6a + 5
(2a² + 7a²) + (3a − 6a) − (4 + 5)
9a⁴ − 3a − 9

4 Combine the like terms in $ab+bc+cd+de-ab+2bc+e$.

Multiplying and Dividing Algebraically

Multiplying and dividing algebraic expressions is somewhat different from adding and subtracting them. When multiplying and dividing, the terms don't have to be exactly alike. You can multiply or divide all variables with the same base — using the laws of exponents (check out Chapter 4 for more information) — and you multiply or divide the number factors.

REMEMBER

If a variable's power is greater in the denominator, then the difference between the two powers is preferably written as a positive power of the base — in the denominator — instead of with a negative exponent in the numerator. For example:

$$\frac{18a^3b^{12}}{3a^7b^4} = 6a^{3-7}b^{12-4} = 6a^{-4}b^8 = \frac{6b^8}{a^4}$$

EXAMPLE

Q. $(4x^2y^2z^3)(3xy^4z^3) =$

A. $\mathbf{12x^3y^6z^6}$. The product of 4 and 3 is 12. Multiply the x's to get $x^2(x) = x^3$. Multiply the y's and then the z's and you get $y^2(y^4) = y^6$ and $z^3(z^3) = z^6$. Each variable has its own power determined by the factors multiplied together to get it.

Q. $\frac{32x^4y^3z}{64x^2y^7} =$

A. $\mathbf{\frac{x^2z}{2y^4}}$. The power of x in the numerator is greater than that in the denominator, and y has the greater power in the denominator. The only factor of z is in the numerator, so it stays there.

$$\frac{32x^4y^3z}{64x^2y^7} = \frac{{}^{1}\not{32}x^{4-2}y^{3-7}z}{{}_{2}\not{64}} = \frac{x^2y^{-4}z}{2} = \frac{x^2z}{2y^4}$$

5 Multiply $(3x)(2x^2)$.

6 Multiply $(4y^2)(-x^4y)$.

7 Multiply $(6x^3y^2z^2)(8x^3y^4z)$.

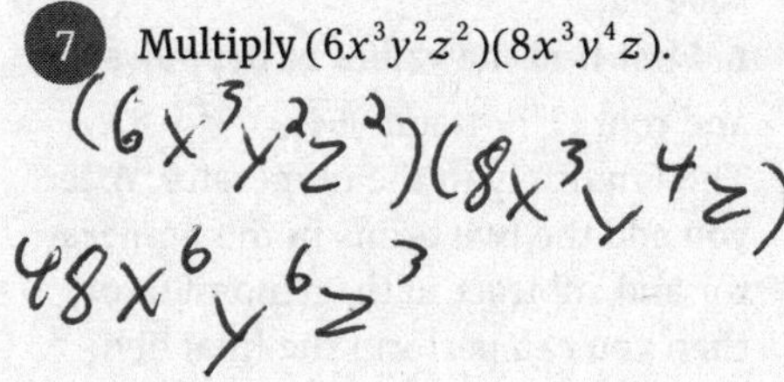

8 Divide (write all exponents as positive numbers) $\frac{10x^2y^3}{-5xy^2}$.

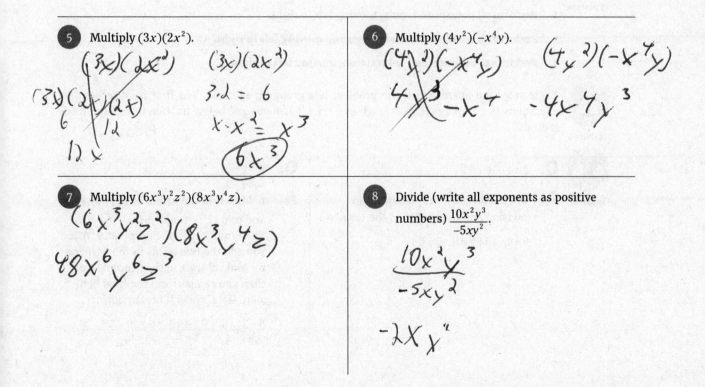

9 Divide (write all exponents as positive numbers) $\frac{24x}{3x^4}$.

10 Divide (write all exponents as positive numbers) $\frac{13x^3y^4}{26x^8y^3}$.

Incorporating Order of Operations

Because much of algebra involves symbols for numbers, operations, relationships, and groupings, are you really surprised that *order* is something special, too? Order helps you solve problems by making sure that everyone doing the problem follows the same procedure and gets the same answer. Order is how mathematicians have been able to communicate — agreeing on these same conventions. The *order of operations* is just one of many such agreements that have been adopted.

REMEMBER

When you perform operations on algebraic expressions and you have a choice between one or more operations to perform, use the following order:

1. **Perform all powers and roots, moving left to right.**
2. **Perform all multiplication and division, moving left to right.**
3. **Perform all addition and subtraction, moving left to right.**

WARNING

These rules are *interrupted* if the problem has grouping symbols. You first need to perform operations in grouping symbols, such as ( ), { }, [ ], above and below fraction lines, and inside radicals.

EXAMPLE

Q. $2\times4-10\div5=$

A. 6. First do the multiplication and division and then subtract the results:

$$2\times4-10\div5=8-2=6$$

Q. $\frac{8+2^2\times5}{\sqrt{64}-1}=$

A. 4. First find the values of the power and root ($2^2=4$ and $\sqrt{64}=\sqrt{8^2}=8$). Then multiply in the numerator. After you add the two terms in the numerator and subtract in the denominator, then you can perform the final division. Here's how it breaks down:

$$\frac{8+2^2\times5}{\sqrt{64}-1}=\frac{8+4\times5}{8-1}=\frac{8+20}{8-1}=\frac{28}{7}=4$$

11 $5+3\times4^2+6\div2-5\sqrt{9}=$

12 $\dfrac{6\times8-4^2}{2^3+8\left(3^2-1\right)}=$

13 $2\times3^3+3\left(2^2-5\right)=$

14 $\dfrac{4^2+3^2}{9(4)-11}=$

Evaluating Expressions

Evaluating an expression means that you want to change it from a bunch of letters and numbers to a specific value — some number. After you solve an equation or inequality, you want to go back and check to see whether your solution really works — so you evaluate the expression. For example, if you let $x=2$ in the expression $3x^2-2x+1$, you replace all the x's with 2's and apply the order of operations when doing the calculations. In this case, you get $3(2)^2-2(2)+1=3(4)-4+1=12-4+1=9$. Can you see why knowing that you square the 2 before multiplying by the 3 is so important? If you multiply by the 3 first, you end up with that first term being worth 36 instead of 12. It makes a big difference.

EXAMPLE

Q. Evaluate $\dfrac{5y-y^2}{2x}$ when $y=-4$ and $x=-3$.

A. **6**

$$\frac{5y-y^2}{2x}=\frac{5(-4)-(-4)^2}{2(-3)}=\frac{5(-4)-16}{2(-3)}$$

$$=\frac{-20-16}{-6}=\frac{-36}{-6}=6$$

EXAMPLE

Q. Evaluate $\dfrac{n!}{r!(n-r)!}$ when $n = 8$ and $r = 3$.

A. **56**. What's with this exclamation (the $n!$)? The exclamation indicates an operation called a *factorial.* This operation has you multiply the number in front of the ! by every positive whole number smaller than it. You see a lot of factorials in statistics and higher mathematics. The order of operations is important here, too.

$$\frac{n!}{r!(n-r)!} = \frac{8!}{3!(8-3)!} = \frac{8!}{3!5!}$$
$$= \frac{8 \cdot 7 \cdot 6 \cdot 5 \cdot 4 \cdot 3 \cdot 2 \cdot 1}{3 \cdot 2 \cdot 1 \cdot 5 \cdot 4 \cdot 3 \cdot 2 \cdot 1} =$$
$$\frac{8 \cdot 7 \cdot 6 \cdot \cancel{5} \cdot \cancel{4} \cdot \cancel{3} \cdot \cancel{2} \cdot 1}{3 \cdot 2 \cdot 1 \cdot \cancel{5} \cdot \cancel{4} \cdot \cancel{3} \cdot \cancel{2} \cdot 1} =$$
$$\frac{8 \cdot 7 \cdot \cancel{6}}{\cancel{3} \cdot \cancel{2} \cdot 1} = \frac{56}{1} = 56$$

15 Evaluate $3x^2$ if $x = -2$.

16 Evaluate $9y - y^2$ if $y = -1$.

17 Evaluate $-(3x - 2y)$ if $x = 4$ and $y = 3$.

18 Evaluate $6x^2 - xy$ if $x = 2$ and $y = -3$.

19 Evaluate $\frac{2x+y}{x-y}$ if $x=4$ and $y=1$.

20 Evaluate $\frac{x^2-2x}{y^2+2y}$ if $x=3$ and $y=-1$.

21 Evaluate $\frac{-b+\sqrt{b^2-4ac}}{2a}$ if $a=3$, $b=-2$, and $c=-1$.

22 Evaluate $\frac{n!}{r!}+\frac{n!}{r!(n-r)!}$ if $n=5$ and $r=2$.

Answers to Problems on Algebraic Expressions

This section provides the answers (in bold) to the practice problems in this chapter.

1. Combine the like terms in $4a+3ab-2ab+6a$. The answer is $\mathbf{10a+ab}$.

   $4a+3ab-2ab+6a=(4a+6a)+(3ab-2ab)=10a+ab$

2. Combine the like terms in $3x^2y-2xy^2+4x^3-8x^2y$. The answer is $\mathbf{-5x^2y-2xy^2+4x^3}$.

   $3x^2y-2xy^2+4x^3-8x^2y=(3x^2y-8x^2y)-2xy^2+4x^3=-5x^2y-2xy^2+4x^3$

3. Combine the like terms in $2a^2+3a-4+7a^2-6a+5$. The answer is $\mathbf{9a^2-3a+1}$.

   $2a^2+3a-4+7a^2-6a+5=(2a^2+7a^2)+(3a-6a)+(-4+5)=9a^2-3a+1$

4. Combine the like terms in $ab+bc+cd+de-ab+2bc+e$. The answer is $\mathbf{3bc+cd+de+e}$.

   $ab+bc+cd+de-ab+2bc+e=(ab-ab)+(bc+2bc)+cd+de+e=0+3bc+cd+de+e$

5. Multiply $(3x)(2x^2)$. The answer is $\mathbf{6x^3}$.

   $(3x)(2x^2)=(3\cdot 2)(x\cdot x^2)=6x^3$

6. Multiply $(4y^2)(-x^4y)$. The answer is $\mathbf{-4x^4y^3}$.

   $(4y^2)(-x^4y)=-4x^4(y^2)(y)=-4x^4y^3$

7. Multiply $(6x^3y^2z^2)(8x^3y^4z)$. The answer is $\mathbf{48x^6y^6z^3}$.

   $(6x^3y^2z^2)(8x^3y^4z)=(6\cdot 8)(x^3\cdot x^3)(y^2\cdot y^4)(z^2\cdot z)=48x^6y^6z^3$

8. Divide (write all exponents as positive numbers) $\dfrac{10x^2y^3}{-5xy^2}$. The answer is $\mathbf{-2xy}$.

   $\dfrac{10x^2y^3}{-5xy^2}=\dfrac{{}^{2}\cancel{10}x^{2-1}y^{3-2}}{-\cancel{5}_{-1}}=-2xy$

9. Divide (write all exponents as positive numbers) $\dfrac{24x}{3x^4}$. The answer is $\mathbf{\dfrac{8}{x^3}}$.

   $\dfrac{24x}{3x^4}=8x^{1-4}=8x^{-3}=\dfrac{8}{x^3}$ or $\dfrac{24x}{3x^4}=\dfrac{8}{x^{4-1}}=\dfrac{8}{x^3}$

10. Divide (write all exponents as positive numbers) $\dfrac{13x^3y^4}{26x^8y^3}$. The answer is $\mathbf{\dfrac{y}{2x^5}}$.

    $\dfrac{13x^3y^4}{26x^8y^3}=\dfrac{x^{3-8}y^{4-3}}{2}=\dfrac{x^{-5}y^1}{2}=\dfrac{y}{2x^5}$ or $\dfrac{13x^3y^4}{26x^8y^3}=\dfrac{y^{4-3}}{2x^{8-3}}=\dfrac{y^1}{2x^5}=\dfrac{y}{2x^5}$

11. $5+3\times 4^2+6\div 2-5\sqrt{9}=\mathbf{41}$

    $5+3\times 4^2+6\div 2-5\sqrt{9}=5+3\times 16+6\div 2-5(3)=5+48+3-15=56-15=41$

12. $\dfrac{6\times 8-4^2}{2^3+8(3^2-1)}=\mathbf{\dfrac{4}{9}}$

    $\dfrac{6\times 8-4^2}{2^3+8(3^2-1)}=\dfrac{6\times 8-16}{8+8(9-1)}=\dfrac{6\times 8-16}{8+8(8)}=\dfrac{48-16}{8+64}=\dfrac{32}{72}=\dfrac{{}^{4}\cancel{32}}{{}_{9}\cancel{72}}=\dfrac{4}{9}$

13. $2\times3^3+3(2^2-5)=\mathbf{51}$

$2\times3^3+3(2^2-5)=2\times27+3(4-5)=2\times27+3(-1)=54-3=51$

14. $\dfrac{4^2+3^2}{9(4)-11}=\mathbf{1}$

$\dfrac{4^2+3^2}{9(4)-11}=\dfrac{16+9}{9(4)-11}=\dfrac{16+9}{36-11}=\dfrac{25}{25}=1$

15. Evaluate $3x^2$ if $x=-2$. The answer is **12**.

$3x^2=3(-2)^2=3\times4=12$

16. Evaluate $9y-y^2$ if $y=-1$. The answer is **−10**.

$9y-y^2=9(-1)-(-1)^2=-9-1=-10$

17. Evaluate $-(3x-2y)$ if $x=4$ and $y=3$. The answer is **−6**.

$-(3x-2y)=-[3(4)-2(3)]=-[12-6]=-6$

18. Evaluate $6x^2-xy$ if $x=2$ and $y=-3$. The answer is **30**.

$6x^2-xy=6(2)^2-(2)(-3)=6(4)-(2)(-3)=24+6=30$

19. Evaluate $\dfrac{2x+y}{x-y}$ if $x=4$ and $y=1$. The answer is **3**.

$\dfrac{2x+y}{x-y}=\dfrac{2\times4+1}{4-1}=\dfrac{8+1}{4-1}=\dfrac{9}{3}=3$

20. Evaluate $\dfrac{x^2-2x}{y^2+2y}$ if $x=3$ and $y=-1$. The answer is **−3**.

$\dfrac{x^2-2x}{y^2+2y}=\dfrac{3^2-2\times3}{(-1)^2+2(-1)}=\dfrac{9-6}{1-2}=\dfrac{3}{-1}=-3$

21. Evaluate $\dfrac{-b+\sqrt{b^2-4ac}}{2a}$ if $a=3$, $b=-2$ and $c=-1$. The answer is **1**.

$$\frac{-b+\sqrt{b^2-4ac}}{2a}=\frac{-(-2)+\sqrt{(-2)^2-4(3)(-1)}}{2(3)}=\frac{2+\sqrt{4-(-12)}}{6}=\frac{2+\sqrt{16}}{6}=\frac{2+4}{6}=\frac{6}{6}=1$$

22. Evaluate $\dfrac{n!}{r!}+\dfrac{n!}{r!(n-r)!}$ if $n=5$ and $r=2$. The answer is **70**.

$$\frac{n!}{r!}+\frac{n!}{r!(n-r)!}=\frac{5!}{2!}+\frac{5!}{2!(5-2)!}=\frac{5!}{2!}+\frac{5!}{2!3!}=\frac{5\cdot4\cdot3\cdot\cancel{2}\cdot1}{\cancel{2}\cdot1}+\frac{5\cdot4\cdot\cancel{3}\cdot\cancel{2}\cdot1}{2\cdot1\cdot\cancel{3}\cdot\cancel{2}\cdot1}=\frac{60}{1}+\frac{20}{2}=60+10=70$$

2

Changing the Format of Expressions

IN THIS PART . . .

Further your skills in multiplying more than one term.

Use long division to simplify algebraic expressions.

Get a handle on factoring.

Practice factoring binomials.

Focus on factoring trinomials and special polynomials.

FOIL

» Squaring and cubing binomials

» Calling on Pascal to raise binomials to many powers

» Incorporating special rules when multiplying

Chapter 7

Specializing in Multiplication Matters

In Chapter 6, I cover the basics of multiplying algebraic expressions. In this chapter, I expand those processes to multiplying by more than one term. When performing multiplications involving many terms, it's helpful to understand how to take advantage of special situations, like multiplying the sum and difference of the same two values, such as $(xy+16)(xy-16)$, and raising a binomial to a power, such as $(a+3)^4$, which seem to pop up frequently. Fortunately, various procedures have been developed to handle such situations with ease.

You also see the nitty-gritty of multiplying factor by factor and term by term (the long way) compared to the neat little trick called FOIL. With this information, you'll be able to efficiently and correctly multiply expressions in many different types of situations. You'll also be able to expand expressions using multiplication so that you can later go backward and factor expressions back into their original multiplication forms.

Distributing One Factor over Many

When you *distribute* Halloween candy, you give one piece to each costumed person. When you *distribute* some factor over several terms, you take each factor (multiplier) on the outside of a grouping symbol and multiply it by each term (all separated by + or −) inside the grouping symbol.

REMEMBER

The distributive rule is

$$a(b+c) = ab+ac \quad \textbf{and} \quad a(b-c) = ab-ac$$

In other words, if you multiply a value times a sum or difference within a grouping symbol such as $2(x+3)$, you multiply every term inside by the factor outside. In this case, multiply the x and 3 each by 2 to get $2x+6$.

EXAMPLE

Q. Distributing: $6x(3x^2+5x-2) =$

A. $\mathbf{18x^3+30x^2-12x}$. Now for the details: $6x(3x^2+5x-2) = 6x(3x^2)+6x(5x) -6x(2) = 18x^3+30x^2-12x$

Q. Distributing: $3abc(2a^2bc+5abc^2 -2abd) =$

A. $\mathbf{6a^3b^2c^2 + 15a^2b^2c^3 - 6a^2b^2cd}$. The details: $3abc\left(2a^2bc+5abc^2-2abd\right) = 3abc\left(2a^2bc\right)+3abc\left(5abc^2\right) -3abc\left(2abd\right)$

1 Distribute $x(8x^3-3x^2+2x-5)$.

2 Distribute $x^2y(2xy^2+3xyz+y^2z^3)$.

3 Distribute $-4y(3y^4-2y^2+5y-5)$.

4 Distribute $x^{1/2}y^{-1/2}\left(x^{3/2}y^{1/2}+x^{1/2}y^{3/2}\right)$.

Curses, FOILed again — or not

A common process found in algebra is that of multiplying two binomials together. A *binomial* is an expression with two terms such as $x+7$. One possible way to multiply the binomials together is to distribute the two terms in the first binomial over the two terms in the second.

TIP

But some math whiz came up with a great acronym, *FOIL*, which translates to F for First, O for Outer, I for Inner, and L for Last. This acronym helps you save time and makes multiplying binomials easier. These letters refer to the terms' positions in the product of two binomials.

When you FOIL the product $(a+b)(c+d)$

- » The product of the **F**irst terms is *ac.*
- » The product of the **O**uter terms is *ad.*
- » The product of the **I**nner terms is *bc.*
- » The product of the **L**ast terms is *bd.*

The result is then $ac+ad+bc+bd$. Usually *ad* and *bc* are like terms and can be combined.

EXAMPLE

Q. Use FOIL to multiply $(x-8)(x-9)$.

A. $\mathbf{x^2-17x+72}$. Using FOIL, multiply the First, the Outer, the Inner, and the Last and then combine the like terms: $(x-8)(x-9)$

$$= x^2+x(-9)+(-8)x+72$$
$$= x^2-9x-8x+72 = x^2-17x+72$$

Q. Use FOIL to multiply $(2y^2+3)(y^2-4)$.

A. $\mathbf{2y^4-5y^2-12}$. Using FOIL, multiply the First, the Outer, the Inner, and the Last and then combine the like terms: $(2y^2+3)(y^2-4)$

$$= 2y^2\cdot y^2+2y^2(-4)+3\cdot y^2+3(-4)$$
$$= 2y^4-8y^2+3y^2-12 = 2y^4-5y^2-12$$

5 Use FOIL to multiply $(2x+1)(3x-2)$.

6 Use FOIL to multiply $(x-7)(3x+5)$.

7 Use FOIL to multiply $(x^2-2)(x^2-4)$.

8 Use FOIL to multiply $(3x+4y)(4x-3y)$.

Squaring binomials

You can always use FOIL or the distributive law to square a binomial, but there's a helpful pattern that makes the work quicker and easier. You square the first and last terms, and then you put twice the product of the terms between the two squares.

REMEMBER

The squares of binomials are

$$(a+b)^2 = a^2 + 2ab + b^2 \quad \textbf{and} \quad (a-b)^2 = a^2 - 2ab + b^2$$

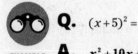

EXAMPLE

Q. $(x+5)^2 =$

A. $\boldsymbol{x^2 + 10x + 25}$. The 10x is twice the product of the x and 5: $(x+5)^2 = (x)^2 + 2(x)(5) + (5)^2 = x^2 + 10x + 25$

Q. $(3y-7)^2 =$

A. $\boldsymbol{9y^2 - 42y + 49}$. The 42y is twice the product of 3y and 7. And because the 7 is negative, the Inner and Outer products are, too: $(3y-7)^2 = (3y)^2 - 2(3y)(7) + (7)^2 = 9y^2 - 42y + 49$

9 $(x+3)^2 =$

10 $(2y-1)^2 =$

11 $(3a-2b)^2 =$

12 $(5xy+z)^2 =$

Multiplying the sum and difference of the same two terms

When you multiply two binomials together, you can always just FOIL them. You save yourself some work, though, if you recognize when the terms in the two binomials are the same — except for the sign between them. If they're the sum and difference of the same two numbers, then their product is just the difference between the squares of the two terms.

REMEMBER

The product of $(a+b)(a-b)$ is a^2-b^2.

This special product occurs because applying the FOIL method results in two opposite terms that cancel one another out: $(a+b)(a-b)=a^2-ab+ab-b^2=a^2-b^2$.

EXAMPLE

Q. $(x+5)(x-5)=$

A. x^2-25

Q. $(3ab^2-4)(3ab^2+4)=$

A. $9a^2b^4-16$

13 $(x+3)(x-3)=$

14 $(2x-7)(2x+7)=$

15 $(a^3-3)(a^3+3)=$

16 $(2x^2h+9)(2x^2h-9)=$

Cubing binomials

To *cube* something in algebra is to multiply it by itself and then multiply the result by itself again. When cubing a binomial, you have a couple of options. With the first option, you square the binomial and then multiply the original binomial times the square. This process involves distributing and then combining the like terms. Not a bad idea, but I have a better one.

When two binomials are cubed, two patterns occur.

- In the first pattern, the *coefficients* (numbers in front of and multiplying each term) in the answer start out as 1-3-3-1. The first coefficient is 1, the second is 3, the third is 3, and the last is 1.
- The other pattern is that the powers on the variables decrease and increase by ones. The powers of the first term in the binomial go down by one with each step, and the powers of the second term go up by one each time.

REMEMBER

To cube a binomial, follow this rule:

The cube of $(a+b)$, $(a+b)^3$, is $a^3+3a^2b+3ab^2+b^3$.

When one or more of the variables has a coefficient, then the powers of the coefficient get incorporated into the pattern, and the 1-3-3-1 seems to disappear.

EXAMPLE

Q. $(y+4)^3 =$

A. $\mathbf{y^3+12y^2+48y+64}$. The answer is built by incorporating the two patterns — the 1-3-3-1 of the coefficients and powers of the two terms. $(y+4)^3 = y^3+3y^2(4^1)+3y(4^2)+4^3$ $= y^3+12y^2+48y+64$. Notice how the powers of y go down one step each term. Also, the powers of 4, starting with the second term, go up one step each time. The last part of using this method is to simplify each term.

The 1-3-3-1 pattern gets lost when you do the simplification, but it's still part of the answer — just hidden. *Note:* In binomials with a subtraction in them, the terms in the answer will have alternating signs: +, –, +, –.

Q. $(2x-3)^3$

A. Starting with the 1-3-3-1 pattern and adding in the multipliers, $(2x-3)^3$ $=(2x)^3+3(2x)^2(-3)^1+3(2x)(-3)^2$ $+(-3)^3 = \mathbf{8x^3-36x^2+54x-27}$.

 17 $(x+1)^3 =$

 18 $(y-2)^3 =$

19 $(3z+1)^3 =$

20 $(5-2y)^3 =$

Creating the Sum and Difference of Cubes

A lot of what you do in algebra is to take advantage of patterns, rules, and quick tricks. Multiply the sum and difference of two values together, for example, and you get the difference of squares. Another pattern gives you the sum or difference of two cubes. These patterns are actually going to mean a lot more to you when you do the factoring of binomials, but for now, just practice with these patterns.

REMEMBER

Here's the rule: If you multiply a binomial times a particular *trinomial* — one that has the squares of the two terms in the binomial as well as the opposite of the product of them, such as $(y-5)(y^2+5y+25)$ — you get the sum or difference of two perfect cubes.

$$(a+b)(a^2-ab+b^2)=a^3+b^3 \quad \textbf{and} \quad (a-b)(a^2+ab+b^2)=a^3-b^3$$

EXAMPLE

Q. $(y+3)(y^2-3y+9)=$

A. $\mathbf{y^3+27}$. If you don't believe me, multiply it out: Distribute the binomial over the trinomial and combine like terms. You find all the *middle* terms pairing up with their opposites and becoming 0, leaving just the two cubes.

Q. $(5y-1)(25y^2+5y+1)=$

A. $\mathbf{125y^3-1}$. The number 5 cubed is 125, and −1 cubed is −1. The other terms in the product drop out because of the opposites that appear there.

21 $(x-2)(x^2+2x+4)=$

22 $(y+1)(y^2-y+1)=$

23 $(2z+5)(4z^2-10z+25)=$

24 $(3x-2)(9x^2+6x+4)=$

Raising binomials to higher powers

The nice pattern for cubing binomials, 1-3-3-1, gives you a start on what the coefficients of the different terms are — at least what they start out to be before simplifying the terms. Similar patterns also exist for raising binomials to the fourth power, fifth power, and so on. They're all based on mathematical *combinations* and are easily pulled out with Pascal's Triangle. Check out Figure 7-1 to see a small piece of Pascal's Triangle with the powers of the binomial identified.

					1						$(a+b)^0$
				1		1					$(a+b)^1$
			1		2		1				$(a+b)^2$
		1		3		3		1			$(a+b)^3$
	1		4		6		4		1		$(a+b)^4$
1		5		10		10		5		1	$(a+b)^5$

FIGURE 7-1: Pascal's Triangle can help you find powers of binomials.

EXAMPLE

Q. Refer to Figure 7-1 and use the coefficients from the row for the fourth power of the binomial to raise $(x-3y)$ to the fourth power, $(x-3y)^4$.

A. $\mathbf{x^4-12x^3y+54x^2y^2-108xy^3+81y^4}$

$(x-3y)^4=(x+(-3y))^4$

Insert the coefficients 1-4-6-4-1 from the row in Pascal's Triangle. (Actually, the 1's are understood.)

$=x^4+4x^3(-3y)^1+6x^2(-3y)^2$
$+4x^1(-3y)^3+(-3y)^4$

$=x^4+4x^3(-3y)+6x^2(9y^2)$
$+4x(-27y^3)+(81y^4)$

$=x^4-12x^3y+54x^2y^2-108xy^3+81y^4$

Q. Raise $(2x-1)$ to the sixth power, $(2x-1)^6$.

A. $\mathbf{64x^6-192x^5+240x^4-160x^3+60x^2}$
$\mathbf{-12x+1}$

Insert the coefficients 1-6-15-20-15-6-1 from the row in Pascal's Triangle. (Actually, the 1's are understood.)

$=1(2x)^6+6(2x)^5(-1)^1+15(2x)^4(-1)^2$
$+20(2x)^3(-1)^3+15(2x)^2(-1)^4$
$+6(2x)^1(-1)^5+1(-1)^6$

$=64x^6+6(32x^5)(-1)+15(16x^4)(1)$
$+20(80x^3)(-1)+15(4x^2)(1)+6(2x)(-1)$
$+1(1)$

$=64x^6-192x^5+240x^4-160x^3+60x^2$
$-12x+1$

Notice how, in the first step, the first term has decreasing powers of the exponent, and the second term has increasing powers. The last step has alternating signs. This method may seem rather complicated, but it still beats multiplying it out the long way.

25 $(x+1)^4=$

26 $(2y-1)^4=$

27 $(z-1)^5=$

28 $(3z+2)^5=$

Answers to Problems on Multiplying Expressions

This section provides the answers (in bold) to the practice problems in this chapter.

1. Distribute $x(8x^3-3x^2+2x-5)$. The answer is $\mathbf{8x^4-3x^3+2x^2-5x}$.

$$x(8x^3-3x^2+2x-5)=x(8x^3)-x(3x^2)+x(2x)-x(5)=8x^4-3x^3+2x^2-5x$$

2. Distribute $x^2y(2xy^2+3xyz+y^2z^3)$. The answer is $\mathbf{2x^3y^3+3x^3y^2z+x^2y^3z^3}$.

$$\begin{aligned}x^2y(2xy^2+3xyz+y^2z^3)&=x^2y(2xy^2)+x^2y(3xyz)+x^2y(y^2z^3)\\&=2x^3y^3+3x^3y^2z+x^2y^3z^3\end{aligned}$$

3. Distribute $-4y(3y^4-2y^2+5y-5)$. The answer is $\mathbf{-12y^5+8y^3-20y^2+20y}$.

$$\begin{aligned}-4y(3y^4-2y^2+5y-5)&=(-4y)(3y^4-2y^2+5y-5)\\&=(-4y)(3y^4)-(-4y)(2y^2)+(-4y)(5y)-(-4y)(5)\\&=-12y^5+8y^3-20y^2+20y\end{aligned}$$

4. Distribute $x^{1/2}y^{-1/2}(x^{3/2}y^{1/2}+x^{1/2}y^{3/2})$. The answer is $\mathbf{x^2+xy}$.

$$\begin{aligned}x^{1/2}y^{-1/2}(x^{3/2}y^{1/2}+x^{1/2}y^{3/2})&=x^{1/2}y^{-1/2}(x^{3/2}y^{1/2})+x^{1/2}y^{-1/2}(x^{1/2}y^{3/2})=\\&=x^{1/2+3/2}y^{-1/2+1/2}+x^{1/2+1/2}y^{-1/2+3/2}=x^2y^0+x^1y^1=x^2+xy\end{aligned}$$

5. Use FOIL to multiply $(2x+1)(3x-2)$. The answer is $\mathbf{6x^2-x-2}$.

$$(2x+1)(3x-2)=6x^2-4x+3x-2=6x^2-x-2$$

6. Use FOIL to multiply $(x-7)(3x+5)$. The answer is $\mathbf{3x^2-16x-35}$.

$$(x-7)(3x+5)=3x^2+5x-21x-35=3x^2-16x-35$$

7. Use FOIL to multiply $(x^2-2)(x^2-4)$. The answer is $\mathbf{x^4-6x^2+8}$.

$$(x^2-2)(x^2-4)=x^4-4x^2-2x^2+8=x^4-6x^2+8$$

8. Use FOIL to multiply $(3x+4y)(4x-3y)$. The answer is $\mathbf{12x^2+7xy-12y^2}$.

$$(3x+4y)(4x-3y)=12x^2-9xy+16xy-12y^2=12x^2+7xy-12y^2$$

9. $(x+3)^2=\mathbf{x^2+6x+9}$

$$(x+3)^2=x^2+2(x)(3)+3^2=x^2+6x+9$$

10. $(2y-1)^2=\mathbf{4y^2-4y+1}$

$$(2y-1)^2=(2y)^2-2(2y)(1)+1^2=4y^2-4y+1$$

11 $(3a-2b)^2 = \mathbf{9a^2 - 12ab + 4b^2}$

$(3a-2b)^2 = (3a)^2 - 2(3a)(2b) + (2b)^2 = 9a^2 - 12ab + 4b^2$

12 $(5xy+z)^2 = \mathbf{25x^2y^2 + 10xyz + z^2}$

$(5xy+z)^2 = (5xy)^2 + 2(5xy)(z) + z^2 = 25x^2y^2 + 10xyz + z^2$

13 $(x+3)(x-3) = \mathbf{x^2 - 9}$

14 $(2x-7)(2x+7) = \mathbf{4x^2 - 49}$

15 $(a^3-3)(a^3+3) = \mathbf{a^6 - 9}$

$(a^3-3)(a^3+3) = (a^3)^2 - 3^2 = a^6 - 9$

16 $(2x^2h+9)(2x^2h-9) = \mathbf{4x^4h^2 - 81}$

$(2x^2h+9)(2x^2h-9) = (2x^2h)^2 - 9^2 = 4x^4h^2 - 81$

17 $(x+1)^3 = \mathbf{x^3 + 3x^2 + 3x + 1}$

$(x+1)^3 = x^3 + 3(x^2)1 + 3(x)1^2 + 1^3 = x^3 + 3x^2 + 3x + 1$

18 $(y-2)^3 = \mathbf{y^3 - 6y^2 + 12y - 8}$

$$(y-2)^3 = y^3 + 3(y^2)(-2) + 3(y)(-2)^2 + (-2)^3$$
$$= y^3 - 6y^2 + 12y - 8$$

19 $(3z+1)^3 = \mathbf{27z^3 + 27z^2 + 9z + 1}$

$(3z+1)^3 = (3z)^3 + 3(3z)^2(1) + 3(3z)(1)^2 + 1^3 = 27z^3 + 27z^2 + 9z + 1$

20 $(5-2y)^3 = \mathbf{125 - 150y + 60y^2 - 8y^3}$

$$(5-2y)^3 = 5^3 + 3(5)^2(-2y) + 3(5)(-2y)^2 + (-2y)^3$$
$$= 125 - 150y + 60y^2 - 8y^3$$

21 $(x-2)(x^2+2x+4) = \mathbf{x^3 - 8}$

22 $(y+1)(y^2-y+1) = \mathbf{y^3 + 1}$

23 $(2z+5)(4z^2-10z+25) = \mathbf{8z^3 + 125}$

$(2z+5)(4z^2-10z+25) = (2z)^3 + 5^3$ by $(a+b)(a^2-ab+b^2) = a^3 + b^3$ with $a = 2z$ and $b = 5$.

$= 8z^2 + 125$

(24) $(3x-2)(9x^2+6x+4)=\mathbf{27x^3-8}$

$$\begin{aligned}(3x-2)(9x^2+6x+4)&=(3x)^3-2^3 \text{ by } (a-b)(a^2+ab+b^2)=a^3-b^3 \text{ with } a=3x \text{ and } b=2.\\&=27x^3-8\end{aligned}$$

(25) $(x+1)^4=\mathbf{x^4+4x^3+6x^2+4x+1}$

$$(x+1)^4=x^4+4x^3(1)+6x^2(1)^2+4x(1)^3+1^4=x^4+4x^3+6x^2+4x+1$$

(26) $(2y-1)^4=\mathbf{16y^4-32y^3+24y^2-8y+1}$

$$\begin{aligned}(2y-1)^4&=[2y+(-1)]^4\\&=(2y)^4+4(2y)^3(-1)+6(2y)^2(-1)^2+4(2y)(-1)^3+(-1)^4\\&=16y^4-32y^3+24y^2-8y+1\end{aligned}$$

(27) $(z-1)^5=\mathbf{z^5-5z^4+10z^3-10z^2+5z-1}$

$$\begin{aligned}(z-1)^5&=[z+(-1)]^5\\&=z^5+5z^4(-1)+10z^3(-1)^2+10z^2(-1)^3+5z(-1)^4+(-1)^5 \text{ (Use Pascal line 1-5-10-10-5-1.)}\\&=z^5-5z^4+10z^3-10z^2+5z-1\end{aligned}$$

(28) $(3z+2)^5=\mathbf{243z^5+810z^4+1{,}080z^3+720z^2+240z+32}$

$$\begin{aligned}(3z+2)^5&=(3z)^5+5(3z)^4(2)+10(3z)^3(2)^2+10(3z)^2(2)^3+5(3z)(2)^4+2^5\\&=243z^5+10(81z^4)+40(27z^3)+80(9z^2)+80(3z)+32\\&=243z^5+810z^4+1{,}080z^3+720z^2+240z+32\end{aligned}$$

» Working with binomial and trinomial divisors

» Simplifying the process with synthetic division

Chapter 8

Dividing the Long Way to Simplify Algebraic Expressions

Using long division to simplify algebraic expressions with variables and constants has many similarities to performing long division with just numbers. The variables do add an interesting twist (besides making everything look like alphabet soup) — with the exponents and different letters to consider. But the division problem is still made up of a *divisor, dividend,* and *quotient* (what divides in, what's divided into, and the answer). And one difference between traditional long division and algebraic division is that, in algebra, you usually write the remainders as algebraic fractions.

Dividing by a Monomial

Dividing an expression by a *monomial* (one term) can go one of two ways.

- Every term in the expression is evenly divisible by the divisor.
- One or more terms in the expression don't divide evenly.

If a fraction divides evenly — if every term can be divided by the divisor — the denominator and numerator have a common factor. For instance, in the first example in this section, the denominator, $6y$, divides every term in the numerator. To emphasize the common factor business, I first factor the numerator by dividing out the $6y$, and then I reduce the fraction.

As nice as it would be if algebraic expressions always divided evenly, that isn't always the case. Often, you have one or more terms in the expression — in the fraction's numerator — that don't contain all the factors in the divisor (denominator). When this happens, the best strategy is to break up the problem into as many fractions as there are terms in the numerator. In the end, though, the method you use is pretty much dictated by what you want to do with the expression when you're done.

EXAMPLE

Q. $\frac{24y^2-18y^3+30y^4}{6y}=$

A. $y(4-3y+5y^2)$

The numerator contains a factor matching the denominator.

$$\frac{24y^2-18y^3+30y^4}{6y}=\frac{6y^2\left(4-3y+5y^2\right)}{6y}$$
$$=\frac{\cancel{6y}\cdot y\left(4-3y+5y^2\right)}{\cancel{6y}}$$
$$=y\left(4-3y+5y^2\right)$$

Q. $\frac{40x^4-32x^3+20x^2-12x+3}{4x}=$

A. $10x^3-8x^2+5x-3+\frac{3}{4x}$

The last term doesn't have a factor of $4x$, so you break up the numerator into separate fractions for the division.

$$\frac{40x^4-32x^3+20x^2-12x+3}{4x}$$
$$=\frac{40x^4}{4x}-\frac{32x^3}{4x}+\frac{20x^2}{4x}-\frac{12x}{4x}+\frac{3}{4x}$$
$$=\frac{{}^{10}\cancel{40}x^{\cancel{4}3}}{\cancel{4}\cancel{x}}-\frac{{}^{8}\cancel{32}x^{\cancel{3}2}}{\cancel{4}\cancel{x}}+\frac{{}^{5}\cancel{20}x^{\cancel{2}1}}{\cancel{4}\cancel{x}}-\frac{{}^{3}\cancel{12}\cancel{x}}{\cancel{4}\cancel{x}}+\frac{3}{4x}$$
$$=10x^3-8x^2+5x-3+\frac{3}{4x}$$

1. $\frac{4x^3-3x^2+2x}{x}=$

2. $\frac{8y^4+12y^5-16y^6+40y^8}{4y^4}=$

3 $\frac{6x^5 - 2x^3 + 4x + 1}{x} =$

4 $\frac{15x^3y^4 + 9x^2y^2 - 12xy}{3xy^2} =$

Dividing by a Binomial

Dividing by a *binomial* (two terms) in algebra means that those two terms, as a unit or grouping, have to divide into another expression. After dividing, if you find that the division doesn't have a remainder, then you know that the divisor was actually a factor of the original expression. When dividing a binomial into another expression, you always work toward getting rid of the *lead term* (the first term — the one with the highest power) in the original polynomial and then the new terms in the division process. See the following example for a clearer picture of this concept.

This example shows a dividend that starts with a third-degree term and is followed by terms in decreasing powers (second degree, first degree, and zero degree, which is a *constant* — just a number with no variable). If your dividend is missing any powers that are lower than the lead term, you need to fill in the spaces with zeros to keep your division lined up.

Also, if you have a remainder, remember to write that remainder as the numerator of a fraction with the divisor in the denominator.

Q. $x-4\overline{)x^3-9x^2+27x-28} =$

EXAMPLE

To divide by a binomial, follow these steps:

1. **Eliminate the lead term.**

   To do this, you determine what value you must multiply the first term in the divisor by to match the lead term. If the first term in the divisor is x and the lead term is x^3, as it is in this example, you must multiply by x^2, so write x^2 over the lead term in the quotient and then multiply each term in the divisor by that value.

2. **Subtract the two values by multiplying (in algebra, *subtract* means to change the signs and add; see Chapter 2 for more information).**

3. **Bring down the rest of the terms in the dividend. Notice that, at this point, you have a new lead term.**

4. **Eliminate the new lead term, as explained in Step 1.**

5. **Subtract again and bring down the other terms.**

6. **Repeat Steps 1 through 5 until you run out of terms.**

   If the problem divides evenly (that is, it doesn't have a remainder), you know that the divisor is a factor of the dividend.

A. x^2-5x+7

1. **Because the lead term is x^3, you multiply by x^2 to match lead term.**

$$\begin{array}{r} x^2 \\ x-4\overline{)x^3-9x^2+27x-28} \\ x^3-4x^2 \end{array}$$

2. **Subtract the two expressions.**

3. **Bring down the rest of the terms in the dividend.**

$$\begin{array}{r} x^2 \\ x-4\overline{)x^3-9x^2+27x-28} \\ \underline{-\left(x^3-4x^2\right)} \\ -5x^2+27x-28 \end{array}$$

Notice that your new lead term is $-5x^2$.

4. **Multiply by $-5x$ to match the new lead term.**

5. **Subtract again and bring down the other terms.**

$$\begin{array}{r} x^2-5x \\ x-4\overline{)x^3-9x^2+27x-28} \\ \underline{-\left(x^3-4x^2\right)} \\ -5x^2+27x-28 \\ \underline{-\left(-5x^2+20x\right)} \\ 7x-28 \end{array}$$

6. **Repeat Steps 1 through 5 until you run out of terms.**

$$\begin{array}{r} x^2-5x+7 \\ x-4\overline{)x^3-9x^2+27x-28} \\ \underline{-\left(x^3-4x^2\right)} \\ -5x^2+27x-28 \\ -\left(5x^2+20x\right) \\ 7x-28 \\ \underline{-(7x-28)} \\ 0 \end{array}$$

Because there's no remainder, you know that $x-4$ was a factor of the dividend.

5 $x+2\overline{)x^3+7x^2+3x-14} =$

6 $x-3\overline{)x^4-2x^3-5x^2+7x-3} =$

7 $3x-4\overline{)12x^3-10x^2-17x+12} =$

8 $x^2+1\overline{)x^6-3x^5+x^4-2x^3-3x^2+x-3} =$

Dividing by Polynomials with More Terms

Even though dividing by monomials or binomials is the most commonly found division task in algebra, you may run across the occasional opportunity to divide by a *polynomial* with three or more terms.

The process isn't really much different from that used to divide binomials. You just have to keep everything lined up correctly and fill in the blanks if you find missing powers. Any remainder is written as a fraction.

EXAMPLE

Q. $(9x^6 - 4x^5 + 3x^2 - 1) \div (x^2 - 2x + 1) =$

The fourth, third, and first powers are missing, so you put in zeros. Don't forget to distribute the negative sign when subtracting each product.

A. $\mathbf{9x^4 + 14x^3 + 9x^2 + 24x + 32 + \dfrac{40x - 33}{x^2 - 2x + 1}}$

Here's what the division looks like:

$$
\begin{array}{r}
9x^4 + 14x^3 + 19x^2 + 24x + 32 \\
x^2 - 2x + 1 \overline{\big)\, 9x^6 - 4x^5 + 0 + 0 + 3x^2 + 0 - 1} \\
\underline{-\left(9x^6 - 18x^5 + 9x^4\right)} \\
14x^5 - 9x^4 + 0 + 3x^2 + 0 - 1 \\
\underline{-\left(14x^5 - 28x^4 + 14x^3\right)} \\
+19x^4 - 14x^3 + 3x^2 + 0 - 1 \\
\underline{-\left(19x^4 - 38x^3 + 19x^2\right)} \\
+24x^3 - 16x^2 + \ 0 \ - 1 \\
\underline{-\left(24x^3 - 48x^2 + 24x\right)} \\
32x^2 - 24x - 1 \\
\underline{-\left(32x^2 - 64x + 32\right)} \\
+40x - 33
\end{array}
$$

9 $(x^4 - 2x^3 + x^2 - 7x - 2) \div (x^2 + 3x - 1) =$

10 $(x^6 + 6x^4 - 4x^2 + 21) \div (x^4 - x^2 + 3) =$

Simplifying Division Synthetically

Dividing polynomials by binomials is a very common procedure in algebra. The division process allows you to determine factors of an expression and roots of an equation. A quick, easy way of dividing a polynomial by a binomial of the form $x+a$ or $x-a$ is called *synthetic division.* Notice that these two binomials each have a coefficient of 1, the variable to the first degree, and a number being added or subtracted. Examples are $x+4$ or $x-7$.

REMEMBER

To perform *synthetic division,* you use just the *coefficients* (the numbers multiplying the variables, *x*'s) of the polynomial's terms being divided and the *opposite* of the number in the binomial.

EXAMPLE

Q. $(x^4 - 3x^3 + x - 4) \div (x+1) =$

1. **Place the opposite of the number in the divisor (–1 in this case) in front of the problem, in a little offset that looks like ⌋. Then write the coefficients in order, using zeros to hold the place(s) of any powers that are missing.**
2. **Bring down the first coefficient (put it below the horizontal line) and then multiply it times the number in front. Write the result under the second coefficient and add the two numbers; put the result on the bottom.**
3. **Take this new result (the –4 in this problem) and multiply it times the number in front; then add the answer to the next coefficient.**
4. **Repeat this multiply-add process all the way down the line.**
5. **The result on the bottom of your work is the list of coefficients in the answer — plus the remainder, if you have one.**

A. $x^3 - 4x^2 + 4x - 3 - \frac{1}{x+1}$

1. **The opposite of +1 goes in front. The coefficients are written in order.**

   –1⌋ 1 –3 0 1 –4

2. **Bring down the first coefficient; multiply it times the number in front. Write the result under the second coefficient, and add.**

   –1⌋ 1 –3 0 1 –4
   –1
   ―――――――
   1 –4

3. **Take the –4 and multiply it by number in front; add the answer to the next coefficient.**

   –1⌋ 1 –3 0 1 –4
   –1 4
   ―――――――
   1 –4 4

4. **Repeat until finished.**

   –1⌋ 1 –3 0 1 –4
   – 1 4 –4 3
   ―――――――
   1 –4 4 –3 –1

The answer uses the coefficients, in order, starting with one degree less than the polynomial that was divided. The last number is the remainder, and it goes over the divisor in a fraction. So to write the answer, the first 1 below the line corresponds to a 1 in front of x^3, then a –4 in front of x^2, and so on. The last –1 is the remainder, which is written in the numerator over the divisor, $x+1$.

11 $(x^4 - 2x^3 - 4x^2 + x + 6) \div (x - 3) =$

12 $(2x^4 + x^3 - 7x^2 + 5) \div (x + 2) =$

Answers to Problems on Division

This section provides the answers (in bold) to the practice problems in this chapter.

1) $\frac{4x^3-3x^2+2x}{x} = \mathbf{4x^2-3x+2}$

$$\frac{4x^3-3x^2+2x}{x} = \frac{\cancel{x}\left(4x^2-3x+2\right)}{\cancel{x}} = 4x^2-3x+2$$

2) $\frac{8y^4+12y^5-16y^6+40y^8}{4y^4} = \mathbf{2+3y-4y^2+10y^4}$

$$\frac{8y^4+12y^5-16y^6+40y^8}{4y^4} = \frac{\cancel{4y^4}\left(2+3y-4y^2+10y^4\right)}{\cancel{4y^4}}$$
$$= 2+3y-4y^2+10y^4$$

3) $\frac{6x^5-2x^3+4x+1}{x} = \mathbf{6x^4-2x^2+4+\frac{1}{x}}$

$$\frac{6x^5-2x^3+4x+1}{x} = \frac{6x^5}{x} - \frac{2x^3}{x} + \frac{4x}{x} + \frac{1}{x}$$
$$= 6x^4-2x^2+4+\frac{1}{x}$$

4) $\frac{15x^3y^4+9x^2y^2-12xy}{3xy^2} = \mathbf{5x^2y^2+3x-\frac{4}{y}}$

$$\frac{15x^3y^4+9x^2y^2-12xy}{3xy^2} = \frac{15x^3y^4}{3xy^2} + \frac{9x^2y^2}{3xy^2} - \frac{12xy}{3xy^2}$$
$$= \frac{{}^5\cancel{15}x^{\cancel{3}^2}y^{\cancel{4}^2}}{\cancel{3}\cancel{x}\cancel{y^2}} + \frac{{}^3\cancel{9}x^{\cancel{2}^1}\cancel{y^2}}{\cancel{3}\cancel{x}\cancel{y^2}} - \frac{{}^4\cancel{12}\cancel{x}\cancel{y}}{\cancel{3}\cancel{x}y^{\cancel{2}^1}} = 5x^2y^2+3x-\frac{4}{y}$$

5) $x+2\overline{)x^3+7x^2+3x-14} = \mathbf{x^2+5x-7}$

$$\begin{array}{r}
x^2+5x-7 \\
x+2\overline{)\;x^3+7x^2+3x-14} \\
\underline{-\left(x^3+2x^2\right)} \qquad\quad \\
5x^2+3x \qquad \\
\underline{-\left(5x^2+10x\right)} \qquad \\
-7x-14 \\
\underline{-(-7x-14)} \\
0
\end{array}$$

(6) $x-3\overline{)x^4-2x^3-5x^2+7x-3}=\mathbf{x^3+x^2-2x+1}$

$$\begin{array}{r l}
 & x^3+x^2-2x+1 \\
x-3\,\big) & \overline{x^4-2x^3-5x^2+7x-3} \\
 & \underline{-(x^4-3x^3)} \\
 & \quad x^3-5x^2 \\
 & \quad \underline{-(x^3-3x^2)} \\
 & \qquad -2x^2+7x \\
 & \qquad \underline{-(-2x^2+6x)} \\
 & \qquad\qquad x-3 \\
 & \qquad\qquad \underline{-(-x-3)} \\
 & \qquad\qquad\qquad 0
\end{array}$$

(7) $3x-4\overline{)12x^3-10x^2-17x+12}=\mathbf{4x^2+2x-3}$

$$\begin{array}{r l}
 & 4x^2+2x-3 \\
3x-4\,\big) & \overline{12x^3-10x^2-17x+12} \\
 & \underline{-(12x^3-16x^2)} \\
 & \quad 6x^2-17x \\
 & \quad \underline{-(6x^2-8x)} \\
 & \qquad -9x+12 \\
 & \qquad \underline{-(-9x+12)} \\
 & \qquad\qquad 0
\end{array}$$

(8) $x^2+1\overline{)x^6-3x^5+x^4-2x^3-3x^2+x-3}=\mathbf{x^4-3x^3+x-3}$

$$\begin{array}{r l}
 & x^4-3x^3+x-3 \\
x^2+1\,\big) & \overline{x^6-3x^5+x^4-2x^3-3x^2+x-3} \\
 & \underline{-(x^6\qquad +x^4)} \\
 & \quad -3x^5\qquad -2x^3 \\
 & \quad \underline{-(-3x^5\qquad -3x^3)} \\
 & \qquad\qquad x^3-3x^2+x \\
 & \qquad\qquad \underline{-(x^3\qquad +x)} \\
 & \qquad\qquad\quad -3x^2\qquad -3 \\
 & \qquad\qquad\quad \underline{-(-3x^2\qquad -3)} \\
 & \qquad\qquad\qquad\qquad 0
\end{array}$$

(9) $(x^4-2x^3+x^2-7x-2)\div(x^2+3x-1)=\mathbf{x^2-5x+17+\frac{-63x+15}{x^2+3x-1}}$

$$
\begin{array}{r}
x^2-5x+17 \\
x^2+3x-1 \overline{) \; x^4-2x^3+x^2-7x-2} \\
-(x^4+3x^3-x^2) \qquad\qquad \\
\hline
-5x^3+2x^2-7x \quad \\
-(-5x^3-15x^2+5x) \quad \\
\hline
17x^2-12x-2 \\
-(17x^2+51x-17) \\
\hline
-63x+15
\end{array}
$$

(10) $(x^6+6x^4-4x^2+21)\div(x^4-x^2+3)=\mathbf{x^2+7}$

$$
\begin{array}{r}
x^2+7 \qquad\qquad\qquad \\
x^4-x^2+3 \overline{) \; x^6+0+6x^4+0-4x^2+0+21} \\
-(x^6 \quad -x^4 \quad +3x^2) \qquad\quad \\
\hline
7x^4 \quad -7x^2 \quad +21 \\
-(7x^4 \quad -7x^2 \quad +21) \\
\hline
0
\end{array}
$$

Don't forget to use 0 as a placeholder when one of the powers is missing.

(11) $(x^4-2x^3-4x^2+x+6)\div(x-3)=\mathbf{x^3+x^2-x-2}$

3	1	−2	−4	1	6
		3	3	−3	−6
	1	1	−1	−2	0

So $x^3+x^2-x-2+\frac{0}{x-3}$

$=x^3+x^2-x-2$

(12) $(2x^4+x^3-7x^2+5)\div(x+2)=\mathbf{2x^3-3x^2-x+2+\frac{1}{x+2}}$

Use the following breakdown to solve the problem:

−2	2	1	−7	0	5
		−4	6	2	−4
	2	−3	−1	2	1

Write the remainder as a fraction with the divisor in the denominator of the fraction.

» Determining the greatest common factor (GCF)

» Using factors to reduce algebraic fractions

Chapter 9
Figuring on Factoring

Factoring an expression amounts to changing the form from a bunch of addition and subtraction to a simpler expression that uses multiplication and division. The change from an unfactored form to a factored form creates a single term — all tied together by the multiplication and division — that you can use when performing other processes. Here are some of the other tasks in algebra that require a factored form: reducing or simplifying fractions (see Chapter 3), solving equations (see Chapters 12–15), solving inequalities (see Chapter 16), and graphing functions (see Chapter 21).

Pouring Over Prime Factorizations

A *prime factorization* of a number is a listing of all the prime numbers whose product is that number. Of course, you first have to recognize which numbers are the prime numbers. The first 25 prime numbers are: 2, 3, 5, 7, 11, 13, 17, 19, 23, 29, 31, 37, 41, 43, 47, 53, 59, 61, 67, 71, 73, 79, 83, 89, and 97. Don't worry about memorizing them. Infinitely many more primes exist, but these smaller numbers (and, actually, usually just the first ten) are the most commonly used ones when doing prime factorizations.

TIP

To write the prime factorization of a number, start by writing that number as the product of two numbers and then writing each of those two numbers as products, and so on, until you have only prime numbers in the product.

By convention, prime factorizations are written with the prime factors going from the smallest to the largest. The specific order helps when you're trying to find common factors in two or three (or more) different numbers.

EXAMPLE

Q. Find the prime factorization of 360.

A. $360 = 2^3 \times 3^2 \times 5$

$360 = 10 \times 36 = 2 \times 5 \times 6 \times 6$
$= 2 \times 5 \times 2 \times 3 \times 2 \times 3 = 2^3 \times 3^2 \times 5$

Q. Find the prime factorization of 90.

A. $90 = 2 \times 3^2 \times 5$

$90 = 9 \times 10 = 3 \times 3 \times 2 \times 5 = 2 \times 3^2 \times 5$

You can start the multiplication in different ways. For example, maybe you started writing 90 as the product of 6 and 15. How you start doesn't matter. You'll always end up with the same answer.

1 Write the prime factorization of 24.

2 Write the prime factorization of 100.

3 Write the prime factorization of 256.

4 Write the prime factorization of 3,872.

Factoring Out the Greatest Common Factor

The first line of attack (and the easiest to perform) when factoring an expression is to look for the *greatest common factor* (GCF), or the largest factor that will divide all terms in the expression evenly. You want a factor that divides each of the terms and, at the same time, doesn't leave any common factor in the resulting terms. The goal is to take out as many factors as possible. More than one step may be required to completely accomplish this feat, but the end result is a GCF times terms that are *relatively prime* (have no factor in common).

EXAMPLE

Q. Find the GCF and factor the expression. $30x^4y^2 - 20x^5y^3 + 50x^6y$.

A. $\mathbf{10x^4y(3y - 2xy^2 + 5x^2)}$. If you divide each term by the greatest common factor, which is $10x^4y$, and put the results of the divisions in parentheses, the factored form is $30x^4y^2 - 20x^5y^3 + 50x^6y = 10x^4y(3y - 2xy^2 + 5x^2)$. It's like doing this division, with each fraction reducing to become a term in the parentheses:

$$\frac{30x^4y^2 - 20x^5y^3 + 50x^6y}{10x^4y}$$
$$= \frac{30x^4y^2}{10x^4y} - \frac{20x^5y^3}{10x^4y} + \frac{50x^6y}{10x^4y}$$

Q. Factor out the GCF: $8a^{3/2} - 12a^{1/2}$.

A. $\mathbf{4a^{1/2}(2a - 3)}$. Dealing with fractional exponents can be tricky. Just remember that the same rules apply to fractional exponents as with whole numbers. You subtract the exponents.

$$\frac{8a^{3/2}}{4a^{1/2}} - \frac{12a^{1/2}}{4a^{1/2}} = \frac{{}^{2}\not{8}a^{3/2}}{{}_{1}\not{4}a^{1/2}} - \frac{{}^{3}\not{12}a^{1/2}}{{}_{1}\not{4}a^{1/2}}$$
$$= 2a^{3/2-1/2} - 3a^{1/2-1/2} = 2a^1 - 3a^0$$

Now write the common factor, $4a^{1/2}$, outside the parentheses and the results of the division inside.

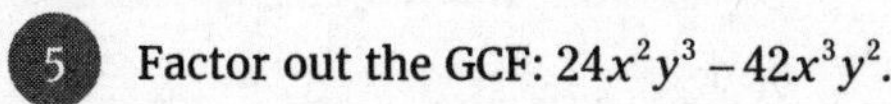

5 Factor out the GCF: $24x^2y^3 - 42x^3y^2$.

6 Factor out the GCF: $9z^{-4} + 15z^{-2} - 24z^{-1}$.

7 Factor out the GCF: $16a^2b^3c^4 - 48ab^4c^2$.

8 Factor out the GCF: $16x^{-3}y^4 + 20x^{-4}y^3$.

Reducing Algebraic Fractions

The basic principles behind reducing fractions with numbers and reducing fractions with variables and numbers remain the same. You want to find something that divides both the *numerator* (the top of the fraction) and *denominator* (bottom of the fraction) evenly and then leave the results of the division as the new numerator and new denominator.

When the fraction has two or more terms in the numerator, denominator, or both, you first have to factor out the GCF before you can reduce. And when the algebraic fraction has just multiplication and division in the numerator and denominator, the reducing part is pretty easy. Just divide out the common factors as shown in the following example.

EXAMPLE

Q. Reduce the fraction: $\frac{14x^3y}{21xy^4}$.

A. $\mathbf{\frac{2x^2}{3y^3}}$

In this fraction, the GCF is $7xy$:

$$\frac{14x^3y}{21xy^4} = \frac{{}^{2}\cancel{14}x^{\cancel{3}2}\cancel{y}}{{}_{3}\cancel{21}\cancel{x}\,y^{\cancel{4}3}} = \frac{2x^2}{3y^3}$$

Q. Reduce the fraction: $\frac{15y^3-15y^2}{6y^5-6y^4}$.

A. $\mathbf{\frac{5}{2y^2}}$

First find the GCF of the numerator and denominator; it's $3y^2(y-1)$:

$$\frac{15y^3-15y^2}{6y^5-6y^4} = \frac{15y^2(y-1)}{6y^4(y-1)}$$

$$= \frac{{}^{5}\cancel{15}\cancel{y^2}\cancel{(y-1)}}{{}_{2}\cancel{6}y^{\cancel{4}2}\cancel{(y-1)}} = \frac{5}{2y^2}$$

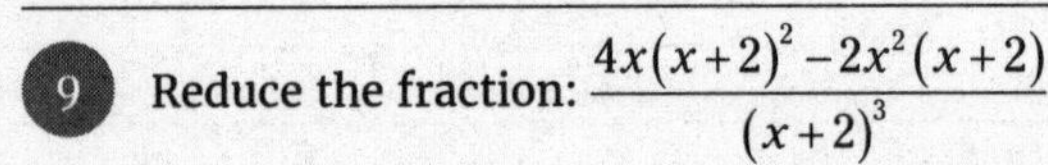

9 Reduce the fraction: $\frac{4x(x+2)^2-2x^2(x+2)}{(x+2)^3}$.

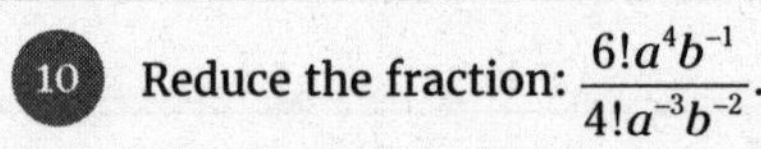

10 Reduce the fraction: $\frac{6!a^4b^{-1}}{4!a^{-3}b^{-2}}$.

11 Reduce the fraction: $\frac{14a^2b-21a}{28ab^2}$.

12 Reduce the fraction: $\frac{6w^3(w+1)-8w^4(w+1)^3}{10w^5(w+1)^3}$.

13 Reduce the fraction: $\frac{9{,}009x^{4/3}y^2-7{,}007x^{7/3}y}{4{,}004x^{1/3}y}$.

14 Reduce the fraction: $\frac{8a^2b^3(c^2+1)^4-6a^3b^2(c^2+1)^3+14a^4b(c^2+1)^2}{4a^3b^2(c^2+1)^2-10a^4b^3(c^2+1)^3}$.

Answers to Problems on Factoring Expressions

This section provides the answers (in bold) to the practice problems in this chapter.

1. Write the prime factorization of 24. The answer is $\mathbf{2^3 \times 3}$.

   $24 = 4 \times 6 = 2 \times 2 \times 2 \times 3 = 2^3 \times 3$

2. Write the prime factorization of 100. The answer is $\mathbf{2^2 \times 5^2}$.

   $100 = 4 \times 25 = 2 \times 2 \times 5 \times 5 = 2^2 \times 5^2$

3. Write the prime factorization of 256. The answer is $\mathbf{2^8}$.

   $256 = 4 \times 64 = 4 \times 8 \times 8 = (2 \times 2)(2 \times 2 \times 2)(2 \times 2 \times 2) = 2^8$

4. Write the prime factorization of 3,872. The answer is $\mathbf{2^5 \times 11^2}$.

   $3{,}872 = 4 \times 968 = 4 \times (8 \times 121) = (2 \times 2)(2 \times 2 \times 2)(11 \times 11) = 2^5 \times 11^2$

5. Factor out the GCF: $24x^2y^3 - 42x^3y^2$. The answer is $\mathbf{6x^2y^2(4y - 7x)}$.

6. Factor out the GCF: $9z^{-4} + 15z^{-2} - 24z^{-1}$. The answer is $\mathbf{3z^{-4}\left(3 + 5z^2 - 8z^3\right)}$.

TIP

When factoring negative exponents, you factor out the smallest power, which is the most negative power, or the number farthest to the left on the number line. In this case, –4 is the smallest power. Notice that the powers in the parentheses are all non-negative.

7. Factor out the GCF: $16a^2b^3c^4 - 48ab^4c^2$. The answer is $\mathbf{16ab^3c^2\left(ac^2 - 3b\right)}$.

8. Factor out the GCF: $16x^{-3}y^4 + 20x^{-4}y^3$. The answer is $\mathbf{4x^{-4}y^3\left(4xy + 5\right)}$. The greatest common factor includes the negative exponent on the x factor. Remember that –4 is smaller than –3; subtract the exponents when dividing.

9. Reduce the fraction: $\dfrac{4x(x+2)^2 - 2x^2(x+2)}{(x+2)^3}$. The answer is $\mathbf{\dfrac{2x\left(x^2+4\right)}{(x+2)^2}}$. All three terms have the common factor $(x+2)$.

   $$\frac{4x(x+2)^2 - 2x^2(x+2)}{(x+2)^3} = \frac{(x+2)\left[4x(x+2) - 2x^2\right]}{(x+2)^3} = \frac{\cancel{(x+2)}\left[4x^2 + 8x - 2x^2\right]}{(x+2)^{\cancel{3}2}}$$

   $$= \frac{2x^2 + 8x}{(x+2)^2} = \frac{2x(x+4)}{(x+2)^2}$$

10. Reduce the fraction: $\dfrac{6!a^4b^{-1}}{4!a^{-3}b^{-2}}$. The answer is $\mathbf{30a^7b}$.

    $$\frac{6!a^4b^{-1}}{4!a^{-3}b^{-2}} = \frac{6 \cdot 5 \cdot 4 \cdot 3 \cdot 2 \cdot 1a^4b^{-1}}{4 \cdot 3 \cdot 2 \cdot 1a^{-3}b^{-2}} = \frac{6 \cdot 5 \cdot \cancel{4} \cdot \cancel{3} \cdot \cancel{2} \cdot \cancel{1} \cdot a^{4-(-3)}b^{-1-(-2)}}{\cancel{4} \cdot \cancel{3} \cdot \cancel{2} \cdot \cancel{1} \cdot \cancel{a^{3}}\,\cancel{b^{2}}} = \frac{30a^7b^1}{1}$$

    For a refresher on factorials, refer to Chapter 6.

11. Reduce the fraction: $\dfrac{14a^2b - 21a}{28ab^2}$. The answer is $\mathbf{\dfrac{2ab-3}{4b^2}}$.

    $$\frac{14a^2b - 21a}{28ab^2} = \frac{7a(2ab-3)}{28ab^2} = \frac{\cancel{7}\,\cancel{a}(2ab-3)}{{}_4\cancel{28}\,\cancel{a}b^2} = \frac{2ab-3}{4b^2}$$

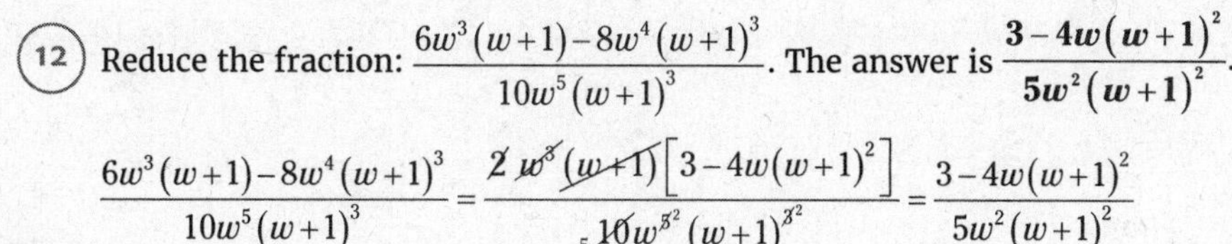

12) Reduce the fraction: $\frac{6w^3(w+1)-8w^4(w+1)^3}{10w^5(w+1)^3}$. The answer is $\mathbf{\frac{3-4w(w+1)^2}{5w^2(w+1)^2}}$.

$$\frac{6w^3(w+1)-8w^4(w+1)^3}{10w^5(w+1)^3}=\frac{\cancel{2}\,\cancel{w^3}\,\cancel{(w+1)}\left[3-4w(w+1)^2\right]}{{}_5\cancel{10}w^{\cancel{5}2}(w+1)^{\cancel{3}2}}=\frac{3-4w(w+1)^2}{5w^2(w+1)^2}$$

WARNING

Even though the answer appears to have a common factor in the numerator and denominator, you can't reduce it. The numerator has two terms, and the first term, the 3, doesn't have that common factor in it.

13) Reduce the fraction: $\frac{9{,}009x^{4/3}y^2-7{,}007x^{7/3}y}{4{,}004x^{1/3}y}$. The answer is $\mathbf{\frac{x(9y-7x)}{4}}$.

$$\frac{9{,}009x^{4/3}y^2-7{,}007x^{7/3}y}{4{,}004x^{1/3}y}=\frac{1{,}001x^{4/3}y(9y-7x^1)}{4(1{,}001)x^{1/3}y}$$

WARNING

When factoring the terms in the numerator, be careful with the subtraction of the fractions. These fractional exponents are found frequently in higher mathematics and behave just as you see here. I put the exponent of 1 on the x in the numerator just to emphasize the result of the subtraction of exponents. Continuing,

$$=\frac{\cancel{1{,}001}x^{\cancel{4/3}\,1}\,\cancel{y}(9y-7x^1)}{4\cancel{(1{,}001)}\cancel{x^{1/3}}\,\cancel{y}}=\frac{x(9y-7x)}{4}$$

14) Reduce the fraction: $\frac{8a^2b^3(c^2+1)^4-6a^3b^2(c^2+1)^3+14a^4b(c^2+1)^2}{4a^3b^2(c^2+1)^2-10a^4b^3(c^2+1)^3}$. The answer is

$\mathbf{\frac{4b^2(c^2+1)^2-3ab(c^2+1)+7a^2}{ab\left[2-5ab(c^2+1)\right]}}$.

Factor the numerator and denominator separately and then reduce by dividing by the common factors in each:

$$\frac{8a^2b^3(c^2+1)^4-6a^3b^2(c^2+1)^3+14a^4b(c^2+1)^2}{4a^3b^2(c^2+1)^2-10a^4b^3(c^2+1)^3}=\frac{2a^2b(c^2+1)^2\left[4b^2(c^2+1)^2-3a^1b^1(c^2+1)^1+7a^2\right]}{2a^3b^2(c^2+1)^2\left[2-5ab(c^2+1)\right]}$$

$$=\frac{\cancel{2}\,\cancel{a^2}\,\cancel{b}\,\cancel{(c^2+1)^2}\left[4b^2(c^2+1)^2-3a^1b^1(c^2+1)^1+7a^2\right]}{\cancel{2}a^{\cancel{3}1}b^{\cancel{2}1}\,\cancel{(c^2+1)^2}\left[2-5ab(c^2+1)\right]}=\frac{4b^2(c^2+1)^2-3ab(c^2+1)^1+7a^2}{ab\left[2-5ab(c^2+1)\right]}$$

» Dicing up the cubes — their sums and differences

» Using multiple factoring techniques

Chapter 10
Taking the Bite Out of Binomial Factoring

You have several different choices when factoring a *binomial* (an expression that is the sum or difference of two terms):

- Factor out a greatest common factor (GCF).
- Write the expression as the product of two binomials — one the sum of the two roots and the other the difference of those same two roots.
- Write the expression as the product of a binomial and *trinomial* (an expression with three terms) — one with the sum or difference of the cube roots and the other with squares of the roots and a product of the roots.
- Use two or more of the above.

In this chapter, you find how to recognize which type of factorization to use and how to change from two terms to one by factoring the expression. I cover GCF in Chapter 9, if you need a refresher. The other procedures are new to this chapter.

Factoring the Difference of Squares

REMEMBER

When a binomial is the difference of two perfect squares, you can factor it into the product of the sum and difference of the square roots of those two terms:

$a^2 - b^2 = (a+b)(a-b)$

EXAMPLE

Q. Factor: $4x^2 - 81$.

A. $\mathbf{(2x+9)(2x-9)}$. The square root of $4x^2$ is $2x$, and the square root of 81 is 9.

Q. Factor: $25 - 36x^4y^2z^6$.

A. $\mathbf{(5+6x^2yz^3)(5-6x^2yz^3)}$. The square of $6x^2yz^3$ is $36x^4y^2z^6$. Notice that each exponent is doubled in the square.

1. Factor: $x^2 - 25$.

2. Factor: $64a^2 - y^2$.

3. Factor: $49x^2y^2 - 9z^2w^4$.

4. Factor: $100x^{1/2} - 81y^{1/4}$.

Factoring Differences and Sums of Cubes

REMEMBER

When you have two perfect squares, you can use the special factoring rule if the operation is subtraction. With cubes, though, both sums and differences factor into the product of a binomial and a trinomial.

$$a^3 - b^3 = (a-b)(a^2+ab+b^2) \quad \textbf{and} \quad a^3+b^3=(a+b)(a^2-ab+b^2)$$

Here's the pattern: First, you write the sum or difference of the two cube roots corresponding to the sum or difference of cubes; second, you multiply the binomial containing the roots by a trinomial composed of the squares of those two cube roots and the *opposite* of the product of them. If the binomial has a + sign, the middle term of the trinomial is –. If the binomial has a – sign, then the middle term in the trinomial is +. The two squares in the trinomial are always positive.

EXAMPLE

Q. Factor: $x^3 - 27$.

A. $\mathbf{(x-3)(x^2+3x+9)}$

$x^3 - 27 = (x-3)(x^2 + x\cdot 3 + 3^2) =$
$(x-3)(x^2+3x+9)$

Q. Factor: $125 + 8y^3$.

A. $\mathbf{(5+2y)(25-10y+4y^2)}$

$125 + 8y^3 = (5+2y)(5^2 - 5\cdot 2y +$
$[2y]^2) = (5+2y)(25-10y+4y^2)$

5 Factor: $x^3 + 1$.

6 Factor: $8 - y^3$.

7 Factor: $27z^3 + 125$.

8 Factor: $64x^3 - 343y^6$.

Making Factoring a Multiple Mission

Many factorization problems in mathematics involve more than one type of factoring process. You may find a GCF in the terms, and then you may recognize that what's left is the difference of two cubes. You sometimes factor the difference of two squares just to find that one of those binomials is the difference of two new squares.

TIP

Solving these problems is really like figuring out a gigantic puzzle. You discover how to conquer it by applying the factorization rules. In general, first look for a GCF. Life is much easier when the numbers and powers are smaller because they're easier to deal with and work out in your head.

EXAMPLE

Q. Factor: $4x^6 + 108x^3$.

A. $\mathbf{4x^3(x+3)(x^2-3x+9)}$. First, take out the GCF, $4x^3$. Then factor the sum of the cubes in the parentheses:

$$4x^6 + 108x^3 = 4x^3(x^3+27) = 4x^3(x+3)(x^2-3x+9)$$

Q. Factor: $y^8 - 256$.

A. $\mathbf{(y^4+16)(y^2+4)(y+2)(y-2)}$. You can factor this problem as the difference of two squares. Then the second factor factors again and again:

$$y^8 - 256 = (y^4+16)(y^4-16) = (y^4+16)(y^2+4)(y^2-4) = (y^4+16)(y^2+4)(y+2)(y-2)$$

9 Completely factor: $36x^2 - 100y^2$.

10 Completely factor: $80y^4 - 10y$.

11 Completely factor: $10{,}000x^4 - 1$.

12 Completely factor: $x^{-4} + x^{-7}$.

Answers to Problems on Factoring

This section provides the answers (in bold) to the practice problems in this chapter.

1. Factor: $x^2 - 25$. The answer is $\mathbf{(x+5)(x-5)}$.

2. Factor: $64a^2 - y^2$. The answer is $\mathbf{(8a+y)(8a-y)}$.

3. Factor: $49x^2y^2 - 9z^2w^4$. The answer is $\mathbf{(7xy+3zw^2)(7xy-3zw^2)}$.

4. Factor: $100x^{1/2} - 81y^{1/4}$. The answer is $\mathbf{(10x^{1/4}+9y^{1/8})(10x^{1/4}-9y^{1/8})}$.

   When looking at the exponents, you see that ½ is twice the fraction ¼, and ¼ is twice the fraction ⅛.

5. Factor: $x^3 + 1$. The answer is $\mathbf{(x+1)(x^2-x+1)}$.

6. Factor: $8 - y^3$. The answer is $\mathbf{(2-y)(4+2y+y^2)}$.

   $$8 - y^3 = (2-y)(2^2+2y+y^2) = (2-y)(4+2y+y^2)$$

It's nice to have a list of the first ten cubes handy when factoring the sum or difference of cubes: 1, 8, 27, 64, 125, 216, 343, 512, 729, 1000.

TIP

7. Factor: $27z^3 + 125$. The answer is $\mathbf{(3z+5)(9z^2-15z+25)}$.

   $$\begin{aligned} 27z^3 + 125 &= (3z+5)\left[(3z)^2 - 3z(5) + 5^2\right] \\ &= (3z+5)(9z^2 - 15z + 25) \end{aligned}$$

8. Factor: $64x^3 - 343y^6$. The answer is $\mathbf{(4x-7y^2)(16x^2+28xy^2+49y^4)}$.

   Did you remember that $7^3 = 343$?

   $$\begin{aligned} 64x^3 - 343y^6 &= (4x-7y^2)\left[(4x)^2 + (4x)(7y^2) + (7y^2)^2\right] \\ &= (4x-7y^2)(16x^2+28xy^2+49y^4) \end{aligned}$$

9. Completely factor: $36x^2 - 100y^2$. The answer is $\mathbf{4(3x+5y)(3x-5y)}$.

   $$36x^2 - 100y^2 = 4(9x^2 - 25y^2) = 4(3x+5y)(3x-5y)$$

10. Completely factor: $80y^4 - 10y$. The answer is $\mathbf{10y(2y-1)(4y^2+2y+1)}$.

    $$\begin{aligned} 80y^4 - 10y &= 10y(8y^3 - 1) \\ &= 10y(2y-1)\left[(2y)^2 + 2y(1) + 1^2\right] \\ &= 10y(2y-1)(4y^2+2y+1) \end{aligned}$$

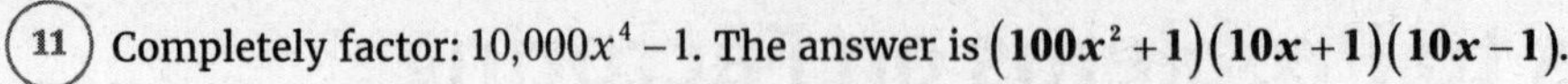

(11) Completely factor: $10{,}000x^4 - 1$. The answer is $\mathbf{(100x^2+1)(10x+1)(10x-1)}$.

$$10{,}000x^4 - 1 = (100x^2+1)(100x^2-1) = (100x^2+1)(10x+1)(10x-1)$$

(12) Completely factor: $x^{-4} + x^{-7}$. The answer is $\mathbf{x^{-7}(x+1)(x^2-x+1)}$.

$$x^{-4} + x^{-7} = x^{-7}(x^3+1) = x^{-7}(x+1)(x^2-x+1)$$

You first take out the GCF, which involves the most negative exponent. The resulting binomial in the parentheses is the sum of two perfect cubes.

REMEMBER

You may have been tempted to go right into the difference of cubes because 125 is a perfect cube. It's always more desirable, though, to factor out large numbers when possible.

» Reversing FOIL for a factorization

» Assigning terms to groups to factor them

» Making use of multiple methods to factor

Chapter 11

Factoring Trinomials and Special Polynomials

In Chapter 10, you find the basic ways to factor a *binomial* (an expression with two terms). *Factoring* means to change the expression from several terms to one expression connected by multiplication and division. When dealing with a polynomial with four terms, such as $x^4 - 4x^3 - 11x^2 - 6x$, the four terms become one when you write the factored form using multiplication: $x(x+1)^2(x-6)$. The factored form has many advantages, especially when you want to simplify fractions, solve equations, or graph functions.

When working with an algebraic expression with three terms (a *trinomial*) or more terms, you have a number of different methods available for factoring it. You generally start with the greatest common factor (GCF) and then apply one or more of the other techniques if necessary. This chapter covers the different methods and provides several sample questions for you to try.

Focusing First on the Greatest Common Factor (GCF)

In any factoring problem, first you want to find a common factor — if one exists. If you find a GCF for the terms in the expression, then you divide every term by that common factor and write the expression as the product of the common factor and the results of each division.

EXAMPLE

Q. Factor out the GCF:
$28x^2y - 21x^3y^2 + 35x^5y^3$.

A. $\mathbf{7x^2y(4 - 3xy + 5x^3y^2)}$

You divide every term by the GCF, $7x^2y$.

$$\frac{28x^2y}{7x^2y} - \frac{21x^3y^2}{7x^2y} + \frac{35x^5y^3}{7x^2y}$$

$$= \frac{{}^4\cancel{28}\cancel{x^2}\cancel{y}}{\cancel{7}\cancel{x^2}\cancel{y}} - \frac{{}^3\cancel{21}x^{\cancel{3}1}y^{\cancel{2}1}}{\cancel{7}\cancel{x^2}\cancel{y}} + \frac{{}^5\cancel{35}x^{\cancel{5}3}y^{\cancel{3}2}}{\cancel{7}\cancel{x^2}\cancel{y}}$$

$$= 4 - 3x^1y^1 + 5x^3y^2$$

Q. Factor out the binomial GCF:
$3(x-5)^4 + 2a(x-5)^3 - 11a^2(x-5)^2$.

A. $\mathbf{(x-5)^2[3(x-5)^2 + 2a(x-5) - 11a^2]}$

The GCF is the square of the binomial, $(x-5)^2$. This example has three terms with a varying number of factors, or powers, of the binomial $(x-5)$ in each term.

1. Factor out the GCF: $8x^3y^2 - 4x^2y^3 + 14xy^4$.

2. Factor out the GCF: $36w^4 - 24w^3 - 48w^2$.

3. Factor out the GCF:
$15(x-3)^3 + 60x^4(x-3)^2 + 5(x-3)$.

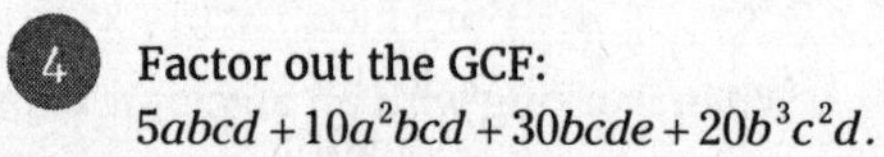

4. Factor out the GCF:
$5abcd + 10a^2bcd + 30bcde + 20b^3c^2d$.

"Un"wrapping the FOIL

The FOIL method helps you when you're multiplying two binomials. (See Chapter 7 for some problems that use this process.) When factoring, you *unFOIL*, which reverses the process to tell you which two binomials were multiplied together in the first place. The task in this chapter is to first recognize that a trinomial has been created by multiplying two binomials together and then *factor* it — figure out what those binomials are and write the product of them.

TIP

The general procedure for performing unFOIL includes these steps:

1. **Write the trinomial in descending powers of a variable.**
2. **Find all the possible combinations of factors whose product gives you the first term in the trinomial.**
3. **Find all the possible sets of factors whose product gives you the last term in the trinomial.**
4. **Try different combinations of those choices of factors in the binomials so that the middle term is the result of combining the outer and inner products.**

EXAMPLE

Q. Factor $2x^2 - 5x - 3$.

A. $(2x+1)(x-3)$

1. **The trinomial is already written with descending powers.**
2. **The only possible factors for $2x^2$ are $2x$ and x.**
3. **The only possible factors for the last term are 3 and 1.**
4. **Work on creating the middle term.** Because the last term is *negative*, you want to find a way to arrange the factors so that the outer and inner products have a *difference* of $5x$. You do this by placing the $2x$ and 3 so they multiply one another: $(2x\ 1)(x\ 3)$. When deciding on the placement of the signs, use a + and a –, and situate them so that the middle term is negative. Putting the – sign in front of the 3 results in a $-6x$ and a $+1x$. Combining them gives you the $-5x$.

Q. Factor $12y^2 - 17y + 6$.

A. $(4y-3)(3y-2)$. The factors of the first term are either y and $12y$, $2y$ and $6y$, or $3y$ and $4y$. The factors of the last term are either 1 and 6 or 2 and 3. The last term is *positive*, so the outer and inner products have to have a *sum* of $17y$. The signs between the terms are negative (two positives multiplied together give you a positive) because the sign of the middle term in the original problem is negative.

5 Factor $x^2 - 8x + 15$.

6 Factor $y^2 - 6y - 40$.

7 Factor $2x^2 + 3x - 2$.

8 Factor $4z^2 + 12z + 9$.

9 Factor $w^2 - 16$.

10 Factor $12x^2 - 8x - 15$.

Factoring Quadratic-Like Trinomials

A *quadratic-like* trinomial has a first term whose power on the variable is twice that in the second term. The last term is a constant. In general, these trinomials are of the form $ax^{2n} + bx^n + c$. If these trinomials factor, then the factorizations look like $(dx^n + e)(fx^n + g)$. Notice that the power on the variables in the factored form matches the power of the middle term in the original trinomial.

To factor a quadratic-like trinomial, you treat it as if it were $ax^2 + bx + c$, with the same rules applying to unFOILing and just using the higher powers on the variables.

EXAMPLE

Q. Factor $6x^4 + 13x^2 - 28$.

A. $\mathbf{(3x^2 - 4)(2x^2 + 7)}$. Treat this problem as if it is the trinomial $6x^2 + 13x - 28$. You have to find factors for the first term, involving the 6, and factors for the last term, involving the 28. The middle term, with the 13, has to be the difference between the outer and inner products. Using $3x^2$ from the first term and 7 from the last term, you get a product of $21x^2$. Then, using $2x^2$ from the first and 4 from the last, you get $8x^2$. The difference between 21 and 8 is 13. Get the factors aligned correctly and the signs inserted in the right places.

Q. Factor $5x^{-6} - 36x^{-3} + 36$.

A. $\mathbf{(5x^{-3} - 6)(x^{-3} - 6)}$. Don't let the negative exponents throw you. The middle term has an exponent that's half the first term's exponent. Think of the trinomial as being like $5x^2 - 36x + 36$. It works!

11 Factor $x^{10} + 4x^5 + 3$.

12 Factor $4y^{16} - 9$.

13 Factor $x^{-8} - 7x^{-4} - 8$.

14 Factor $2z^{1/3} - 7x^{1/6} + 3$.

Factoring Trinomials Using More than One Method

You can factor trinomials by taking out a GCF or by using the unFOIL method, and sometimes you can use both of these methods in one expression. Even better, you often get to apply the rules for factoring binomials on one or more of the factors you get after unFOILing. In general, first take out the common factor to make the terms in the expression simpler and the numbers smaller. Then look for patterns in the trinomial that results.

EXAMPLE

Q. Factor $9x^4 - 18x^3 - 72x^2$.

A. $\mathbf{9x^2(x-4)(x+2)}$. First take out the common factor, $9x^2$, and write the product with that common factor outside the parentheses: $9x^2(x^2 - 2x - 8)$. You can then factor the trinomial inside the parentheses.

Q. Factor $3x^5 - 15x^3 + 12x$.

A. $\mathbf{3x(x-1)(x+1)(x-2)(x+2)}$. First take out the common factor, $3x$, and write the product with that common factor outside the parentheses: $3x(x^4 - 5x^2 + 4)$. You can then factor the quadratic-like trinomial inside the parentheses to get $3x(x^2 - 1)(x^2 - 4)$. The two binomials then each factor into the difference of squares.

EXAMPLE

Q. Factor $(x-3)^3+(x-3)^2-30(x-3)$.

A. $\mathbf{(x-3)[(x-8)(x+3)]}$. Remember, the GCF can be a binomial. First, factor out the binomial $(x-3)$, which gives you $(x-3)[(x-3)^2+(x-3)-30]$. Then you have two options. This example uses the first option (the next example has the other option): You can square the first term in the brackets and then simplify the expression that results by combining like terms: $(x-3)[x^2-6x+9+x-3-30]=(x-3)[x^2-5x-24]$. Now you can factor the trinomial in the brackets.

Q. Factor $(x-3)^3+(x-3)^2-30(x-3)$ using a quadratic-like pattern.

A. $\mathbf{(x-3)[(x-8)(x+3)]}$. Yes, this is the same problem and same answer as shown in the preceding example. This time, after factoring out the binomial, you use the quadratic-like pattern to factor the expression inside the bracket. Beginning with $(x-3)[(x-3)^2+(x-3)-30]$, think of the $(x-3)$ expressions as being y's, and you see y^2+y-30, which is a trinomial that factors into $(y+6)(y-5)$. Replace the y's with the binomials, and you have $(x-3+6)(x-3-5)$, which simplifies into $(x+3)(x-8)$. You get the same answer.

15 Completely factor $5y^3-5y^2-10y$.

16 Completely factor $x^6-18x^5+81x^4$.

17 Completely factor $3x^2(x-2)^2+9x(x-2)^2-12(x-2)^2$.

18 Completely factor $a^2\left(x^2-25\right)-15a\left(x^2-25\right)+14\left(x^2-25\right)$.

19 Completely factor $40y^{1/4} + y^{1/8} - 15$.

20 Completely factor $x^{-3} - 10x^{-2} + 24x^{-1}$.

Factoring by Grouping

The expression $2axy + 8x - 3ay - 12$ has four terms — terms that don't share a single common factor. But you notice that the first two terms have a common factor of $2x$, and the last two terms have a common factor of -3. What to do, what to do!

Don't worry. This problem suggests that factoring by *grouping* may be an option. Expressions that can be factored by grouping have two distinct characteristics:

- A common factor (or factorable expression) occurs in each pairing or grouping of terms.
- The factorization of each individual grouping results in a new GCF common to each group.

Demonstrating this process with some examples makes it easier to understand:

EXAMPLE

Q. Factor by grouping: $2axy+8x-3ay-12$.

A. $(ay+4)(2x-3)$. Factor $2x$ out of the first two terms and -3 out of the second two terms: $2x(ay+4)-3(ay+4)$. You can see how you now have two terms, instead of four, and the two new terms have a common factor of $(ay+4)$. If you factor out a 3 instead of a -3, the second term becomes $3(-ay-4)$, which doesn't have the same $(ay+4)$ as the first. For factoring by grouping to work, the two new common factors have to be exactly the same.

Q. Factor by grouping: $2a^3x-a^3y-6b^2x+3b^2y+2cx-cy$.

A. $(2x-y)(a^3-3b^2+c)$. This type of factoring by grouping can also work with six terms. First, find the common factor in each pair of terms. Factor a^3 out of the first two terms, $-3b^2$ out of the second two terms, and c out of the last two: $a^3(2x-y)-3b^2(2x-y)+c(2x-y)$. Notice that, with the middle pairing, if you factor out $3b^2$ instead of $-3b^2$, you don't have the same common factor as the other two pairings: The signs are wrong. The new trinomial doesn't factor, but you should always check in case another factorization possibility is lurking in the background.

21 Factor by grouping: $ab^2+2ab+b+2$.

22 Factor by grouping: $xz^2-5z^2+3x-15$.

23 Factor by grouping: $n^{4/3}-2n^{1/3}+n-2$.

24 Factor by grouping: $x^2y^2+3y^2+x^2y+3y-6x^2-18$.

Putting All the Factoring Together

Factoring an algebraic expression is somewhat like buying presents when the holidays roll around. When you buy presents, you categorize (family, friend, or acquaintances?) and purchase items based on those categories so that the end result — complete satisfaction — doesn't break the bank. In terms of factoring algebraic expressions, you categorize (is an expression two terms, three terms, or more terms?) and then choose a procedure that works for that category. If you have two terms, for example, you may get to factor them as the difference of squares or cubes or the sum of cubes. If you have three terms, you may be able to factor the expression as the product of two binomials. With four or more terms, grouping may work. In any case, you first want to look for the GCF. Your goal? A completely satisfactory result that doesn't use too much brain power.

EXAMPLE

Q. Completely factor $8x^3+56x^2-240x$.

A. $\mathbf{8x(x+10)(x-3)}$. The first thing you always look for is a common factor. In this case, it's 8x that you can factor out: $8x(x^2+7x-30)$. Then you can use the unFOIL method on the trinomial in the parentheses. Finally, write the answer as the factor 8x times the product of the two binomials from the trinomial.

Q. Completely factor $3x^5-75x^3+24x^2-600$.

A. $\mathbf{3[(x+5)(x-5)(x+2)(x^2-2x+4)]}$

1. **Factor out the common factor of 3.**

   $3(x^5-25x^3+8x^2-200)$

2. **Factor by grouping.**

   Take x^3 out of the first two terms and 8 out of the last two terms. Then factor out the common factor of the two terms, the binomial.

   $3\left[x^3(x^2-25)+8(x^2-25)\right]$

   $3\left[(x^2-25)(x^3+8)\right]$

   The first factor in the brackets is the difference of perfect squares. The second factor is the sum of perfect cubes.

3. **Factor each of the two binomials in the parentheses to find the answer.**

   $(x^2-25)=(x-5)(x+5)$

   $(x^3+8)=(x+2)(x^2-2x+4)$

   $3[(x^2-25)(x^3+8)]=3[(x-5)(x+5)$
   $(x+2)(x^2-2x+4)]$

Refer to Chapter 10 if you need a refresher on binomial factorizations.

25 Completely factor $5x^3 - 80x$.

26 Completely factor $y^5 - 9y^3 + y^2 - 9$.

27 Completely factor $3x^5 - 66x^3 - 225x$.

28 Completely factor $8a^3b^2 - 32a^3 - b^2 + 4$.

29 Completely factor $4m^5 - 4m^4 - 36m^3 + 36m^2$.

30 Completely factor $10y^{19/3} + 350y^{10/3} + 2160y^{1/3}$.

Answers to Problems on Factoring Trinomials and Other Expressions

This section provides the answers (in bold) to the practice problems in this chapter.

1. Factor out the GCF: $8x^3y^2 - 4x^2y^3 + 14xy^4$. The answer is $\mathbf{2xy^2\left(4x^2 - 2xy + 7y^2\right)}$.

2. Factor out the GCF: $36w^4 - 24w^3 - 48w^2$. The answer is $\mathbf{12w^2(3w^2 - 2w - 4)}$.

3. Factor out the GCF: $15(x-3)^3 + 60x^4(x-3)^2 + 5(x-3)$.

   The answer is $\mathbf{5(x-3)\left(12x^5 - 36x^4 + 3x^2 - 18x + 28\right)}$.

   $15(x-3)^3 + 60x^4(x-3)^2 + 5(x-3) = 5(x-3)\left[3(x-3)^2 + 12x^4(x-3) + 1\right]$

   The trinomial in the brackets doesn't factor as a quadratic-like expression, so you need to expand each term by multiplying and simplifying.

   $5(x-3)\left[\left(3(x-3)^2 + 12x^4(x-3) + 1\right)\right] = 5(x-3)\left[3\left(x^2 - 6x + 9\right) + 12x^4(x-3) + 1\right]$

   $= 5(x-3)\left[3x^2 - 18x + 27 + 12x^5 - 36x^4 + 1\right] = 5(x-3)\left[12x^5 - 36x^4 + 3x^2 - 18x + 28\right]$

4. Factor out the GCF: $5abcd + 10a^2bcd + 30bcde + 20b^3c^2d$. The answer is $\mathbf{5bcd\left(a + 2a^2 + 6e + 4b^2c\right)}$.

5. Factor $x^2 - 8x + 15$. The answer is $\mathbf{(x-5)(x-3)}$, considering 15 and 1, or 5 and 3 for the factors of 15.

6. Factor $y^2 - 6y - 40$. The answer is $\mathbf{(y-10)(y+4)}$, which needs opposite signs with factors of 40 to be either 40 and 1, 20 and 2, 10 and 4, or 8 and 5.

7. Factor $2x^2 + 3x - 2$. The answer is $\mathbf{(2x-1)(x+2)}$.

8. Factor $4z^2 + 12z + 9$. The answer is $\mathbf{(2z+3)^2}$.

   $4z^2 + 12z + 9 = (2z+3)(2z+3) = (2z+3)^2$

9. Factor $w^2 - 16$. The answer is $\mathbf{(w+4)(w-4)}$, which is a difference of squares.

10. Factor $12x^2 - 8x - 15$. The answer is $\mathbf{(6x+5)(2x-3)}$.

11. Factor $x^{10} + 4x^5 + 3$. The answer is $\mathbf{\left(x^5+3\right)\left(x^5+1\right)}$.

12. Factor $4y^{16} - 9$. The answer is $\mathbf{\left(2y^8+3\right)\left(2y^8-3\right)}$, which is a difference of squares.

13. Factor $x^{-8} - 7x^{-4} - 8$. The answer is $\mathbf{\left(x^{-4}-8\right)\left(x^{-4}+1\right)}$.

14. Factor $2z^{1/3} - 7x^{1/6} + 3$. The answer is $\mathbf{\left(2z^{1/6}-1\right)\left(z^{1/6}-3\right)}$. Twice $1/6$ is $1/3$.

15 Completely factor $5y^3 - 5y^2 - 10y$. The answer is $\mathbf{5y(y-2)(y+1)}$.

The GCF is 5y. Factor that out first.

$$5y^3 - 5y^2 - 10y = 5y(y^2 - y - 2) = 5y(y-2)(y+1)$$

16 Completely factor $x^6 - 18x^5 + 81x^4$. The answer is $\mathbf{x^4(x-9)^2}$.

$$x^6 - 18x^5 + 81x^4 = x^4(x^2 - 18x + 81) = x^4(x-9)(x-9) = x^4(x-9)^2$$

17 Completely factor $3x^2(x-2)^2 + 9x(x-2)^2 - 12(x-2)^2$. The answer is $\mathbf{3(x-2)^2(x+4)(x-1)}$.

First, divide out the GCF, $3(x-2)^2$. Then you have a factorable trinomial in the parentheses.

$$3x^2(x-2)^2 + 9x(x-2)^2 - 12(x-2)^2 = 3(x-2)^2(x^2 + 3x - 4) = 3(x-2)^2(x+4)(x-1)$$

18 Completely factor $a^2(x^2 - 25) - 15a(x^2 - 25) + 14(x^2 - 25)$. The answer is $\mathbf{(x+5)(x-5)(a-14)(a-1)}$.

The GCF is $(x^2 - 25)$, which is the difference of squares.

$$\begin{aligned} a^2(x^2 - 25) - 15a(x^2 - 25) + 14(x^2 - 25) &= (x^2 - 25)(a^2 - 15a + 14) \\ &= (x+5)(x-5)(a-14)(a-1) \end{aligned}$$

19 Completely factor $40y^{1/4} + y^{1/8} - 15$. The answer is $\mathbf{(8y^{1/8} + 5)(5y^{1/8} - 3)}$.

The quadratic-like trinomial has fractional exponents with the exponent $\frac{1}{4}$ being twice the exponent $\frac{1}{8}$. The factors of 40 are 1 and 40, 2 and 20, 4 and 10, 5 and 8. The factors of 15 are 1 and 15, 3 and 5. You have to find a combination of factors that gives you a difference of 1 for the middle term. Using the 8 and 5 with the 3 and 5 does the trick.

The product of the outer terms is 24, and the product of the inner terms is 25: (8 5)(5 3).

20 Completely factor $x^{-3} - 10x^{-2} + 24x^{-1}$. The answer is $\mathbf{x^{-3}(6x-1)(4x-1)}$.

First divide by the GCF to get $x^{-3}(1 - 10x^1 + 24x^2)$. You can factor the trinomial as it's written or rearrange the expression to read $x^{-3}(24x^2 - 10x + 1)$. Now the trinomial factors, and you get $x^{-3}(6x-1)(4x-1)$.

21 Factor by grouping: $ab^2 + 2ab + b + 2$. The answer is $\mathbf{(b+2)(ab+1)}$.

$$ab^2 + 2ab + b + 2 = ab(b+2) + 1(b+2) = (b+2)(ab+1)$$

22 Factor by grouping: $xz^2 - 5z^2 + 3x - 15$. The answer is $\mathbf{(x-5)(z^2+3)}$.

$$xz^2 - 5z^2 + 3x - 15 = z^2(x-5) + 3(x-5) = (x-5)(z^2+3)$$

23 Factor by grouping: $n^{4/3} - 2n^{1/3} + n - 2$. The answer is $\mathbf{(n-2)(n^{1/3}+1)}$.

The GCF of the first two terms is $n^{1/3}$. The GCF of the last two terms is just 1. So $n^{4/3} - 2n^{1/3} + n - 2 = n^{1/3}(n^1 - 2) + 1(n-2) = (n-2)(n^{1/3}+1)$.

24 Factor by grouping: $x^2y^2 + 3y^2 + x^2y + 3y - 6x^2 - 18$. The answer is $\mathbf{(x^2+3)(y+3)(y-2)}$.

$$\begin{aligned} x^2y^2 + 3y^2 + x^2y + 3y - 6x^2 - 18 &= y^2(x^2+3) + y(x^2+3) - 6(x^2+3) \\ &= (x^2+3)(y^2 + y - 6) \\ &= (x^2+3)(y+3)(y-2) \end{aligned}$$

25 Completely factor $5x^3 - 80x$. The answer is $\mathbf{5x(x+4)(x-4)}$. First factor $5x$ out of each term: $5x(x^2 - 16)$. Then you can factor the binomial as the sum and difference of the same two terms.

26 Completely factor $y^5 - 9y^3 + y^3 - 9$. The answer is $\mathbf{(y+3)(y-3)(y+1)(y^2-y+1)}$.

$$\begin{aligned} y^5 - 9y^3 + y^2 - 9 &= y^3\left(y^2 - 9\right) + 1\left(y^2 - 9\right) \\ &= \left(y^2 - 9\right)\left(y^3 + 1\right) \\ &= (y+3)(y-3)(y+1)\left(y^2 - y + 1\right) \end{aligned}$$

27 Completely factor $3x^5 - 66x^3 - 225x$. The answer is $\mathbf{3x(x+5)(x-5)(x^2+3)}$.

$$\begin{aligned} 3x^5 - 66x^3 - 225x &= 3x\left(x^4 - 22x^2 - 75\right) \\ &= 3x\left(x^2 - 25\right)\left(x^2 + 3\right) \\ &= 3x(x+5)(x-5)\left(x^2 + 3\right) \end{aligned}$$

28 Completely factor $8a^3b^2 - 32a^3 - b^2 + 4$. The answer is $\mathbf{(b+2)(b-2)(2a-1)(4a^2+2a+1)}$.

$$\begin{aligned} 8a^3b^2 - 32a^3 - b^2 + 4 &= 8a^3\left(b^2 - 4\right) - 1\left(b^2 - 4\right) \\ &= \left(b^2 - 4\right)\left(8a^3 - 1\right) \\ &= (b+2)(b-2)(2a-1)\left(4a^2 + 2a + 1\right) \end{aligned}$$

29 Completely factor $4m^5 - 4m^4 - 36m^3 + 36m^2$. The answer is $\mathbf{4m^2(m-1)(m+3)(m-3)}$.

$$\begin{aligned} 4m^5 - 4m^4 - 36m^3 + 36m^2 &= 4m^2\left(m^3 - m^2 - 9m + 9\right) \\ &= 4m^2\left[m^2(m-1) - 9(m-1)\right] \\ &= 4m^2\left[(m-1)\left(m^2 - 9\right)\right] \\ &= 4m^2(m-1)(m+3)(m-3) \end{aligned}$$

30 Completely factor $10y^{19/3} + 350y^{10/3} + 2160y^{1/3}$. The answer is $\mathbf{10y^{1/3}(y+2)(y^2-2y+4)(y+3)(y^2-3y+9)}$.

$$\begin{aligned} 10y^{19/3} + 350y^{10/3} + 2160y^{1/3} &= 10y^{1/3}\left(y^6 + 35y^3 + 216\right) \\ &= 10y^{1/3}\left(y^6 + 35y^3 + 8 \times 27\right) \\ &= 10y^{1/3}\left(y^3 + 8\right)\left(y^3 + 27\right) \\ &= 10y^{1/3}(y+2)\left(y^2 - 2y + 4\right)(y+3)\left(y^2 - 3y + 9\right) \end{aligned}$$

3

Seek and Ye Shall Find . . . Solutions

IN THIS PART . . .

Lock in your linear equation skills.

Work with quadratic equations.

Utilize techniques to make reasonable guesses at solutions when working with polynomials.

Rock at radical and absolute value equations.

Tackle problems dealing with inequalities.

» Making grouping symbols and fractions work

» Putting proportions in their place

Chapter 12

Lining Up Linear Equations

Linear equations are algebraic equations that have no powers on the variables that are greater than the first power. The most common (and easiest) way of solving linear equations is to perform operations or other manipulations so that the variable you're solving for is on one side of the equation and the numbers or other letters and symbols are on the other side of the equation. You want to get the variable alone so that you can finish with a statement, such as $x = 4$ or $y = 2a$. Because linear equations involve just the first degree (power one) of the variable, you look for just one answer.

This chapter provides you with the different setups or situations where linear equations are usually found — and what to do when you find them.

Using the Addition/Subtraction Property

One of the most basic properties of equations is that you can add or subtract the same amount from each side of the equation and not change the balance or *equality*. The equation is still a true statement (as long as it started out that way) after adding or subtracting the same from each side. You use this property to get all the terms with the variable you want to solve for to one side and all the other letters and numbers to the other side so that you can solve the equation for the value of the variable.

TIP

You can check the solution by putting the answer back in the original equation to see whether it gives you a true statement.

EXAMPLE

Q. Solve for $x: x+7=11$

A. $\mathbf{x=4}$. Subtract 7 from each side (same as adding –7 to each side), like this:

$$\begin{array}{rl} x+7 &= 11 \\ -7 &- 7 \\ \hline x \quad &= 4 \end{array}$$

Q. Solve for $y: 8y-2=7y-10$

A. $\mathbf{y=-8}$. First add $-7y$ to each side to get rid of the variable on the right (this moves the variable to the left with the other variable term) and then add 2 to each side to get rid of the –2 (gets the numbers together on the right). This is what the process looks like:

$$\begin{array}{rcl} 8y-2 &=& 7y-10 \\ -7y & & -7y \\ \hline y-2 &=& -10 \\ +2 & & +2 \\ \hline y &=& -8 \end{array}$$

1 Solve for $x: x+4=15$.

2 Solve for $y: y-2=11$.

3 Solve for $x: 5x+3=4x-1$.

4 Solve for $y: 2y+9+6y-8=4y+5+3y-11$.

Using the Multiplication/Division Property

Another property of equations is that when you multiply or divide both sides by the same number (but not zero), then the equation is still an *equality*; it's still a true statement. You can use this multiplication/division property alone or with the addition/subtraction property to help solve equations for the value of the variable.

EXAMPLE

Q. Solve for x: $-3x = -45$.

A. $x = 15$. **Divide each side by –3 to determine what x is:**

$$\frac{\cancel{-3}x}{\cancel{-3}} = \frac{-45}{-3}$$
$$x = 15$$

Q. Solve for y: $\frac{y}{5} = 12$.

A. $y = 60$. **Multiply each side by 5 to solve the equation for y:**

$$\cancel{5} \cdot \frac{y}{\cancel{5}} = 12 \cdot 5$$
$$y = 60$$

5 Solve for x: $6x = 24$.

6 Solve for y: $-4y = 20$.

7 Solve for z: $\frac{z}{3} = 11$.

8 Solve for w: $\frac{w}{-4} = -2$.

Putting Several Operations Together

The different properties of equations that allow you to add the same number to each side or multiply each side by the same number (except zero) are the backbone of solving linear equations. More often than not, you have to perform several different operations to solve a particular equation. In the cases where the problem just has the operations of addition, subtraction, multiplication, and division (and there aren't any grouping symbols to change the rules), you first do all the addition and subtraction to get the variables on one side and the numbers on the other side. Then you can multiply or divide to get the variable by itself.

REMEMBER

The side you move the variable to really doesn't matter. Many people like to have the variable on the left, so you can read $x = 2$ as "x equals 2." Writing $2 = x$ is just as correct. You may prefer having the variable on one side in one equation and on the other side in another equation — depending on which side makes for less awkward operations or keeps the variable with a positive factor.

EXAMPLE

Q. Solve for $x: 6x - 3 + 2x = 9x + 1 - 4x + 8$.

A. $x = 4$

1. **Simplify each side of the equation by combining like terms.**

$$8x - 3 = 5x + 9$$

2. **Add 3 to and subtract 5x from each side.**

$$\begin{aligned} 8x - 3 &= 5x + 9 \\ +3 \quad &\quad +3 \\ \hline 8x \quad &= 5x + 12 \\ -5x \quad &\quad -5x \\ \hline 3x \quad &= \quad 12 \end{aligned}$$

3. **Divide each side by 3 to get $x = 4$.**

$$\frac{\cancel{3}x}{\cancel{3}} = \frac{\cancel{12}^4}{\cancel{3}_1}$$

$$x = 4$$

Q. Solve for y: $\frac{2y}{3} + 1 = \frac{4y}{3} + 5$.

A. $-6 = y$

1. **By subtracting $\frac{2y}{3}$ from each side and subtracting 5 from each side, you get**

$$\begin{aligned} \frac{2y}{3} + 1 &= \frac{4y}{3} + 5 \\ -\frac{2y}{3} \quad &\quad -\frac{2y}{3} \\ \hline 1 &= \frac{2y}{3} + 5 \\ -5 \quad &\quad -5 \\ \hline -4 &= \frac{2y}{3} \end{aligned}$$

2. **Multiply each side by 3 and then divide each side by 2.**

$$3(-4) = \frac{2y}{\cancel{3}} \cdot \cancel{3}$$

$$-12 = 2y$$

$$\frac{-12}{2} = \frac{\cancel{2}y}{\cancel{2}}$$

$$-6 = y$$

Another way to do the last two operations in just one is to multiply each side of the equation by the reciprocal of $2/3$, which is $3/2$.

9 Solve for $x: 3x - 4 = 5$.

10 Solve for y: $8 - \frac{y}{2} = 7$.

11 Solve for $x: 5x - 3 = 8x + 9$.

12 Solve for z: $\frac{z}{6} - 3 = z + 7$.

13 Solve for $y: 4y + 16 - 3y = 7 + 3y$.

14 Solve for x: $\frac{3x}{4} - 2 = \frac{9x}{4} + 13$.

Solving Linear Equations with Grouping Symbols

The most general procedure to use when solving linear equations is to add and subtract first and then multiply or divide. This general rule is interrupted when the problem contains grouping symbols such as ( ), [ ], { }. (See Chapter 2 for more on grouping symbols.) If the equation has grouping symbols (and this includes fractions with many-termed numerators), you need to perform whatever operation is indicated by the grouping symbol before carrying on with the other rules.

REMEMBER

If you perform an operation on the grouping symbol, then every term in the grouping symbol has to have that operation performed on it.

EXAMPLE

Q. 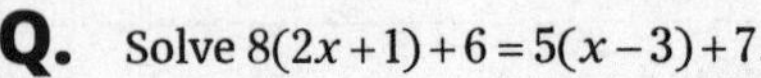 Solve $8(2x+1)+6=5(x-3)+7$.

A.  $x=-2$

1. **Distribute the 8 over the two terms in the left parentheses and the 5 over the two terms in the right parentheses.**

   You get the equation $16x+8+6=5x-15+7$.

2. **Combine the two numbers on each side of the equation.**

   You get $16x+14=5x-8$.

3. **Subtract 5*x* and 14 from each side; then divide each side by 11.**

$$\begin{array}{rcr} 16x+14 & = & 5x-8 \\ -5x-14 & & -5x-14 \\ \hline 11x & = & -22 \end{array}$$

$$\frac{\cancel{11}x}{\cancel{11}}=\frac{-22}{11}$$

$$x=-2$$

Q. Solve $\frac{x-5}{4}+3=x+4$.

A. $x=-3$. First multiply each term on both sides of the equation by 4:

$$\cancel{4}\left(\frac{x-5}{\cancel{4}}\right)+4(3)=4(x)+4(4)$$

$$x-5+12=4x+16$$

Combine the like terms on the left. Then subtract 4*x* from each side and subtract 7 from each side; finally, divide each side by −3.

$$\begin{array}{rcr} x+7 & = & 4x+16 \\ -4x-7 & & -4x-7 \\ \hline -3x & = & 9 \end{array}$$

$$\frac{\cancel{-3}x}{\cancel{-3}}=\frac{9}{-3}$$

$$x=-3$$

15 Solve for $x: 3(x-5)=12$.

16 Solve for $y: 4(y+3)+7=3$.

17 Solve for x: $\frac{4x+1}{3}=x+2$.

18 Solve for $y: 5(y-3)-3(y+4)=1-6(y-4)$.

19 Simplify the quadratic equation to create a linear equation and then solve for $x: x(3x+1)-2=3x^2-5$.

20 Simplify the quadratic equation to create a linear equation and then solve for $x: (x-3)(x+4)=(x+1)(x-2)$.

Working It Out with Fractions

Fractions aren't everyone's favorite thing, although it's hard to avoid them in everyday life or in algebra. Fractions in algebraic equations can complicate everything, so just getting rid of fractions is often easier than trying to deal with finding common denominators several times in the same problem.

Two general procedures work best when dealing with algebraic fractions.

- If you can easily isolate a single term with the fraction on one side, do the necessary addition and subtraction, and then multiply each side of the equation by the denominator of the fraction (be sure to multiply *each* term in the equation by that denominator).
- If the equation has more than one fraction, find a common denominator for *all* the terms and then multiply each side of the equation by this common denominator. Doing so, in effect, gets rid of all the fractions.

EXAMPLE

Q. Solve $\frac{2x-1}{3}+4=7$ by isolating the fractional term on the left.

A. $x=5$

1. **Subtract 4 from each side.**

$$\begin{aligned} \frac{2x-1}{3}+4&=7 \\ -4&-4 \\ \hline \frac{2x-1}{3}\quad&=3 \end{aligned}$$

2. **Multiply each side by 3.**

$$\not{3}\left(\frac{2x-1}{\not{3}}\right)=3(3)$$

$$2x-1=9$$

Now the problem is in a form ready to solve.

3. **Add 1 to each side and divide each side by 2.**

$$\begin{aligned} 2x-1&=9 \\ +1\ &+1 \\ \hline 2x\quad&=10 \end{aligned}$$

$$\frac{\not{2}x}{\not{2}}=\frac{10}{2}$$

$$x=5$$

Q. This time, use the second procedure from the bulleted list to solve $\frac{x}{4}+15=1-\frac{3x}{2}$.

A. $x=-8$

1. **Determine the common denominator for the fractions, which is 4.**

2. **Multiply each term in the equation by 4.**

$$4\left(\frac{x}{4}\right)+4(15)=4(1)-4\left(\frac{3x}{2}\right)$$

Doing so eliminates all the fractions after you reduce them.

$$\not{4}\left(\frac{x}{\not{4}}\right)+4(15)=4(1)-\not{4}^{2}\left(\frac{3x}{\not{2}}\right)$$

$$x+60=4-6x$$

3. **Add 6x to each side and subtract 60 from each side. Then finish solving by dividing by 7.**

$$\begin{aligned} x+60 &= \ 4-6x \\ +6x-60 &\ \ -60+6x \\ \hline 7x\quad &=-56 \end{aligned}$$

$$\frac{\not{7}x}{\not{7}}=\frac{-56}{7}$$

$$x=-8$$

21 Solve for x: $\frac{x+1}{5}-1=3$.

22 Solve for x: $\frac{2x}{3}-\frac{3x}{4}=1$.

23 Solve for y: $\frac{2(y+3)}{5}-1=\frac{3(y-3)}{4}$.

24 Solve for x: $\frac{x}{2}+\frac{x}{3}+\frac{x}{6}=6$.

25 Simplify the rational equation by multiplying each term by y. Then solve the resulting linear equation for y: $\frac{4}{y}-\frac{6}{y}=1$.

26 Simplify the rational equation by multiplying each term by z. Then solve the resulting linear equation for z: $\frac{1}{3z}-\frac{1}{2z}=\frac{1}{6}$.

Solving Proportions

A *proportion* is actually an equation with two fractions set equal to one another. The proportion $\frac{a}{b} = \frac{c}{d}$ has the following properties:

- The cross products are equal: $ad = bc$.
- If the proportion is true, then the *flip* of the proportion is also true: $\frac{b}{a} = \frac{d}{c}$.
- You can reduce vertically or horizontally: $\frac{a \cdot \cancel{k}}{b \cdot \cancel{k}} = \frac{c}{d}$ or $\frac{a \cdot \cancel{k}}{b} = \frac{c \cdot \cancel{k}}{d}$.

You solve proportions that are algebraic equations by cross-multiplying, flipping, reducing, or using a combination of two or more of the processes. The flipping part of solving proportions usually occurs when you have the variable in the denominator and can do a quick solution by first flipping the proportion and then multiplying by a number.

EXAMPLE

Q. Solve for *x*: $\frac{2x}{16} = \frac{3x+5}{28}$.

A. $x = 10$

1. **First, reduce horizontally through the denominators. Then cross-multiply.**

$$\frac{2x}{{}_4\cancel{16}} = \frac{3x+5}{\cancel{28}_7}$$
$$2x(7) = 4(3x+5)$$
$$14x = 12x + 20$$

2. **Subtract 12*x* from each side. Then divide each side by 2.**

$$14x = 12x + 20$$
$$-12x - 12x$$
$$2x = 20$$
$$\frac{\cancel{2}x}{\cancel{2}} = \frac{{}^{10}\cancel{20}}{{}_1\cancel{2}}$$
$$x = 10$$

Q. Solve for *x*: $\frac{6}{10} = \frac{12}{x-5}$.

A. $x = 25$

1. **Flip the proportion to get $\frac{10}{6} = \frac{x-5}{12}$.**

2. **Reduce through the denominators and then multiply each side by 2. (You could reduce vertically in the first fraction, too, but dividing by 6 in the denominators is a better choice.)**

$$\frac{10}{\cancel{6}} = \frac{x-5}{\cancel{12}_2}$$
$$2 \cdot \frac{10}{1} = \frac{x-5}{\cancel{2}} \cdot \cancel{2}$$
$$10(2) = x - 5$$
$$20 = x - 5$$
$$+5 = +5$$
$$25 = x$$

27 Solve for x: $\frac{x}{8} = \frac{9}{12}$.

28 Solve for y: $\frac{20}{y} = \frac{30}{33}$.

29 Solve for z: $\frac{z+4}{32} = \frac{35}{56}$.

30 Solve for y: $\frac{6}{27} = \frac{8}{2y+6}$.

Answers to Problems on Solving Linear Equations

This section provides the answers (in bold) to the practice problems in this chapter.

1. Solve for x: $x+4=15$. The answer is $\boldsymbol{x=11}$.

$$\begin{array}{rcl} x+4 &=& 15 \\ -4 && -4 \\ \hline x &=& 11 \end{array}$$

2. Solve for y: $y-2=11$. The answer is $\boldsymbol{y=13}$.

$$\begin{array}{rcl} y-2 &=& 11 \\ +2 && +2 \\ \hline y &=& 13 \end{array}$$

3. Solve for x: $5x+3=4x-1$. The answer is $\boldsymbol{x=-4}$.

$$\begin{array}{rcl} 5x+3 &=& 4x-1 \\ -4x && -4x \\ \hline x+3 &=& -1 \\ -3 && -3 \\ \hline x &=& -4 \end{array}$$

4. Solve for y: $2y+9+6y-8=4y+5+3y-11$. The answer is $\boldsymbol{y=-7}$. By combining like terms, you get

$$\begin{array}{rcl} 8y+1 &=& 7y-6 \\ -7y && -7y \\ \hline y+1 &=& -6 \\ -1 && -1 \\ \hline y &=& -7 \end{array}$$

5. Solve for x: $6x=24$. The answer is $\boldsymbol{x=4}$.

$$6x=24$$
$$\frac{6x}{6}=\frac{24}{6}$$
$$x=4$$

6. Solve for y: $-4y=20$. The answer is $\boldsymbol{y=-5}$.

$$-4y=20$$
$$\frac{-4y}{-4}=\frac{20}{-4}$$
$$y=-5$$

7. Solve for z: $\frac{z}{3} = 11$. The answer is $\boldsymbol{z = 33}$.

$$\begin{aligned} \frac{z}{3} &= 11 \\ 3\left(\frac{z}{3}\right) &= (3)(11) \\ z &= 33 \end{aligned}$$

8. Solve for w: $\frac{w}{-4} = -2$. The answer is $\boldsymbol{w = 8}$.

$$\begin{aligned} \frac{w}{-4} &= -2 \\ (-4)\left(\frac{w}{-4}\right) &= (-4)(-2) \\ w &= 8 \end{aligned}$$

9. Solve for x: $3x - 4 = 5$. The answer is $\boldsymbol{x = 3}$.

$$\begin{array}{r} 3x - 4 = 5 \\ \underline{\quad +4 + 4} \\ 3x \quad = 9 \\ \frac{3x}{3} = \frac{9}{3} \\ x = 3 \end{array}$$

10. Solve for y: $8 - \frac{y}{2} = 7$. The answer is $\boldsymbol{y = 2}$.

$$\begin{array}{r} 8 - \frac{y}{2} = 7 \\ \underline{-8 \qquad -8} \\ -\frac{y}{2} = -1 \\ (-2)\left(-\frac{y}{2}\right) = (-2)(-1) \\ y = 2 \end{array}$$

11. Solve for x: $5x - 3 = 8x + 9$. The answer is $\boldsymbol{x = -4}$.

$$\begin{array}{r} 5x - 3 = 8x + 9 \\ \underline{-5x - 9 - 5x - 9} \\ 12 = 3x \\ \frac{-12}{3} = x \\ -4 = x \end{array}$$

12 Solve for z: $\frac{z}{6}-3=z+7$. The answer is $\boldsymbol{z=-12}$.

$$\begin{array}{r}\frac{z}{6}-3=z+7\\ \underline{-\frac{z}{6}-7-\frac{z}{6}-7}\\ -10=\frac{5z}{6}\end{array}$$

Note that $z-\frac{z}{6}=\frac{6z}{6}-\frac{z}{6}=\frac{5z}{6}$.

$$(6)(-10)=\left(\frac{5z}{6}\right)(6)$$
$$-60=5z$$
$$\frac{5z}{5}=\frac{-60}{5}$$
$$z=-12$$

13 Solve for y: $4y+16-3y=7+3y$. The answer is $\boldsymbol{y={}^{9}/_{2}}$. Combine like terms and then solve:

$$\begin{array}{rl}y+16= & 7+3y\\ \underline{-3y-16} & \underline{-16-3y}\\ -2y & =-9\end{array}$$
$$\frac{-2y}{-2}=\frac{-9}{-2}$$
$$y=\frac{9}{2}$$

14 Solve for x: $\frac{3x}{4}-2=\frac{9x}{4}+13$. The answer is $\boldsymbol{x=-10}$.

$$\begin{array}{rl}\frac{3x}{4}-2= & \frac{9x}{4}+13\\ \underline{-\frac{9x}{4}+2} & \underline{-\frac{9x}{4}+2}\\ -\frac{6x}{4} & = \quad 15\end{array}$$
$$-\frac{3x}{2}=15$$
$$(2)\left(-\frac{3x}{2}\right)=(2)(15)$$
$$-3x=30$$
$$\frac{-3x}{-3}=\frac{30}{-3}$$
$$x=-10$$

15. Solve for x: $3(x-5)=12$. The answer is $\boldsymbol{x=9}$.

$$\begin{aligned}3(x-5)&=12\\3x-15&=12\\+15&+15\\\hline 3x&=27\\\frac{3x}{3}&=\frac{27}{3}\\x&=9\end{aligned}$$

16. Solve for y: $4(y+3)+7=3$. The answer is $\boldsymbol{y=-4}$.

$$\begin{aligned}4(y+3)+7&=3\\4y+12+7&=3\\4y+19&=3\\-19&-19\\\hline 4y&=-16\\\frac{4y}{4}&=\frac{-16}{4}\\y&=-4\end{aligned}$$

17. Solve for x: $\frac{4x+1}{3}=x+2$. The answer is $\boldsymbol{x=5}$.

$$\begin{aligned}\frac{4x+1}{3}&=x+2\\(3)\left(\frac{4x+1}{3}\right)&=(3)(x+2)\\4x+1&=3x+6\\-3x-1&\quad-3x-1\\\hline x&=5\end{aligned}$$

18. Solve for y: $5(y-3)-3(y+4)=1-6(y-4)$. The answer is $\boldsymbol{y={}^{13}\!/_{2}}$.

$$\begin{aligned}5(y-3)-3(y+4)&=1-6(y-4)\\5y-15-3y-12&=1-6y+24\\2y-27&=-6y+25\\+6y+27&\quad+6y+27\\\hline 8y&=52\\\frac{8y}{8}&=\frac{52}{8}\\y&=\frac{13}{2}\end{aligned}$$

19. Solve for x: $x(3x+1)-2=3x^2-5$. The answer is $\boldsymbol{x=-3}$.

$$\begin{aligned}x(3x+1)-2&=3x^2-5\\3x^2+x-2&=3x^2-5\\-3x^2\quad+2&\quad-3x^2+2\\\hline x&=-3\end{aligned}$$

(20) Solve for x: $(x-3)(x+4)=(x+1)(x-2)$. The answer is $\boldsymbol{x=5}$.

$$\begin{aligned}(x-3)(x+4)&=(x+1)(x-2)\\ x^2+x-12&=x^2-x-2\\ -x^2+x+12&\quad -x^2+x+12\\ \hline 2x&=10\\ \frac{2x}{2}&=\frac{10}{2}\\ x&=5\end{aligned}$$

(21) Solve for x: $\frac{(x+1)}{5}-1=3$. The answer is $\boldsymbol{x=19}$.

$$\begin{aligned}\frac{(x+1)}{5}-1&=3\\ +1&\ +1\\ \hline \frac{x+1}{5}&=4\\ 5\cdot\left(\frac{x+1}{5}\right)&=(5)(4)\\ x+1&=20\\ -1&\ -1\\ \hline x&=19\end{aligned}$$

(22) Solve for x: $\frac{2x}{3}-\frac{3x}{4}=1$. The answer is $\boldsymbol{x=-12}$. Twelve is a common denominator, so

$$\begin{aligned}\cancel{12}^{4}\left(\frac{2x}{\cancel{3}}\right)-\cancel{12}^{3}\left(\frac{3x}{\cancel{4}}\right)&=(12)(1)\\ 8x-9x&=12\\ -x&=12\\ \frac{-x}{-1}&=\frac{12}{-1}\\ x&=-12\end{aligned}$$

(23) Solve for y: $\frac{2(y+3)}{5}-1=\frac{3(y-3)}{4}$. The answer is $\boldsymbol{y=7}$. Twenty is a common denominator, so

$$\begin{aligned}\cancel{20}^{4}\cdot\left[\frac{2(y+3)}{\cancel{5}}\right]-(20)(1)&=\cancel{20}^{5}\cdot\left[\frac{3(y-3)}{\cancel{4}}\right]\\ 8(y+3)-20&=15(y-3)\\ 8y+24-20&=15y-45\\ 8y+4&=15y-45\\ -8y+45&\ -8y+45\\ \hline 49&=7y\\ \frac{7y}{7}&=\frac{49}{7}\\ y&=7\end{aligned}$$

(24) Solve for x: $\frac{x}{2}+\frac{x}{3}+\frac{x}{6}=6$. The answer is $\boldsymbol{x}=\mathbf{6}$. A common denominator is 6, so

$$\begin{aligned}6\cdot\left(\frac{x}{2}\right)+6\cdot\left(\frac{x}{3}\right)+6\cdot\left(\frac{x}{6}\right)&=(6)(6)\\3x+2x+x&=36\\6x&=36\\\frac{6x}{6}&=\frac{36}{6}\\x&=6\end{aligned}$$

(25) Solve for y: $\frac{4}{y}-\frac{6}{y}=1$. The answer is $\boldsymbol{y}=\mathbf{-2}$. The common denominator is y, so

$$\begin{aligned}\cancel{y}\cdot\left(\frac{4}{\cancel{y}}\right)-\cancel{y}\cdot\left(\frac{6}{\cancel{y}}\right)&=(y)(1)\\4-6&=y\\-2&=y\end{aligned}$$

(26) Solve for z: $\frac{1}{3z}-\frac{1}{2z}=\frac{1}{6}$. The answer is $z=\mathbf{-1}$. A common denominator is $6z$, so

$$\begin{aligned}\cancel{6z}^{2}\cdot\left(\frac{1}{\cancel{3z}}\right)-\cancel{6z}^{3}\cdot\left(\frac{1}{\cancel{2z}}\right)&=\cancel{6}z\cdot\left(\frac{1}{\cancel{6}}\right)\\2-3&=z\\-1&=z\end{aligned}$$

(27) Solve for x: $\frac{x}{8}=\frac{9}{12}$. The answer is $\boldsymbol{x}=\mathbf{6}$. Reduce by dividing the denominators by 4 and the right fractions by 3. Then cross-multiply.

$$\frac{x}{{}_{2}\cancel{8}}=\frac{9}{\cancel{12}_{3}}\rightarrow\frac{x}{2}=\frac{\cancel{9}^{3}}{\cancel{3}_{1}}\rightarrow\frac{x}{2}=\frac{3}{2}\rightarrow x=6$$

(28) Solve for y: $\frac{20}{y}=\frac{30}{33}$. The answer is $\boldsymbol{y}=\mathbf{22}$. Reduce through the numerators. Then flip.

$$\begin{aligned}\frac{{}^{2}\cancel{20}}{y}&=\frac{\cancel{30}^{3}}{33}\\\frac{y}{2}&=\frac{33}{3}\\\frac{y}{2}&=\frac{\cancel{33}^{11}}{\cancel{3}}\\y&=22\end{aligned}$$

(29) Solve for z: $\frac{z+4}{32}=\frac{35}{56}$. The answer is $\boldsymbol{z=16}$. **Reduce the fraction on the right by dividing the numerator and denominator by 7. Then reduce through the denominators before you cross-multiply:**

$$\frac{z+4}{32}=\frac{35}{56}=\frac{\cancel{35}^{5}}{\cancel{56}_{8}}=\frac{5}{8}$$

$$\frac{z+4}{{}_4\cancel{32}}=\frac{5}{{}_1\cancel{8}}$$

$$(z+4)\cdot 1=4\cdot 5$$

$$z+4=20$$

$$z=16$$

(30) Solve for y: $\frac{6}{27}=\frac{8}{2y+6}$. The answer is $\boldsymbol{y=15}$. **Flip to get $\frac{27}{6}=\frac{2y+6}{8}$ and solve by reducing the fraction on the left and then cross-multiplying:**

$$\frac{\cancel{27}^{9}}{\cancel{6}_{2}}=\frac{2y+6}{8}$$

$$9(8)=2(2y+6)$$

$$72=4y+12$$

$$60=4y$$

$$\frac{60}{4}=\frac{4y}{4}$$

$$15=y$$

Yes, you could also have reduced through the denominators, but when the numbers are small enough, it's just as quick to skip that step.

- Solving quadratic equations by factoring
- Enlisting the quadratic formula
- Completing the square to solve quadratics
- Dealing with the impossible

Chapter 13

Muscling Up to Quadratic Equations

A *quadratic equation* is an equation that is usually written as $ax^2 + bx + c = 0$ where *b*, *c*, or both *b* and *c* may be equal to 0, but *a* is *never* equal to 0. The solutions of quadratic equations can be two real numbers, one real number, or no real number at all. (*Real numbers* are all the whole numbers, fractions, negatives and positives, radicals, and irrational decimals. Imaginary numbers are something else again!)

When solving quadratic equations, the most useful form for the equation is one in which the equation is equal to 0 and the terms are written in decreasing powers of the variable. When set equal to zero, you can factor for a solution or use the quadratic formula. An exception to this rule, though, is when you have just a squared term and a number, and you want to use the *square root rule.* (Say *that* three times quickly.) I go into further detail about all these procedures in this chapter.

For now, strap on your boots and get ready to answer quadratic equations. This chapter offers you plenty of chances to get your feet wet.

Using the Square Root Rule

REMEMBER

You can use the *square root rule* when a quadratic equation has just the squared term and a number — no term with the variable to the first degree. This rule says that if $x^2 = k$, then $x = \pm\sqrt{k}$, as long as k isn't a negative number. The tricky part here — what most people trip on — is in remembering to use the "plus or minus" symbol so that both solutions are identified.

EXAMPLE

Q. Use the square root rule to solve: $7x^2 = 28$.

A. $\boldsymbol{x = \pm 2}$ **(which is the same as $\boldsymbol{x = 2}$ or $\boldsymbol{x = -2}$).** First divide each side by 7 to get $x^2 = 4$. Then find the square root of 4 to get the answer.

Q. Use the square root rule to solve: $3y^2 - 75 = 0$.

A. $\boldsymbol{y = \pm 5}$ **(which is the same as $\boldsymbol{y = 5}$ or $\boldsymbol{y = -5}$).** Before using the square root rule, first add 75 to each side to get the number on the right. Then divide each side by 3 to get $y^2 = 25$. Finally, find the square root of 25 to get the answer.

1 Use the square root rule to solve: $x^2 = 9$.

2 Use the square root rule to solve: $5y^2 = 80$.

3 Use the square root rule to solve: $z^2 - 100 = 0$.

4 Use the square root rule to solve: $20w^2 - 125 = 0$.

Solving by Factoring

The quickest and most efficient way of solving a quadratic equation that has three terms is to factor it (if it can be factored) and then use the *multiplication property of zero* (MPZ) to solve for the solutions. The MPZ says that, if the product $ab = 0$, then either a or b must be equal to 0. You use this property on the factored form of a quadratic equation to set the two linear factors equal to 0 and solve those simple equations for the value of the variable.

REMEMBER

Sometimes when you factor the quadratic, you get two identical factors. That's because the quadratic was a perfect square. You still get two answers, but they're the same number, which is called a *double root*.

EXAMPLE

Q. Solve for x by factoring: $18x^2 + 21x - 60 = 0$.

A. $\boldsymbol{x = 4/3}$ **or** $\boldsymbol{x = -5/2}$. The factored form of the original equation is $3(6x^2 + 7x - 20) = 3(3x - 4)(2x + 5) = 0$. When the product of three factors is zero, then one or more of the factors must be equal to zero. The first factor here, the 3, is certainly not equal to zero, so you move on to the next factor, $3x - 4$, and set it equal to zero to solve for the solution. You use the same process with the last factor, $2x + 5$. Only the variables can take on a value to make the factor equal to 0. That's why, when you set the last two factors equal to 0, you solve those equations and get the answers.

$$3x - 4 = 0 \quad \text{or} \quad 2x + 5 = 0$$
$$3x = 4 \qquad 2x = -5$$
$$x = \frac{4}{3} \qquad x = \frac{-5}{2}$$

Q. Solve for x by factoring: $4x^2 - 48x = 0$.

A. $\boldsymbol{x = 0}$ **or** $\boldsymbol{x = 12}$. You don't need a constant term (it's technically 0 in this case) in order for this process to work. Just factor out the GCF $4x$ from each term in the equation.

$$4x(x - 12) = 0$$

The two factors, set equal to 0 give you

$$4x = 0 \quad \text{or} \quad x - 12 = 0$$
$$x = \frac{0}{4} = 0 \qquad x = 12$$

5 Solve for x by factoring: $x^2 - 2x - 15 = 0$.

6 Solve for x by factoring: $3x^2 - 25x + 28 = 0$.

7 Solve for y by factoring: $4y^2 - 9 = 0$.

8 Solve for z by factoring: $z^2 + 64 = 16z$.

9 Solve for y by factoring: $y^2 + 21y = 0$.

10 Solve for x by factoring: $12x^2 = 24x$.

11 Solve for z by factoring: $15z^2 + 14z = 0$.

12 Solve for y by factoring: $\frac{1}{4}y^2 = \frac{2}{3}y$.

Using the Quadratic Formula

You can use the quadratic formula to solve a quadratic equation, regardless whether the terms can be factored. Factoring and using the MPZ is almost always easier, but you'll find the quadratic formula most useful when the equation can't be factored or the equation has numbers too large to factor in your head.

REMEMBER

If a quadratic equation appears in its standard form, $ax^2 + bx + c = 0$, then the quadratic formula gives you the solutions to that equation. You can find the solutions by using the following formula:

$$x = \frac{-b \pm \sqrt{b^2 - 4ac}}{2a}$$

If you use the quadratic formula on a quadratic that can be factored, then the number under the *radical* (the square root symbol) always turns out to be a perfect square, and no radical appears in the solution. If the equation isn't factorable, then your answer — a perfectly good one, mind you — has radicals in it. If the number under the radical turns out to be negative, then that equation doesn't have a real solution. If you want to know more about this real versus imaginary situation, look at the "Dealing with Impossible Answers" section later in this chapter.

EXAMPLE

Q. Use the quadratic formula to solve: $2x^2 + 11x - 21 = 0$ with $a = 2$, $b = 11$, and $c = -21$.

A. $x = 3/2$ **or** $x = -7$. Fill in the formula and simplify to get

$$x = \frac{-11 \pm \sqrt{11^2 - 4(2)(-21)}}{2(2)}$$
$$= \frac{-11 \pm \sqrt{121 - (-168)}}{4}$$
$$= \frac{-11 \pm \sqrt{289}}{4} = \frac{-11 \pm 17}{4}$$
$$= \frac{-11 + 17}{4} \quad \text{or} \quad \frac{-11 - 17}{4}$$
$$= \frac{6}{4} \quad \text{or} \quad \frac{-28}{4}$$
$$= \frac{3}{2} \quad \text{or} \quad -7$$

Because the 289 under the radical is a perfect square, you could have solved this problem by factoring.

Q. Use the quadratic formula to solve: $x^2 - 8x + 2 = 0$.

A. $x = 4 + \sqrt{14}$ **or** $x = 4 - \sqrt{14}$. The quadratic equation is already in the standard form, with $a = 1$, $b = -8$, and $c = 2$. Fill in the formula with those values and simplify:

$$x = \frac{-(-8) \pm \sqrt{(-8)^2 - 4(1)(2)}}{2(1)}$$
$$= \frac{8 \pm \sqrt{64 - (8)}}{2}$$
$$= \frac{8 \pm \sqrt{56}}{2} = \frac{8 \pm \sqrt{4}\sqrt{14}}{2}$$
$$= \frac{8 \pm 2\sqrt{14}}{2} = \frac{{}^{4}\not{8} \pm \not{2}\sqrt{14}}{\not{2}}$$
$$= 4 \pm \sqrt{14}$$

13 Use the quadratic formula to solve: $x^2 - 5x - 6 = 0$.

14 Use the quadratic formula to solve: $6x^2 + 13x = -6$.

15 Use the quadratic formula to solve: $x^2 - 4x - 6 = 0$.

16 Use the quadratic formula to solve: $2x^2 + 9x = 2$.

17 Use the quadratic formula to solve: $3x^2 - 5x = 0$. ***Hint:*** When there's no constant term, let $c = 0$.

18 Use the quadratic formula to solve: $4x^2 - 25 = 0$. ***Hint:*** Let $b = 0$.

Completing the Square

An alternative to using factoring or the quadratic formula to solve a quadratic equation is a method called *completing the square*. Admittedly, this is seldom the method of choice, but the technique is used when dealing with conic sections in higher mathematics courses. I include it here to give you some practice using it on some nice quadratic equations.

Here are the basic steps you follow to complete the square:

1. **Rewrite the quadratic equation in the form** $ax^2 + bx = -c$.
2. **Divide every term by** ***a*** **(if** ***a*** **isn't equal to 1).**
3. **Add** $\left(\frac{b}{2a}\right)^2$ **to each side of the equation.**

   This is essentially just half the *x* term's newest coefficient squared.
4. **Factor on the left (it's now a perfect square trinomial).**
5. **Take the square root of each side of the equation.**
6. **Solve for** ***x*****.**

EXAMPLE

Q. Use completing the square to solve $x^2 - 4x - 5 = 0$.

A. $x = 5$, $x = -1$. Working through the steps:

1. **Rewrite the equation as** $x^2 - 4x = 5$.
2. **No division is necessary.**
3. **Add** $\left(\frac{-4}{2}\right)^2 = 4$ **to each side to get** $x^2 - 4x + 4 = 5 + 4 = 9$.
4. **Factor on the left,** $(x-2)^2 = 9$.
5. **Find the square root of each side:**

   $$\sqrt{(x-2)^2} = \pm\sqrt{9}$$
   $$x - 2 = \pm 3$$

   You only need use the ± in front of the radical on the right. Technically, it belongs on both sides, but because you end up with two pairs of the same answer, just one ± is enough.
6. **Solve for** ***x*** **by adding 2 to each side of the equation:** $x = 2 \pm 3$**, giving you** $x = 5$ **or** $x = -1$.

Q. Use completing the square to solve $2x^2 + 10x - 3 = 0$.

A. $x = \frac{-5 \pm \sqrt{31}}{2}$. Working through the steps:

1. **Rewrite the equation as** $2x^2 + 10x = 3$.
2. **Divide each term by 2:** $x^2 + 5x = \frac{3}{2}$.
3. **Add** $\left(\frac{5}{2}\right)^2 = \frac{25}{4}$ **to each side to get** $x^2 + 5x + \frac{25}{4} = \frac{3}{2} + \frac{25}{4} = \frac{31}{4}$.
4. **Factor on the left,** $\left(x + \frac{5}{2}\right)^2 = \frac{31}{4}$.

   Notice that the constant in the binomial is the number that got squared in Step 3.
5. **Find the square root of each side:**

   $$\sqrt{\left(x+\frac{5}{2}\right)^2} = \pm\sqrt{\frac{31}{4}}$$
   $$x + \frac{5}{2} = \pm\sqrt{\frac{31}{2}}$$
6. **Solve for** ***x*****:**

   $$x = -\frac{5}{2} \pm \frac{\sqrt{31}}{2}$$
   $$= \frac{-5 \pm \sqrt{31}}{2}$$

19 Use completing the square to solve for x in $3x^2+11x-4=0$.

20 Use completing the square to solve for x in $x^2+6x+2=0$.

Dealing with Impossible Answers

REMEMBER

The square root of a negative number doesn't exist — as far as real numbers are concerned. When you encounter the square root of a negative number as you're solving quadratic equations, it means that the equation doesn't have a real solution.

You can report your answers when you end up with negatives under the radical by using *imaginary numbers* (or numbers that are indicated with an *i* to show that they aren't real). With imaginary numbers, you let $\sqrt{-1}=i$. Then you can simplify the radical using the imaginary number as a factor. Don't worry if you're slightly confused about imaginary numbers. This concept is more advanced than most of the algebra problems you'll encounter in this book and during Algebra I. For now, just remember that using *i* allows you to make answers more complete; imaginary numbers let you finish the problem.

EXAMPLE

Q. Rewrite $\sqrt{-9}$, using imaginary numbers.

A. $3i$. Split up the value under the radical into two factors:

$$\sqrt{-9} = \sqrt{(-1)9} = \sqrt{-1}\sqrt{9}$$
$$= i \cdot 3 \text{ or } 3i$$

Q. Rewrite $-6 \pm \sqrt{-48}$, using imaginary numbers.

A. $-6 \pm 4i\sqrt{3}$. You can write the value under the radical as the product of three factors:

$$\begin{aligned}-6 \pm \sqrt{-48} &= -6 \pm \sqrt{-1}\sqrt{16}\sqrt{3}\\ &= -6 \pm i \cdot 4\sqrt{3}\\ &= -6 \pm 4i\sqrt{3}\end{aligned}$$

The last two lines of the equation look almost identical. Putting the i after the 4 is just a mathematical convention, a preferred format. It doesn't change the value at all.

21 Rewrite $\sqrt{-4}$ as a product with a factor of i.

22 Rewrite $6 \pm \sqrt{-96}$ as an expression with a factor of i.

Answers to Problems on Solving Quadratic Equations

This section provides the answers (in bold) to the practice problems in this chapter.

1. Use the square root rule to solve: $x^2 = 9$. The answer is $\mathbf{x = \pm 3}$.

2. Use the square root rule to solve: $5y^2 = 80$. The answer is $\mathbf{y = \pm 4}$.

$$5y^2 = 80$$
$$\frac{5y^2}{5} = \frac{80}{5}$$
$$y^2 = 16$$
$$y = \pm 4$$

3. Use the square root rule to solve: $z^2 - 100 = 0$. The answer is $\mathbf{z = \pm 10}$.

$$z^2 - 100 = 0$$
$$\underline{\quad +100 \quad +100}$$
$$z^2 = 100$$
$$z = \pm 10$$

4. Use the square root rule to solve: $20w^2 - 125 = 0$. The answer is $\mathbf{w = \pm \frac{5}{2}}$.

$$20w^2 - 125 = 0$$
$$\underline{\quad +125 \quad +125}$$
$$20w^2 = 125$$
$$\frac{20w^2}{20} = \frac{125}{20}$$
$$w^2 = \frac{25}{4}$$
$$w = \pm \frac{5}{2}$$

5. Solve for x by factoring: $2x^2 - 2x - 15 = 0$. The answer is $\mathbf{x = 5}$ **or** $\mathbf{x = -3}$.

$$x^2 - 2x - 15 = 0$$
$$(x-5)(x+3) = 0$$
$$x - 5 = 0,\ x = 5$$
$$\text{or}\ x + 3 = 0,\ x = -3$$

6. Solve for x by factoring: $3x^2 - 25x + 28 = 0$. The answer is $\boldsymbol{x = \frac{4}{3}}$ **or** $\boldsymbol{x = 7}$.

$$3x^2 - 25x + 28 = 0$$
$$(3x - 4)(x - 7) = 0$$
$$3x - 4 = 0,\ 3x = 4,\ x = \frac{4}{3}$$
$$\text{or } x - 7 = 0,\ x = 7$$
$$x = \frac{4}{3}, 7$$

7. Solve for y by factoring: $4y^2 - 9 = 0$. The answer is $\boldsymbol{y = \pm\frac{3}{2}}$.

$$4y^2 - 9 = 0$$
$$(2y + 3)(2y - 3) = 0$$
$$2y + 3 = 0, 2y = -3, y = -\frac{3}{2}$$
$$\text{or } 2y - 3 = 0, 2y = 3, y = \frac{3}{2}$$
$$y = \pm\frac{3}{2}$$

You could also have used the square root rule on this problem.

8. Solve for z by factoring: $z^2 + 64 = 16z$. The answer is $\boldsymbol{z = 8}$ **or** $\boldsymbol{z = 8}$**, which is a double root.**

$$z^2 + 64 = 16z$$
$$z^2 - 16z + 64 = 0$$
$$(z - 8)(z - 8) = 0$$
$$z - 8 = 0, z = 8$$
$$\text{or } z - 8 = 0, z = 8$$

9. Solve for y by factoring: $y^2 + 21y = 0$. The answer is $\boldsymbol{y = 0}$ **or** $\boldsymbol{y = -21}$.

$$y^2 + 21y = 0$$
$$y(y + 21) = 0$$
$$y = 0$$
$$\text{or } y + 21 = 0, y = -21$$
$$y = 0,\ -21$$

10. Solve for x by factoring: $12x^2 = 24x$. The answer is $\boldsymbol{x = 0}$ **or** $\boldsymbol{x = 2}$.

$$12x^2 = 24x$$
$$12x^2 - 24x = 0$$
$$12x(x - 2) = 0$$
$$12x = 0, x = 0$$
$$\text{or } x - 2 = 0, x = 2$$
$$x = 0, 2$$

11 Solve for z by factoring: $15z^2 + 14z = 0$. The answer is $\mathbf{z = 0}$ **or** $\mathbf{z = -\frac{14}{15}}$.

$$15z^2 + 14z = 0$$
$$z(15z + 14) = 0$$
$$z = 0$$
$$\text{or } 15z + 14 = 0,\ 15z = 14,\ z = -\frac{14}{15}$$
$$z = 0, -\frac{14}{15}$$

12 Solve for y by factoring: $\frac{1}{4}y^2 = \frac{2}{3}y$. The answer is $\mathbf{y = 0}$ **or** $\mathbf{y = \frac{8}{3}}$.

$\frac{1}{4}y^2 = \frac{2}{3}y$ has 12 as a common denominator, so

$$12\left(\frac{1}{4}y^2\right) = 12\left(\frac{2}{3}y\right)$$
$$3y^2 = 8y$$
$$3y^2 - 8y = 0$$
$$y(3y - 8) = 0$$
$$y = 0 \quad \text{or} \quad 3y - 8 = 0$$
$$3y = 8$$
$$y = \frac{8}{3}$$

13 Use the quadratic formula to solve: $x^2 - 5x - 6 = 0$. The answer is $\mathbf{x = 6}$ **or** $\mathbf{x = -1}$.

$$x^2 - 5x - 6 = 0$$
$$x = \frac{-(-5) \pm \sqrt{(-5)^2 - 4(1)(-6)}}{2(1)} = \frac{5 \pm \sqrt{25 + 24}}{2}$$
$$x = \frac{5 \pm \sqrt{49}}{2} = \frac{5 \pm 7}{2}$$
$$x = \frac{5 + 7}{2} = \frac{12}{2} = 6 \quad \text{or} \quad x = \frac{5 - 7}{2} = \frac{-2}{2} = -1$$
$$x = 6, -1$$

14 Use the quadratic formula to solve: $6x^2 + 13x = -6$. The answer is $\mathbf{x = -\frac{2}{3}}$ **or** $\mathbf{x = -\frac{3}{2}}$.

First, rewrite in the standard form:

$$6x^2 + 13x + 6 = 0$$
$$x = \frac{-(13) \pm \sqrt{(13)^2 - 4(6)(6)}}{2(6)} = \frac{-13 \pm \sqrt{169 - 144}}{12}$$
$$= \frac{-13 \pm \sqrt{25}}{12} = \frac{-13 \pm 5}{12}$$
$$x = \frac{-13 + 5}{12} = \frac{-8}{12} = -\frac{2}{3} \quad \text{or} \quad x = \frac{-13 - 5}{12} = \frac{-18}{12} = -\frac{3}{2}$$

(15) Use the quadratic formula to solve: $x^2 - 4x - 6 = 0$. The answer is $\mathbf{2 \pm \sqrt{10}}$.

$x^2 - 4x - 6 = 0$

$$x = \frac{-(-4) \pm \sqrt{(-4)^2 - 4(1)(-6)}}{2(1)} = \frac{4 \pm \sqrt{16+24}}{2}$$

$$x = \frac{4 \pm \sqrt{40}}{2} = \frac{4 \pm 2\sqrt{10}}{2} = 2 \pm \sqrt{10}$$

(16) Use the quadratic formula to solve $2x^2 + 9x = 2$. The answer is $\mathbf{\frac{-9 \pm \sqrt{97}}{4}}$. First rewrite the equation in standard form.

$2x^2 + 9x - 2 = 0$

$$x = \frac{-(9) \pm \sqrt{(9)^2 - 4(2)(-2)}}{2(2)} = \frac{-9 \pm \sqrt{81+16}}{4} = \frac{-9 \pm \sqrt{97}}{4}$$

(17) Use the quadratic formula to solve: $3x^2 - 5x = 0$. The answer is $\boldsymbol{x = \frac{5}{3}}$ **or** $\boldsymbol{x = 0}$.

$3x^2 - 5x = 0$

$$x = \frac{-(-5) \pm \sqrt{(-5)^2 - 4(3)(0)}}{2(3)} = \frac{5 \pm \sqrt{25}}{6} = \frac{5 \pm 5}{6}$$

$$x = \frac{5+5}{6} = \frac{10}{6} = \frac{5}{3} \text{ or } x = \frac{5-5}{6} = \frac{0}{6} = 0$$

$$x = \frac{5}{3}, 0$$

Note: **You could have factored the quadratic:** $x(3x-5) = 3x^2 - 5x = 0$.

(18) Use the quadratic formula to solve: $4x^2 - 25 = 0$. The answer is $\boldsymbol{x = \pm\frac{5}{2}}$.

$4x^2 - 25 = 0$

$$x = \frac{-(0) \pm \sqrt{(0)^2 - 4(4)(-25)}}{2(4)} = \frac{\pm\sqrt{16 \cdot 25}}{8} = \pm\frac{4 \cdot 5}{8} = \pm\frac{5}{2}$$

(19) Use completing the square to solve for x in $3x^2 + 11x - 4 = 0$. The answer is $\boldsymbol{x = 1/3}$ **or** $\boldsymbol{x = -4}$.

$$3x^2 + 11x = 4$$

$$x^2 + \frac{11}{3}x = \frac{4}{3}$$

$$x^2 + \frac{11}{3}x + \left(\frac{11}{6}\right)^2 = \frac{4}{3} + \left(\frac{11}{6}\right)^2$$

$$x^2 + \frac{11}{3}x + \frac{121}{36} = \frac{4}{3} + \frac{121}{36} = \frac{169}{36}$$

$$\left(x + \frac{11}{6}\right)^2 = \frac{169}{36}$$

$$x + \frac{11}{6} = \pm\sqrt{\frac{169}{36}} = \pm\frac{13}{6}$$

$$x = -\frac{11}{6} \pm \frac{13}{6} = \frac{-11 \pm 13}{6}$$

$$x = \frac{2}{6} = \frac{1}{3} \text{ or } x = \frac{-24}{6} = -4$$

20 Use completing the square to solve for x in $x^2+6x+2=0$. The answer is $\mathbf{x=-3+\sqrt{7}}$ **or** $\mathbf{x=-3-\sqrt{7}}$.

$$\begin{aligned}
x^2+6x&=-2\\
x^2+6x+\left(\frac{6}{2}\right)^2&=-2+\left(\frac{6}{2}\right)^2\\
x^2+6x+9&=-2+9=7\\
(x+3)^2&=7\\
\sqrt{(x+3)^2}&=\pm\sqrt{7}\\
x+3&=\pm\sqrt{7}\\
x&=-3\pm\sqrt{7}
\end{aligned}$$

21 Rewrite $\sqrt{-4}$ as a product with a factor of i. The answer is $\mathbf{2i}$.

$$\sqrt{-4}=\sqrt{(-1)(4)}=\sqrt{-1}\sqrt{4}=i(2)=2i$$

22 Rewrite $6\pm\sqrt{-96}$ as an expression with a factor of i. The answer is $\mathbf{6\pm 4i\sqrt{6}}$.

$$6\pm\sqrt{-96}=6\pm\sqrt{(-1)(16)(6)}=6\pm\sqrt{-1}(4)\sqrt{6}=6\pm i\left(4\sqrt{6}\right)=6\pm 4i\sqrt{6}$$

- Making educated guesses about solutions
- Finding solutions by factoring
- Recognizing patterns to make factoring and solutions easier

Chapter 14

Yielding to Higher Powers

Polynomial equations are equations involving the sum (or difference) of terms where the variables have exponents that are whole numbers. (Trinomials are special types of polynomials; I thoroughly cover solving trinomial equations in Chapter 13.) Solving polynomial equations involves setting polynomials equal to zero and then figuring out which values create true statements. You can use the solutions to polynomial equations to solve problems in calculus, algebra, and other mathematical areas. When you're graphing polynomials, the solutions show you where the curve intersects with the *x*-axis — either crossing it or just touching it at that point. Rather than just taking some wild guesses as to what the solutions might be, you can utilize some of the available techniques that help you make more reasonable guesses as to what the solutions are and then confirm your guess with good algebra.

This chapter provides several examples of these techniques and gives you ample opportunities to try them out.

Determining How Many Possible Roots

Mathematician René Descartes came up with his *rule of signs*, which allows you to determine the number of real roots that a polynomial equation may have. The *real roots* are the *real* numbers that make the equation a true statement. This rule doesn't tell you for sure how many roots there are; it just tells you the maximum number there *could* be. (If this number is less than the maximum number of roots, then it's less than that by two or four or six, and so on.)

To use Descartes's rule, first write the polynomial in decreasing powers of the variable; then do the following:

- To determine the maximum possible *positive roots,* count how many times the signs of the terms change from positive to negative or vice versa.
- To determine the possible number of *negative roots,* replace all the *x*'s with negative *x*'s. Simplify the terms and count how many times the signs change.

EXAMPLE

Q. How many possible real roots are there in $3x^5+5x^4-x^3+2x^2-x+4=0$?

A. **At most four positive and one negative.** The sign changes from positive to negative to positive to negative to positive. That's four changes in sign, so you have a maximum of four positive real roots. If it doesn't have four, then it could have two. If it doesn't have two, then it has none. You step down by twos. Now count the number of possible negative real roots in that same polynomial by replacing all the *x*'s with negative *x*'s and counting the number of sign changes:

$$3(-x)^5+5(-x)^4-(-x)^3+2(-x)^2-(-x)$$
$$+4=-3x^5+5x^4+x^3+2x^2+x+4=0$$

This version only has one sign change — from negative to positive, which means that it has one negative real root. You can't go down by two from that, so one negative real root is the only choice.

Q. How many possible real roots are there in $6x^4+5x^3+3x^2+2x-1=0$?

A. **One positive and three or one negative.** Count the number of sign changes in the original equation. It has only one sign change, so there's exactly one positive real root. Change the function by replacing all the *x*'s with negative *x*'s and count the changes in sign:

$$6(-x)^4+5(-x)^3+3(-x)^2+2(-x)-1$$
$$=6x^4-5x^3+3x^2-2x-1=0$$

It has three sign changes, which means that it has three or one negative real roots.

1. Count the number of possible positive and negative real roots in $x^5 - x^3 + 8x^2 - 8 = 0$.

2. Count the number of possible positive and negative real roots in $8x^5 - 25x^4 - x^2 + 25 = 0$.

Applying the Rational Root Theorem

In the preceding section, you discover that Descartes's rule of signs counts the possible number of *real* roots. Now you see a rule that helps you figure out just what those real roots are, when they're rational numbers.

REMEMBER

Real numbers can be either rational or irrational. *Rational* numbers are numbers that have fractional equivalents; that is, they can be written as fractions. *Irrational* numbers can't be written as fractions; they have decimal values that never repeat and never end.

The *rational root theorem* says that, if you have a polynomial equation written in the form $a_n x^n + a_{n-1}x^{n-1} + a_{n-2}x^{n-2} + \ldots + a_1 x^1 + a_0 = 0$, then you can make a list of all the possible *rational* roots by looking at the first term and the last term. Any rational roots must be able to be written as a fraction with a factor of the *constant* (the last term or a_0) in the numerator of the fraction and a factor of the lead coefficient (a_n) in the denominator.

For example, in the equation $4x^4 - 3x^3 + 5x^2 + 9x - 3 = 0$, the factors of the constant are $+3, -3, +1, -1$ and the factors of the coefficient of the first term are $+4, -4, +2, -2, +1, -1$. The following list includes all the ways that you can create a fraction with a factor of the constant in the numerator and a factor of the lead coefficient in the denominator:

$$\pm 3/4, \pm 3/2, \pm\frac{3}{1}, \pm\frac{1}{4}, \pm\frac{1}{2}, \pm\frac{1}{1}$$

Of course, the two fractions with 1 in the denominator are actually whole numbers, when you simplify. This abbreviated listing represents all the possible ways to combine +3 and –3 and +4 and –4, and so on, to create all the possible fractions. It's just quicker to use the ± notation than to write out every single possibility.

Although this new list has 12 candidates for solutions to the equation, it's really relatively short when you're trying to run through all the possibilities. Many of the polynomials start out with a 1 as the coefficient of the first term, which is great news when you're writing your list because that means the only rational numbers you're considering are whole numbers — the denominators are 1.

EXAMPLE

Q. Determine all the possible rational solutions of this equation: $2x^6 - 4x^3 + 5x^2 + x - 30 = 0$.

A. $\pm 30, \pm 15, \pm 10, \pm 6, \pm 5, \pm 3, \pm 2, \pm 1, \pm \frac{15}{2}, \pm \frac{5}{2}, \pm \frac{3}{2}, \pm \frac{1}{2}$

The factors of the constant are $\pm 30, \pm 15, \pm 10, \pm 6, \pm 5, \pm 3, \pm 2, \pm 1$ and the factors of the lead coefficient are $\pm 2, \pm 1$. You create the list of all the numbers that could be considered for roots of the equation by dividing each of the factors of the constant by the factors of the lead coefficient. The numbers shown in the answer don't include repeats or unfactored fractions.

Q. Determine all the possible rational solutions of the equation: $x^6 - x^3 + x^2 + x - 1 = 0$.

A. ± 1

Yes, even though Descartes tells you that there could be as many as three positive and one negative real root, the only possible rational roots are $+1$ or -1.

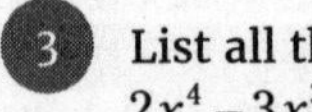

3 List all the possible rational roots of $2x^4 - 3x^3 - 54x + 81 = 0$.

4 List all the possible rational roots of $8x^5 - 25x^3 - x^2 + 25 = 0$.

Using the Factor/Root Theorem

Algebra has a theorem that says if the binomial $x - c$ is a factor of a polynomial (it divides the polynomial evenly, with no remainder), then c is a root or solution of the polynomial. You may say, "Okay, so what?" Well, this property means that you can use the very efficient method of synthetic division to solve for solutions of polynomial equations.

Use synthetic division to try out all those rational numbers that you listed as possibilities for roots of a polynomial. (See Chapter 8 for more on synthetic division.) If $x - c$ is a factor (and c is a root), then you won't have a remainder (the remainder is 0) when you perform synthetic division.

EXAMPLE

Q. Check to see whether the number 2 is a root of the following polynomial:

$x^6 - 6x^5 + 8x^4 + 2x^3 - x^2 - 7x + 2 = 0$

A. **Yes, it's a root**. Use the 2 and the coefficients of the polynomial in a synthetic division problem:

$$\begin{array}{r|rrrrrrr} 2 & 1 & -6 & 8 & 2 & -1 & -7 & 2 \\ & & 2 & -8 & 0 & 4 & 6 & -2 \\ \hline & 1 & -4 & 0 & 2 & 3 & -1 & 0 \end{array}$$

The remainder is 0, so $x - 2$ is a factor, and 2 is a root or solution. The quotient of this division is $x^5 - 4x^4 + 2x^2 + 3x - 1$, which you write using the coefficients along the bottom. When writing the factorization, make sure you start with a variable that's one degree lower than the one that was divided into. This new polynomial ends in a -1 and has a lead coefficient of 1, so the only possible solutions when setting the quotient equal to zero are 1 or -1.

Q. Check to see whether 1 or -1 is a solution of the new equation.

A. **Neither is a solution**. First, try 1:

$$\begin{array}{r|rrrrrr} 1 & 1 & -4 & 0 & 2 & 3 & -1 \\ & & 1 & -3 & -3 & -1 & 2 \\ \hline & 1 & -3 & -3 & -1 & 2 & 1 \end{array}$$

That 1 didn't work; the remainder isn't 0. Now, try -1:

$$\begin{array}{r|rrrrrr} -1 & 1 & -4 & 0 & 2 & 3 & -1 \\ & & -1 & 5 & -5 & 3 & -6 \\ \hline & 1 & -5 & 5 & -3 & 6 & -7 \end{array}$$

It doesn't work, either. The only rational solution of the original equation is 2.

5 Check to see whether -3 is a root of $x^4 - 10x^2 + 9 = 0$.

6 Check to see whether $3/2$ is a root of $2x^4 - 3x^3 - 54x + 81 = 0$.

Solving by Factoring

When determining the solutions for polynomials, many techniques are available to help you determine what those solutions are — if any solutions exist. One method that is usually the quickest, though, is factoring and using the *multiplication property of zero (MPZ)*. (Check out Chapter 13 for more ways to use the MPZ.) Not all polynomials lend themselves to factoring, but when they do, using this method is to your advantage. And don't forget to try synthetic division and the factor theorem if you think you have a potential solution.

EXAMPLE

Q. Find the real solutions of $x^4 - 81 = 0$.

A. $\boldsymbol{x = 3}$ **or** $\boldsymbol{x = -3}$. Do you recognize that the two numbers are both perfect squares? Factoring the binomial into the sum and difference of the roots, you get $(x^2 - 9)(x^2 + 9) = 0$. The first factor of this factored form is also the difference of perfect squares. Factoring again, you get $(x-3)(x+3)(x^2+9) = 0$. Now, to use the MPZ, set the first factor equal to 0 to get $x - 3 = 0$, $x = 3$. Set the second factor equal to 0, $x + 3 = 0$, $x = -3$. The last factor doesn't cooperate: $x^2 + 9 = 0$, $x^2 = -9$. A perfect square can't be negative, so this factor has no solution. If you go back to the original equation and use Descartes's rule of signs (see "Determining How Many Possible Roots" earlier in this chapter), you see that it has one real positive root and one real negative root, which just confirms that prediction.

Q. Find the real solutions of $x^4 + 2x^3 - 125x - 250 = 0$.

A. $\boldsymbol{x = -2}$ **or** $\boldsymbol{x = 5}$. You can factor by grouping to get $x^3(x+2) - 125(x+2) = (x+2)(x^3 - 125) = 0$. The second factor is the difference of perfect cubes, which factors into $(x+2)(x-5)(x^2 + 5x + 25) = 0$. The trinomial factor in this factorization never factors any more, so only the first two factors yield solutions: $x + 2 = 0$, $x = -2$ and $x - 5 = 0$, $x = 5$.

But suppose that, instead of factoring, you make a guess (after determining with Descartes's rule of signs that only one positive real root and three or one negative real roots are possible). You go with a negative guess (go with the odds). How about trying –2?

$$\begin{array}{r|rrrrr} -2 & 1 & 2 & 0 & -125 & -250 \\ & & -2 & 0 & 0 & 250 \\ \hline & 1 & 0 & 0 & -125 & 0 \end{array}$$

The –2 is a solution (no surprise there), and the factored form is $(x+2)(x^3 - 125) = 0$. The difference of cubes gives you that same solution of $x = 5$. You can use both synthetic division and factoring in the same problem!

7 Solve by factoring: $x^4 - 16 = 0$.

8 Solve by factoring: $x^4 - 3x^3 + 3x^2 - x = 0$.

9 Solve by factoring: $x^3 + 5x^2 - 16x - 80 = 0$.

10 Solve by factoring: $x^6 - 9x^4 - 16x^2 + 144 = 0$.

Solving Powers That Are Quadratic-Like

A special classification of equations, called *quadratic-like*, lends itself to solving by factoring using unFOIL. These equations have three terms:

- A variable term with a particular power
- Another variable with a power half that of the first term
- A constant

A way to generalize these characteristics is with the equation $ax^{2n} + bx^n + c = 0$. In Chapter 11, you find details on factoring these quadratic-like trinomials, which then allows you to solve the related equations.

EXAMPLE

Q. Solve for $x : x^8 - 17x^4 + 16 = 0$.

A. $\mathbf{x = 1}$ **or** $\mathbf{x = -1}$ **or** $\mathbf{x = 2}$ **or** $\mathbf{x = -2}$

1. **Factor the expression:**

   $(x^4 - 1)(x^4 - 16) = 0$.

2. **Factor each of the binomials.**

   You can factor $x^4 - 1$ into $(x^2 - 1)(x^2 + 1)$. You can factor $x^4 - 16$ into $(x^2 - 4)(x^2 + 4)$.

3. **Factor the binomials that are still the difference of perfect squares.**

   $(x^2 - 1)(x^2 + 1) = (x - 1)(x + 1)(x^2 + 1)$
   $x^4 - 16 = (x - 2)(x + 2)(x^2 + 4)$

4. **Set the complete factorization equal to 0.**

   $(x - 1)(x + 1)(x^2 + 1)(x - 2)(x + 2)$
   $(x^2 + 4) = 0$

   The four real solutions of the original equation are $x = 1,\ -1,\ 2$, and -2. The two factors that are the sums of perfect squares don't provide any real roots.

Q. Solve for y: $y^{2/3} + 5y^{1/3} + 6 = 0$.

A. $\mathbf{y = -8}$ **or** $\mathbf{y = -27}$. This example involves fractional exponents. Notice that the power on the first variable is twice that of the second.

1. **Factor the expression.**

   $(y^{1/3} + 2)(y^{1/3} + 3) = 0$

2. **Take the first factor and set it equal to 0.**

   $y^{1/3} + 2 = 0$

3. **Add -2 to each side and cube each side of the equation.**

   $$y^{1/3} = -2$$
   $$\left(y^{1/3}\right)^3 = (-2)^3$$
   $$y = -8$$

4. **Follow the same steps with the other factor.**

   $$\left(y^{1/3}\right)^3 = (-3)^3$$
   $$y = -27$$

11 **Solve the equation:** $x^4 - 13x^2 + 36 = 0$.

12 **Solve the equation:** $x^{10} - 31x^5 - 32 = 0$.

13 **Solve the equation:** $y^{4/3} - 17y^{2/3} + 16 = 0$.

14 **Solve the equation:** $z^{-2} + z^{-1} - 12 = 0$.

Answers to Problems on Solving Higher Power Equations

This section provides the answers (in bold) to the practice problems in this chapter.

1. Count the number of possible positive and negative real roots in $x^5 - x^3 + 8x^2 - 8 = 0$. The answer: **Three or one positive roots and two or no negative roots.** The original equation has three sign changes, so there are three or one possible positive real roots. Then substituting $-x$ for each x, you get $(-x)^5 - (-x)^3 + 8(-x)^2 - 8 = -x^5 + x^3 + 8x^2 - 8$, and you have two sign changes, meaning there are two negative roots or none at all.

2. Count the number of possible positive and negative real roots in $8x^5 - 25x^4 - x^2 + 25 = 0$. The answer: **Two or no positive roots and one negative root.** The original equation has two sign changes (from positive to negative to positive), so there are two or no positive roots. Substituting $-x$ for each x, you get $8(-x)^5 - 25(-x)^4 - (-x)^2 + 25 = -8x^5 - 25x^4 - x^2 + 25$, which has one sign change and one negative root.

3. List all the possible rational roots of $2x^4 - 3x^3 - 54x + 81 = 0$. The answer: **The possible rational roots are** $\pm\mathbf{81}, \pm\mathbf{27}, \pm\mathbf{9}, \pm\mathbf{3}, \pm\mathbf{1}, \pm\frac{\mathbf{81}}{\mathbf{2}}, \pm\frac{\mathbf{27}}{\mathbf{2}}, \pm\frac{\mathbf{9}}{\mathbf{2}}, \pm\frac{\mathbf{3}}{\mathbf{2}}, \pm\frac{\mathbf{1}}{\mathbf{2}}$. The constant term is 81. Its factors are $\pm 81, \pm 27, \pm 9, \pm 3, \pm 1$. The lead coefficient is 2 with factors $\pm 2, \pm 1$.

4. List all the possible rational roots of $8x^5 - 25x^3 - x^2 + 25 = 0$. **The possible rational roots are** $\pm\mathbf{25}, \pm\mathbf{5}, \pm\mathbf{1}, \pm\frac{\mathbf{25}}{\mathbf{8}}, \pm\frac{\mathbf{25}}{\mathbf{4}}, \pm\frac{\mathbf{25}}{\mathbf{2}}, \pm\frac{\mathbf{5}}{\mathbf{8}}, \pm\frac{\mathbf{5}}{\mathbf{4}}, \pm\frac{\mathbf{5}}{\mathbf{2}}, \pm\frac{\mathbf{1}}{\mathbf{8}}, \pm\frac{\mathbf{1}}{\mathbf{4}}, \pm\frac{\mathbf{1}}{\mathbf{2}}$. The constant term is 25, having factors $\pm 25, \pm 5, \pm 1$. The lead coefficient is 8 with factors $\pm 8, \pm 4, \pm 2, \pm 1$.

5. Check to see whether –3 is a root of $x^4 - 10x^2 + 9 = 0$. The answer: **Yes.** Rewrite the equation with the coefficients showing in front of the variables:
$x^4 - 10x^2 + 9 = 1(x^4) + 0(x^3) - 10(x^2) + 0(x) + 9$.

$$\begin{array}{r|rrrrr} -3 & 1 & 0 & -10 & 0 & 9 \\ & & -3 & 9 & 3 & -9 \\ \hline & 1 & -3 & -1 & 3 & 0 \end{array}$$

Because the remainder is 0, the equation has a root of –3 and a factor of $(x+3)$.

6. Check to see whether $3/2$ is a root of $2x^4 - 3x^3 - 54x + 81 = 0$. The answer: **Yes.** Writing in the coefficients of the terms, you get $2x^4 - 3x^3 + 0(x^2) - 54x + 81 = 0$. Note that 3 is a factor of 81 and 2 is a factor of 2, so $3/2$ is a possible rational root:

$$\begin{array}{r|rrrrr} \frac{3}{2} & 2 & -3 & 0 & -54 & 81 \\ & & 3 & 0 & 0 & -81 \\ \hline & 2 & 0 & 0 & -51 & 0 \end{array}$$

The remainder is 0, so $3/2$ is a root (solution), and $\left(x - 3/2\right)$ or $(2x - 3)$ is a factor.

7 Solve by factoring: $x^4 - 16 = 0$. The answer is $\boldsymbol{x = \pm 2}$. First factor the binomial as the difference and sum of the same two values; then factor the first of these factors the same way:

$$x^4 - 16 = (x^2 - 4)(x^2 + 4) = (x-2)(x+2)(x^2+4) = 0$$

$x = 2$ or $x = -2$ are the real solutions. So $x = \pm 2$. ***Note:*** $x^2 + 4 = 0x = \pm 2$ has no real solutions.

8 Solve by factoring: $x^4 - 3x^3 + 3x^2 - x = 0$. The answer is $\boldsymbol{x = 0, 1}$. First factor out x from each term to get $x(x^3 - 3x^2 + 3x - 1) = 0$. You may recognize that the expression in the parentheses is a perfect cube. But just in case that hasn't occurred to you, try using synthetic division with the guess $x = 1$.

1⌋	1	−3	3	−1
		1	−2	1
	1	−2	1	0

The factored form now reads $x(x-1)(x^2 - 2x + 1) = 0$. The trinomial in the parentheses is a perfect square, so the final factored form is $x(x-1)^3 = 0$. So $x = 0, 1$, and 1 is a *triple root*.

9 Solve by factoring: $x^3 + 5x^2 - 16x - 80 = 0$. The answer is $\boldsymbol{x = \pm 4, -5}$. Factor by grouping:
$x^3 + 5x^2 - 16x - 80 = x^2(x+5) - 16(x+5) = (x^2 - 16)(x+5) = (x-4)(x+4)(x+5) = 0$
So $x - 4 = 0$, $x = 4$; $x + 4 = 0$, $x = -4$; or $x + 5 = 0$, $x = -5$. Therefore, $x = \pm 4, -5$.

10 Solve by factoring: $x^6 - 9x^4 - 16x^2 + 144 = 0$. The answer is $\boldsymbol{x = \pm 2, \pm 3}$. First you get $x^6 - 9x^4 - 16x^2 + 144 = x^4(x^2 - 9) - 16(x^2 - 9) = 0$ by grouping. Then $(x^4 - 16)(x^2 - 9) = (x^2 - 4)(x^2 + 4)(x^2 - 9) = (x-2)(x+2)(x^2+4)(x-3)(x+3) = 0$. So $x = 2$, $x = -2$, $x = 3$ or $x = -3$ give the real solutions. Therefore, $x = \pm 2, \pm 3$.

11 Solve the equation: $x^4 - 13x^2 + 36 = 0$. The answer is $\boldsymbol{x = \pm 3, \pm 2}$.

$$x^4 - 13x^2 + 36 = (x^2 - 9)(x^2 - 4) = 0$$

You can continue factoring or use the square root rule.

$x^2 - 9 = 0$, $x^2 = 9$, $x = \pm 3$; or $x^2 - 4 = 0$, $x^2 = 4$, $x = \pm 2$. Therefore $x = \pm 3, \pm 2$.

12 Solve the equation: $x^{10} - 31x^5 - 32 = 0$. The answer is $\boldsymbol{x = 2, -1}$.

$$x^{10} - 31x^5 - 32 = (x^5 - 32)(x^5 + 1) = 0$$

So $x^5 - 32 = 0$, $x^5 = 32$, $x = 2$; or $x^5 + 1 = 0$, $x^5 = -1$, $x = -1$. Therefore, $x = 2, -1$.

13 Solve the equation: $y^{4/3} - 17y^{2/3} + 16 = 0$. The answer is $\boldsymbol{y = 1, 64}$.

$y^{4/3} - 17y^{2/3} + 16 = (y^{2/3} - 1)(y^{2/3} - 16) = 0$, so

$y^{2/3} - 1 = 0$, $y^{2/3} = 1$, $\left(y^{2/3}\right)^{3/2} = 1^{3/2}, y = 1$

or $y^{2/3} - 16 = 0$, $y^{2/3} = 16$, $\left(y^{2/3}\right)^{3/2} = 16^{3/2} = \left(\sqrt{16}\right)^3 = 64$. Therefore, $y = 1$ or $y = 64$.

(14) **Solve the equation: $z^{-2}+z^{-1}-12=0$. The answer is $z = \frac{1}{3}, -\frac{1}{4}$.**

$z^{-2}+z^{-1}-12=\left(z^{-1}-3\right)\left(z^{-1}+4\right)=0$, so

$z^{-1}-3=0,\ z^{-1}=3,\ \frac{1}{z}=3,\ 1=3z,\ z=\frac{1}{3}$

or $z^{-1}+4=0,\ z^{-1}=-4,\ \frac{1}{z}=-4,\ 1=-4z,\ z=-\frac{1}{4}$

Therefore, $z=\frac{1}{3},-\frac{1}{4}$.

(and making them nice)

» **Being absolutely sure of absolute value**

» **Checking for extraneous solutions**

Chapter 15
Reeling in Radical and Absolute Value Equations

Radical equations and absolute values are just what their names suggest. *Radical equations* contain one or more *radicals* (square root or other root symbols), and *absolute value equations* have an *absolute value operation* (two vertical bars that say to give the distance from 0). Although they're two completely different types of equations, radical equations and absolute value equations do have something in common: You change both into linear or quadratic equations (see Chapters 12 and 13) and then solve them. After all, going back to something familiar makes more sense than trying to develop (and then remember) a bunch of new rules and procedures.

What's different is *how* you change these two types of equations. I handle each type separately in this chapter and offer practice problems for you.

Squaring Both Sides to Solve Radical Equations

If your radical equation has just one radical term, then you solve it by isolating that radical term on one side of the equation and the other terms on the opposite side, and then squaring both sides. After solving the resulting equation, be sure to check your answer or answers to be sure you actually have a solution.

WARNING

Watch out for *extraneous roots*. These false answers crop up in several mathematical situations where you change from one type of equation to another in the course of solving the original equation. In this case, it's the squaring that can introduce *extraneous* or false roots. Creating these false roots happens because the square of a positive number or its opposite (negative) gives you the same positive number.

For example, if you start with the simple statement that $x = 2$ and then square both sides, you get $x^2 = 4$. Now take the square root of both sides, and you get $x = \pm 2$. All of a sudden you have an extraneous root because the -2 got included (it wasn't part of the original statement).

Squaring both sides to get these false answers may sound like more trouble than it's worth, but this procedure is still much easier than anything else. You really can't avoid the extraneous roots; just be aware that they can occur so you don't include them in your answer.

REMEMBER

When squaring both sides in radical equations, you can encounter one of three possible outcomes: (1) both of the solutions work, (2) neither solution works, or (3) just one of the two solutions works because the other solution turns out to be extraneous.

Check out the following examples to see how to handle an extraneous root in a radical equation.

EXAMPLE

Q. Solve for x: $\sqrt{x+10} + x = 10$

A. $x = 6$

1. **Isolate the radical term by subtracting x from each side. Then square both sides of the equation.**

$$\sqrt{x+10} = 10 - x$$
$$\left(\sqrt{x+10}\right)^2 = (10-x)^2$$
$$x + 10 = 100 - 20x + x^2$$

2. **To solve this quadratic equation, subtract x and 10 from each side so that the equation is set equal to zero. Then simplify and then factor it.**

$$0 = x^2 - 21x + 90$$
$$= (x-15)(x-6)$$

Two solutions appear, $x = 15$ or $x = 6$.

3. **Check for an extraneous solution.**

In this case, substituting the solutions, you see that the 6 works, but the 15 doesn't.

$$x = 15 \rightarrow \sqrt{15+10} + 15 \stackrel{?}{=} 10$$
$$\sqrt{25} + 15 \neq 10$$
$$x - 6 \rightarrow \sqrt{6+10} + 6 \stackrel{?}{=} 10$$
$$\sqrt{16} + 6 = 10$$

Q. Solve for *x*: $\sqrt{3x+10}-x=4$

A. $x=-2$ **or** $x=-3$. It's unusual to have both answers from the quadratic work in the original radical equation.

1. **Isolate the radical term by adding x to each side; then square both sides of the equation.**

$$\sqrt{3x+10}=4+x$$
$$\left(\sqrt{3x+10}\right)^2=(4+x)^2$$
$$3x+10=16+8x+x^2$$

2. **Set the equation equal to 0, simplify, and then factor it.**

$$0=x^2+5x+6$$
$$=(x+2)(x+3)$$

Two solutions appear, $x=-2$ or $x=-3$.

3. **Check for an extraneous solution.**

Substituting the solutions, you see that both numbers work in this case.

$$x=-2\rightarrow\sqrt{3(-2)+10}-(-2)\stackrel{?}{=}4$$
$$\sqrt{4}+2=4$$
$$x=-3\rightarrow\sqrt{3(-3)+10}-(-3)\stackrel{?}{=}4$$
$$\sqrt{1}+3=4$$

1 Solve for *x*: $\sqrt{x-3}=6$.

2 Solve for *x*: $\sqrt{x^2+9}=5$.

3 Solve for *x*: $\sqrt{x+5}+x=1$.

4 Solve for *x*: $\sqrt{x-3}+9=x$.

5 Solve for *x*: $\sqrt{x+7}-7=x$.

6 Solve for *x*: $\sqrt{x-1}=x-1$.

Doubling the Fun with Radical Equations

Some radical equations have two or more radical terms. When you have more than one radical term, solving the equation takes more than one squaring process because, after you square both sides, you still have a radical term. Therefore, to solve a radical equation with multiple radical terms, you square the two sides first, then isolate the remaining radical term on one side, and then square both sides again.

In general, squaring a *binomial* (the sum or difference of two terms) is easier if only one of the two terms is a radical term, so a good technique is to rewrite the equations, putting a radical term on each side before you perform the first squaring process.

EXAMPLE

Q. Solve for x: $\sqrt{5x+11}+\sqrt{x+3}=2$.

A. $x=-2$

1. **Subtract $\sqrt{x+3}$ from each side (doing so places a radical on each side of the equation).**

$$\sqrt{5x+11}=2-\sqrt{x+3}$$

2. **Square both sides, simplify the terms, and get the remaining radical term on one side and all the other terms on the opposite side.**

$$\left(\sqrt{5x+11}\right)^2=\left(2-\sqrt{x+3}\right)^2$$
$$5x+11=4-4\sqrt{x+3}+(x+3)$$
$$4x+4=-4\sqrt{x+3}$$

3. **Each of the terms is divisible by 4. Divide every term by 4 and then square both sides.**

$$x+1=-\sqrt{x+3}$$
$$(x+1)^2=\left(-\sqrt{x+3}\right)^2$$
$$x^2+2x+1=x+3$$

4. **Set the quadratic equation equal to 0, factor it, and solve for the solutions to that equation.**

$$x^2+x-2=0$$
$$(x+2)(x-1)=0$$
$$x=-2 \text{ or } x=1$$

5. **Check the two solutions.**

When you test each solution in the original equation, you find that −2 is a solution but 1 is an extraneous root.

Q. Solve for x: $2\sqrt{x+1}=4-\sqrt{4-x}$.

A. $x=0$

1. **Square both sides. (Be sure to square the 2 in front of the radical before distributing over the other terms.) Simplify and isolate the radical on one side.**

$$\left(2\sqrt{x+1}\right)^2=\left(4-\sqrt{4-x}\right)^2$$
$$4(x+1)=16-8\sqrt{4-x}+(4-x)$$
$$4x+4=20-x-8\sqrt{4-x}$$
$$5x-16=-8\sqrt{4-x}$$

2. **Square both sides.**

$$(5x-16)^2=\left(-8\sqrt{4-x}^{2}\right)$$
$$25x^2-160x+256=64(4-x)$$
$$25x^2-160x+256=256-64x$$

3. **Set the quadratic equation equal to 0, factor it, and solve for the solutions to that equation.**

$$25x^2-96x=0$$
$$x(25x-96)=0$$
$$x=0 \text{ or } x=\frac{96}{25}$$

4. **Check the two solutions.**

When you test each solution in the original equation, you find that 0 is a solution but $^{96}\!/_{25}$ is an extraneous root.

7 Solve for x: $\sqrt{x}+3=\sqrt{x+27}$.

8 Solve for x: $3\sqrt{x+1}-2\sqrt{x-4}=5$.

Solving Absolute Value Equations

An absolute value equation contains the absolute value operation. Seems rather obvious, doesn't it? When solving an absolute value equation, you have to change its form to solve it (just as you do with radical equations; refer to the preceding sections). When solving an absolute value equation in the form $|ax+b|=c$, take the following steps:

1. **Rewrite the original equation as two separate equations and solve the two equations separately for two different answers.**

   The two equations to solve are $ax+b=c$ **or** $ax+b=-c$.

2. **Check the results in the original equation to ensure the answers work.**

   Generally, both answers work, but you need to check the results to be sure the original equation didn't have a nonsense statement (like having a positive equal to a negative) in it.

EXAMPLE

Q. Solve for x: $|4x+5|=3$.

A. $x=-\frac{1}{2}$ **or** $x=-2$. Rewrite the absolute value equation as two different equations: $4x+5=3$ or $4x+5=-3$. Solve $4x+5=3$, which gives $x=-\frac{1}{2}$. Solve $4x+5=-3$, which gives $x=-2$.

Checking the solutions:

$\left|4\left(\frac{-1}{2}\right)+5\right|=|-2+5|=|3|=3$ and

$|4(-2)+5|=|-8+5|=|-3|=3$.

Q. Solve for x: $|3+x|-5=1$.

A. $x=3$ **or** $x=-9$. Before applying the rule to change the absolute value into linear equations, add 5 to each side of the equation. This gets the absolute value by itself, on the left side: $|3+x|=6$.

Now the two equations are $3+x=6$ and $3+x=-6$. The solutions are $x=3$ and $x=-9$, respectively. Checking these answers in the original equation, $|3+3|-5=|6|-5=6-5=1$ and $|3+(-9)|-5=|-6|-5=6-5=1$.

9 Solve for x: $|x-2|=6$.

10 Solve for y: $|3y+2|=4$.

11 Solve for w: $|5w-2|+3=6$.

12 Solve for y: $3|4-y|+2=8$.

13 Solve for x: $|-4x|=12$.

14 Solve for y: $|y+3|+6=2$.

Answers to Problems on Radical and Absolute Value Equations

This section provides the answers (in bold) to the practice problems in this chapter.

1. Solve for x: $\sqrt{x-3}=6$. The answer is $\boldsymbol{x=39}$. First square both sides and then solve for x by adding 3 to each side:

$$\sqrt{x-3}=6 \to \left(\sqrt{x-3}\right)^2=6^2 \to x-3=36 \to x=39$$

Then check: $\sqrt{39-3}\overset{?}{=}6 \to \sqrt{36}=6$

2. Solve for x: $\sqrt{x^2+9}=5$. The answer is $\boldsymbol{x=\pm 4}$. First square both sides and then subtract 9 from each side. Find the square root of each side and check to see whether the answers work:

$$\sqrt{x^2+9}=5 \to \left(\sqrt{x^2+9}\right)^2=5^2 \to x^2+9=25 \to x^2=16 \to x=\pm 4$$

Then check:

$$\sqrt{(4)^2+9}\overset{?}{=}5,\ \sqrt{16+9}\overset{?}{=}5,\ \sqrt{25}\overset{?}{=}5$$
$$\sqrt{(-4)^2+9}\overset{?}{=}5,\ \sqrt{16+9}\overset{?}{=}5,\ \sqrt{25}\overset{?}{=}5$$

3. Solve for x: $\sqrt{x+5}+x=1$. The answer is $\boldsymbol{x=-1}$. First move x to the right side:

$$\sqrt{x+5}+x=1 \to \sqrt{x+5}=1-x$$

$$\left(\sqrt{x+5}\right)^2=(1-x)^2 \to x+5=1-2x+x^2 \to 0=x^2-3x-4$$
$$(x-4)(x+1)=0 \to x-4=0 \to x=4 \text{ or } x+1=0 \to x=-1$$

Check: $x=4: \sqrt{4+5}+4\overset{?}{=}1, \sqrt{9}+4\overset{?}{=}1, 3+4\neq 1$. So 4 isn't a solution; it's extraneous.

Check: $x=-1: \sqrt{(-1)+5}+(-1)\overset{?}{=}1,\ \sqrt{4}-1\overset{?}{=}1,\ 2-1=1$. So $x=-1$ is the only solution.

4. Solve for x: $\sqrt{x-3}+9=x$. The answer is $\boldsymbol{x=12}$. First subtract 9 from each side and then square both sides. Set the quadratic equal to 0 to factor and solve for x:

$$\sqrt{x-3}+9=x \to \sqrt{x-3}=x-9 \to \left(\sqrt{x-3}\right)^2=(x-9)^2,$$
$$x-3=x^2-18x+81 \to 0=x^2-19x+84 \to (x-12)(x-7)=0$$

Using the multiplication property of zero (see Chapter 13), you have $x-12=0,\ x=12$ or $x-7=0,\ x=7$.

Check: $x=12: \sqrt{12-3}+9\overset{?}{=}12 \to \sqrt{9}+9\overset{?}{=}12 \to 3+9=12$

Check: $x=7: \sqrt{7-3}+9\overset{?}{=}7 \to \sqrt{4}+9\overset{?}{=}7 \to 2+9\neq 7$

5 Solve for x: $\sqrt{x+7}-7=x$. The answer is both $\boldsymbol{x=-7}$ **and** $\boldsymbol{x=-6}$.

First add 7 to each side. Then square both sides, set the equation equal to 0, and solve for x:

$$\sqrt{x+7}-7=x \rightarrow \sqrt{x+7}=x+7 \rightarrow \left(\sqrt{x+7}\right)^2=(x+7)^2$$
$$x+7=x^2+14x+49 \rightarrow 0=x^2+13x+42 \rightarrow (x+7)(x+6)=0$$

Using the multiplication property of zero (see Chapter 13), you have $x+7=0,\ x=-7$ or $x+6=0,\ x=-6$.

$$\text{Check}: x=-7: \sqrt{(-7)+7}-7 \stackrel{?}{=} -7 \rightarrow \sqrt{0}-7 \stackrel{?}{=} -7 \rightarrow 0-7=-7$$

$$\text{Check}: x=-6: \sqrt{(-6)+7}-7 \stackrel{?}{=} -6 \rightarrow \sqrt{1}-7 \stackrel{?}{=} -6 \rightarrow 1-7=-6$$

6 Solve for x: $\sqrt{x-1}=x-1$. The answer is both $\boldsymbol{x=1}$ **and** $\boldsymbol{x=2}$. First square both sides of the equation; then set it equal to 0 and factor:

$$\left(\sqrt{x-1}\right)^2=(x-1)^2 \rightarrow x-1=x^2-2x+1 \rightarrow 0=x^2-3x+2$$
$$0=(x-1)(x-2) \rightarrow x=1 \text{ or } x=2$$

$$\text{Check}: x=1: \sqrt{1-1} \stackrel{?}{=} 1-1 \rightarrow 0=0$$

$$\text{Check}: x=2: \sqrt{2-1} \stackrel{?}{=} 2-1 \rightarrow 1=1$$

7 Solve for x: $\sqrt{x}+3=\sqrt{x+27}$. The answer is $\boldsymbol{x=9}$. First square both sides of the equation. Then keep the radical term on the left and subtract x and 9 from each side. Before squaring both sides again, divide by 6:

$$\sqrt{x}+3=\sqrt{x+27} \rightarrow \left(\sqrt{x}+3\right)^2=\left(\sqrt{x+27}\right)^2$$
$$\left(\sqrt{x}\right)^2+6\sqrt{x}+9=x+27 \rightarrow x+6\sqrt{x}+9=x+27 \rightarrow 6\sqrt{x}=18 \rightarrow \sqrt{x}=3$$

Square both sides of the new equation: $\left(\sqrt{x}\right)^2=3^2, x=9$

Check: $x=9: \sqrt{9}+3 \stackrel{?}{=} \sqrt{9+27} \rightarrow 3+3=6=\sqrt{36}$

8 Solve for x: $3\sqrt{x+1}-2\sqrt{x-4}=5$. The answer is $\boldsymbol{x=8}$. First move a radical term to the right, square both sides, simplify, and, finally, isolate the radical term on the right. You can then divide each side by 5:

$$3\sqrt{x+1}-2\sqrt{x-4}=5 \rightarrow 3\sqrt{x+1}=2\sqrt{x-4}+5 \rightarrow \left(3\sqrt{x+1}\right)^2=\left(2\sqrt{x-4}+5\right)^2$$
$$9(x+1)=4(x-4)+20\sqrt{x-4}+25 \rightarrow 9x+9=4x-16+20\sqrt{x-4}+25$$
$$9x+9=4x+9+20\sqrt{x-4} \rightarrow 5x=20\sqrt{x-4} \rightarrow x=4\sqrt{x-4}$$

Square both sides again, set the equation equal to 0, and factor:

$$(x)^2=\left(4\sqrt{x-4}\right)^2 \rightarrow x^2=16(x-4) \rightarrow x^2=16x-64 \rightarrow x^2-16x+64=0,\ (x-8)^2=0$$

Using the multiplication property of zero (see Chapter 13), you have $x-8=0,\ x=8$.

Check: $x=8: 3\sqrt{8+1}-2\sqrt{8-4} \stackrel{?}{=} 5 \rightarrow 3\sqrt{9}-2\sqrt{4} \stackrel{?}{=} 5 \rightarrow 3(3)-2(2)=9-4=5$

9. Solve for $x: |x-2|=6$. The answer is $\boldsymbol{x=8}$ **and** $\boldsymbol{x=-4}$. First remove the absolute value symbol by setting what's inside equal to both positive and negative 6. Then solve the two linear equations that can be formed:

   $$|x-2|=6 \to x-2=\pm 6 \to x=2\pm 6 \to x=2+6=8 \text{ or } x=2-6=-4$$

   Check: $x=8: |8-2|=|6|=6$, and $x=-4: |(-4)-2|=|-6|=6$

10. Solve for $y: |3y+2|=4$. The answer is $\boldsymbol{y=\frac{2}{3}}$ **and** $\boldsymbol{y=-2}$. First remove the absolute value symbol by setting what's inside equal to both positive and negative 4. Then solve the two linear equations that can be formed:

    $$|3y+2|=4 \to 3y+2=\pm 4 \to 3y=-2\pm 4$$
    $$3y=-2+4 \to 3y=2, y=\tfrac{2}{3} \text{ and } 3y=-2-4 \to 3y=-6,\ y=-2$$

    Check: $y=\frac{2}{3}: \left|3\left(\frac{2}{3}\right)+2\right|=|2+2|=|4|=4$, and $y=-2: |3(-2)+2|=|-6+2|=|-4|=4$

11. Solve for w: $|5w-2|+3=6$. The answer is $\boldsymbol{w=1}$ **and** $\boldsymbol{w=-\frac{1}{5}}$. First subtract 3 from each side. Then remove the absolute value symbol by setting what's inside equal to both positive and negative 3:

    $$|5w-2|+3=6 \to |5w-2|=6-3=3 \to 5w-2=\pm 3 \to 5w=2\pm 3$$

    The two linear equations that are formed give you two different answers:

    $$5w=2+3 \to 5w=5,\ w=1 \text{ and } 5w=2-3 \to 5w=-1,\ w=-\frac{1}{5}$$

12. Solve for y: $3|4-y|+2=8$. The answer is $\boldsymbol{y=6}$ **and** $\boldsymbol{y=2}$. First subtract 2 from each side. Then divide each side by 3:

    $$3|4-y|+2=8 \to 3|4-y|=6 \to |4-y|=2$$

    Then rewrite without the absolute value symbol by setting the expression inside the absolute value equal to positive or negative 2: $4-y=\pm 2;\ 4\pm 2=y$. Then simplify the resulting linear equations:

    $$y=4+2=6 \text{ or } y=4-2=2$$

13. Solve for x: $|-4x|=12$. The answer is $\boldsymbol{x=3}$ **and** $\boldsymbol{x=-3}$. First rewrite the equation without the absolute value symbol:

    $$|-4x|=12 \to -4x=\pm 12$$
    $$-4x=12 \to x=\frac{12}{4}=-3 \textit{ and } -4x=-12 \to x=\frac{-12}{4}=3$$

14. Solve for y: $|y+3|+6=2$. **This equation doesn't have an answer**. Here's why:

    $$|y+3|+6=2 \to |y+3|=-4 \to y+3=\pm 4 \to y=-3\pm 4,\ y=1 \text{ or } y=-7$$

    Check $y=1: |(1)+3|+6=|4|+6=10\neq 2$, and $y=-7: |(-7)+3|+6=|-4|+6=4+6=10\neq 2$

WARNING

Note that $|y+3|=-4$ is impossible because $|y+3|\geq 0$ can never equal a negative number.

» Solving linear and quadratic inequalities

» Getting the most out of absolute value inequalities

» Working with compound inequalities

Chapter 16
Getting Even with Inequalities

An *inequality* is a mathematical statement that says that some expression is bigger or smaller than another expression. Sometimes the inequality also includes an equal sign with the inequality sign to show that you want *something bigger than or equal to,* or *smaller than or equal to.*

REMEMBER

The good news about solving inequalities is that nearly all the rules are the same as solving an equation — with one big difference. The difference in applying rules comes in when you're multiplying or dividing both sides of an inequality by negative numbers. If you pay attention to what you're doing, you shouldn't have a problem.

This chapter covers everything from basic inequalities and linear equalities to the more challenging quadratic, absolute value, and complex inequalities. Take a deep breath. I offer you plenty of practice problems so you can work out any kinks.

Using the Rules to Work on Inequality Statements

REMEMBER

Working with inequalities really isn't that difficult if you just keep a few rules in mind. The following rules deal with inequalities (assume that *c* is some number):

- If $a > b$, then adding *c* to each side or subtracting *c* from each side doesn't change the sense (direction of the inequality), and you get $a \pm c > b \pm c$.
- If $a > b$, then multiplying or dividing each side by a *positive c* doesn't change the sense, and you get $a \cdot c > b \cdot c$ or $\frac{a}{c} > \frac{b}{c}$.
- If $a > b$, then multiplying or dividing each side by a *negative c* does change the sense (reverses the direction), and you get $a \cdot c < b \cdot c$ or $\frac{a}{c} < \frac{b}{c}$.
- If $a > b$, then reversing the terms reverses the sense, and you get $b < a$.

EXAMPLE

Q. Starting with $-20 < 7$, perform the following operations: Add 5 to each side, multiply each side by -2, change the number order, and then divide each side by 6.

A. $-4 < 5$

$$-20 < 7$$

$$-20 + 5 < 7 + 5 \rightarrow -15 < 12$$

Adding 5 didn't change the sense.

$$-15(-2) > 12(-2) \rightarrow 30 > -24$$

Multiplying by -2 reverses the sense.

$$30 > -24 \rightarrow -24 < 30$$

Flip-flopping the terms to put the numbers in order from smaller to larger reverses the sense.

$$\frac{-24}{6} < \frac{30}{6} \rightarrow -4 < 5$$

Dividing by a positive number does nothing to the direction of the sense.

1 Starting with $5 > 2$, add 4 to each side and then divide each side by -3; simplify the result.

2 Starting with $5 \geq 1$, multiply each side by -4; then divide each side by -2 and simplify the result.

Rewriting Inequalities by Using Interval Notation

Interval notation is an alternate form for writing inequality statements. Interval notation uses brackets and parentheses instead of greater than or less than signs. Many books in higher mathematics courses use interval notation; I show it here so you'll be acquainted with the notation. In general, you use parentheses to indicate that the number is *not* included in the statement and brackets to show that it *is* included (with greater than or equal to and less than or equal to signs). I show you several examples of interval notation versus inequality notation.

EXAMPLE

Q. Write $x \le 6$ and $x > -4$, using interval notation.

A. $\left(-\infty, \mathbf{6}\right]$ **and** $\left(\mathbf{-4}, \infty\right)$

$x \le 6$ becomes $\left(-\infty, 6\right]$. The numbers that x represents have no boundary as they get smaller, so $-\infty$ is used. The 6 is included, and a bracket indicates that.

$x > -4$ becomes $\left(-4, \infty\right)$. The -4 isn't included, so a parenthesis is used. You always use a parenthesis with infinity or negative infinity because there's no *end number.*

Q. Write $-5 < x \le 3$ and $4 < x < 7$, using interval notation.

A. $\left(\mathbf{-5, 3}\right]$ **and** $\left(\mathbf{4, 7}\right)$

$-5 < x \le 3$ becomes $\left(-5, 3\right]$. The number -5 isn't included, so a parenthesis is used. The 3 is included, so a bracket is used.

$4 < x < 7$ becomes (4,7). Neither 4 nor 7 is included, so parentheses are used. A caution here: The interval (4,7) looks like the coordinates for the point (4,7) in graphing. You have to be clear (use some actual words) to convey what you're trying to write when you use the two parentheses for intervals.

3 Write $x > 7$, using interval notation.

4 Write $2 \le x \le 21$, using interval notation.

Solving Linear Inequalities

Solving linear inequalities involves pretty much the same process as solving linear equations: Move all the variable terms to one side and the number to the other side. Then multiply or divide to solve for the variable. The tricky part is when you multiply or divide by a negative number. Because this special situation doesn't happen frequently, people tend to forget it. ***Remember:*** If you multiply both sides of $-x < -3$ by -1, the inequality becomes $x > 3$; you have to reverse the sense.

Another type of linear inequality has the linear expression sandwiched between two numbers, like $-1 < 8 - x \leq 4$. The main rule here is that whatever you do to one section of the inequality, you do to all the others. For more on this, go to "Solving Complex Inequalities," later in this chapter.

EXAMPLE

Q. Solve for x: $5 - 3x \geq 14 + 6x$.

A. $\mathbf{x \leq -1}$ **or** $\mathbf{(-\infty, -1]}$. Subtract $6x$ from each side and subtract 5 from each side; then divide by -9:

$$\begin{aligned} 5 - 3x &\geq 14 - 6x \\ -5 - 6x\ &\ \ -5 - 6x \\ \hline -9x &\geq 9 \\ \frac{-9x}{-9} &\leq \frac{9}{-9} \\ x &\leq -1 \end{aligned}$$

Note that you can do this problem another way to avoid division by a negative number. See the next example for the alternate method.

Q. Solve for x: $5 - 3x \geq 14 + 6x$

A. $\mathbf{x \leq -1}$ **or** $\mathbf{(-\infty, -1]}$. Add $3x$ to each side and subtract 14 from each side. Then divide by 9. This is the same answer, if you reverse the inequality and the numbers.

$$\begin{aligned} 5 - 3x &\geq 14 + 6x \\ +3x\ &\ \ +3x \\ \hline 5 &\geq 14 + 9x \\ -14\ &\ \ -14 \\ \hline -9 &\geq 9x \\ -1 &\geq x \end{aligned}$$

5 Solve for y: $4 - 5y \leq 19$.

6 Solve for x: $3(x + 2) > 4x + 5$.

7 Solve for x: $-5 < 2x + 3 \le 7$.

8 Solve for x: $3 \le 7 - 2x < 11$.

Solving Quadratic Inequalities

REMEMBER

When an inequality involves a quadratic expression, you have to resort to a completely different type of process to solve it than that used for linear inequalities. The quickest and most efficient method to find a solution is to use a number line.

After finding the *critical numbers* (where the expression changes from positive to negative or vice versa), you use a number line and place some + and – signs to indicate what's happening to the factors. (See Chapter 1 for some background info on the number line and where numbers fall on it.)

EXAMPLE

Q. Solve the inequality $x^2 - x > 12$.

A. $x < -3$, $x > 4$ **or** $(-\infty, -3), (4, \infty)$

1. **Subtract 12 from each side to set it greater than 0.**
2. **Factor the quadratic and determine the *zeros*. (These are the *critical numbers*.)**

   You want to find out what values of *x* make the different factors equal to 0 so that you can separate intervals on the number line into positive and negative portions for each factor.

   $$x^2 - x - 12 > 0$$
   $$(x-4)(x+3) > 0$$

   The two critical numbers are 4 and –3; they're the numbers that make the expression equal to 0.

3. **Mark these two numbers on the number line.**

4. **Look to the left of the –3, between the –3 and 4, and then to the right of the 4 and indicate, on the number line, what the signs of the factors are in those intervals.**

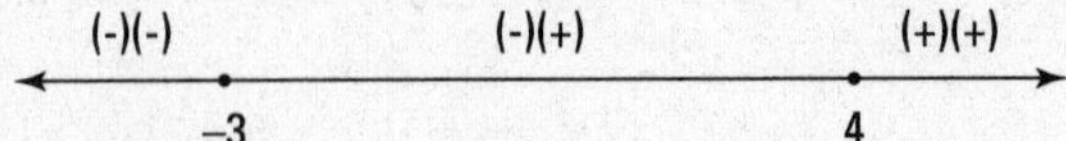

When you replace the x with any number smaller than –3, the factor $(x-4)$ is negative, and the factor $(x+3)$ is also negative. When you choose a number between –3 and 4 — say 0, for instance — the factor $(x-4)$ is negative, and the factor $(x+3)$ is positive. When you replace the x with any number bigger than 4, the factor $(x-4)$ is positive, and the factor $(x+3)$ is also positive.

Recall that, when you multiply an even number of negative numbers, the product is positive, and when the number of negative numbers is odd, the product is negative. The inequality asks for when the product is positive; according to the signs on the line, this is when $x<-3$ (when a negative is multiplied by a negative) or $x>4$ (when a positive is multiplied by a positive).

9 Solve for x: $(x+7)(x-1)>0$.

10 Solve for x: $x^2-x\le 20$.

11 Solve for x: $3x^2\ge 9x$.

12 Solve for x: $x^2-25\ge 0$.

Dealing with Polynomial and Rational Inequalities

The same process that gives you solutions to quadratic inequalities is used to solve some other types of inequality problems (see "Solving Quadratic Inequalities" earlier in this chapter for more info). You use the number line process for polynomials (higher degree expressions) and for rational expressions (fractions where a variable ends up in the denominator).

EXAMPLE

Q. Solve for *x*: $(x+3)(x+2)(x-1)^2(x-8)\le 0$.

A. $\boldsymbol{x \le -3, -2 \le x \le 8}$ **or** $(-\infty,-3],[2,8]$. The polynomial is already factored (thank goodness). So set each factor equal to 0 to determine where the factors might change from positive to negative or vice versa (critical numbers). Place the zeros on a number line, test each factor in each interval on the number line, and determine the sign of the expression in that interval. Use that information to solve the problem.

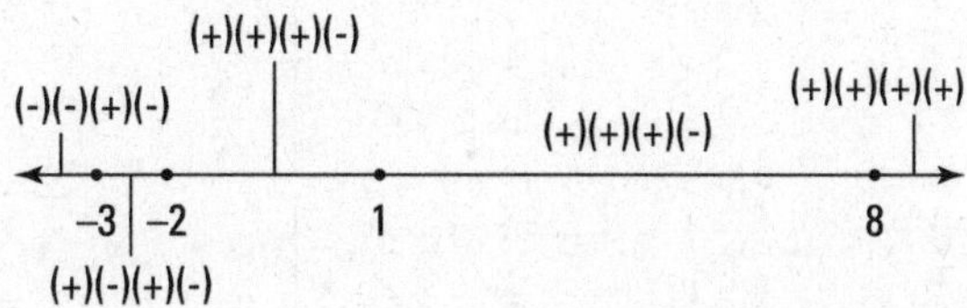

The solution consists of all the numbers that make the expression either negative or equal to 0. The product is negative when you have an odd number of negative factors. Notice that the sign of the product didn't change when *x* went from smaller than 1 to larger than 1. That's because that factor was squared, making that factor either positive or 0 all the time.

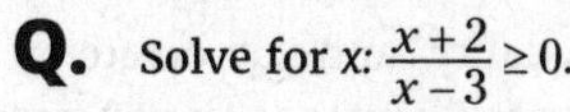

Q. Solve for *x*: $\dfrac{x+2}{x-3}\ge 0$.

A. $\boldsymbol{x \le -2, x > 3}$ **or** $(-\infty,-2],(3,\infty)$. Solving an inequality with a fraction works pretty much the same way as solving one with a polynomial. Find all the zeros of the factors, put them on a number line, and check for the sign of the result. The only thing you need to be careful of is not including some number that would result in a 0 factor in the denominator. The sign can change from one side to the other of that number; you just can't use it in your answer. See this number line for clarification.

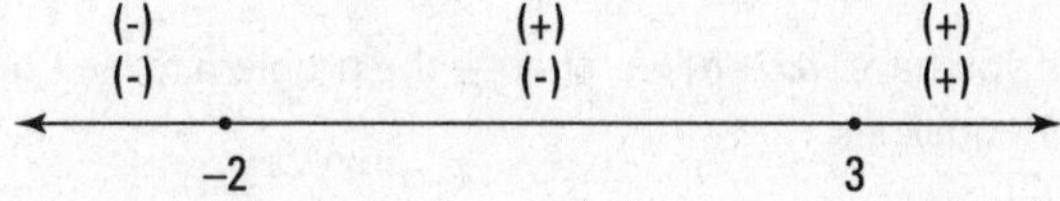

Remember the rule for dividing a signed number is the same as it is in multiplication. According to the sign line, the fraction is positive for numbers smaller than −2 or for numbers greater than +3. Also, you get a 0 when $x=-2$.

13 Solve for x: $x(x-1)(x+2) \geq 0$.

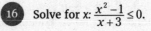

14 Solve for x: $x^3 - 4x^2 + 4x - 16 \leq 0$.

15 Solve for x: $\frac{5+x}{x} > 0$.

16 Solve for x: $\frac{x^2-1}{x+3} \leq 0$.

Solving Absolute Value Inequalities

Put the absolute value function together with an inequality, and you create an *absolute value inequality.* When solving absolute value equations (refer to Chapter 15, if you need a refresher), you rewrite the equations without the absolute value function in them. To solve absolute value inequalities, you also rewrite the form to create simpler inequality problems — types you already know how to solve. Solve the new problem or problems for the solution to the original.

REMEMBER

You need to keep two different situations in mind. (Always assume that the c is a positive number or 0.) In the following list, I show only the rules for > and <, but the same holds if you're working with $\leq$ or $\geq$:

- If you have $|ax+b| > c$, change the problem to $ax+b > c$ or $ax+b < -c$ and solve the two inequalities.
- If you have $|ax+b| < c$, change the problem to $-c < ax+b < c$ and solve the one compound inequality.

EXAMPLE

Q. Solve for x: $|9x-5|>4$.

A. $x<\frac{1}{9}$, $x>1$ **or** $\left(-\infty,\frac{1}{9}\right),(1,\infty)$. Change the absolute value inequality to the two separate inequalities $9x-5>4$ or $9x-5<-4$. Solving the two inequalities, you get the two solutions $9x>9$, $x>1$ or $9x<1$, $x<\frac{1}{9}$. So numbers bigger than 1 or smaller than $\frac{1}{9}$ satisfy the original statement.

Q. Solve for x: $|9x-5|<4$.

A. $\frac{1}{9}<x<1$ **or** $\left(\frac{1}{9},1\right)$. This is like the first example, except that the sense has been turned around. Rewrite the inequality as $-4<9x-5<4$. Solving it, the solution is $1<9x<9$, $\frac{1}{9}<x<1$. The inequality statement says that all the numbers between $\frac{1}{9}$ and 1 work. Notice that the interval in this answer is what was left out in writing the solution to the problem when the inequality was reversed.

17 Solve for x: $|4x-3|<5$.

18 Solve for x: $5|7x-4|+1>6$.

Solving Complex Inequalities

A *complex inequality* — one with more than two sections (intervals or expressions sandwiched between inequalities) to it — could be just compound and have variables in the middle, or they can have variables in more than one section where adding and subtracting can't isolate the variable in one place. When this happens, you have to break up the inequality into solvable sections and write the answer in terms of what the different solutions share.

EXAMPLE

Q. Solve for x: $1 \le 4x - 3 < 3x + 7$.

A. $\mathbf{1 \le x < 10}$ **or [1, 10)**. Break it up into the two separate problems: $1 \le 4x - 3$ and $4x - 3 < 3x + 7$. Solve the first inequality $1 \le 4x - 3$ to get $1 \le x$. Solve the second inequality $4x - 3 < 3x + 7$ to get $x < 10$. Putting these two answers together, you get that x must be some number both bigger than or equal to 1 *and* smaller than 10.

Q. Solve for x: $2x < 3x + 1 \le 5x - 2$.

A. $\mathbf{x \ge 3/2}$ **or** $\mathbf{\left(3/2, \infty\right]}$. Break the inequality up into two separate problems. The solution to $2x < 3x + 1$ is $-1 < x$, and the solution to $3x + 1 \le 5x - 2$ is $3/2 \le x$. The two solutions overlap, with all the common solutions lying to the right of and including $3/2$.

19 Solve for x: $6 \le 5x + 1 < 2x + 10$.

20 Solve for x: $-6 \le 4x - 3 < 5x + 1$.

Answers to Problems on Working with Inequalities

This section provides the answers (in bold) to the practice problems in this chapter.

1. Starting with $5 > 2$, add 4 to each side and then divide by -3. The answer is $\mathbf{-3 < -2}$.

$$5 > 2$$
$$5 + 4 > 2 + 4 \rightarrow 9 > 6$$
$$\frac{9}{-3} < \frac{6}{-3} \rightarrow -3 < -2$$

2. Starting with $5 \geq 1$, multiply each side by -4 and then divide each side by -2. The answer is $\mathbf{10 > 2}$, because you reverse the sense twice.

$$5 \geq 1$$
$$5(-4) < 1(-4) \rightarrow -20 < -4$$
$$\frac{-20}{-2} > \frac{-4}{-2} \rightarrow 10 > 2$$

3. Write $x > 7$, using interval notation. The answer is $\mathbf{(7, \infty)}$.

4. Write $2 \leq x \leq 21$, using interval notation. The answer is **[2, 21]**.

5. Solve for y: $4 - 5y \leq 19$. The answer is $\boldsymbol{y \geq -3}$ **or** $\mathbf{[-3, \infty)}$. Subtract 4 and then divide by -5:

$$\begin{aligned} 4 - 5y &\leq 19 \\ \underline{-4 \quad} & \underline{\;\; -4} \\ -5y &\leq 15 \\ \frac{-5y}{-5} &\geq \frac{15}{-5} \\ y &\geq -3 \end{aligned}$$

6. Solve for x: $3(x+2) > 4x + 5$. The answer is $\mathbf{1 > \boldsymbol{x}}$ **or** $\mathbf{(-\infty, 1)}$.

$$\begin{aligned} 3(x+2) &> 4x + 5 \\ 3x + 6 &> 4x + 5 \\ \underline{-3x - 5} & \underline{\; -3x - 5} \\ 1 &> x \text{ or } x < 1 \end{aligned}$$

7. Solve for x: $-5 < 2x + 3 \leq 7$. The answer is $\mathbf{-4 < \boldsymbol{x} \leq 2}$ **or** $\mathbf{(-4, 2]}$.

$$\begin{aligned} -5 < 2x &+ 3 \leq 7 \\ \underline{-3 \qquad} & \underline{-3 - 3} \\ -8 < 2x & \quad \leq 4 \\ \frac{-8}{2} < \frac{2x}{2} & \quad \leq \frac{4}{2} \\ -4 < x & \quad \leq 2 \end{aligned}$$

8. Solve for x: $3 \le 7-2x < 11$. The answer is $\mathbf{2 \ge x > -2}$ **(or** $\mathbf{-2 < x \le 2}$**) or** $\mathbf{(-2,2]}$. First subtract 7 and then divide by –2 to get the answer:

$$\begin{array}{l} 3 \le 7-2x < 11 \\ \underline{-7-7 \qquad -7} \\ -4 \le -2x < 4 \\ \frac{-4}{-2} \ge \frac{-2x}{-2} > \frac{4}{-2} \\ 2 \ge x > -2 \text{ or } -2 < x \le 2 \end{array}$$

9. Solve for x: $(x+7)(x-1) > 0$. The answer is $\mathbf{x > 1, x < -7}$ **or** $\mathbf{(-\infty,-7),\ (1,\infty)}$.

$x+7=0$ when $x=-7$, and $x-1=0$ when $x=1$, as shown on the following number line.

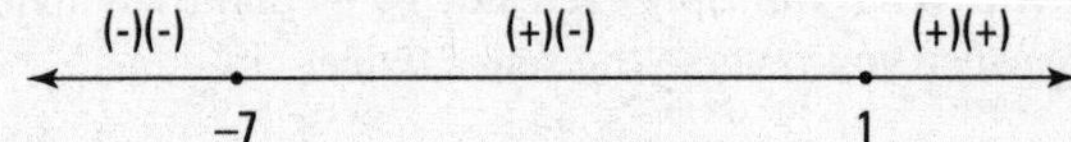

If $x>1$, then both factors are positive. If $-7<x<1$, then $x+7$ is positive, but $x-1$ is negative, making the product negative. If $x<-7$ then both factors are negative, and the product is positive. So $x>1$ or $x<-7$.

10. Solve for x: $x^2 - x \le 20$. The answer is $\mathbf{-4 \le x \le 5}$ **or** $\mathbf{[-4,\ 5]}$. First subtract 20 from both sides; then factor the quadratic and set the factors equal to 0 to find the values where the factors change signs:

$$x^2 - x \le 20 \to x^2 - x - 20 \le 0 \to (x-5)(x+4) \le 0$$

$x-5=0$ when $x=5$, and $x+4=0$ when $x=-4$, as shown on the following number line.

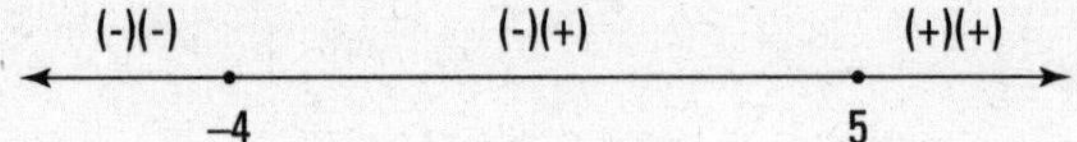

If $x>5$, then $x-5>0$ and $x+4>0$, making the product positive. If $-4<x<5$ then $x-5<0$, and $x+4>0$, resulting in a product that's negative. If $x<-4$, then both factors are negative, and the product is positive. So the product is negative only if $-4<x<5$. But the solutions of $(x-5)(x+4)=0$ are $x=5$, $x=-4$. Including these two values, the solution is then $-4 \le x \le 5$.

11. Solve for x: $3x^2 \ge 9x$. The answer is $\mathbf{x \ge 3,\ x \le 0}$ **or** $\mathbf{(-\infty,0],\ [3,\infty)}$. First subtract 9x from each side. Then factor the quadratic and set the factors equal to 0:

$$3x^2 \ge 9x \to 3x^2 - 9x \ge 0 \to 3x(x-3) \ge 0$$

$3x(x-3)=0$ when $x=0,\ x=3$, as shown on the following number line.

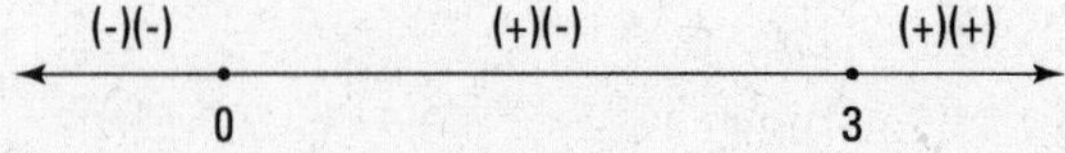

If $x > 3$, both factors are positive, and $3x(x-3) > 0$. If $0 < x < 3$, then $3x > 0$ and $x - 3 < 0$, making the product negative. If $x < 0$, both factors are negative, and $3x(x-3) > 0$. When $x = 0$ or $x - 3$, $3x(x-3) = 0$. Include those in the solution to get $x \geq 3$ or $x \leq 0$.

12 Solve for *x*: $x^2 - 25 \geq 0$. The answer is $\boldsymbol{x \geq 5,\ x \leq -5}$ **or** $\boldsymbol{(-\infty, -5], [5, \infty)}$. First set the expression equal to 0 to help find the factors:

$x^2 - 25 \geq 0 \rightarrow (x-5)(x+5) \geq 0$

The critical numbers are 5 and –5. Place them on the number line.

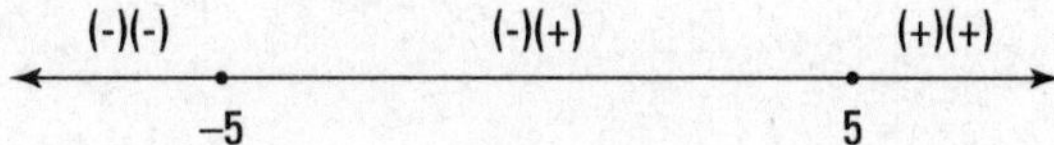

From the figure, $x^2 - 25 > 0$ when $x > 5$ or $x < -5$. When $x = \pm 5$, $x^2 - 25 = 0$. So $x \geq 5$ or $x \leq -5$.

13 Solve for *x*: $x(x-1)(x+2) \geq 0$. The answer is $\boldsymbol{x \geq 1, -2 \leq x \leq 0}$ **or** $\boldsymbol{[-2, 0], [1, \infty)}$. First set the factored expression equal to 0. Put these values on the number line:

$x(x-1)(x+2) \geq 0 \rightarrow x(x-1)(x+2) = 0$, when $x = 0, 1, -2$

(-)(-)(-) (-)(-)(+) (+)(-)(+) (+)(+)(+)

–2 0 1

Assign signs to each of the four regions to get the answer $x \geq 1$ or $-2 \leq x \leq 0$.

14 Solve for *x*: $x^3 - 4x^2 + 4x - 16 \leq 0$. The answer is $\boldsymbol{x \leq 4}$ **or** $\boldsymbol{(-\infty, 4]}$. First factor the expression by grouping. Then set the factors equal to 0.

$x^3 - 4x^2 + 4x - 16 \leq 0 \rightarrow x^2(x-4) + 4(x-4) \leq 0$

$(x^2 + 4)(x-4) \leq 0$

The factored form is equal to 0 only if $x = 4$. Put this number on the number line.

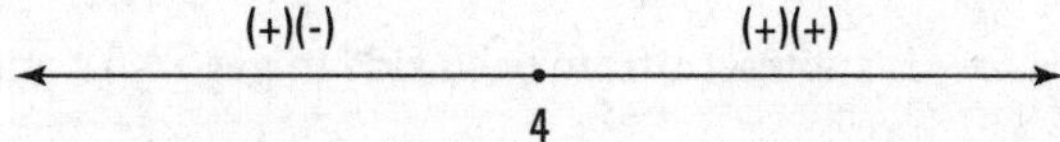

Assign signs to each interval to get the answer $x \leq 4$.

15 Solve for *x*: $\frac{5+x}{x} > 0$. The answer is $\boldsymbol{x > 0, x < -5}$ **or** $\boldsymbol{(-\infty, -5), (0, \infty)}$.

$\frac{5+x}{x} > 0$ when the numerator $5 + x = 0$, $x = -5$. When the denominator $x = 0$, $\frac{5+x}{x}$ is undefined, so place $x = 0$ and $x = -5$ on the number line.

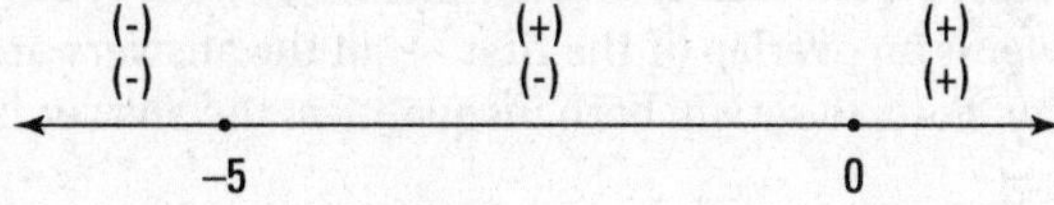

Assign signs to each of the three intervals to get the answer: $x > 0$ or $x < -5$.

16 Solve for x: $\frac{x^2-1}{x+3} \le 0$. The answer is $-1 \le x \le 1$, $x < -3$ or $(-\infty, -3), [-1, 1]$.

$$\frac{x^2-1}{x+3} \le 0 \to \frac{(x-1)(x+1)}{x+3} \le 0$$

The fraction equals 0 when $x = 1$ or $x = -1$, and it's undefined when $x = -3$.

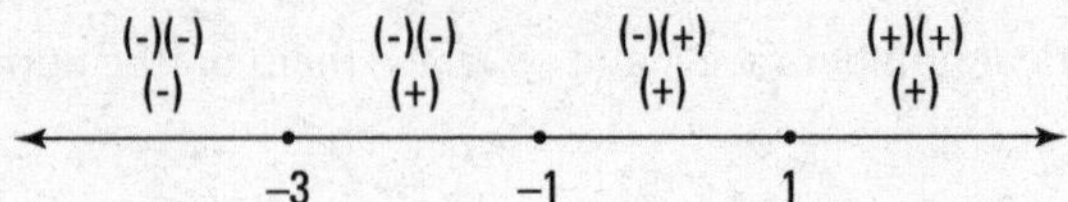

Assign signs to each of the four intervals. So $\frac{(x-1)(x+1)}{x+3} < 0$ when $-1 < x < 1$ or $x < -3$. But $\frac{(x-1)(x+1)}{x+3} = 0$ only when $x = 1$ or $x = -1$, not at $x = -3$. So the way to write these answers all together with inequality symbols is $-1 \le x \le 1$ or $x < -3$.

17 Solve for x: $|4x-3| < 5$. The answer is $-\frac{1}{2} < x < 2$ or $\left(-\frac{1}{2}, 2\right)$. First, rewrite the absolute value as an inequality. Then use the rules for solving inequalities to isolate x in the middle and determine the answer:

$$|4x-3| < 5 \to -5 < 4x-3 < 5$$

Adding 3 to each section gives you $-2 < 4x < 8$. Then divide each section by 4 to get $-\frac{1}{2} < x < 2$.

18 Solve for x: $5|7x-4|+1 > 6$. The answer is $x > \frac{5}{7}$, $x < \frac{3}{7}$ or $\left(-\infty, \frac{3}{7}\right), \left(\frac{5}{7}, \infty\right)$. Before rewriting the absolute value, it has to be alone, on the left side. First, add –1 to each side: $5|7x-4|+1 > 6 \to 5|7x-4| > 5$. Then divide each side by 5 to get $|7x-4| > 1$. Now you can rewrite the absolute value as two inequality statements. Each statement is solved by performing operations that end up as x greater than or less than some value. Add 4 to each side to get $7x-4 > 1$ or $7x-4 < -1 \to 7x > 5$ or $7x < 3$. And finally divide by 7 to get $x > \frac{5}{7}$ or $x < \frac{3}{7}$.

19 Solve for x: $6 \le 5x+1 < 2x+10$. The answer is $1 \le x < 3$ or $[1, 3)$. First separate $6 \le 5x+1 < 2x+10$ into $6 \le 5x+1$ and $5x+1 < 2x+10$.

When $6 \le 5x+1$, subtract 1 from each side to get $5 \le 5x$ and then divide each side by 5 to get $1 \le x$.

When $5x+1 < 2x+10$, subtract 1 from each side and subtract $2x$ from each side to get $3x < 9$ and then divide each side by 3 to get $x < 3$. So $1 \le x$ and $x < 3$, which gives the answer $1 \le x < 3$. This part of the answer includes the first part, also.

20 Solve for x: $-6 \le 4x-3 < 5x+1$. The answer is $-\frac{3}{4} \le x$ or $\left(-\frac{3}{4}, \infty\right]$. First separate $-6 \le 4x-3 < 5x+1$ into $-6 \le 4x-3$ and $4x-3 < 5x+1$. Solving the first inequality, add 3 to each side to get $-3 \le 4x$. Then divide each side by 4 to get $-\frac{3}{4} \le x$. Solving the other inequality, you subtract 1 from each side and subtract $4x$ from each side to get $-4 < x$. This second part of the answer is an overlap of the first — all the answers are already covered in the first inequality. For x to satisfy both inequalities, the answer is only $-\frac{3}{4} \le x$ or $x \ge -\frac{3}{4}$.

4

Solving Story Problems and Sketching Graphs

IN THIS PART . . .

Work with various formulas.

Try your hand at basic story problems.

Get a stronger handle on relating values in story problems.

Tackle story problems dealing with quality and quantity.

Practice plotting graphs.

» **Introducing perimeter, area, and volume formulas**

» **Computing interest and percentages**

Chapter 17
Facing Up to Formulas

Just as a cook refers to a recipe when preparing delectable concoctions, algebra uses formulas to whip up solutions. In the kitchen, a cook relies on the recipe to turn equal amounts of jalapeños, cream cheese, and beans into a zippy dip. In algebra, a *formula* is an equation that expresses some relationship you can count on to help you concoct such items as the diagonal distance across a rectangle or the amount of interest paid on a loan.

Formulas such as $I = Prt$, $A = \pi r^2$, and $d = rt$ are much more compact than all the words needed to describe them. And as long as you know what the letters stand for, you can use these formulas to solve problems.

Working with formulas is easy. You can apply them to so many situations in algebra and in real life. Most formulas become old, familiar friends. Plus a certain comfort comes from working with formulas, because you know they never change with time, temperature, or relative humidity.

This chapter provides you several chances to work through some of the more common formulas and to tweak areas where you may need a little extra work. The problems are pretty straightforward, and I tell you which formula to use. In Chapter 18, you get to make decisions as to when and if to use a formula, or whether you get to come up with an equation all on your own.

Working with Formulas

A *formula* is an equation that expresses some known relationship between given quantities. You use formulas to determine how much a dollar is worth when you go to another country. You use a formula to figure out how much paint to buy when redecorating your home.

Sometimes, solving for one of the variables in a formula is advantageous if you have to repeat the same computation over and over again. In each of the examples and practice exercises, you use the same rules from solving equations, so you see familiar processes in familiar formulas. The examples in this section introduce you to various formulas and then show you how to use them to solve problems.

EXAMPLE

Q. The formula for changing from degrees Celsius, °C, to degrees Fahrenheit, °F, is $F=\frac{9}{5}C+32$. What is the temperature in degrees Fahrenheit when it's 25 degrees Celsius?

A. **77°F**. Replace *C* with 25, multiply by $9/5$, and then add 32.

$$F=\frac{9}{\cancel{5}}\left(\cancel{25}^{5}\right)+32=45+32=77$$

Q. Use the formula for changing Celsius to Fahrenheit to find the average body temperature in degrees Celsius.

A. **37°C**. First solve for *C* by subtracting 32 from each side of the formula and then multiplying by $5/9$.

$$F-32=\frac{9}{5}C$$

$$\frac{5}{9}(F-32)=\frac{\cancel{5}}{\cancel{9}}\cdot\frac{\cancel{9}}{\cancel{5}}C$$

$$C=\frac{5}{9}(F-32)$$

Now replace *F* with 98.6 (average normal body temperature) and compute *C*.

$$C=\frac{5}{9}(98.6-32)=\frac{5}{9}(66.6)$$

$$=\frac{333.0}{9}=37$$

1 The simple interest formula is $I=Prt$, where *I* is the interest earned, *P* is the principal or what you start with, *r* is the interest rate written as a decimal, and *t* is the amount of time in years. Find *I* if the principal, *P*, is $10,000, the rate, *r* is 2%, and the time, *t*, is 4 years.

2 The simple interest formula is $I=Prt$. Solve for *t* so you can find out how long it takes for $10,000 to earn $1,000 interest when the rate is 2%.

3 The formula for the perimeter of a rectangle is $P = 2(l + w)$. Find the perimeter, P, when the length is 7 feet and the width is one yard.

4 The formula for the area of a trapezoid is $A = \frac{1}{2}h(b_1 + b_2)$. Solve for h so you can determine how high a trapezoid is if the area is 56 square centimeters and the two bases are 6 cm and 8 cm.

Deciphering Perimeter, Area, and Volume

When a problem involves perimeter, area, or volume, take the formula and fill in what you know. Where do you find the formulas? One place is in this book, of course (they're sprinkled throughout the chapters). Geometry books and almanacs also have formulas. Or you can do like my neighbors and call me. (Just not during dinnertime, please.)

In general, *perimeter* is a linear measure of the distance around a figure, *area* is a square measure of how many squares tile the inside of a figure, and *volume* is a cubic measure of how many cubes it takes to fill a three-dimensional figure.

Using perimeter formulas to get around

The *perimeter* of a figure is the distance around its outside. So how do you apply perimeter? You can always just add up the measures of the sides, or you can use perimeter formulas when the amount of fencing you need is for a rectangular yard, or the railing is around a circular track, or the amount of molding is around an octagonal room.

You don't need to memorize all the perimeter formulas; just realize that there are formulas for the perimeters of standard-shaped objects. Perimeter formulas are helpful for doing the needed computing, and you can alter them to solve for the desired value. Other formulas are available in geometry books, almanacs, and books of math tables.

Here are the perimeter (P) formulas for rectangles, squares, and triangles:

» **Rectangle:** $P = 2(l + w)$, where l is the length and w is the width.

» **Square:** $P = 4s$, where s represents the length of a side.

» **Triangle:** $P = a + b + c$, where a, b, and c are the sides.

EXAMPLE

Q. If you know that the perimeter of a particular rectangle is 20 yards and that the length is 8 yards, then what is the width?

A. **2 yards**. You can find a rectangle's perimeter by using the formula $P = 2(l + w)$ where l and w are the length and width of the rectangle. Substitute what you know into the formula and solve for the unknown. In this case, you know P and l. The formula now reads $20 = 2(8 + w)$. Divide each side of the equation by 2 to get $10 = 8 + w$. Subtract 8 from each side, and you get the width, w, of 2 yards.

Q. A. isosceles triangle has a perimeter of 40 yards and two equal sides, each 5 yards longer than the base. How long is the base?

A. **The base is 10 yards long.** First, you can write the triangle's perimeter as $P = 2s + b$. The two equal sides, s, are 5 yards longer than the base, b, which means you can write the lengths of the sides as $b + 5$. Putting $b + 5$ in for the s in the formula and putting the 40 in for P, the problem now involves solving the equation $40 = 2(b + 5) + b$. Distribute the 2 to get $40 = 2b + 10 + b$. Simplify on the right to get $40 = 3b + 10$. Subtracting 10 from each side gives you $30 = 3b$. Dividing by 3, you get $10 = b$. So the base is 10 yards. The two equal sides are then 15 yards each. If you add the two 15-yard sides to the 10-yard base, you get (drum roll, please) $15 + 15 + 10 = 40$, the perimeter.

5 If a rectangle has a length that's 3 inches greater than twice the width, and if the perimeter of the rectangle is 36 inches, then what is its length?

6 You have 400 feet of fencing to fence in a rectangular yard. If the yard is 30 feet wide and you're going to use all 400 feet to fence in the yard, then how long is the yard?

A square and an *equilateral* triangle (all three sides equal in length) have sides that are the same length. If the sum of their perimeters is 84 feet, then what is the perimeter of the square?

A triangle has one side that's twice as long as the shortest side, and a third side that's 8 inches longer than the shortest side. Its perimeter is 60 inches. What are the lengths of the three sides?

Squaring off with area formulas

You measure the area of a figure in square inches, square feet, square yards, and so on. Some of the more commonly found figures, such as rectangles, circles, and triangles, have standard area formulas. Obscure figures even have formulas, but they aren't used very often, especially in an algebra class. Here are the area formulas for rectangles, squares, circles, and triangles:

- **Rectangle:** $A = lw$, where *l* and *w* represent the length and width
- **Square:** $A = s^2$, where *s* represents the length of a side
- **Circle:** $A = \pi r^2$, where *r* is the radius
- **Triangle:** $A = \frac{1}{2}bh$, where *b* is the base and *h* is the height

EXAMPLE

Q. Find the area of a circle with a circumference of 1,256 feet.

A. **125,600 square feet**. You're told that the distance around the outside (*circumference*) of a circular field is 1,256 feet. The formula for the circumference of a circle is $C = \pi d = 2\pi r$, which says that the circumference is π (about 3.14) times the diameter or two times π times the radius. To find the area of a circle, you need the formula $A = \pi r^2$. So to find the area of this circular field, you first find the radius by putting the 1,256 feet into the circumference formula: $1,256 = 2\pi r$. Replace the π with 3.14 and solve for *r*:

$$\frac{1,256}{2\pi} = \frac{\cancel{2\pi} r}{\cancel{2\pi}}$$

$$r = \frac{1,256}{2\pi} \approx \frac{1,256}{2(3.14)} = \frac{1,256}{6.28} = 200$$

The radius is 200 feet. Putting that into the area formula, you get that the area is 125,600 square feet.

$$A = \pi r^2 \approx 3.14(200)^2 = 3.14(40,000)$$
$$= 125,600$$

Q. A builder is designing a house with a square room. If she increases the sides of the room by 8 feet, the area increases by 224 square feet. What are the dimensions of the expanded room?

A. **18 by 18 feet**. You can find the area of a square with $A = s^2$, where s is the length of the sides. Start by letting the original room have sides measuring s feet. Its area is $A = s^2$. The larger room has sides that measure $s + 8$ feet. Its area is $A = (s+8)^2$. The difference between these two areas is 224 feet, so subtract the smaller area from the larger and write the equation showing the 224 as a difference: $(s+8)^2 - s^2 = 224$. Simplify the left side of the equation: $s^2 + 16s + 64 - s^2 = 16s + 64 = 224$. Subtract 64 from each side and then divide by 16: $16s = 160 \rightarrow \frac{\cancel{16}s}{\cancel{16}} = \frac{160}{16} = 10$.

The original room has walls measuring 10 feet. Eight feet more than that is 18 feet.

9 If a rectangle is 4 inches longer than it is wide and the area is 60 square inches, then what are the dimensions of the rectangle?

10 You can find the area of a trapezoid with $A = \frac{1}{2}h(b_1 + b_2)$. Determine the length of the base b_1 if the trapezoid has an area of 30 square yards, a height of 5 yards, and the base b_2 of 3 yards.

11 The perimeter of a square is 40 feet. What is its area? (Remember: $P = 4s$ and $A = s^2$.)

12 You can find the area of a triangle with $A = \frac{1}{2}bh$, where the base and the height are perpendicular to one another. If a right triangle has legs measuring 10 inches and 24 inches and a hypotenuse of 26 inches, what is its area?

Working with volume formulas

The *volume* of an object is a three-dimensional measurement. In a way, you're asking, "How many little cubes can I fit into this object?" Cubes won't fit into spheres, pyramids, or other structures with slants and curves, so you have to accept that some of these little cubes are getting shaved off or cut into pieces to fit. Having a formula is much easier than actually sitting and trying to fit all those little cubes into an often large or unwieldy object. Here are the important volume formulas:

- **Box (rectangular prism):** $V = lwh$
- **Sphere:** $V = \frac{4}{3}\pi r^3$
- **Cylinder:** $V = \pi r^2 h$

EXAMPLE

Q. What are the possible dimensions of a refrigerator that has a capacity of 8 cubic feet?

A. **It could be 1 foot deep, 1 foot wide, and 8 feet high, or it could be 2 feet deep, 2 feet wide, and 2 feet high (there are lots of answers).** A refrigerator with these suggested dimensions isn't very efficient — or easy to find. Maybe 1 foot deep by 2 feet wide by 4 feet high would be better. More likely than not, it's something more like $1\frac{1}{2} \times 2 \times 2\frac{2}{3}$ feet.

Q. Find the volume of an orange traffic cone that's 30 inches tall and has a diameter of 18 inches.

A. **A little more than 2,543 cubic inches.** A right circular cone (that's what those traffic cones outlining a construction area look like) has a volume you can find if you know its radius and its height. The formula is $V = \frac{1}{3}\pi r^2 h$. As you can see, the multiplier π is in this formula because the base is a circle. Use 3.14 as an estimate of π; because the diameter is 18 inches, use 9 inches for the radius. To find this cone's volume, put those dimensions into the formula to get $V = \frac{1}{3}(3.14)(9)^2(30) = 2{,}543.4$. The cone's volume is over 2,500 cubic inches.

13 You can find the volume of a box (right rectangular prism) with $V = lwh$. Find the height of the box if the volume is 200 cubic feet and the square base is 5 feet on each side (length and width are each 5).

14 The volume of a sphere (ball) is $V = \frac{4}{3}\pi r^3$, where r is the *radius* of the sphere — the measure from the center to the outside. What is the volume of a sphere with a radius of 6 inches?

15 You can find the volume of a right circular cylinder (soda pop can) with $V = \pi r^2 h$, where r is the radius, and h is the height of the cylinder — the distance between the two circular bases (the top and bottom of the can). Which has the greater volume: a cylinder with a radius of 6 cm and a height of 9 cm or a cylinder with a radius of 9 cm and a height of 4 cm?

16 The volume of a cube is 216 cubic centimeters. What is the new volume if you double the length of each side?

Getting Interested in Using Percent

Percentages are a form of leveling the playing field. They're great for comparing ratios of numbers that have different bases. For example, if you want to compare the fact that 45 men out of 80 bought a Kindle with the fact that 33 women out of 60 bought a Kindle, you can change both of these to percentages to determine who is more likely to buy a Kindle. (In this case, it's $56\frac{1}{4}\%$ men and 55% women.)

To change a ratio or fraction to a percent, divide the part by the whole (numerator by denominator) and multiply by 100. For instance, in the case of the Kindles, you divide 45 by 80 and get 0.5625. Multiplying that by 100, you get 56.25 which you can write as $56\frac{1}{4}\%$.

Percents also show up in interest formulas because you earn interest on an investment or pay interest on a loan based on a percentage of the initial amount. The formula for simple interest is $I = Prt$, which is translated as "Interest earned is equal to the principal invested times the interest rate (written as a decimal) times time (the number of years)."

Compare the total amount of money earning simple interest with the total you'd have if you invested in an account that compounded interest. *Compounding* means that the interest is added to the initial amount at certain intervals, and the interest is then figured on the new sum. The formula for compound interest is $A = P\left(1+\frac{r}{n}\right)^{nt}$. The A is the total amount — the principal plus the interest earned. The P is the principal, the r is the interest rate written as a decimal, the n is the number of times each year that compounding occurs, and the t is the number of years.

EXAMPLE

Q. How much money do you have after 5 years if you invest $1,000 at 4% simple interest?

A. **$1,200**. Multiplying 1,000(0.04)(5), you get that you'll earn $200 in simple interest. Add that to the amount you started with for a total of $1,200.

Q. How much money will you have if you invest that same $1,000 at 4% for 5 years compounded quarterly (4 times each year)?

A. **$1,220.19**. Putting the numbers in the formula, you get $A = 1{,}000\left(1+\frac{0.04}{4}\right)^{4(5)}$. Using a calculator, the result comes out to be $1,220.19. True, that's not all that much more than using simple interest, but the more money you invest, the bigger difference it makes.

17 If 60% of the class has the flu and that 60% is 21 people, then how many are in the class?

18 How much simple interest will you earn on $4,000 invested at 3% for 10 years? What is the total amount of money at the end of the 10 years?

19 How much money will be in an account that started with $4,000 and earned 3% compounded quarterly for 10 years?

20 If you earned $500 in simple interest on an investment that was deposited at 2% interest for 5 years, how much had you invested?

Answers to Problems on Using Formulas

The following are the answers (in bold) to the practice problems in this chapter.

1. The simple interest formula is $I = Prt$. Find I if the principal, P, is \$10,000, the rate, r, is 2%, and the time, t, is 4 years. The answer is **\$800.**

   Inserting the numbers into the formula (and changing 2% to the decimal equivalent 0.02), you get $I = 10{,}000(0.02)4 = 800$.

2. The simple interest formula is $I = Prt$. Solve for t so you can find out how long it takes for \$10,000 to earn \$1,000 interest when the rate is 2%. The answer is **5 years.**

   Solving for t, you divide each side of the formula by Pr:

   $$I = Prt \rightarrow \frac{I}{Pr} = \frac{\cancel{Pr}t}{\cancel{Pr}} \rightarrow \frac{I}{Pr} = t$$

   Plug the values into the new equation and solve:

   $$t = \frac{I}{Pr} = \frac{1{,}000}{10{,}000(0.02)} = \frac{1{,}000}{200} = 5$$

3. The formula for the perimeter of a rectangle is $P = 2(l + w)$. Find the perimeter, P, when the length is 7 feet and the width is one yard. The answer is **20 feet.**

   The length and width are in different units. Changing one yard to 3 feet and substituting into the formula, you get $P = 2(7 + 3) = 2(10) = 20$.

4. The formula for the area of a trapezoid is $A = \frac{1}{2}h(b_1 + b_2)$. Solve for h so you can determine how high a trapezoid is if the area is 56 square centimeters and the two bases are 6 cm. and 8 cm. The answer is **8 cm.**

   To solve for h, multiply each side of the formula by 2 and the divide by the sum in the parentheses:

   $$2A = \cancel{2}\left(\frac{1}{\cancel{2}}\right)h(b_1 + b_2) \rightarrow 2A = h(b_1 + b_2) \rightarrow \frac{2A}{(b_1 + b_2)} = \frac{h\cancel{(b_1 + b_2)}}{\cancel{(b_1 + b_2)}} = h$$

   Now use the new formula to solve for h: $h = \frac{2A}{(b_1 + b_2)} = \frac{2(56)}{6 + 8} = \frac{2(56)}{14} = \frac{2(\cancel{56}^{4})}{\cancel{14}} = 8$

5. If a rectangle has a length that's 3 inches greater than twice the width, and if the perimeter of the rectangle is 36 inches, then what is its length? **The length is 13 inches.** Use this figure to help you solve this problem.

   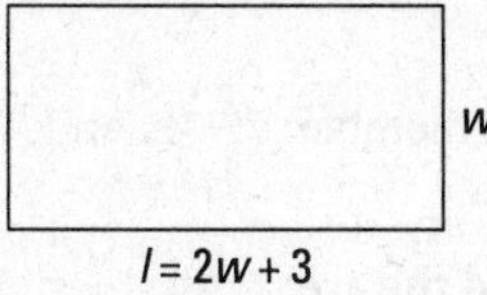

   Let w = the width of the rectangle, which makes the length, $l = 3 + 2w$. A rectangle's perimeter is $P = 2(l + w)$. Substituting in $3 + 2w$ for the l in this formula and replacing P with 36, you get $36 = 2(3 + 2w + w)$. Simplifying, you get $36 = 2(3w + 3)$. Now divide each side of the equation by

2 to get $18 = 3w + 3$. Subtract 3 from each side: $15 = 3w$. Divide each side by 3 to get $5 = w$. The length is $3 + 2w = 3 + 2(5) = 13$. The rectangle is 5 inches by 13 inches.

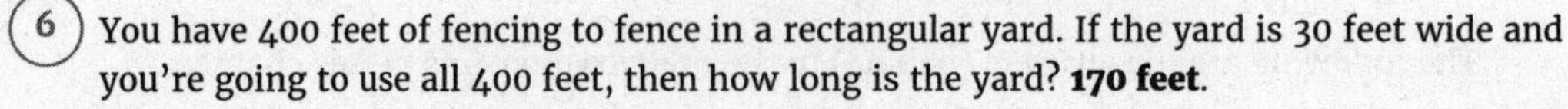

6 You have 400 feet of fencing to fence in a rectangular yard. If the yard is 30 feet wide and you're going to use all 400 feet, then how long is the yard? **170 feet.**

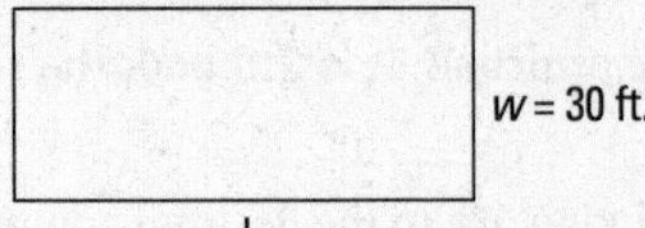

You know that the total distance around the yard (its perimeter) is 400 and the width of the yard is 30, so plug those values into the formula $P = 2(l + w)$ to get $400 = 2(l + 30)$. Divide by 2 to get $200 = l + 30$ and then subtract 30 from each side to get $200 - 30 = l$. So $l = 170$ feet.

7 A square and an *equilateral* triangle (all three sides equal in length) have sides that are the same length. If the sum of their perimeters is 84 feet, then what is the perimeter of the square? **48 feet.**

The perimeter of the square is $4l$, and the perimeter of the equilateral triangle is $3l$. Adding these together, you get $4l + 3l = 7l = 84$ feet. Dividing each side of $7l = 84$ by 7 gives you $l = 12$ feet. So the perimeter of the square is $4(12) = 48$ feet.

8 A triangle has one side that's twice as long as the shortest side and a third side that's 8 inches longer than the shortest side. Its perimeter is 60 inches. What are the lengths of the three sides? **13 inches, 26 inches, 21 inches.**

This problem doesn't need a special perimeter formula. The perimeter of a triangle is just the sum of the measures of the three sides. Letting the shortest side be x, twice that is 2x, and 8 more than that is $x + 8$. Add the three measures together to get $x + 2x + x + 8 = 60$, which works out to be $4x + 8 = 60$, or $4x = 52$. Dividing by 4 to $x = 13$. Twice that is 26, and eight more than that is 21.

9 If a rectangle is 4 inches longer than it is wide and the area is 60 square inches, what are the dimensions of the rectangle? **6 inches by 10 inches.**

Using the area formula for a rectangle, $A = lw$, and letting $l = w + 4$, you get the equation $w(w + 4) = 60$. Simplifying, setting the equation equal to 0, and then factoring gives you $w^2 + 4w = 60 \rightarrow w^2 + 4w - 60 = 0 \rightarrow (w + 10)(w - 6) = 0$. The two solutions of the equation are -10 and 6. Only the $+6$ makes sense, so the width is 6, and the length is 4 more than that, or 10.

10 You can find the area of a trapezoid with $A = \frac{1}{2}h(b_1 + b_2)$. Determine the length of the base b_1 if the trapezoid has an area of 30 square yards, a height of 5 yards, and the base b_2 of 3 yards. **9 yards.**

Plug in the values and then multiply each side by two: $A = \frac{1}{2}h(b_1 + b_2) \rightarrow 30\frac{1}{2}(5)(b_1 + 3) \rightarrow$ $60 = (5)(b_1 + 3)$. Then divide each side by 5 to get $12 = b_1 + 3$. Do the math to find that $12 - 3 = b_1$, so $b_1 = 9$ yards.

11 The perimeter of a square is 40 feet. What is its area? (Remember: $P = 4s$ and $A = s^2$.) **100 square feet.**

Dividing each side of $40 = 4s$ by 4, you get $10 = s$. Now find the area with $A = s^2$. Yes, 100 square feet is correct.

12 You can find the area of a triangle with $A = \frac{1}{2}bh$ where the base (b) and the height (h) are perpendicular to one another. If a right triangle has legs of 10 inches and 24 inches and a hypotenuse of 26 inches, then what is its area? **120 square inches.**

In a right triangle, the hypotenuse is always the longest side, and the two legs are perpendicular to one another. Use the measures of the two legs for your base and height, so $A = \frac{1}{2}(10)(24) = 120$.

13 You can find the volume of a box with $V = lwh$. Find the height if the volume is 200 cubic feet and the square base is 5 feet on each side (length and width are each 5). **8 feet.**

Replace the V with 200 and replace the l and w each with 5 to get $200 = 5(5)h = 25h$. Dividing each side of $200 = 25h$ by 25, you get $h = 8$. So the height is 8 feet.

14 The volume of a sphere (ball) is $V = \frac{4}{3}\pi r^3$, where r is the *radius* of the sphere — the measure from the center to the outside. What is the volume of a sphere with a radius of 6 inches? **904.32 cubic inches.**

Substituting in the 6 for r, you get $V = \frac{4}{3}(3.14)(6^3) = 904.32$ cubic inches.

15 You can find the volume of a right circular cylinder (soda pop can) with $V = \pi r^2 h$, where r is the radius and h is the height of the cylinder — the distance between the two circular bases (the top and bottom of the can). Which has the greater volume: a cylinder with a radius of 6 cm and a height of 9 cm or a cylinder with a radius of 9 cm and a height of 4 cm? **Neither, the volumes are the same.**

The first volume is $V = \pi(6^2)(9) = 324\pi \text{ cm}^3$.

The second volume is $V = \pi(9^2)(4) = 324\pi \text{ cm}^3$.

So they have the same volume, namely $324(3.14) = 1{,}017.36$ cubic centimeters.

16 The volume of a cube is 216 cubic centimeters. What is the new volume if you double the length of each side? **1,728 cm³.**

First, find the lengths of the edges of the original cube. If $s =$ the length of the edge of the cube, then use the formula for the volume of a cube $(V = s^3)$.

$$216 = s^3 \rightarrow c = \sqrt[3]{216} = 6$$

Doubling the length of the edge for the new cube results in sides of $2(6) = 12$ centimeters. So the volume of the new cube is $V = 12^3 = 1{,}728 \text{ cm}^3$.

17 If 60% of the class has the flu and that 60% is 21 people, then how many are in the class? **35 people.**

Let $x =$ the number of people in the class. Then 60% of x is 21, which is written $0.60x = 21$. Divide each side by 0.60, and you get that $x = 35$ people.

18 How much simple interest will you earn on \$4,000 invested at 3% for 10 years? What is the total amount of money the end of the 10 years? **\$1,200 and \$5,200.**

Use the formula $I = Prt$, where the principal (P) is 4,000, the rate (r) is 0.03, and the time (t) is 10: $I = 4{,}000(0.03)(10) = \$1{,}200$. Add this amount to the original \$4,000 to get a total of \$5,200.

19 How much money will be in an account that started with \$4,000 and earned 3% compounded quarterly for 10 years? **\$5,393.39.**

Use the formula for compound interest: $A = P\left(1+\frac{r}{n}\right)^{nt}$. (***Note:*** Compare this total amount with the total using simple interest, in problem 18. In that problem, the total is $\$4,000 + 1,200 = \$5,200$.) In the compound interest formula, $P = 4,000$, $r = 0.03$, $n = 4$, and $t = 10$.

$$A = 4,000\left(1+\frac{0.03}{4}\right)^{4(10)} = 4,000(1+0.0075)^{40} = 5,393.3944 = \$5,393.39$$

So you do slightly better by letting the interest compound.

20 If you earned \$500 in simple interest for an investment that was deposited at 2% interest for 5 years, how much had you invested? **\$5,000.**

Use $I = Prt$ where $I = 500$, $r = 0.02$, and $t = 5$. Putting the numbers into the formula, $500 = P(0.02)(5) = P(0.1)$. Divide each side of $500 = P(0.1)$ by 0.1, and you get that $P = 5,000$, or the amount that was invested.

» Tackling geometric structures

» Moving along with distance problems

Chapter 18

Making Formulas Work in Basic Story Problems

Algebra students often groan and moan when they see story problems. You "feel their pain," you say? It's time to put the myth to bed that story problems are too challenging. You know you're facing a story problem when you see a bunch of words followed by a question. And the trick to doing story problems is quite simple. Change the words into a solvable equation, solve that equation (now a familiar friend), and then answer the question based on the equation's solution. Coming up with the equation is often the biggest challenge. However, some story problems have a formula built into them to help. Look for those first.

One technique for being successful with story problems is to start writing. Take your pencil and draw a picture of what's going on. Next, read the last sentence. No, this isn't a book where you don't want to go to the end and spoil the rest of the story. The last sentence has the biggest clue; it tells you what you're solving for. Take that pencil and start assigning letters (variables) to the different values in the problem. Just remember that a letter has to represent a number, not a person or thing.

Take a deep breath. Grab your pencil. Charge!

Applying the Pythagorean Theorem

Pythagoras, the Greek mathematician, is credited for discovering the wonderful relationship between the lengths of the sides of a *right triangle* (a triangle with one 90 degree angle). The Pythagorean theorem is $a^2 + b^2 = c^2$. If you square the length of the two shorter sides of a right triangle and add them, then that sum equals the square of the longest side (called the *hypotenuse*), which is always across from the right angle. Right triangles show up frequently in story problems, so when you recognize them, you have an instant, built-in equation to work with on the problem.

EXAMPLE

Q. I have a helium-filled balloon attached to the end of a 500-foot string. My friend, Keith, is standing directly under the balloon, 300 feet away from me. (And yes, the ground is perfectly level, as it always is in these hypothetical situations — at least until you get into higher math.) These dimensions form a right triangle, with the string as the hypotenuse. Here's the question: How high up is the balloon?

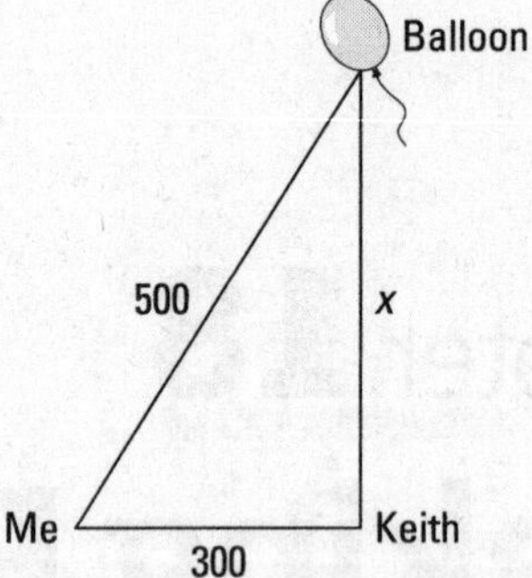

A. **400 feet up**. Identify the parts of the right triangle in this situation and substitute the known values into the Pythagorean theorem. Refer to the picture.

The 500-foot string forms the hypotenuse, so the equation reads $300^2 + x^2 = 500^2$. Solving for x,

$$90{,}000 + x^2 = 250{,}000$$
$$x^2 = 250{,}000 - 90{,}000 = 160{,}000$$
$$x = \pm\sqrt{160{,}000} = \pm 400$$

You only use the positive solution to this equation because a negative answer doesn't make any sense.

1. Jack's recliner is in the corner of a rectangular room that measures 10 feet by 24 feet. His television is in the opposite corner. How far is Jack (his head, when the recliner is wide open) from the television? (***Hint:*** Assume that the distance across the room is the hypotenuse of a right triangle.)

2. Sammy's house is 1,300 meters from Tammy's house — straight across the lake. The paths they need to take to get to one another's house (and not get wet) form a right angle. If the path from Sammy's house to the corner is 1,200 meters, then how long is the path from the corner to Tammy's house?

3 A ladder from the ground to a window that's 24 feet above the ground is placed 7 feet from the base of the building, forming a right triangle. How long is the ladder, if it just reaches the window?

4 Calista flew 400 miles due north and then turned due east and flew another 90 miles. How far is she from where she started?

Using Geometry to Solve Story Problems

Geometry is a subject that has something for everyone. It has pictures, formulas, proofs, and practical applications for the homeowner. The perimeter, area, and volume formulas are considered to be a part of geometry. But geometry also deals in angle measures, parallel lines, congruent triangles, polygons and similar figures, and so forth. The different properties that you find in the study of geometry are helpful in solving many story problems.

Story problems that use geometry are some of the more popular (if you can call any story problem popular) because they come with ready-made equations from the formulas. Also, you can draw a picture to illustrate the problem. I'm a very visual person, and I find pictures and labels on the pictures to be very helpful.

EXAMPLE

Q. The opposite angles in a parallelogram are equal, and the adjacent angles in the parallelogram are *supplementary* (add up to 180 degrees). If one of the angles of a parallelogram measures 20 degrees more than three times another angle, then how big is the larger of the two angles?

A. **140 degrees.** The two angles have different measures, so they must be adjacent to one another. The sum of adjacent angles is 180. Let *x* represent the measure of the smaller angle. Then, because the larger angle is *20 degrees more than three times* the smaller, you can write its measure as $20+3x$. Represent this in an equation in which the two angle measures are added together and the sum is 180: $x+20+3x=180$. Simplifying and subtracting 20 from each side, you get $4x=160$. Divide by 4 to get $x=40$. Putting 40 in for *x* in the measure $20+3x$, you get $20+120=140$.

Q. An *isosceles triangle* has two sides that have the same measure. In a particular isosceles triangle that has a perimeter of 27 inches, the base (the side with a different measure) is 1 foot more than twice the measure of either of the other two sides. How long is the base?

A. **14 inches.** The perimeter of the isosceles triangle is $x+x+1+2x=27$. The *x* represents the lengths of the two congruent sides, and $1+2x$ is the measure of the base. Simplifying and subtracting 1 from each side of the equation, you get $4x=26$. Dividing by 4, you get $x=6\,{}^1\!/_2$ inches. The base is equal to $1+2\left(6\,{}^1\!/_2\right)=1+13=14$.

5 The sum of the measures of the angles of a triangle is 180 degrees. In a certain triangle, one angle is 10 degrees greater than the smallest angle, and the biggest angle is 15 times as large as the smallest. What is the measure of that biggest angle?

6 A *pentagon* is a five-sided polygon. In a certain pentagon, one side is twice as long as the smallest side, another side is 6 inches longer than the smallest side, the fourth side is 2 inches longer than two times the smallest side, and the fifth side is half as long as the fourth side. If the perimeter of the pentagon is 65 inches, what are the lengths of the five sides?

7 The sum of the measures of the angles in a *quadrilateral* (a polygon with 4 sides) adds up to 360 degrees. If one of the angles is twice as big as the smallest and the other two angles are both three times as big as the smallest, then what is the measure of that smallest angle?

8 The sum of the measures of all the angles in any polygon can be found with the formula $A = 180(n-2)$, where n is the number of sides that the polygon has. How many sides are there on a polygon where the sum of the measures is 1,080 degrees?

9 Two figures are similar when they're exactly the same shape — their corresponding angles are exactly the same measure, but the corresponding sides don't have to be the same length. When two figures are similar, their corresponding sides are proportional (all have the same ratio to one another). In the figure, triangle ABC is similar to triangle DEF, with AB corresponding to DE and BC corresponding to EF.

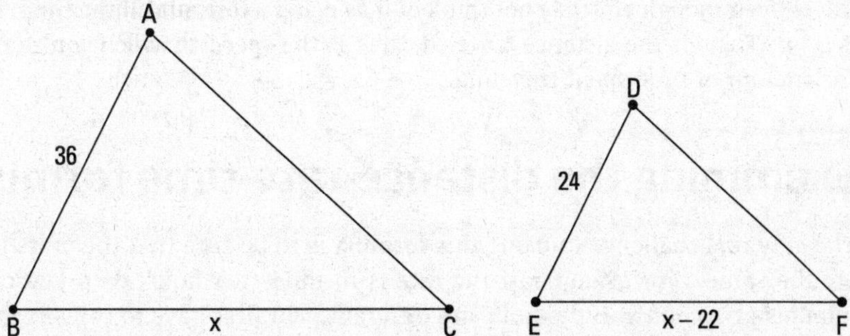

If side EF is 22 units smaller than side BC, then what is the measure of side BC?

10 The exterior angle of a triangle lies along the same line as the interior angle it's next to. See the following figure.

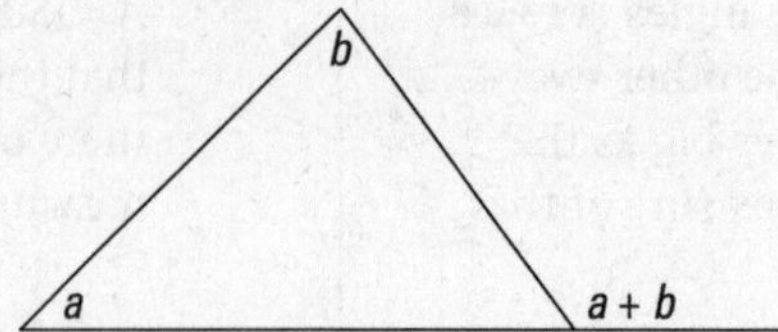

The measure of an exterior angle of a triangle is always equal to the sum of the other two interior angles. If one of the nonadjacent angles in a triangle measures 30 degrees, and if the exterior angle measures 70 degrees less than twice the measure of the other nonadjacent angle, then how big is that exterior angle?

Putting Distance, Rate, and Time in a Formula

The distance-rate-time formula is probably the formula you're most familiar with from daily life — even though you may not think of it as using a formula all the time. The distance formula is $d = rt$. The d is the distance traveled, the r is the speed at which you're traveling, and the t is the amount of time spent traveling.

Examining the distance-rate-time formula

WARNING

The only real challenge in using this formula is to be sure that the units in the different parts are the same. (For example, if the rate is in miles per hour, then you can't use the time in minutes or seconds.) If the units are different, you first have to convert them to an equivalent value before you can use the formula.

EXAMPLE

Q. How long does it take for light from the sun to reach Earth? (***Hint:*** The sun is 93 million miles from Earth, and light travels at 186,000 miles per second.)

A. **About $8\frac{1}{3}$ minutes**. Using $d = rt$ and substituting the distance (93 million miles) for d and 186,000 for r, you get $93{,}000{,}000 = 186{,}000t$. Dividing each side by 186,000, t comes out to be 500 seconds. Divide 500 seconds by 60 seconds per minute, and you get $8\frac{1}{3}$ minutes.

Q. How fast do you go to travel 200 miles in 300 minutes?

A. **Average 40 mph**. Assume you're driving over the river and through the woods, you need to get to Grandmother's house by the time the turkey is done, which is in 300 minutes. It's 200 miles to Grandmother's house. Because your speedometer is in miles per hour, change the 300 minutes to hours by dividing by 60, which gives you 5 hours. Fill the values into the distance formula, $200 = 5r$. Dividing by 5, it looks like you have to average 40 miles per hour.

11 How long will it take you to travel 600 miles if you're averaging 50 mph?

12 What was your average speed (just using the actual driving time) if you left home at noon, drove 200 miles, stopped for an hour to eat, drove another 130 miles, and arrived at your destination at 7 p.m.?

Going the distance with story problems

Distance problems use, as you would expect, the distance formula, $d = rt$. There are two traditional types of distance problems. Recognizing them for what they are makes life so much easier.

One type of distance problem involves setting two distances *equal to* one another. The usual situation is that one person is traveling at one speed and another person is traveling at another speed, and they end up at the same place at the same time. The other traditional distance problem involves *adding* two distances together, giving you a total distance apart. That's it. All you have to do is determine whether you're equating or adding!

EXAMPLE

Q. Angelina left home traveling at an average of 40 mph. Brad left the same place an hour later, traveling at an average of 60 mph. How long did it take for Brad to catch up to Angelina?

A. **2 hours**. This type of problem is where you set the distances equal to one another. You don't know what the distance is, but you know that the rate times the time of each must equal the same thing. So let t represent the amount of time that Angelina traveled and set Angelina's distance, $40t$, equal to Brad's distance, $60(t-1)$. (Remember, he traveled one less hour than Angelina did.) Then solve the equation $40t = 60(t-1)$. Distribute the 60 on the right, giving you $40t = 60t - 60$. Subtract $60t$ from each side, resulting in $-20t = -60$. Divide by -20, and you get that $t = 3$. Angelina traveled for 3 hours at 40 mph, which is 120 miles. Brad traveled for 2 hours at 60 mph, which is also 120 miles.

Q. One train leaves Kansas City traveling due east at 45 mph. A second train leaves Kansas City three hours later, traveling due west at 60 mph. When are they 870 miles apart?

A. **10 hours after the first train left**. This type of problem is where you add two distances together. Let t represent the time that the first train traveled and $45t$ represent the distance that the first train traveled. This is rate times time, which equals the distance. The second train didn't travel as long; its time will be $t-3$, so represent its distance as $60(t-3)$. Set the equation up so that the two distances are added together and the sum is equal to 870: $45t + 60(t-3) = 870$. Distribute the 60 on the left and simplify the terms to get $105t - 180 = 870$. Add 180 to each side to get $105t = 1{,}050$. Divide each side by 105, and you have $t = 10$ hours.

13 Kelly left school at 4 p.m. traveling at 25 mph. Ken left at 4:30 p.m., traveling at 30 mph, following the same route as Kelly. At what time did Ken catch up with Kelly?

14 A Peoria Charter Coach bus left the bus terminal at 6 a.m. heading due north and traveling at an average of 45 mph. A second bus left the terminal at 7 a.m., heading due south and traveling at an average of 55 mph. When were the buses 645 miles apart?

15 Geoffrey and Grace left home at the same time. Geoffrey walked east at an average rate of 2.5 mph. Grace rode her bicycle due south at 6 mph until they were 65 miles apart. How long did it take them to be 65 miles apart?

16 Melissa and Heather drove home for the holidays in separate cars, even though they live in the same place. Melissa's trip took two hours longer than Heather's because Heather drove an average of 20 mph faster than Melissa's 40 mph. How far did they have to drive?

Answers to Making Formulas Work in Basic Story Problems

The following are the answers (in bold) to the practice problems in this chapter.

1. Jack's recliner is in the corner of a rectangular room that measures 10 feet by 24 feet. His television is in the opposite corner. How far is Jack (his head, when the recliner is wide open) from the television? (*Hint:* Assume that the distance across the room is the hypotenuse of a right triangle.) **26 feet.**

$$\begin{aligned} 10^2 + 24^2 &= c^2 \\ 100 + 576 &= c^2 \\ c^2 &= 676 = 26^2 \\ c &= 26 \end{aligned}$$

2. Sammy's house is 1,300 meters from Tammy's house — straight across the lake. The paths they need to take to get to one another's house (and not get wet) form a right angle. If the path from Sammy's house to the corner is 1,200 meters, then how long is the path from the corner to Tammy's house? **500 meters.**

$$\begin{aligned} 1{,}200^2 + b^2 &= 1{,}300^2 \\ 1{,}440{,}000 + b^2 &= 1{,}690{,}000 \\ b^2 &= 1{,}690{,}000 - 1{,}440{,}000 = 250{,}000 = 500^2 \\ b &= 500 \end{aligned}$$

3. A ladder from the ground to a window that's 24 feet above the ground is placed 7 feet from the base of the building. How long is the ladder, if it just reaches the window? **25 feet.** Check out the following figure.

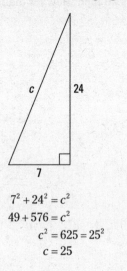

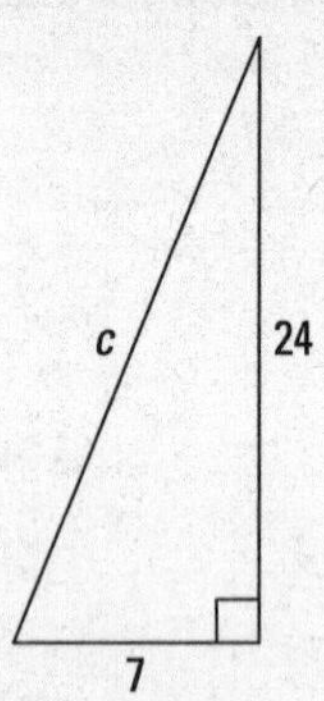

$$\begin{aligned} 7^2 + 24^2 &= c^2 \\ 49 + 576 &= c^2 \\ c^2 &= 625 = 25^2 \\ c &= 25 \end{aligned}$$

4. Calista flew 400 miles due north and then turned due east and flew another 90 miles. How far is she from where she started? **410 miles**. See the following figure.

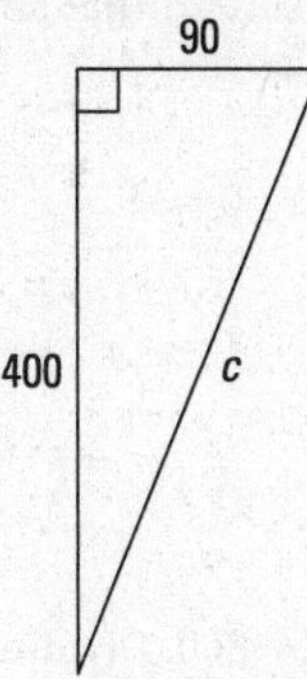

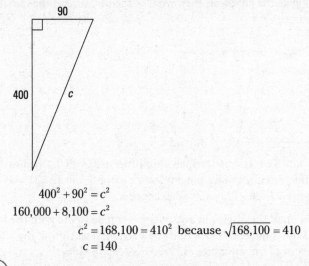

$$400^2 + 90^2 = c^2$$
$$160{,}000 + 8{,}100 = c^2$$
$$c^2 = 168{,}100 = 410^2 \text{ because } \sqrt{168{,}100} = 410$$
$$c = 140$$

5. The sum of the measures of the angles of a triangle is 180 degrees. In a certain triangle, one angle is 10 degrees greater than the smallest angle, and the biggest angle is 15 times as large as the smallest. What is the measure of that biggest angle? **150 degrees**. Look at the figure for help.

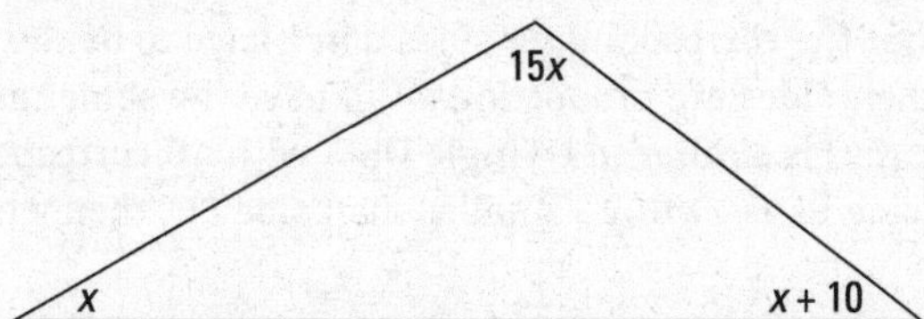

Let x = the measure of the smallest angle in degrees. Then the other two angles measure $x+10$ and 15x. Add them to get $x+x+10+15x=180$. Simplifying on the left, you get $17x+10=180$. Subtract 10 from each side: $17x=170$. Then, dividing by 17, $x=10$ degrees, and the largest angle, which is 15 times as great, is 150 degrees.

To check, find the measure of the other angle, $x+10=10+10=20$. Adding up the three angles, you get $10+20+150=180$.

6. A *pentagon* is a five-sided polygon. In a certain pentagon, one side is twice as long as the smallest side, another side is 6 inches longer than the smallest side, the fourth side is 2 inches longer than two times the smallest side, and the fifth side is half as long as the fourth side. If the perimeter of the pentagon is 65 inches, what are the lengths of the five sides? **8 inches, 16 inches, 14 inches, 18 inches, 9 inches.**

Let x represent the length of the smallest side. Then the second side is 2x long, the third side is $x+6$, the fourth is $2+2x$, and the fifth is $\frac{1}{2}(2+2x)=1+x$. Add up all the sides and set the sum equal to 65: $x+2x+x+6+2+2x+1+x=65$. Simplifying, you get $7x+9=65$. Subtract 9 from each side and divide by 7 to get $x=8$.

7. The sum of the measures of the angles in a *quadrilateral* (a polygon with four sides) adds up to 360 degrees. If one of the angles is twice as big as the smallest and the other two angles are both three times as big as the smallest, then what is the measure of that smallest angle? **40 degrees**. Look at this figure.

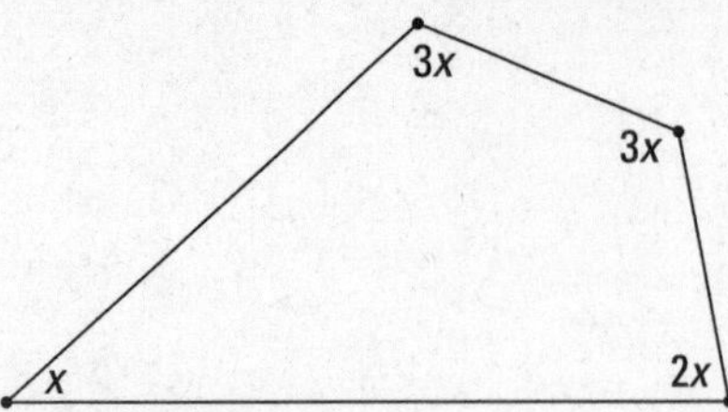

Their sum is 360, so $x+2x+3x+3x=360$, which simplifies to $9x=360$. Dividing by 9, $x=40$ degrees. To check, find the measures of all the angles: $2x=2(40)=80$ and $3x=3(40)=120$. Adding them all up, you get $40+80+120+120=360$ degrees.

8. The sum of the measures of all the angles in any polygon can be found with the formula $A=180(n-2)$, where n is the number of sides that the polygon has. How many sides are there on a polygon where the sum of the measures is 1,080 degrees? **8 sides.**

   Use the formula $A=180(n-2)$, where n is that number you're trying to find. Replace the A with 1,080 to get $1{,}080=180(n-2)$. Divide each side by 180 to get $6=n-2$. Add 2 to each side, and $n=8$. So it's an eight-sided polygon that has that sum for the angles.

9. Two figures are *similar* when they're exactly the same shape — their corresponding angles are exactly the same measure, but the corresponding sides don't have to be the same length. When two figures are similar, their sides are proportional (all have the same ratio to one another). In the figure, triangle ABC is similar to triangle DEF, with AB corresponding to DE and BC corresponding to EF. If side EF is 22 units smaller than side BC, then what is the measure of side BC? **66 units.**

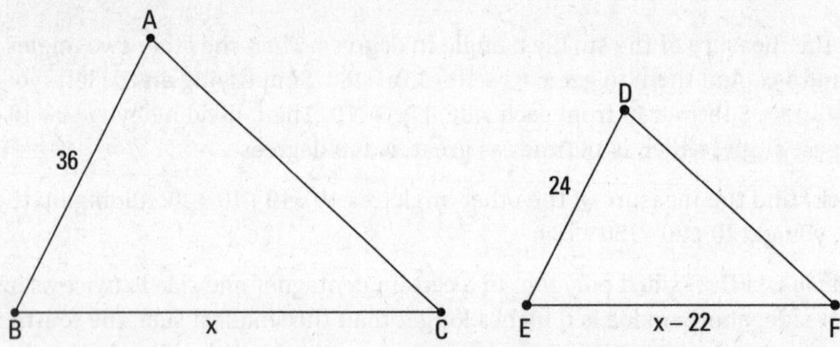

A proportion that represents the relationship between sides of the triangle is $\frac{AB}{DE}=\frac{BC}{EF}$.

Replacing the names of the segments with the respective labels, you get $\frac{36}{24}=\frac{x}{x-22}$. Cross-multiply (refer to Chapter 12 if you need more information on dealing with proportions) to get $36(x-22)=24x$. Distributing on the left, you get $36x-792=24x$. Subtract $24x$ from each side and add 782 to each side for $12x=792$. Dividing by 12, you find that $x=66$. (***Hint:*** The numbers would have been smaller if I had reduced the fraction on the left to $3/2$ before cross-multiplying. The answer is the same, of course.)

10 The measure of an exterior angle of a triangle is always equal to the sum of the other two interior angles. If one of the nonadjacent angles in a triangle measures 30 degrees, and if the exterior angle measures 70 degrees less than twice the measure of the other nonadjacent angle, then how big is that exterior angle? **130 degrees**. Check out the following figure.

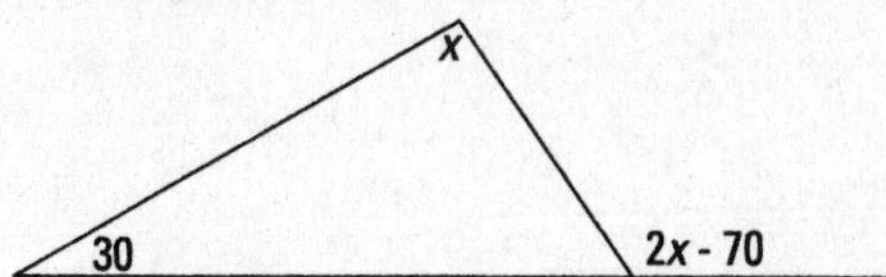

Let $x =$ the measure of a nonadjacent angle. The other nonadjacent interior angle is 30. The exterior angle has measure $2x - 70$. Because the measure of that exterior angle is equal to the sum of the measures of the two nonadjacent interior angles, you can write the equation $2x - 70 = x + 30$. Solving for x, subtract x from each side and add 70 to each side to get $x = 100$. The two nonadjacent interior angles add up to $30 + 100 = 130$. This amount is the same as the measure of the exterior angle. Put 100 in for x in $2x - 70$, $2(100) - 70 = 200 - 70 = 130$.

11 How long will it take you to travel 600 miles if you're averaging 50 mph? **12 hours**.

Use the distance-rate-time formula ($d = rt$) and replace the d with 600 and the r with 50 to get $600 = 50t$. Divide each side by 50 to get $12 = t$.

12 What was your average rate of speed (just using the actual driving time) if you left home at noon, drove 200 miles, stopped for an hour to eat, drove another 130 miles, and arrived at your destination at 7 p.m.? **55 mph**.

Use the formula $d = rt$ where $d = 200 + 330$ total miles, and the time is $t = 7 - 1 = 6$ hours. Substituting into the formula, you get $330 = r(6)$. Divide each side by 6 to get the average rate of speed: $55 = r$.

13 Kelly left school at 4 p.m. traveling at 25 mph. Ken left at 4:30 p.m., traveling at 30 mph, following the same route as Kelly. At what time did Ken catch up with Kelly? **7 p.m.**

Let $t =$ time in hours after 4 p.m. Kelly's distance is $25t$, and Ken's distance is $30\left(t - \frac{1}{2}\right)$, using $t - \frac{1}{2}$ because he left a half hour after 4 p.m.

Ken will overtake Kelly when their distances are equal. So the equation to use is $25t = 30\left(t - \frac{1}{2}\right)$. Distributing on the right gives you $25t = 30t - 15$. Subtract $30t$ from each side to get $-5t = -15$. Divide each side by -5, and $t = 3$. If t is the time in hours after 4 p.m., then $4 + 3 = 7$, or Ken caught up with Kelly at 7 p.m.

14 A Peoria Charter Coach bus left the bus terminal at 6 a.m. heading due north and traveling at an average of 45 mph. A second bus left the terminal at 7 a.m., heading due south and traveling at an average of 55 mph. When were the buses 645 miles apart? **1 p.m.**

Let $t =$ time in hours after 6 a.m. The distance the first bus traveled is $45t$, and the distance the second bus traveled is $55(t - 1)$, which represents 1 hour less of travel time. The sum of their distances traveled gives you their distance apart. So $45t + 55(t - 1) = 645$. Distribute the 55 to get $45t + 55t - 55 = 645$. Combine the like terms on the left and add 55 to each side: $100t = 700$. Divide by 100, $t = 7$. The busses were 645 miles apart 7 hours after the first bus left. Add 7 hours to 6 a.m., and you get 1 p.m.

15 Geoffrey and Grace left home at the same time. Geoffrey walked east at an average rate of 2.5 mph. Grace rode her bicycle due south at 6 mph until they were 65 miles apart. How long did it take them to be 65 miles apart? **10 hours.**

Look at the following figure, showing the distances and directions that Geoffrey and Grace traveled.

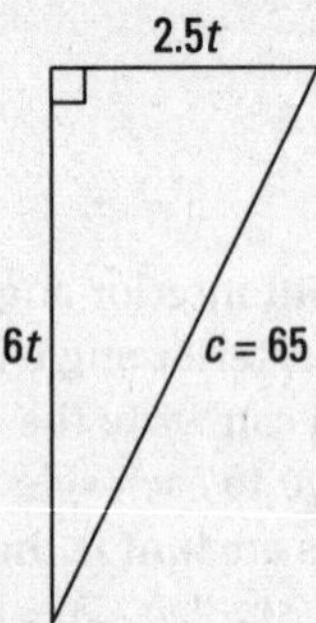

Geoffrey walks $d = rt = 2.5t$ miles, and Grace rides $d = rt = 6t$ miles. Use the Pythagorean theorem:

$$(6t)^2 + (2.5t)^2 = 65^2 \rightarrow 36t^2 + 6.25t^2 = 65^2$$

Multiply each side by 4 to get rid of the decimal:

$$144t^2 + 25t^2 = 4 \times 65^2 \rightarrow 169t^2 = 4 \times 65^2 \rightarrow t^2 = \frac{4 \times 65^2}{169}$$

$$t = \sqrt{\frac{4 \times 65^2}{169}} = \frac{2 \times 65}{13} = \frac{130}{13} = 10 \text{ hours}$$

In 10 hours, Geoffrey will walk $2.5(10) = 25$ miles, and Grace will ride $6(10) = 60$ miles. Plug these values into the Pythagorean theorem: $25^2 + 60^2 = 625 + 3{,}600 = 4{,}225 = 65^2$.

16 Melissa and Heather drove home for the holidays in separate cars, even though they live in the same place. Melissa's trip took two hours longer than Heather's, because Heather drove an average of 20 mph faster than Melissa's 40 mph. How far did they have to drive? **240 miles.**

Because Heather's time is shorter, let t = Heather's time in hours. Heather's distance is $60t$, using $40 + 20$ for her speed. Melissa's distance is $40(t + 2)$, because she took 2 hours longer. Their distances are equal, so $60t = 40(t + 2)$. Distribute the 40 to get $60t = 40t + 80$. Subtract $40t$ from each side: $20t = 80$. Divide by 20 for $t = 4$. Heather's distance is $60(4) = 240$ miles. Melissa's distance is $40(4 + 2) = 40(6) = 240$ miles. It's the same, of course.

IN THIS CHAPTER

» Dealing with age problems

» Counting up consecutive integers

» Working on sharing the workload

Chapter 19
Relating Values in Story Problems

Yes, this is another chapter on story problems. Just in case you're one of those people who are less than excited about the prospect of problems made up of words, I've been breaking these problems down into specific types to help deliver the material logically. Chapter 17 deals with formulas, Chapter 18 gets into geometry and distances, and now this chapter focuses on age problems, consecutive integers, and work problems.

Problems dealing with age and consecutive integers have something in common. You use one or more base values or ages, assigning variables, and you keep adding the same number to each base value. As you work through these problems, you find some recurring patterns, and the theme is to use the same format — pick a variable for a number and add something on to it.

As for work problems, they're a completely different bird. In work problems you need to divvy up the work and add it all together to get the whole job done. The portions usually aren't equal, and the number of participants can vary.

This chapter offers plenty of opportunities for you to tackle these story problems and overcome any trepidation.

Tackling Age Problems

Age problems in algebra don't have anything to do with wrinkles or thinning hair. Algebra deals with age problems very systematically and with an eye to the future. A story problem involving ages usually includes something like "in four years" or "ten years ago." The trick is to have everyone in the problem age the same amount (add four years to each person's age, if needed for example).

WARNING

When establishing your equation, make sure you keep track of how you name your variables. The letter x can't stand for Joe. The letter x can stand for Joe's *age*. If you keep in mind that the variables stand for numbers, the problem — and the process — will all make more sense.

EXAMPLE

Q. Joe's father is twice as old as Joe is. (He hasn't always been and won't be again — think about it: When Joe was born, was his father twice as old as he was?) Twelve years ago, Joe's father was three years older than three times Joe's age. How old is Joe's father now?

A. Joe's father is **42 years old.**

1. **Assign a variable to Joe's age.**

   Let Joe's age be x. Joe's father is twice as old, so Joe's father's age is $2x$.

2. **Continue to read through the problem.**

   Twelve years ago . . . . Both Joe's age and his father's age have to be backed up by 12 years. Their respective ages, 12 years ago, are $x-12$ and $2x-12$.

3. **Take the rest of the sentence where "Joe's father was three years . . . " and change it into an equation, putting an equal sign where the verb is.**

   "Twelve years ago, Joe's father" becomes $2x-12$

   "was" becomes $=$

   "three years older than" becomes $3+$

   "three times Joe's age (12 years ago)" becomes $3(x-12)$

4. **Put this information all together in an equation.**

   $2x-12=3+3(x-12)$

5. **Solve for x.**

   $2x-12=3+3x-36=3x-33$, so $x=21$

   That's Joe's age, so his father is twice that, or 42.

1. **Jack is three times as old as Chloe. Ten years ago, Jack was five times as old as Chloe. How old are Jack and Chloe now?**

2. **Linda is 10 years older than Luke. In ten years, Linda's age will be 30 years less than twice Luke's age. How old is Linda now?**

3. **Avery is six years older than Patrick. In four years, the sum of their ages will be 26. How old is Patrick now?**

4. **Jon is three years older than Jim, and Jim is two years older than Jane. Ten years ago, the sum of their ages was 40. How old is Jim now?**

Tackling Consecutive Integer Problems

When items are *consecutive,* they follow along one after another. An *integer* is a positive or negative whole number, or 0. So put these two things together to get consecutive integers. *Consecutive integers* have patterns — they're evenly spaced. The following three lists are examples of consecutive integers:

Consecutive integers: 5, 6, 7, 8, 9, . . .

Consecutive odd integers: 11, 13, 15, 17, 19, . . .

Consecutive multiples of 8: 48, 56, 64, 72, 80, . . .

After you get one of the integers in a list and are given the rule, then you can pretty much get all the rest of the integers. When doing consecutive integer problems, let x represent one of the integers (usually the first in your list) and then add on 1, 2, or whatever the spacing is to the next number and then add that amount on again to the new number, and so on until you have as many integers as you need.

EXAMPLE

Q. The sum of six consecutive integers is 255. What are they?

A. The integers are **40, 41, 42, 43, 44, and 45**. The first integer in my list is *x*. The next is $x+1$, the one after that is $x+2$, and so on. The equation for this situation reads $x+(x+1)+(x+2)+(x+3)+(x+4)+(x+5)=255$. (***Note:*** The parentheses aren't necessary. I just include them so you can see the separate terms.) Adding up all the *x*'s and numbers, the equation becomes $6x+15=255$. Subtracting 15 from each side and dividing each side by 6, you get $x=40$. Fill the 40 into your original equations to get the six consecutive integers. (If $x=40$, then $x+1=41$, $x+2=42$, and so on.)

Q. The sum of four consecutive odd integers is 8. What are they?

A. The integers are **−1, 1, 3, and 5**. The equation for this problem is $x+(x+2)+(x+4)+(x+6)=8$. It becomes $4x+12=8$. Subtracting 12 and then dividing by 4, you get $x=-1$. You may have questioned using the $+2, +4, +6$ when dealing with odd integers. The first number is −1. Replace the *x* with −1 in each case to get the rest of the answers. The problem designates *x* as an odd integer, and the other integers are all two steps away from one another. It works!

5 The sum of three consecutive integers is 57. What are they?

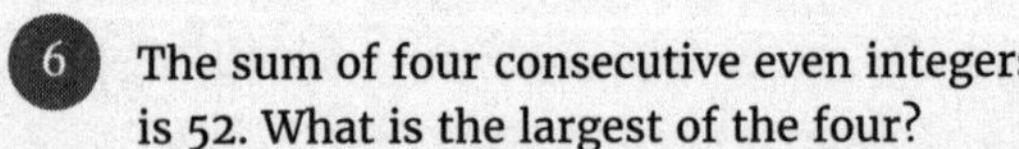

6 The sum of four consecutive even integers is 52. What is the largest of the four?

7 **The sum of three consecutive odd integers is 75. What is the middle number?**

8 **The sum of five consecutive multiples of 4 is 20. What are they?**

9 **The sum of the smallest and largest of three consecutive integers is 126. What is the middle number of those consecutive integers?**

10 **The product of two consecutive integers is 89 more than their sum. What are they?**

Working Together on Work Problems

Work problems in algebra involve doing jobs alone and together. Together is usually better, unless the person you're working with distracts you. I take the positive route and assume that two heads are better than one.

The general format for these problems is to let x represent how long it takes to do the job working together. Follow these steps and you won't even break a sweat when working work problems:

1. **Write the amount that a person can do in one time period as a fraction.**
2. **Multiply that amount by the x.**

   (You've multiplied each fraction that each person can do by the time it takes to do the whole job.)
3. **Add the portions of the job that are completed in one time period together and set the sum equal to 1.**

   (Setting the amount to 1 is 100% of the job.)

EXAMPLE

Q. Meg can clean out the garage in five hours. Mike can clean out the same garage in three hours. How long will the job take if they work together?

A. **Slightly less than two hours**. Let x represent the amount of time it takes to do the cleaning when Meg and Mike work together. Meg can do $\frac{1}{5}$ of the job in one hour, and Mike can do $\frac{1}{3}$ of the job in one hour. The equation to use is $\frac{x}{5}+\frac{x}{3}=1$. Multiply both sides of the equation by the common denominator and add the two fractions together: $15\left(\frac{x}{4}+\frac{x}{3}\right)=15(1)$, or $3x+5x=15$, giving you $8x=15$. Divide by 8, and you have $x=\frac{15}{8}$, just under two hours.

Q. Carlos can wash the bus in seven hours, and when Carlos and Carol work together, they can wash the bus in three hours. How long would it take Carol to wash the bus by herself?

A. **5 hours and 15 minutes**. Let x represent the amount of time it takes Carol to wash the bus by herself. This time, you have the time that it takes working together, so your equation is $\frac{3}{7}+\frac{3}{x}=1$. The common denominator of the two fractions on the left is $7x$. Multiply both sides of the equation by $7x$, simplify, and solve for x.

$$7x\left(\frac{3}{7}+\frac{3}{x}\right)=7x(1)$$

$$\cancel{7}x\left(\frac{3}{\cancel{7}}\right)+7\cancel{x}\left(\frac{3}{\cancel{x}}\right)=7x$$

$$3x+21=7x$$

$$21=4x$$

$$5\frac{1}{4}=x$$

11. Alissa can do the job in three days, and Alex can do the same job in four days. How long will it take if they work together?

12. George can paint the garage in five days, Geanie can paint it in eight days, and Greg can do the job in ten days. How long will painting the garage take if they all work together?

13. Working together, Sam and Helene wrote a company organizational plan in $1\frac{1}{3}$ days. Working alone, it would have taken Sam four days to write that plan. How long would it have taken Helene if she had written it alone?

14. Rancher Biff needs his new fence put up in four days — before the herd arrives. Working alone, it'll take him six days to put up all the fencing. He can hire someone to help. How fast does the hired hand have to work in order for the team to complete the job before the herd arrives?

15. When hose A is running full-strength to fill the swimming pool, it takes 8 hours; when hose B is running full-strength, filling the pool takes 12 hours. How long would it take to fill the pool if both hoses were running at the same time?

16. Elliott set up hose A to fill the swimming pool, planning on it taking 8 hours. But he didn't notice that water was leaking out of the pool through a big crack in the bottom. With just the water leaking, the pool would be empty in 12 hours. How long would filling the pool take with Elliott adding water with hose A and the leak emptying the pool at the same time?

Answers to Relating Values in Story Problems

The following are the answers (in bold) to the practice problems in this chapter.

1. Jack is three times as old as Chloe. Ten years ago, Jack was five times as old as Chloe. How old are Jack and Chloe now? **Chloe is 20, and Jack is 60.**

   Let x = Chloe's present age and $3x$ = Jack's present age. Ten years ago, Chloe's age was $x-10$, and Jack's was $3x-10$. Also ten years ago, Jack's age was 5 times Chloe's age. You can write this equation as $3x-10=5(x-10)$. Distribute the 5 to get $3x-10=5x-50$. Subtract 3x from each side and add 50 to each side, and the equation becomes $40=2x$. Divide by 2 to get $x=20$.

2. Linda is 10 years older than Luke. In ten years, Linda's age will be 30 years less than twice Luke's age. How old is Linda now? **Linda is 40.**

   Let x = Luke's age now. That makes Linda's present age $= x+10$. In ten years, Luke will be $x+10$, and Linda will be $(x+10)+10=x+20$. But at these new ages, Linda's age will be 30 years less than twice Luke's age. This is written as $x+20=2(x+10)-30$. Distribute the 2 to get $x+20=2x+20-30$. Simplifying, $x+20=2x-10$. Subtract x from each side and add 10 to each side to get $x=30$. Luke is 30, and Linda is 40. In ten years, Luke will be 40, and Linda will be 50. Twice Luke's age then, minus 30, is $80-30=50$. It checks.

3. Avery is six years older than Patrick. In four years, the sum of their ages will be 26. How old is Patrick? **Patrick is 6.**

   Let x = Patrick's age now. Then Avery's age $= x+6$. In four years, Patrick will be $x+4$ years old, and Avery will be $x+6+4=x+10$ years old. Write that the sum of their ages in four years: $(x+4)+(x+10)=26$. Simplify on the left to get $2x+14=26$. Subtract 14 from each side: $2x=12$. Divide by 2, and you get $x=6$. Patrick is 6, and Avery is 12. In four years, Patrick will be 10, and Avery will be 16. The sum of 10 and 16 is 26.

4. Jon is three years older than Jim, and Jim is two years older than Jane. Ten years ago, the sum of their ages was 40. How old is Jim now? **Jim is 23.**

   Let x represent Jane's age now. Jim is two years older, so Jim's age is $x+2$. Jon is three years older than Jim, so Jon's age is $(x+2)+3=x+5$. Ten years ago Jane's age was $x-10$, Jim's age was $x+2-10=x-8$, and Jon's age was $x+5-10=x-5$. Add the ages ten years ago together to get 40: $x-10+(x-8)+(x-5)=40$. Simplifying on the left, $3x-23=40$. Add 23 to each side to get $3x=63$. Divide by 3, $x=21$. Jane's age is 21, so Jim's age is $21+2=23$.

5. The sum of three consecutive integers is 57. What are they? **The integers are 18, 19, and 20.**

   Let x = the smallest of the three consecutive integers. Then the other two are $x+1$ and $x+2$. Adding the integers together to get 57, $x+(x+1)+(x+2)=57$, which simplifies to $3x+3=57$. Subtract 3 from each side to get Dividing by 3, $x=18$. $18+19+20=57$, $x=18$.

6. The sum of four consecutive even integers is 52. What is the largest of the four? **16**. The four integers are 16, 14, 12, and 10.

   Let that largest integer $= x$. The other integers will be 2, 4, and 6 smaller, so they can be written with $x-2$, $x-4$, and $x-6$. Adding them, you get $x+(x-2)+(x-4)+(x-6)=52$. Simplifying gives you $4x-12=52$. Add 12 to each side to get $4x=64$. Divide each side by 4, and $x=16$. $16+14+12+10=52$.

7) The sum of three consecutive odd integers is 75. What is the middle number? **25.**

You can add and subtract 2 from that middle integer. Let that integer $= x$. Then the other two are $x+2$ and $x-2$. Add them together: $(x-2)+x+(x+2)=75$. Simplifying, $3x=75$. Divide by 3 to get $x=25$. That's the middle number. The other two are 23 and 27: $23+25+27=75$.

8) The sum of five consecutive multiples of 4 is 20. What are they? **The numbers are –4, 0, 4, 8, and 12.**

Let $x=$ the first of the consecutive multiples of 4. Then the other four are $x+4$, $x+8$, $x+12$, and $x+16$. Add them together: $x+(x+4)+(x+8)+(x+12)+(x+16)=20$. Simplifying on the left, $5x+40=20$. Subtract 40 from each side to get $5x=-20$. Dividing by 5, $x=-4$.

9) The sum of the smallest and largest of three consecutive integers is 126. What is the middle number of those consecutive integers? **63.**

Let $x=$ the smallest of the consecutive integers. Then the other two are $x+1$ and $x+2$. Because the sum of the smallest and largest is 126, you can write it as $x+(x+2)=126$. Simplifying the equation, $2x+2=126$. Subtract 2 from each side to get $2x=124$. Dividing by 2, $x=62$, which is the smallest integer. The middle one is one bigger, so it's 63.

10) The product of two consecutive integers is 89 more than their sum. What are they? **The numbers are 10 and 11 or –9 and –8.**

Let the smaller of the integers $= x$. The other one is then $x+1$. Their product is written $x(x+1)$ and their sum is $x+(x+1)$. Now, to write that their product is 89 more than their sum, the equation is $x(x+1)=89+x+(x+1)$. Distributing the x on the left and simplifying on the right, $x^2+x=2x+90$. Subtract $2x$ and 90 from each side to set the quadratic equation equal to 0: $x^2-x-90=0$. The trinomial on the left side of the equation factors to give you $(x-10)(x+9)=0.x=10$ or $x=-9$. If $x=10$, then $x+1=11$. The product of 10 and 11 is 110. That's 89 bigger than their sum, 21. What if $x=-9$? The next bigger number is then –8. Their product is 72. The difference between their product of 72 and sum of –17 is $72-(-17)=89$. So this problem has two possible solutions.

11) Alissa can do the job in three days, and Alex can do the same job in four days. How long will it take if they work together? **It will take a little less than 2 days working together ($^{12}/_7$ days).**

Let $x=$ the number of days to do the job together. Alissa can do $^1/_3$ of the job in one day and $\frac{1}{3}(x)$ of the job in x days. In x days, as they work together, they're to do 100% of the job. $\frac{1}{3}(x)+\frac{1}{4}(x)=1$, which is 100%. Multiply by 12: $4x+3x=12$, or $7x=12$. Divide by 7: $x=^{12}/_7=1^5/_7$ days to do the job.

Alissa's share is $^1/_3(^{12}/_7)=^4/_7$, and Alex's share is $^1/_4(^{12}/_7)=^3/_7$. Together $^4/_7+^3/_7=1$.

12) George can paint the garage in five days, Geanie can paint it in eight days, and Greg can do the job in ten days. How long will painting the garage take if they all work together? **$2^6/_{17}$ days.**

Let $x=$ the number of days to complete the job together. In x days, George will paint $\frac{1}{5}(x)$ of the garage, Geanie $\frac{1}{8}(x)$ of the garage, and Greg $\frac{1}{10}(x)$ of the garage. The equation for completing the job is $\frac{1}{5}(x)+\frac{1}{10}(x)+\frac{1}{8}(x)=1$. Multiplying through by 40, which is the least common denominator of the fractions, you get $8x+4x+5x=40$. Simplifying, you get $17x=40$. Dividing by 17 gives you $x=^{40}/_{17}=2^6/_{17}$ days to paint the garage. Checking the answer, George's share is $\frac{1}{5}\left(\frac{40}{17}\right)=\frac{8}{17}$, Geanie's share is $\frac{1}{8}\left(\frac{40}{17}\right)=\frac{5}{17}$, and Greg's share is $\frac{1}{10}\left(\frac{40}{17}\right)=\frac{4}{17}$. Together, $\frac{8}{17}+\frac{5}{17}+\frac{4}{17}=\frac{17}{17}$, or 100%.

13. Working together, Sam and Helene wrote a company organizational plan in $1\frac{1}{3}$ days. Working alone, it would have taken Sam four days to write that plan. How long would it have taken Helene, if she had written it alone? **2 days.**

Let x = the number of days for Helene to write the plan alone. So Helene writes $\frac{1}{x}$ of the plan each day. Sam writes $\frac{1}{4}$ of the plan per day. In $1\frac{1}{3}=\frac{4}{3}$ days, they complete the job together. The equation is $\left(\frac{1}{x}\right)\left(\frac{4}{3}\right)+\left(\frac{1}{4}\right)\left(\frac{4}{3}\right)=1$. Multiplying each side by $12x$, the least common denominator, gives you $\left(\frac{4}{3x}\right)(12x)+\left(\frac{4}{12}\right)(12x)=1(12x)$, $16+4x=12x$. Subtract $4x$ from each side to get $16=8x$.

Dividing by 8, $x=2$ days. Helene will complete the job in 2 days. To check this, in $\frac{4}{3}$ days, Sam will do $\frac{1}{4}\left(\frac{4}{3}\right)=\frac{1}{3}$ of the work, and Helene will do $\frac{1}{2}\left(\frac{4}{3}\right)=\frac{2}{3}$. Together, $\frac{1}{3}+\frac{2}{3}=1$ or 100%.

14. Rancher Biff needs his new fence put up in four days — before the herd arrives. Working alone, it'll take him six days to put up all the fencing. He can hire someone to help. How fast does this person have to work in order for the team to complete the job before the herd arrives? **The hired hand must be able to do the job alone in 12 days (or 1/12th of the job each day.)**

Let x = the number of days the hired hand needs to complete the job alone. The hired hand does $\frac{1}{x}$ of the fencing each day, and Biff puts up $\frac{1}{6}$ of the fence each day. In four days, they can complete the project together, so $\left(\frac{1}{x}\right)(4)+\left(\frac{1}{6}\right)(4)=1$. Multiply by the common denominator $6x$: $\left(\frac{4}{x}\right)(6x)+\left(\frac{4}{6}\right)(6x)=(1)(6x)$. Simplifying, $24+4x=6x$. Subtracting $4x$ from each side, $24=2x$.

Dividing by 2, $x=12$. The hired hand must be able to do the job alone in 12 days. Biff can do the job in 6 days, meaning he can do $\frac{1}{6}$ of the job each day. The hired hand must be able to do $\frac{1}{12}$ of the job each day for their combined efforts to complete the job in 4 days. To check this, in four days, Biff does $\left(\frac{1}{6}\right)(4)=\frac{2}{3}$ of the fencing, and the hired hand $\left(\frac{1}{12}\right)(4)=\frac{1}{3}$ of the job.

15. When hose A is running full strength to fill the swimming pool, it takes 8 hours; when hose B is running full strength, it takes 12 hours to fill the swimming pool. How long would it take to fill the pool if both hoses were running at the same time? **4.8 hours.**

Let x represent the amount of time to complete the job. Your equation is $\frac{x}{8}+\frac{x}{12}=1$. Multiplying both sides of the equation by 24, you get $3x+2x=24$. Simplifying and then dividing by 5, you get $5x=24$, $x=4.8$.

16. Elliott set up hose A to fill the swimming pool, planning on it taking 8 hours. But he didn't notice that water was leaking out of the pool through a big crack in the bottom. With just the water leaking, the pool would be empty in 12 hours. How long would filling the pool take with Elliott adding water with hose A and the leak emptying the pool at the same time? **24 hours.**

This time, one of the terms is negative. The leaking water takes away from the completion of the job, making the time longer. Using the equation $\frac{x}{8}+\frac{-x}{12}=1$, where the negative sign represents the loss of water. This becomes $\frac{x}{8}-\frac{x}{12}=1$, multiply both sides of the equation by 24, giving you $3x-2x=24$ or $x=24$.

» Understanding the strength of a solution

» Keeping track of money in piggy banks and interest problems

Chapter 20
Measuring Up with Quality and Quantity Story Problems

The story problems in this chapter have a common theme to them; they deal with *quality* (the strength or worth of an item) and *quantity* (the measure or count) and adding up to a total amount. (Chapters 17, 18, and 19 have other types of story problems.) You encounter quantity and quality problems almost on a daily basis. For instance, if you have four dimes, you know that you have 40 cents. How do you know? You multiply the *quantity*, four dimes, times the *quality*, 10 cents each, to get the total amount of money. And if you have a fruit drink that's 50 percent real juice, then a gallon contains one-half gallon of real juice (and the rest is who-knows-what) — again, multiplying quality times quantity.

In this chapter, take time to practice with these story problems. Just multiply the amount of something, the *quantity*, times the strength or worth of it, *quality*, in order to solve for the total value.

Achieving the Right Blend with Mixtures Problems

Mixtures include what goes in granola, blends of coffee, or the colors of sugarcoated candies in a candy dish. In mixture problems, you often need to solve for some sort of relationship about the mixture: its total value or the amount of each item being blended. Just be sure that the variable represents some number — an amount or value. Bring along an appetite. Many of these problems deal with food.

EXAMPLE

Q. A health store is mixing up some granola that has many ingredients, but three of the basics are oatmeal, wheat germ, and raisins. Oatmeal costs \$1 per pound, wheat germ costs \$3 per pound, and raisins cost \$2 per pound. The store wants to create a base granola mixture of those three ingredients that will cost \$1.50 per pound. (These items serve as the base of the granola; the rest of the ingredients and additional cost will be added later.) The granola is to have nine times as much oatmeal as wheat germ. How much of each ingredient is needed?

A. **Every pound of mixed granola will need $^1/_{16}$ pound of wheat germ, $^9/_{16}$ pound of oatmeal, and $^6/_{16}$ or $^3/_8$ pound of raisins.**

To start this problem, let *x* represent the amount of wheat germ in pounds. Because you need nine times as much oatmeal as wheat germ, you have 9*x* pounds of oatmeal. How much in raisins? The raisins can have whatever's left of the pound after the wheat germ and oatmeal are taken out: $1-(x+9x)$ or $1-10x$ pounds. Now multiply each of these amounts by their respective price: $\$3(x)+\$1(9x)+\$2(1-10x)$. Set this equal to the \$1.50 price multiplied by its amount, as follows: $\$3(x)+\$1(9x)+\$2(1-10x)=\$1.50(1)$. Simplify and solve for *x*: $3x+9x+2-20x=-8x+2=\$1.50$. Subtracting 2 from each side and then dividing each side by 8, gives you $-8x=-0.50$, $x=\frac{-0.50}{-8}=\frac{1}{16}$.

1. Kathy's Kandies features a mixture of chocolate creams and chocolate-covered caramels that sells for \$9 per pound. If creams sell for \$6.75 per pound and caramels sell for \$10.50 per pound, how much of each type of candy should be in a 1-pound mix?

2. Solardollars Coffee is trying new blends to attract more customers. The premium Colombian costs \$10 per pound, and the regular blend costs \$4 per pound. How much of each should the company use to make 100 pounds of a coffee blend that costs \$5.50 per pound?

3. Peanuts cost $2 per pound, almonds cost $3.50 per pound, and cashews cost $6 per pound. How much of each should you use to create a mixture that costs $3.40 per pound, if you have to use twice as many peanuts as cashews?

4. A mixture of jellybeans is to contain twice as many red as yellow, three times as many green as yellow, and twice as many pink as red. Red jelly beans cost $1.50 per pound, yellow cost $3.00 per pound, green cost $4.00, and pink only cost $1.00 per pound. How many pounds of each color jellybean should be in a 10-pound canister that costs $2.20 per pound?

5. A *Very Berry Smoothie* calls for raspberries, strawberries, and yogurt. Raspberries cost $3 per cup, strawberries cost $1 per cup, and yogurt costs $0.50 per cup. The recipe calls for twice as much strawberries as raspberries. How many cups of strawberries are needed to make a gallon of this smoothie that costs $10.10? (***Hint:*** 1 gallon = 16 cups.)

6. A supreme pizza contains five times as many ounces of cheese as mushrooms, twice as many ounces of peppers as mushrooms, twice as many ounces of onions as peppers, and four more ounces of sausage than mushrooms. Mushrooms and onions cost 10 cents per ounce, cheese costs 20 cents per ounce, peppers are 25 cents per ounce, and sausage is 30 cents per ounce. If the toppings are to cost no more than a total of $5.80, then how many ounces of each ingredient can be used?

Concocting the Correct Solution One Hundred Percent of the Time

Solutions problems are sort of like mixtures problems (explained in the preceding section). The main difference is that solutions usually deal in percents — 30%, $27\frac{1}{2}$%, 0%, or even 100%. These last two numbers indicate, respectively, that none of that ingredient is in the solution (0%) or that it's *pure* for that ingredient (100%). You've dealt with these solutions if you've had to add antifreeze or water to your radiator. Or how about adding that frothing milk to your latte mixture?

The general format for these solutions problems is

$$(\%\text{ A} \times \text{amount A}) + (\%\text{ B} \times \text{amount B}) = (\%\text{ C} \times \text{amount C})$$

EXAMPLE

Q. How many gallons of 60% apple juice mix need to be added to 20 gallons of mix that's currently 25% apple juice to bring the new mix up to 32% apple juice?

A. **Five gallons**. To solve this problem, let x represent the unknown amount of 60% apple juice. Using the format of all the percents times the respective amounts, you get $(60\% \times x) + (25\% \times 20\text{gallons}) = [32\% \times (x + 20\text{gallons})]$. Change the percents to decimals, and the equation becomes $0.60x + 0.25(20) = 0.32(x + 20)$. (If you don't care for decimals, you could multiply each side by 100 to change everything to whole numbers.) Now distribute the 0.32 on the right and simplify so you can solve for x:

$$\begin{aligned} 0.60x + 5 &= 0.32x + 6.4 \\ 0.28x &= 1.4 \\ x &= 5 \end{aligned}$$

If you're adding pure alcohol or pure antifreeze or something like this, use 1 (which is 100%) in the equation. If there's no alcohol, chocolate syrup, salt, or whatever in the solution, use 0 (which is 0%) in the equation.

Q. How many quarts of water do you need to add to 4 quarts of lemonade concentrate in order to make the drink 25% lemonade?

A. **12 quarts**. To solve this problem, let x represent the unknown amount of water,which is 0% lemonade. Using the format of all the percents times the respective amounts, you get $(0\% \times x) + (100\% \times 4\text{ quarts}) = [25\% \times (x + 4)\text{quarts}]$. Change the percents to decimals, and the equation becomes $0x + 1.00(4) = 0.25(x + 4)$. When the equation gets simplified, the first term disappears.

$$\begin{aligned} 4 &= 0.25x + 1 \\ 3 &= 0.25x \\ \frac{3}{0.25} &= \frac{0.25x}{0.25} \\ 12 &= x \end{aligned}$$

7 How many quarts of 25% solution do you need to add to 4 quarts of 40% solution to create a 31% solution?

8 How many gallons of a 5% fertilizer solution have to be added to 2 gallons of a 90% solution to create a fertilizer solution that has 15% strength?

9 How many quarts of pure antifreeze need to be added to 8 quarts of 30% antifreeze to bring it up to 50%?

10 How many cups of chocolate syrup need to be added to 1 quart of milk to get a mixture that's 25% syrup?

11 What concentration should 4 quarts of salt water have so that, when it's added to 5 quarts of 40% solution salt water, the concentration goes down to $33\frac{1}{3}\%$?

12 What concentration and amount of solution have to be added to 7 gallons of 60% alcohol to produce 16 gallons of $37\frac{1}{2}\%$ alcohol solution?

Dealing with Money Problems

Story problems involving coins, money, or interest earned all are solved with a process like that used in solutions problems: You multiply a quantity times a quality. In these cases, the qualities are the values of the coins or bills, or they're the interest rate at which money is growing.

EXAMPLE

Q. Gabriella is counting the bills in her cash drawer before the store opens for the day. She has the same number of \$10 bills as \$20 bills. She has two more \$5 bills than \$10 bills, and ten times as many \$1 bills as \$5 bills. She has a total of \$300 in bills. How many of each does she have?

A. **Gabriella has 6 \$10 bills, 6 \$20 bills, 8 \$5 bills, and 80 \$1 bills for a total of \$300.** You can compare everything, directly or indirectly, to the \$10 bills. Let x represent the number of \$10 bills. The number of \$20 bills is the same, so it's x, also. The number of \$5 bills is two more than the number of \$10 bills, so let the number of fives be represented by $x+2$. Multiply $x+2$ by 10 for the number of \$1 bills, $10(x+2)$. Now take each *number* of bills and multiply by the quality or value of that bill. Add them to get \$300:

$$\begin{aligned}10x+20x+5(x+2)+1(10(x+2))&=300\\10x+20x+5x+10+10x+20&=300\\45x+30&=300\\45x&=270\\x&=6\end{aligned}$$

Using $x=6$, the number of \$10 bills and \$20 bills, you get $x+2=8$ for the number of \$5 bills, and $10(x+2)=80$ for the number of \$1 bills.

Q. Jon won the state lottery and has \$1 million to invest. He invests some of it in a highly speculative venture that earns 18% interest. The rest is invested more wisely, at 5% interest. If he earns \$63,000 in simple interest in one year, how much did he invest at 18%?

A. **He invested \$100,000 at 18% interest.** Let x represent the amount of money invested at 18%. Then the remainder, $1{,}000{,}000-x$, is invested at 5%. The equation to use is $0.18x+0.05(1{,}000{,}000-x)=63{,}000$. Distributing the 0.05 on the left and combining terms, you get $0.13x+50{,}000=63{,}000$. Subtract 50,000 from each side, and you get $0.13x=13{,}000$. Dividing each side by 0.13 gives you $x=100{,}000$. It's kind of mind boggling.

13 Carlos has twice as many quarters as nickels and has a total of $8.25. How many quarters does he have?

14 Gregor has twice as many $10 bills as $20 bills, five times as many $1 bills as $10 bills, and half as many $5 bills as $1 bills. He has a total of $750. How many of each bill does he have?

15 Stella has 100 coins in nickels, dimes, and quarters. She has 18 more nickels than dimes and a total of $7.40. How many of each coin does she have?

16 Betty invested $10,000 in two different funds for one year. She invested part at 2% and the rest at 3%. She earned $240 in simple interest. How much did she invest at each rate? (***Hint:*** Use the simple interest formula: $I = Prt$.)

Answers to Problems on Measuring Up with Quality and Quantity

The following are the answers (in bold) to the practice problems in this chapter.

1. Kathy's Kandies features a mixture of chocolate creams and chocolate-covered caramels that sells for \$9 per pound. If creams sell for \$6.75 per pound and caramels sell for \$10.50 per pound, how much of each type of candy should be in a one-pound mix? **0.4 pounds of creams and 0.6 pounds of caramels.**

   Let x represent the amount of chocolate creams in pounds. Then $1-x$ is the pounds of chocolate caramels. In a pound of the mixture, creams cost \$6.75x and caramels $\$10.50(1-x)$. Together, the mixture costs \$9. So

   $$6.75x+10.5(1-x)=9 \rightarrow 6.75x+10.5-10.5x=9 \rightarrow -3.75x+10.5=9$$

   Subtract 10.5 from each side and then divide by -3.75:

   $$-3.75x=-1.5 \rightarrow x=\frac{-1.5}{-3.75}=0.4 \text{ pounds of creams}$$

   To get the amount of caramels, $1-x=1-0.4=0.6$ pounds of caramels. Checking this, the cost of creams is $\$6.75(0.4)=\$2.70$. The cost of caramels is $\$10.50(0.6)=\$6.30$. Adding these together, you get $2.70+6.30=9$ dollars.

2. Solardollars Coffee is trying new blends to attract more customers. The premium Colombian costs \$10 per pound, and the regular blend costs \$4 per pound. How much of each should the company use to make 100 pounds of a coffee blend that costs \$5.50 per pound? **The company needs 25 pounds of Colombian and 75 pounds of regular blend.**

   Let x = the pounds of Colombian coffee at \$10 per pound. Then $100-x=$ pounds of regular blend at \$4 per pound. The cost of 100 pounds of the mixture blend is $\$5.50(100)=\$550$. Use $10x+4(100-x)=550 \rightarrow 10x+400-4x=550 \rightarrow 6x+400=550$.

   Subtract 400 from each side and then divide each side by 6:

   $$6x=150 \rightarrow x=\frac{150}{6}=25$$

   To check, multiply \$10(25) and \$4(75) to get $\$250+\$300=\$550$, as needed.

3. Peanuts cost \$2 per pound, almonds cost \$3.50 per pound, and cashews cost \$6 per pound. How much of each should you use to create a mixture that costs \$3.40 per pound, if you have to use twice as many peanuts as cashews? **$^2/_5$ pounds almonds, $^2/_5$ pounds peanuts, $^1/_5$ pounds cashews.**

Let x = the pounds of cashews at \$6 per pound. Then $2x$ = pounds of peanuts at \$2 per pound. The almonds are then $1-(x+2x)=1-3x$ pounds at \$3.50 per pound. Combine all this and solve:

$$\begin{aligned} 6x+2(2x)+3.5(1-3x)&=3.4\\ 6x+4x+3.5-10.5x&=3.4\\ -0.5x+3.5&=3.4\\ -0.5x&=-0.1\\ x=\frac{-0.1}{-0.5}&=\frac{1}{5}\text{ pounds of cashews} \end{aligned}$$

Use this amount for x and substitute in to get the other weights. You get $2\left(\frac{1}{5}\right)=\frac{2}{5}$ pounds of peanuts and $1-3\left(\frac{1}{5}\right)=1-\frac{3}{5}=\frac{2}{5}$ pounds of almonds.

4 A mixture of jellybeans is to contain twice as many red as yellow, three times as many green as yellow, and twice as many pink as red. Red jelly beans cost \$1.50 per pound, yellow cost \$3.00 per pound, green cost \$4.00, and pink only cost \$1.00 per pound. How many pounds of each color jellybean should be in a 10-pound canister that costs \$2.20 per pound? **1 pound yellow, 2 pounds red, 3 pounds green, and 4 pounds pink jellybeans.**

Let x represent the number of pounds of yellow jellybeans. Then $2x$ is the pounds of red jellybeans, $3x$ is the pounds of green jellybeans, and $2(2x)=4x$ is the pounds of pink jellybeans. Multiplying each quantity times its price and solve:

$$\begin{aligned} x(3.00)+2x(1.50)+3x(4.00)+4x(1.00)&=10(2.20)\\ 3x+3x+12x+4x&=22\\ 22x&=22,\ x=1 \end{aligned}$$

With 1 pound yellow jellybeans, you then know that the mixture has $2(1)=2$ pounds red jellybeans, 3(1) pounds green jellybeans, and 4(1) pounds pink jellybeans. The $1+2+3+4$ pounds adds up to 10 pounds jellybeans.

5 A *Very Berry Smoothie* calls for raspberries, strawberries, and yogurt. Raspberries cost \$3 per cup, strawberries cost \$1 per cup, and yogurt costs \$0.50 per cup. The recipe calls for twice as much strawberries as raspberries. How many cups of strawberries are needed to make a gallon of this smoothie that costs \$10.10? (***Hint:*** 1 gallon = 16 cups.) **1.2 cups.**

Let x = the cups of raspberries at \$3 per cup. Then $2x$ = the cups of strawberries at \$1 per cup. The remainder of the 16 cups of mixture are for yogurt, which comes out to be $16-(x+2x)=16-3x$ cups of yogurt at \$0.50 per cup. The equation you need is

$$\begin{aligned} 3(x)+1(2x)+0.5(16-3x)&=10.10\\ 5x+8-1.5x&=10.1\\ 3.5x+8&=10.1\\ 3.5x&=2.1\\ x=\frac{2.1}{3.5}&=0.6 \end{aligned}$$

The mixture has 0.6 cups of raspberries and $2(0.6)=1.2$ cups of strawberries.

6 A supreme pizza contains five times as many ounces of cheese as mushrooms, twice as many ounces of peppers as mushrooms, twice as many ounces of onions as peppers, and four more ounces of sausage than mushrooms. Mushrooms and onions cost 10 cents per ounce, cheese costs 20 cents per ounce, peppers are 25 cents per ounce, and sausage is 30 cents per ounce. If the toppings are to cost no more than a total of $5.80, then how many ounces of each ingredient can be used? **The mixture has 2 ounces of mushrooms, 10 ounces of cheese, 4 ounces of peppers, 8 ounces of onions, and 6 ounces of sausage.**

Let x represent the number of ounces of mushrooms. Then 5x is the ounces of cheese, 2x is the ounces of peppers, $2(2x)=4x$ is the ounces of onions, and $x+4$ is the ounces of sausage. Multiplying each quantity times its cost (quality) and setting that equal to 580 cents, you get $x(10)+5x(20)+2x(25)+4x(10)+(x+4)(30)=580$. Simplifying, you get $10x+100x+50x+40x+30x+120=580$. Solving for x gives you $230x+120=580$, or $230x=460$. Divide each side by 230 to get $x=2$. So you need 2 ounces of mushrooms, $5(2)=10$ ounces of cheese, $2(2)=4$ ounces of peppers, $4(2)=8$ ounces of onions, and $2+4=6$ ounces of sausage.

7 How many quarts of 25% solution do you need to add to 4 quarts of 40% solution to create a 31% solution? **6 quarts.**

Let x = the quarts of 25% solution needed. Add x quarts of 25% solution to 4 quarts of 40% solution to get $(x+4)$ quarts of 31% solution. Write this as $x(0.25)+4(0.40)=(x+4)(0.31)$. Multiply through by 100 to get rid of the decimals: $25x+4(40)=(x+4)(31)$. Distribute the 31 and simplify on the left: $25x+160=31x+124$. Subtract 25x and 124 from each side to get $36=6x$. Divide by 6 to get $x=6$. The answer is 6 quarts of 25% solution.

8 How many gallons of a 5% fertilizer solution have to be added to 2 gallons of a 90% solution to create a fertilizer solution that has 15% strength? **15 gallons.**

Let x = the gallons of 5% solution. Then $(0.05)x+(0.90)(2)=(0.15)(x+2)$ for the $x+2$ gallons. Multiply through by 100: $5x+(90)(2)=(15)(x+2)$. Simplify each side: $5x+180=15x+30$. Subtract 5x and 30 from each side: $150=10x$ or $x=15$ gallons of 5% solution.

9 How many quarts of pure antifreeze need to be added to 8 quarts of 30% antifreeze to bring it up to 50%? **3.2 quarts.**

Let x = the quarts of pure antifreeze to be added. Pure antifreeze is 100% antifreeze $(100\%=1)$. So $1(x)+(0.30)(8)=(0.50)(x+8)$. Simplify on the left and distribute on the right: $x+2.4=0.5x+4$. Subtract 0.5x and 2.4 from each side: $0.5x=1.6$. Divide by 0.5 to get $x=3.2$ quarts of pure antifreeze.

10 How many cups of chocolate syrup need to be added to 1 quart of milk to get a mixture that's 25% syrup? **$1\frac{1}{3}$ cups.**

Let x = the cups of chocolate syrup needed. (I only use the best quality chocolate syrup, of course, so you know that the syrup is pure chocolate.) 1 quart = 4 cups, and the milk has no chocolate syrup in it. So

$$1(x)+(0)(4)=(0.25)(x+4)$$
$$x=0.25x+1$$
$$0.75x=1$$
$$x=\frac{1}{0.75}=\frac{100}{75}=\frac{4}{3}\text{ cups of chocolate syrup}$$

(11) What concentration should the 4 quarts of salt water have so that, when it's added to 5 quarts of 40% solution salt water, the concentration goes down to 33 $\frac{1}{3}$%? **25%.**

Let x% = the percent of the salt solution in the 4 quarts:

$$\begin{aligned} x(\%)(4)+(40\%)(5) &= \left(33\frac{1}{3}\%\right)(9) \\ 4x+200 &= \left(33\frac{1}{3}\right)(9) \\ 4x+200 &= 300 \\ 4x &= 100 \\ x &= 25 \end{aligned}$$

The 4 quarts must have a 25% salt solution.

(12) What concentration and amount solution have to be added to 7 gallons of 60% alcohol to produce 16 gallons of 37 $\frac{1}{2}$% alcohol solution? **9 gallons of 20% solution.**

To get 16 gallons, 9 gallons must be added to the 7 gallons. Let $x\%$ = the percent of alcohol in the 9 gallons:

$$\begin{aligned} (x\%)(9)+(60\%)(7) &= \left(37\frac{1}{2}\%\right)(16) \\ 9x+420 &= 600 \\ 9x &= 180 \\ x &= \frac{180}{9} = 20 \end{aligned}$$

(13) Carlos has twice as many quarters as nickels and has a total of \$8.25. How many quarters does he have? **30 quarters.**

Let x = the number of nickels. Then $2x$ = the number of quarters. These coins total \$8.25 or 825 cents. So, in cents,

$$\begin{aligned} 5(x)+25(2x) &= 825 \\ 5x+50x &= 825 \\ 55x &= 825 \\ x &= \frac{825}{55} = 15 \end{aligned}$$

Because Carlos has 15 nickels, he must then have 30 quarters.

(14) Gregor has twice as many \$10 bills as \$20 bills, five times as many \$1 bills as \$10 bills, and half as many \$5 bills as \$1 bills. He has a total of \$750. How many of each bill does he have? **10 \$20 bills, 20 \$10 bills, 100 \$1 bills, and 50 \$5 bills.**

Let x = the number of \$20 bills. Then $2x$ = the number of \$10 bills, $5(2x)=10x$ = the number of \$1 bills, and $\frac{1}{2}(10x)=5x$ = the number of \$5 bills. The total in dollars is 750. So the equation should be $20(x)+10(2x)+1(10x)+5(5x)=750$. Simplify on the left to $75x=750$ and $x=10$. Gregor has 10 \$20 bills, 20 \$10 bills, 100 \$1 bills, and 50 \$5 bills.

15) Stella has 100 coins in nickels, dimes, and quarters. She has 18 more nickels than dimes and a total of $7.40. How many of each coin does she have? **40 dimes, 58 nickels, and 2 quarters.**

Let x = the number of dimes. Then $x+18$ = the number of nickels, and the number of quarters is $100-\left[x+(x+18)\right]=82-2x$. These coins total $7.40 or 740 cents:

$$
\begin{aligned}
10(x)+5(x+18)+25\left(100-\left[x+(x+8)\right]\right)&=740\\
10x+5(x+18)+25(82-2x)&=740\\
10x+5x+90+2{,}050-50x&=740\\
2{,}140-35x&=740\\
-35x&=-1{,}400\\
x&=\frac{-1{,}400}{-35}=40
\end{aligned}
$$

So Stella has 40 dimes, 58 nickels, and 2 quarters.

16) Betty invested $10,000 in two different funds. She invested part at 2% and the rest at 3%. She earned $240 in simple interest. How much did she invest at each rate? (***Hint:*** Use the simple interest formula: $I = Prt$.) **Betty has $6,000 invested at 2% and the other $4,000 invested at 3%.**

Let x = the amount invested at 2%. Then the amount invested at 3% is $10{,}000-x$. Betty earns interest of 2% on x dollars and 3% on $10{,}000-x$ dollars. The total interest is $240, so

$$
\begin{aligned}
(0.02)(x)+(0.03)(10{,}000-x)&=240\\
0.02x+300-0.03x&=240\\
-0.01x&=-60\\
x&=\frac{-60}{-0.01}=6{,}000
\end{aligned}
$$

» Computing distances and slopes

» Intercepting and intersecting

» Writing equations of lines

» Graphing basic conics

Chapter 21 Getting a Handle on Graphing

Graphs are as important to algebra as pictures are to books and magazines. A graph can represent data that you've collected, or it can represent a pattern or model of an occurrence. A graph illustrates what you're trying to demonstrate or understand.

The standard system for graphing in algebra is to use the *Cartesian coordinate system*, where points are represented by ordered pairs of numbers; connected points can be lines, curves, or disjointed pieces of graphs.

This chapter can help you sort out much of the graphing mystery and even perfect your graphing skills; just watch out! The slope may be slippery.

Thickening the Plot with Points

Graphing on the Cartesian coordinate system begins by constructing two perpendicular axes, the x-axis (horizontal) and the y-axis (vertical). The Cartesian coordinate system identifies a point by an ordered pair, (x, y). The order in which the coordinates are written matters. The first coordinate, the x, represents how far to the left or right the point is from the *origin*, or where the axes intersect. A positive *x* is to the right; a negative *x* is to the left. The second coordinate, the *y*, represents how far up or down from the origin the point is.

Cartesian coordinates designate where a point is in reference to the two perpendicular axes. To the right and up is positive, to the left and down is negative. Any point that lies on one of the axes has a 0 for one of the coordinates, such as (0, 2) or (−3, 0). The coordinates for the *origin*, the intersection of the axes, are (0, 0).

EXAMPLE

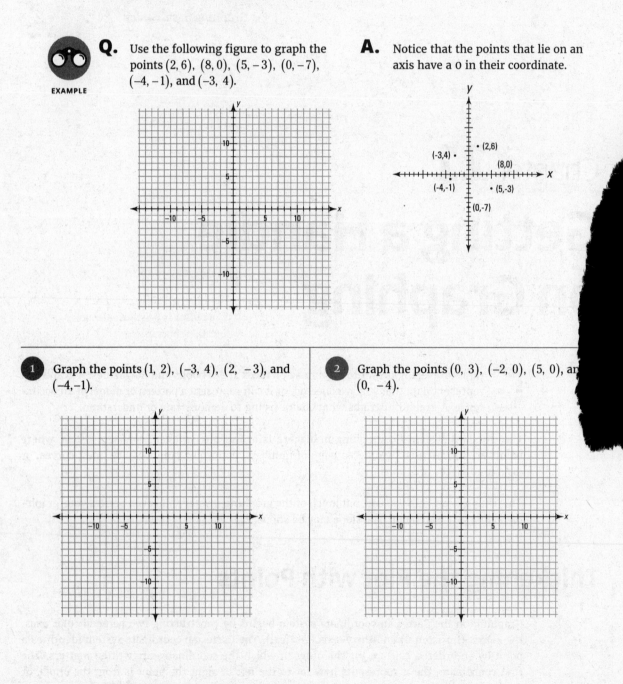

Q. Use the following figure to graph the points (2, 6), (8, 0), (5, −3), (0, −7), (−4, −1), and (−3, 4).

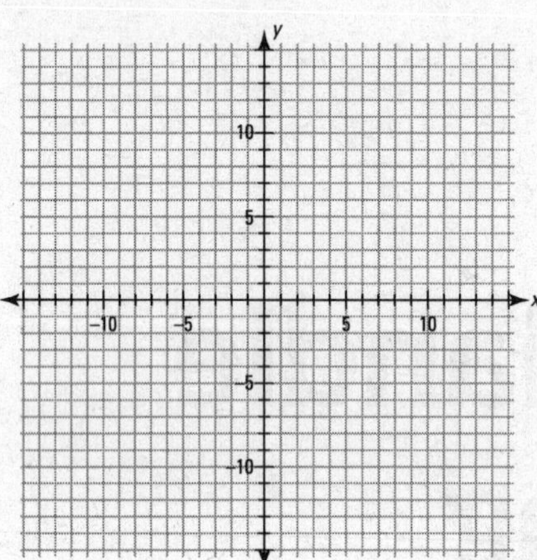

A. Notice that the points that lie on an axis have a 0 in their coordinate.

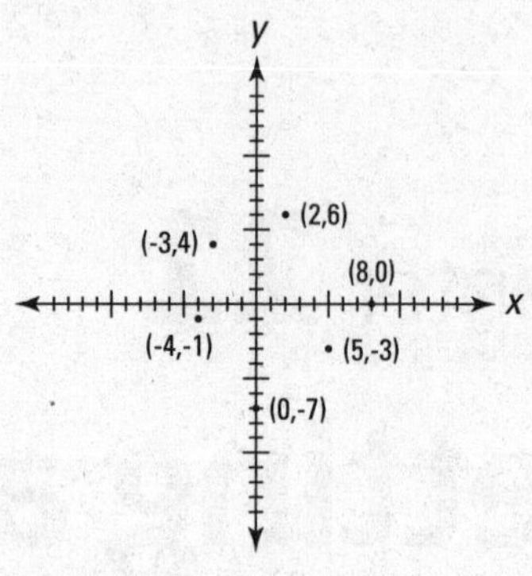

1 Graph the points (1, 2), (−3, 4), (2, −3), and (−4, −1).

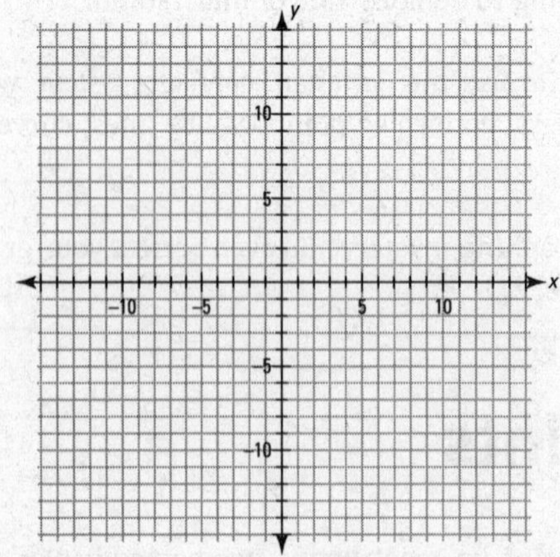

2 Graph the points (0, 3), (−2, 0), (5, 0), an[d] (0, −4).

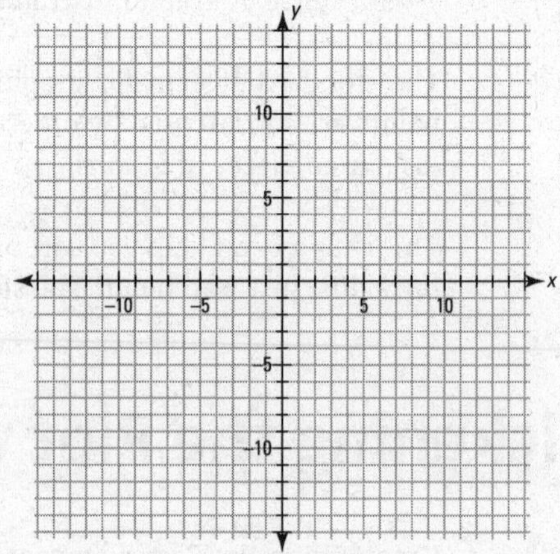

Sectioning Off by Quadrants

Another description for a point is the *quadrant* that the point lies in. The quadrants are referred to in many applications because of the common characteristics of points that lie in the same quadrant. The quadrants are numbered one through four, usually with Roman numerals. Check out Figure 21-1 to see how the quadrants are identified.

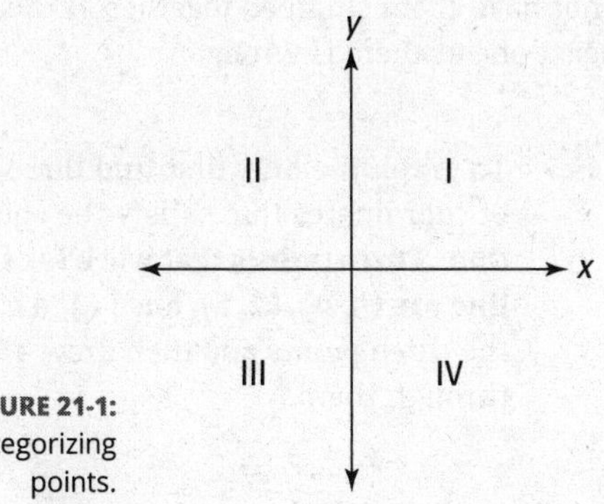

FIGURE 21-1: Categorizing points.

EXAMPLE

Q. Referring to Figure 21-1, describe which coordinates are positive or negative in the different quadrants.

A. **In quadrant I, both the *x* and *y* coordinates are positive numbers. In quadrant II, the *x* coordinate is negative, and the *y* coordinate is positive. In quadrant III, both the *x* and *y* coordinates are negative. In quadrant IV, the *x* coordinate is positive, and the *y* coordinate is negative.**

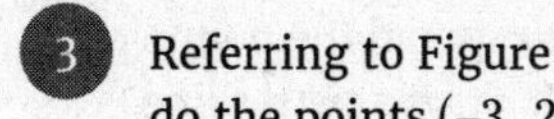

3 Referring to Figure 21-1, in which quadrant do the points $(-3, 2)$ and $(-4, 11)$ lie?

4 Referring to Figure 21-1, in which quadrant do the points $(-4,-1)$ and $(-2,-2)$ lie?

Using Points to Lay Out Lines

One of the most basic graphs you can construct by using the coordinate system is the graph of a straight line. You may remember from geometry that only two points are required to determine a particular line. When graphing lines using points, though, plot three points to be sure that you've graphed the points correctly and put them in the correct positions. You can think of the third point as a sort of a check (like the *check digit* in a UPC Code). The third point can be anywhere, but try to spread out the three points and not have them clumped together. If the three points aren't in a straight line, you know that at least one of them is wrong.

EXAMPLE

Q. Use the following to graph the line represented by the equation $2x+3y=10$.

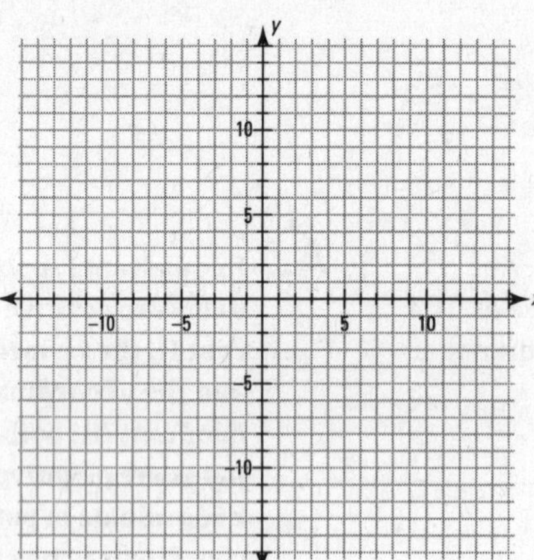

A. To graph the line, first find three sets of coordinates that satisfy the equation. **Three points that work for this line are (5, 0), (2, 2), and** $(-1, 4)$. Plot the three points and then draw a line through them.

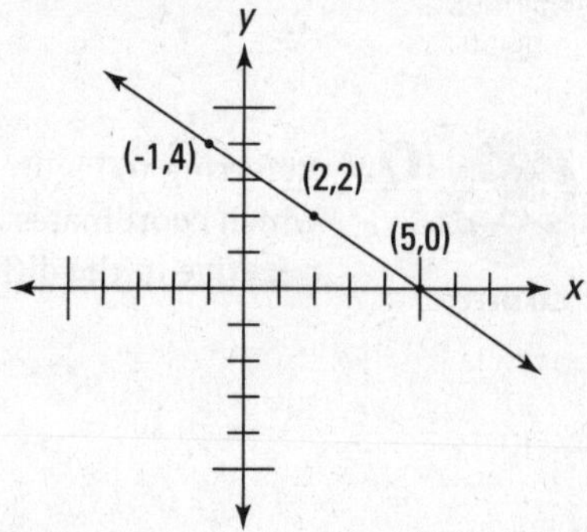

These aren't the only three points you could have chosen. I'm just demonstrating how to spread the points out so that you can draw a better line.

5 Find three points that lie on the line $2x - y = 3$, plot them, and draw the line through them.

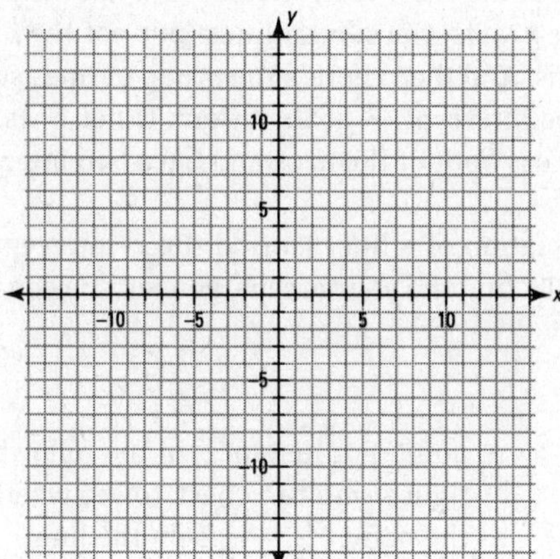

6 Find three points that lie on the line $x + 3y + 6 = 0$, plot them, and draw the line through them.

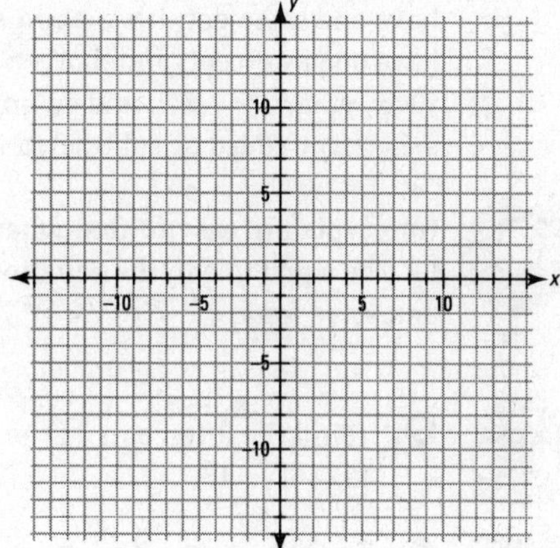

7 Find three points that lie on the line $x = 4$, plot them, and draw the line through them.

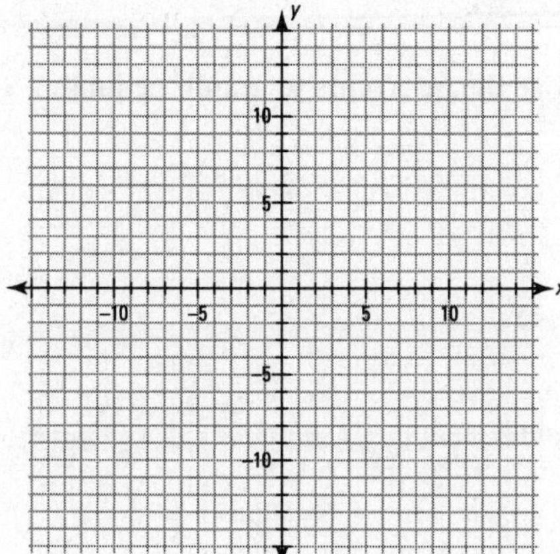

8 Find three points that lie on the line $y = -2$, plot them, and draw the line through them.

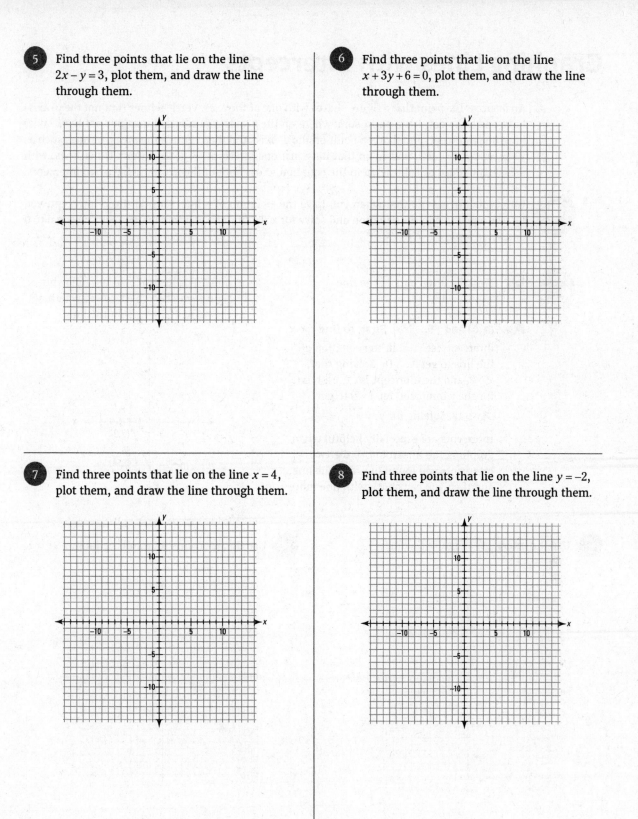

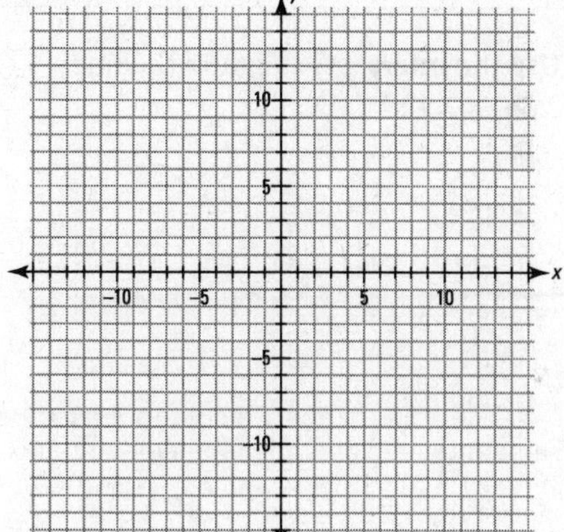

Graphing Lines with Intercepts

An *intercept* is a point that a figure shares with one of the axes. Vertical lines (but not the y-axis) have one intercept; it's a point somewhere on the x-axis. Horizontal lines (but not the x-axis) have one intercept; and that's a point on the y-axis. And then there's the group of lines such as $y = x$, $y = 2x$, $y = -4x$, and so on that have just one intercept — at the origin. Other lines, with a constant added or subtracted in the equation, cross both of the axes and have two intercepts.

TIP

Intercepts are easy to find when you have the equation of a line. To find the x-intercept, you let y be equal to 0 in the equation and solve for x. To find the y-intercept, you let x be equal to 0 and solve for y.

EXAMPLE

Q. Find the intercepts of the line $9x - 4y = 18$.

A. **(2,0) and** $\left(0, -\frac{9}{2}\right)$. First, to find the x intercept, let $y = 0$ in the equation of the line to get $9x = 18$. Solving that, $x = 2$, and the intercept is (2, 0). Next, for the y intercept, let $x = 0$ to get $-4y = 18$. Solving for y, $y = \frac{18}{-4} = -\frac{9}{2}$. Intercepts are especially helpful when graphing the line, too. Use the two intercepts you found to graph the line, and then you can check with one more point. For instance, in the following figure, you can check to see whether the point $\left(\frac{2}{9}, -4\right)$ is on the line.

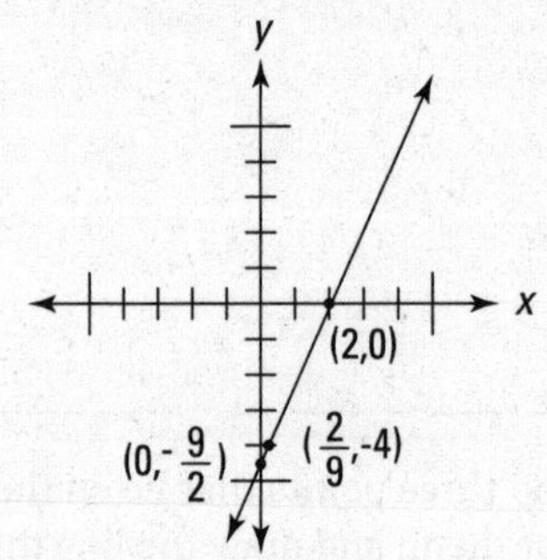

9 Use the intercepts to graph the line $3x + 4y = 12$.

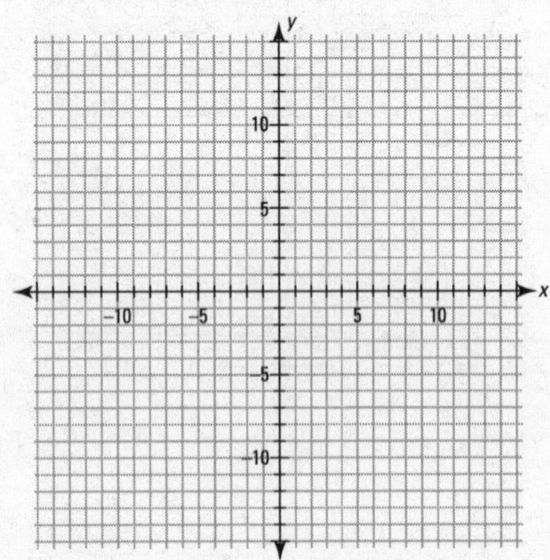

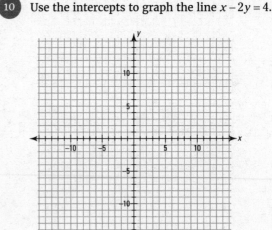

10 Use the intercepts to graph the line $x - 2y = 4$.

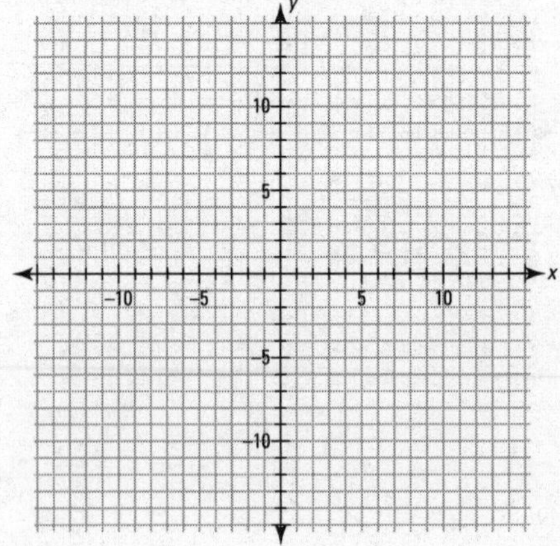

Computing Slopes of Lines

The *slope* of a line is simply a number that describes the steepness of the line and whether it's rising or falling, as the line moves from left to right in a graph. When referring to how steep a line is, when you're given its slope, the general rule is that the farther the number is from 0, the steeper the line. A line with a slope of 7 is much steeper than a line with a slope of 2. And a line whose slope is –6 is steeper than a line whose slope is –3.

To find the slope of a line, you can use two points on the graph of the line and apply the formula $m = \frac{y_2 - y_1}{x_2 - x_1}$. The letter *m* is the traditional symbol for slope; the (x_1, y_1) and (x_2, y_2) are the coordinates of any two points on the line. The point you choose to go first in the formula doesn't really matter. Just be sure to keep the order the same — from the same point — because you can't mix and match.

REMEMBER

A *horizontal* line has a slope of 0, and a vertical line has no slope. To help you remember, picture the sun coming up on the *horizon* — that 0 is just peeking out at you.

EXAMPLE

Q. Find the slope of the line that goes through the two points $(-3, 4)$ and $(1, -8)$ and use the following figure to graph it.

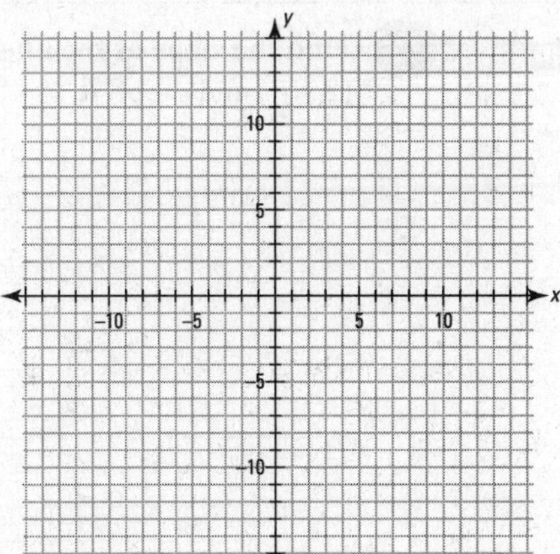

A. **–3**. To find the slope, use $m = \frac{4-(-8)}{-3-1} = \frac{12}{-4} = -3$. The following figure shows a graph of that line. It's fairly steep — any slope greater than 1 or less than –1 is steep. The negative part indicates that the line's falling as you go from left to right. Another description of slope is that the bottom number is the *change in x*, and the top is the *change in y*. Here's how you read a slope of –3: *For every 1 unit you move to the right parallel to the x-axis, you drop down 3 units parallel to the y-axis.*

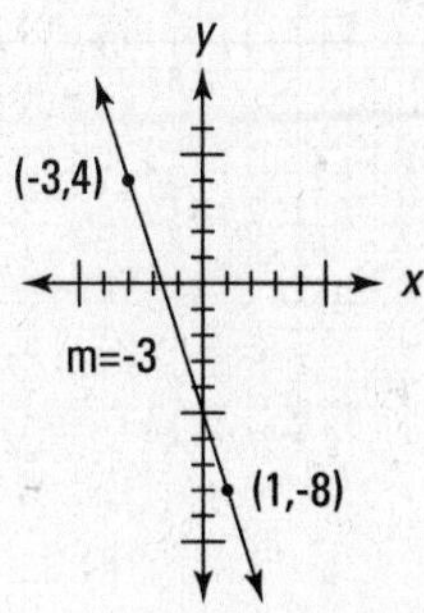

11 Find the slope of the line through the points $(3, 2)$ and $(-4, -5)$ and graph the line.

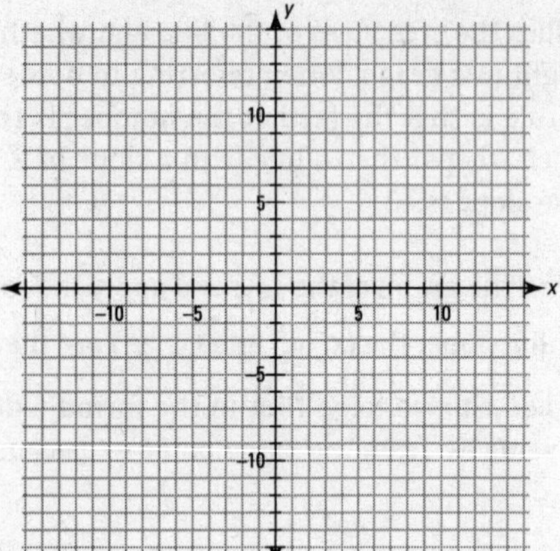

12 Find the slope of the line through the points $(-1, 7)$ and $(1, 3)$ and graph the line.

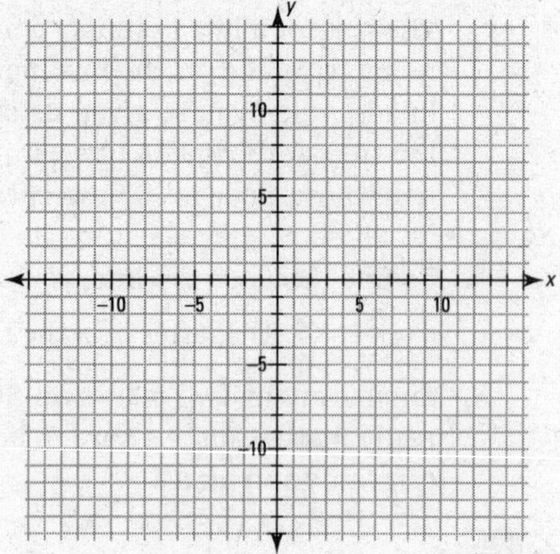

13 Find the slope of the line through $(3, -4)$ and $(5, -4)$ and graph it.

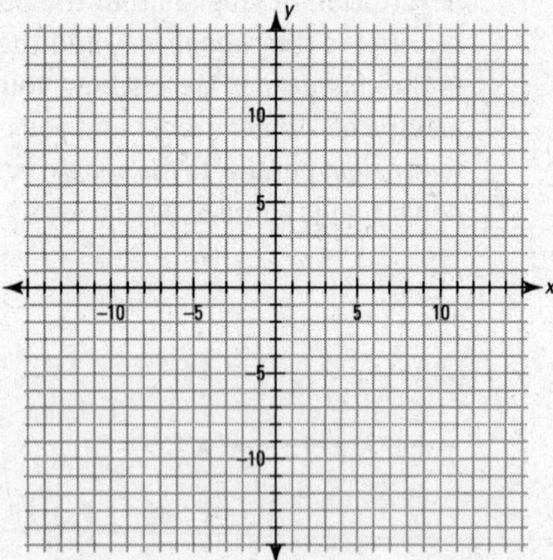

14 Find the slope of the line through $(2, 3)$ and $(2, -8)$ and graph it.

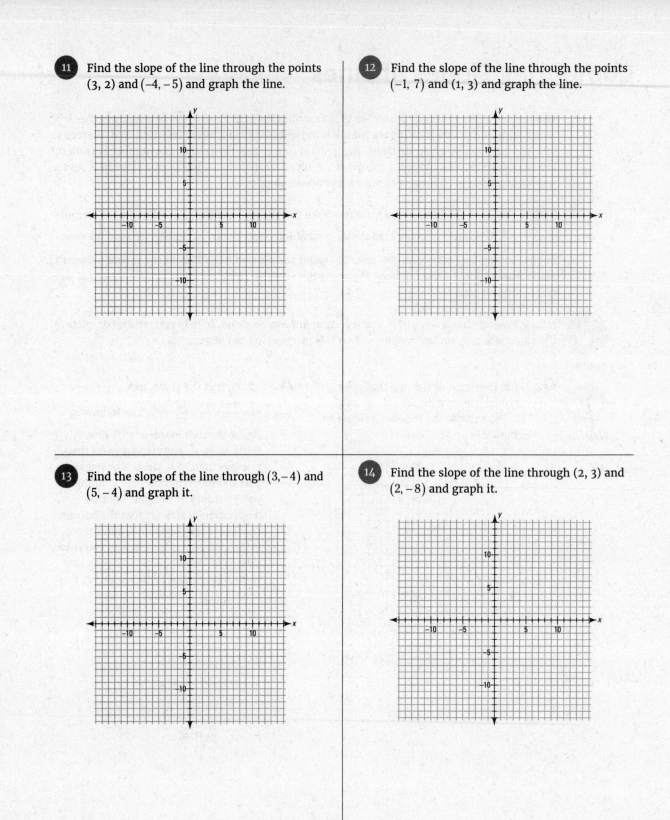

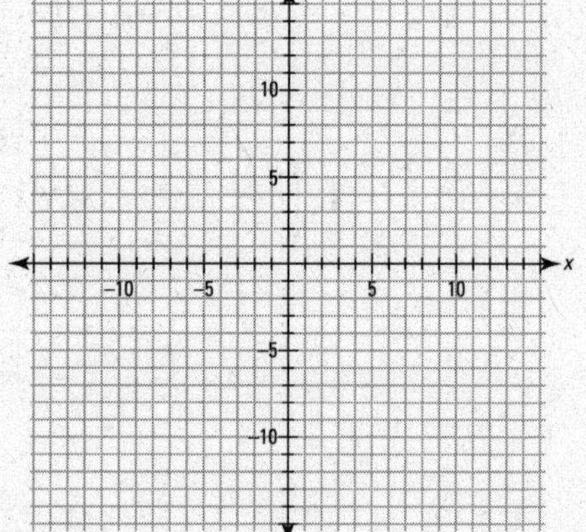

Graphing with the Slope-Intercept Form

Equations of lines can take many forms, but one of the most useful is called the *slope-intercept form*. The numbers for the slope and y-intercept are part of the equation. When you use this form to graph a line, you just plot the y-intercept and use the slope to find another point from there.

REMEMBER

The slope intercept form is $y = mx + b$. The m represents the slope of the line. The b is the y-coordinate of the intercept where the line crosses the y-axis. A line with the equation $y = -3x + 2$ has a slope of -3 and a y-intercept of (0, 2).

Having the equation of a line in the *slope-intercept* form makes graphing the line an easy chore. Follow these steps:

1. **Plot the y-intercept on the y-axis.**
2. **Write the slope as a fraction.**

   Using the equation $y = -3x + 2$, the fraction would be $\frac{-3}{1}$. (If the slope is negative, you put the negative part in the numerator.) The slope has the change in y in the numerator and the change in x in the denominator.
3. **Starting with the y-intercept, count the amount of the change in x (the number in the denominator) to the right of the intercept, and then count up or down from that point (depending on whether the slope is positive or negative), using the number in the numerator.**

   Wherever you end up is another point on the line.
4. **Mark that point and draw a line through the new point and the y-intercept.**

EXAMPLE

Q. Graph $y = -3x + 2$, using the method in the previous steps.

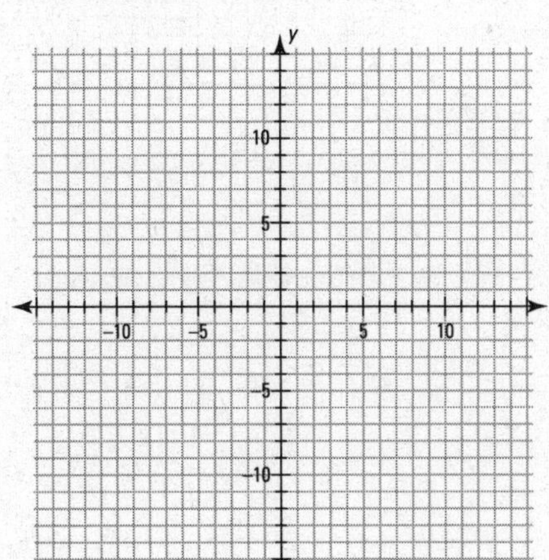

A.

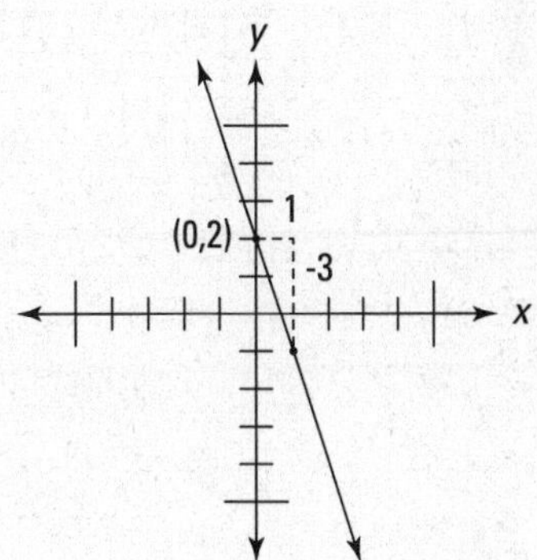

EXAMPLE

Q. Graph $y = \frac{2}{5}x - 1$.

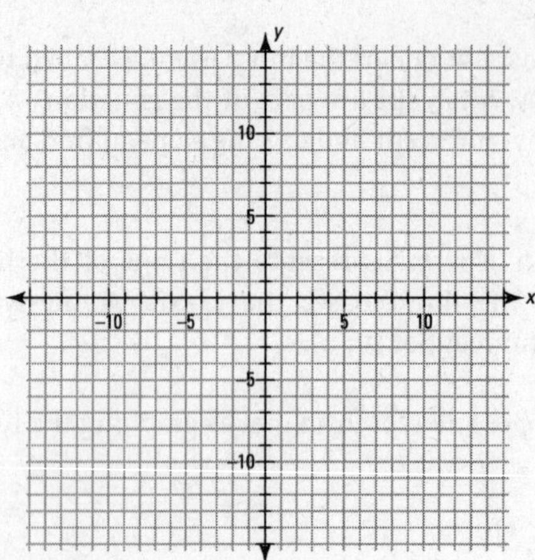

A.

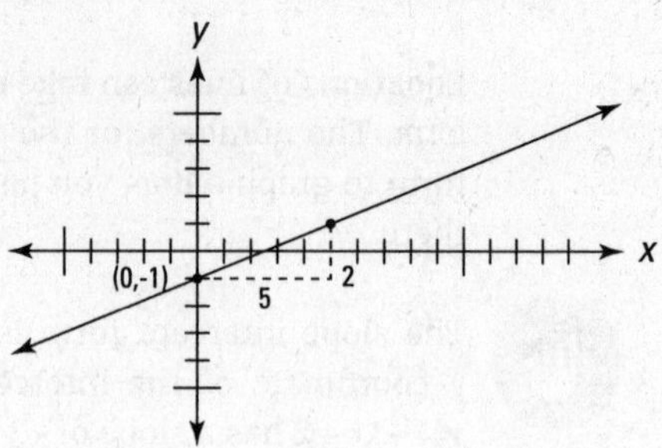

15 **Graph the line $y = -\frac{2}{3}x + 4$, using the y-intercept and slope.**

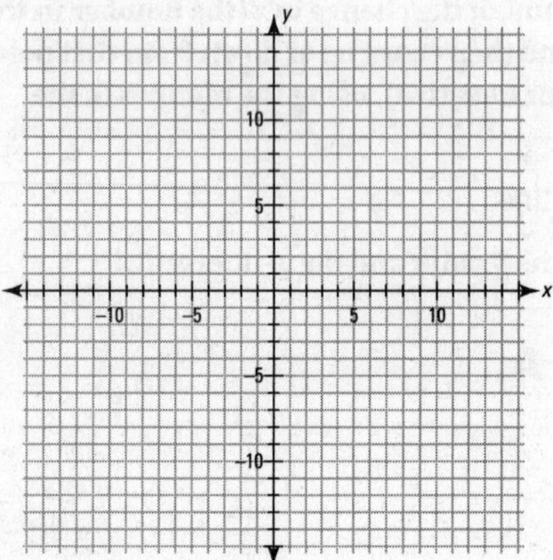

16 **Graph the line $y = 5x - 2$, using the y-intercept and slope.**

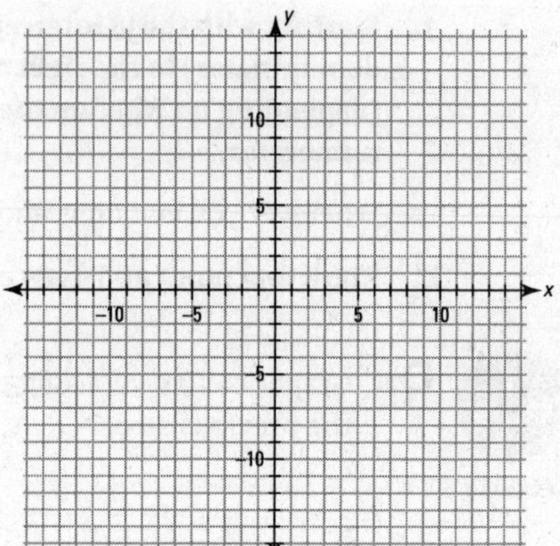

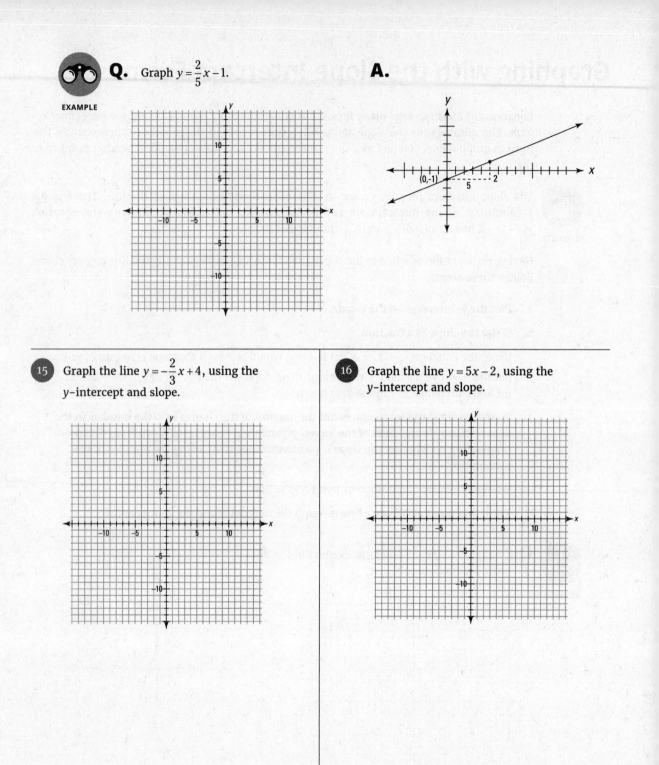

Changing to the Slope-Intercept Form

Graphing lines by using the slope-intercept form is a piece of cake. But what if the equation you're given isn't in that form? Are you stuck with substituting in values and finding coordinates of points that work? Not necessarily. Changing the form of the equation using algebraic manipulations — and then graphing using the new form — is often easier.

REMEMBER

To change the equation of a line to the slope-intercept form, $y = mx + b$, first isolate the term with y in it on one side of the equation and then divide each side by any coefficient of y. You can rearrange the terms so the x term, with the slope multiplier, comes first.

EXAMPLE

Q. Change the equation $3x - 4y = 8$ to the slope-intercept form.

A. $\boldsymbol{y = \frac{3}{4}x - 2}$. First, subtract $3x$ from each side: $-4y = -3x + 8$. Then divide each term by -4:

$$\frac{-4y}{-4} = \frac{-3x}{-4} + \frac{8}{-4}$$

$$y = \frac{3}{4}x - 2$$

This line has a slope of $3/4$ and a y-intercept at $(0, -2)$.

Q. Change the equation $y - 3 = 0$ to the slope-intercept form.

A. $\boldsymbol{y = 3}$. There's no x term, so the slope must be 0. If you want a complete slope-intercept form, you could write the equation as $y = 0x + 3$ to show a slope of 0 and an intercept of (0, 3).

17 Change the equation $8x + 2y = 3$ to the slope-intercept form.

18 Change the equation $4x - y - 3 = 0$ to the slope-intercept form.

Writing Equations of Lines

Up until now, you've been given the equation of a line and been told to graph that line using either two points, the intercepts, or the slope and y-intercept. But how do you re-create the line's equation if you're given either two points (which could be the two intercepts) or the slope and some other point?

REMEMBER

Use the *point-slope* form, $y - y_1 = m(x - x_1)$ to write the equation of a line. The letter m represents the slope of the line, and (x_1, y_1) is any point on the line. After filling in the information, simplify the form.

EXAMPLE

Q. Find the equation of the line that has a slope of 3 and goes through the point (–4, 2).

A. $\mathbf{y = 3x + 14}$. Using the *point-slope* form, you write $y - 2 = 3(x - (-4))$. Simplifying, you get

$$y - 2 = 3(x + 4)$$
$$y - 2 = 3x + 12$$
$$y = 3x + 14$$

Q. Find the equation of the line that goes through the points $(5, -2)$ and $(-4, 7)$.

A. $\mathbf{y = -x + 3}$. First, find the slope of the line. $m = \frac{7-(-2)}{-4-4} = \frac{9}{-9} = -1$. Now use the point slope form with the slope of -1 and with the coordinates of one of the points. It doesn't matter which one, so I chose $(5, -2)$. Filling in the values, $y - (-2) = -1(x - 5)$. Simplifying, you get $y + 2 = -x + 5$ or $y = -x + 3$.

19 Find the equation of the line with a slope of $\frac{1}{3}$ that goes through the point (0, 7).

20 Find the equation of the line that goes through the points $(-3, -1)$ and $(-2, 5)$.

Picking on Parallel and Perpendicular Lines

When two lines are *parallel* to one another, they never touch, and their slopes are exactly the same number. When two lines are *perpendicular* to one another, they cross in exactly one place, creating a 90 degree angle, and their slopes are related in a special way. If two perpendicular lines aren't vertical and horizontal (parallel to the two axes), then their slopes are opposite in sign and the numerical parts are reciprocals. (The *reciprocal* of a number is its flip, what you get when you reverse the numerator and denominator of a fraction.) In other words, if you multiply the values of the two slopes of perpendicular lines together, you always get an answer of –1.

EXAMPLE

Q. Determine how these lines are related: $y=\frac{4}{3}x+1$, $y=\frac{8}{6}x-7$, and $y=\frac{16}{12}x$.

A. **They're parallel.** They're written in slope-intercept form, and all have the same slope. The y-intercepts are the only differences between these three lines.

Q. Determine how these lines are related: $y=-\frac{4}{9}x+3$ and $y=\frac{9}{4}x-19$.

A. **They're perpendicular to one another.** Their slopes are negative reciprocals of one another. It doesn't matter what the y-intercepts are. They can be different or the same.

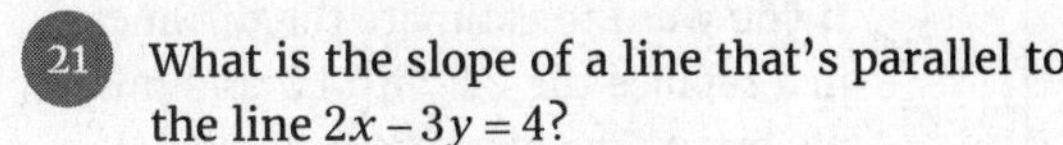

21 What is the slope of a line that's parallel to the line $2x-3y=4$?

22 What is the slope of a line that's perpendicular to the line $4x+2y+7=0$?

Finding Distances between Points

A segment can be drawn between two points that are plotted on the coordinate axes. You can determine the distance between those two points by using a formula that actually incorporates the Pythagorean theorem — it's like finding the length of a hypotenuse of a right triangle. (Check Chapter 18 for more practice with the Pythagorean theorem.) If you want to find the distance between the two points (x_1, y_1) and (x_2, y_2), use the formula $d = \sqrt{(x_2 - x_1)^2 + (y_2 - y_1)^2}$.

EXAMPLE

Q. Find the distance between the points (−8, 2) and (4, 7).

A. **13 units**. Use the distance formula and plug in the coordinates of the points:

$$\begin{aligned} d &= \sqrt{(4-(-8))^2 + (7-2)^2} \\ &= \sqrt{(12)^2 + (5)^2} \\ &= \sqrt{144 + 25} \\ &= \sqrt{169} \\ &= 13 \end{aligned}$$

Of course, not all the distances come out nicely with a perfect square under the radical. When it isn't a perfect square, either simplify the expression or give a decimal approximation (refer to Chapter 5).

Q. Find the distance between the points (4, −3) and (2, 11).

A. **$10\sqrt{2}$ units**. Using the distance formula, you get

$$\begin{aligned} d &= \sqrt{(2-4)^2 + (11-(-3))^2} \\ &= \sqrt{(-2)^2 + (14)^2} \\ &= \sqrt{4 + 196} \\ &= \sqrt{200} = \sqrt{100}\sqrt{2} \\ &= 10\sqrt{2} \end{aligned}$$

If you want to estimate the distance, just replace the $\sqrt{2}$ with 1.4 and multiply by 10. The distance is about 14 units.

23 Find the distance between (3, −9) and (−9, 7).

24 Find the distance between (4, 1) and (−2, 2). Round the decimal equivalent of the answer to two decimal places.

Finding the Intersections of Lines

Two lines will intersect in exactly one point — unless they're parallel to one another. You can find the intersection of lines by careful graphing of the lines or by using simple algebra. Graphing is quick and easy, but it's hard to tell the exact answer if there's a fraction in one or both of the coordinates of the point of intersection.

To use algebra to solve for the intersection, you either add the two equations together (or some multiples of the equations), or you use *substitution*. I show you the substitution method here, because you can use the *slope-intercept* (see the earlier section "Changing to the Slope-Intercept Form") forms of the equations to accomplish the job.

REMEMBER

To find the intersection of two lines, use their slope-intercept forms and set their $mx+b$ portions equal to one another. Solve for x and then find y by putting the x value you found into one of the equations.

EXAMPLE

Q. Find the intersection of the lines $y=3x-2$ and $y=-2x-7$.

A. **(−1, −5)**. Set $3x-2=-2x-7$ and solve for x. Adding $2x$ to each side and adding 2 to each side, you get $5x=-5$. Dividing by 5 gives you $x=-1$. Now substitute -1 for x in either of the original equations. You get $y=-5$. It's really a good idea to do that substitution back into *both* of the equations as a check.

Q. Find the intersection of the lines $x+y=6$ and $2x-y=6$.

A. **(4, 2)**. First, write each equation in the slope-intercept form. The line $x+y=6$ becomes $y=-x+6$, and the line $2x-y=6$ becomes $y=2x-6$. Now, setting $-x+6=2x-6$, you get $-3x=-12$ or $x=4$. Substituting 4 for x in either equation, you get $y=2$.

25 Find the intersection of the lines $y=-4x+7$ and $y=5x-2$.

26 Find the intersection of the lines $3x-y=1$ and $x+2y+9=0$.

Graphing Parabolas and Circles

A *parabola* is a sort of U-shaped curve. It's one of the conic sections. A *circle* is the most easily recognized conic (the other conics are hyperbolas and ellipses). The equations and graphs of parabolas are used to describe all sorts of natural phenomena. For instance, headlight reflectors are formed from parabolic shapes. Circles — well, circles are just circles: handy, easy to deal with, and so symmetric.

An equation for parabolas that open upward or downward is $y = ax^2 + bx + c$, where a isn't 0. If a is a positive number, then the parabola opens upward; a negative a gives you a downward parabola.

REMEMBER

Here are the standard forms for parabolas and circles:

- **Parabola:** $y = a(x-h)^2 + k$
- **Circle:** $(x-h)^2 + (y-k)^2 = r^2$

Notice the h and k in both forms. For the parabola, the coordinates (h, k) tell you where the *vertex* (bottom or top of U-shape) is. For the circle, (h, k) gives you the coordinates of the center of the circle. The r part of the circle's form gives you the radius of the circle.

EXAMPLE

Q. Find the vertex of the parabola $y = -3(x+3)^2 + 7$ and sketch its graph.

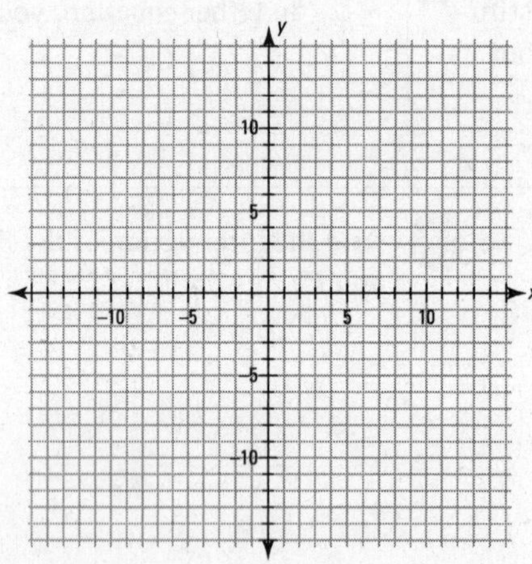

A. **Vertex: (−3, 7); opens downward.**

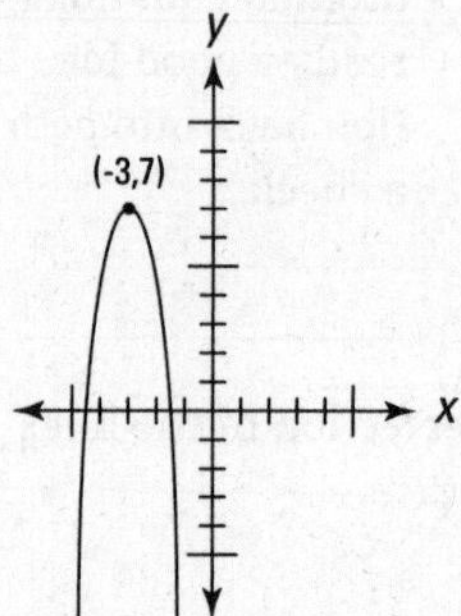

To find the vertex, you need the opposite of 3. The general form has $(x-h)$, which is the same as $(x-(-h))$ to deal with the positive sums in the parentheses. Because a is negative, the parabola opens downward; and a being −3 introduces a steepness, much like the slope of a line. You can plot a few extra points to help with the shape.

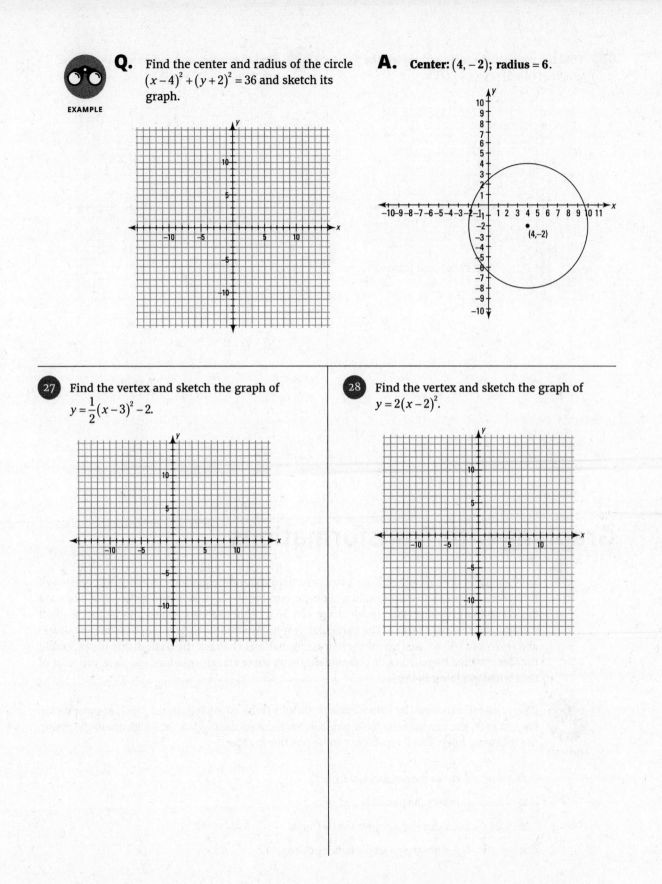

Q. Find the center and radius of the circle $(x-4)^2+(y+2)^2=36$ and sketch its graph.

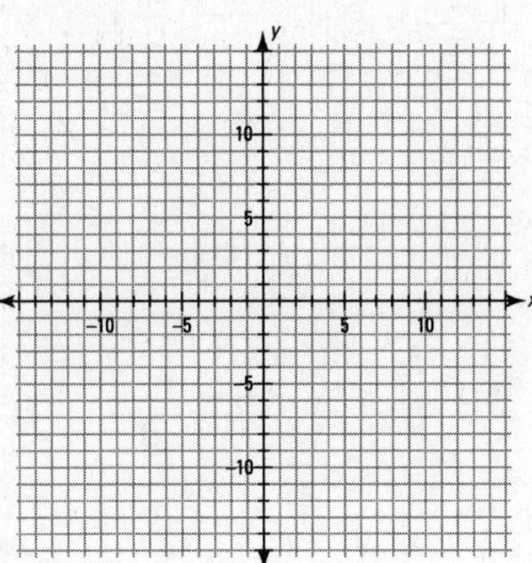

A. **Center:** $(4,-2)$; **radius** $=6$.

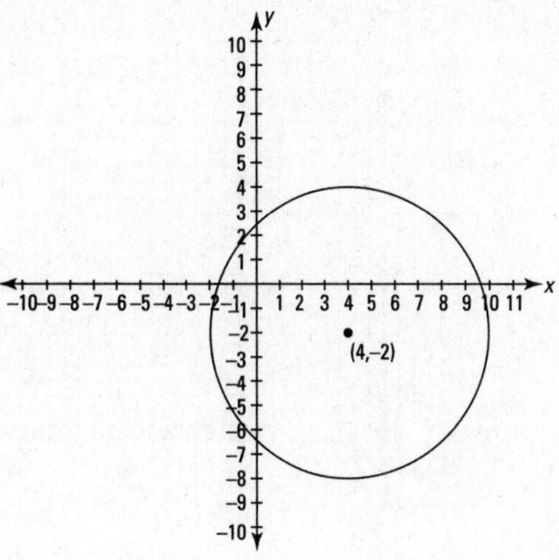

27 Find the vertex and sketch the graph of $y=\frac{1}{2}(x-3)^2-2$.

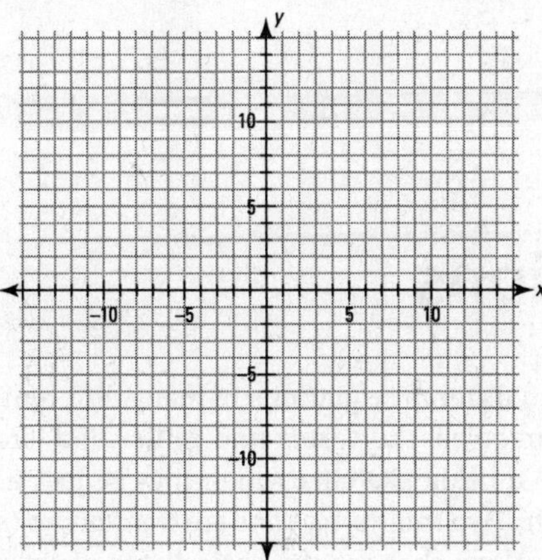

28 Find the vertex and sketch the graph of $y=2(x-2)^2$.

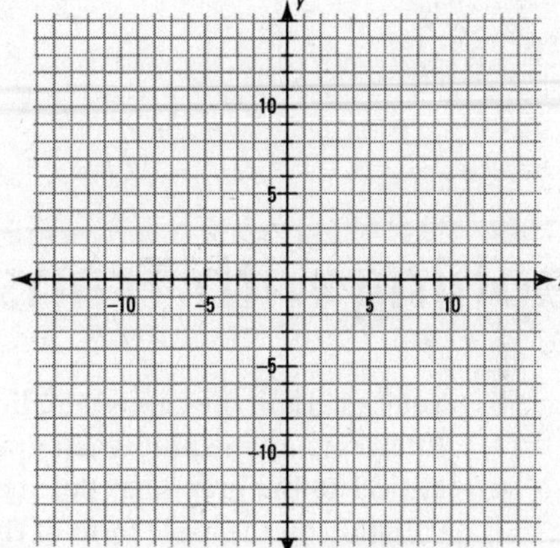

29 Find the center and radius and sketch the graph of $(x+3)^2+(y-4)^2=25$.

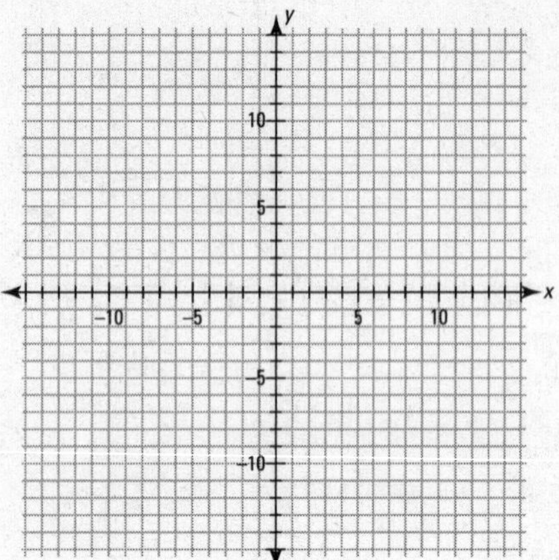

30 Find the center and radius and sketch the graph of $(x-5)^2+(y-2)^2=9$.

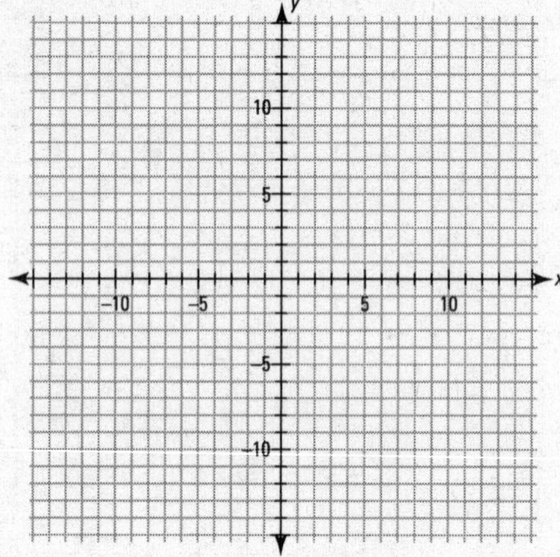

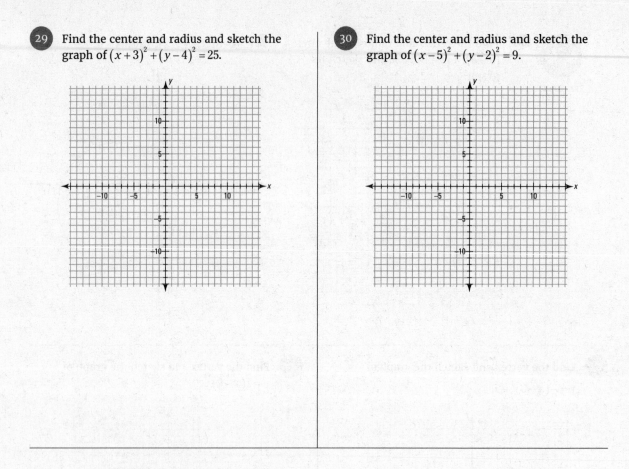

Graphing with Transformations

You can graph the curves and lines associated with different equations in many different ways. Intercepts are helpful when graphing lines or parabolas; the vertex and center of a circle are critical to the graphing. But many curves can be quickly sketched when they're just a slight variation on the basic form of the particular graph. Two *transformations* are *translations* (slides) and *reflections* (flips). Neither of these transformations changes the basic shape of the graph; they just change its position or orientation. Using these transformations can save you a lot of time when graphing figures.

REMEMBER

When a curve is changed by a *translation* or slide, it slides to the left, to the right, or up or down. For instance, you can take the basic parabola with the equation $y=x^2$ and slide it around, using the following rules. The *C* represents some positive number:

- $y=x^2+C$ raises the parabola by *C* units.
- $y=x^2-C$ lowers the parabola by *C* units.
- $y=(x+C)^2$ slides the parabola left by *C* units.
- $y=(x-C)^2$ slides the parabola right by *C* units.

When a curve is changed by a *reflection* or flip, you have a symmetry vertically or horizontally:

- $y = -x^2$ flips the parabola over a horizontal line.
- $y = (-x)^2$ flips the parabola over a vertical line.

TIP

You can change the steepness of a graph by multiplying it by a number. If you multiply the basic function or operation by a positive number greater than 1, then the graph becomes steeper. If you multiply it by a positive number smaller than 1, the graph becomes flatter. Multiplying a basic function by a negative number results in a flip or reflection over a horizontal line. Use these rules when using the parabola:

- $y = kx^2$: Parabola becomes steeper when k is positive and greater than 1.
- $y = kx^2$: Parabola becomes flatter when k is positive and smaller than 1.

EXAMPLE

Q. Use the basic graph of $y = x^2$ to graph $y = -3x^2 + 1$.

A.

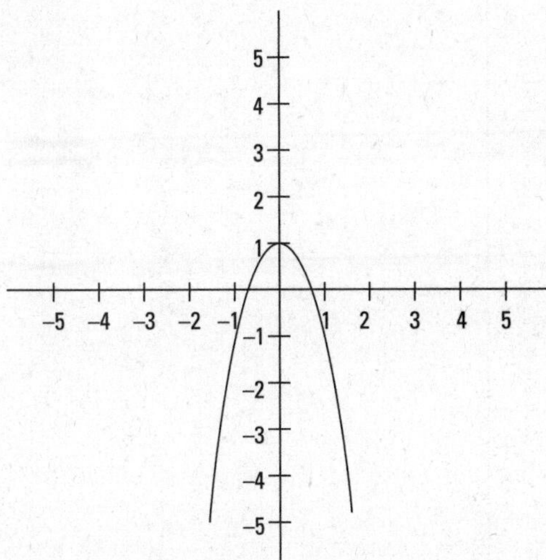

The multiplier -3 flips the parabola over the x-axis and makes it steeper. The $+1$ raises the vertex up one unit.

Q. Use the basic graph of $y = x^2$ to graph $y = (x+1)^2 - 3$.

A.

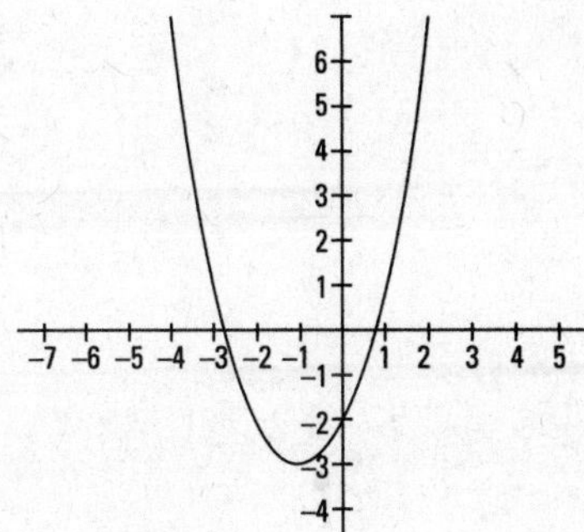

The -3 lowers the parabola by three units. The $+1$ inside the parentheses slides the parabola one unit to the left. Compare this graphing technique with the method of graphing using the vertex, explained in the earlier section "Graphing Parabolas and Circles."

31 Sketch the graph of $y = (x - 4)^2$.

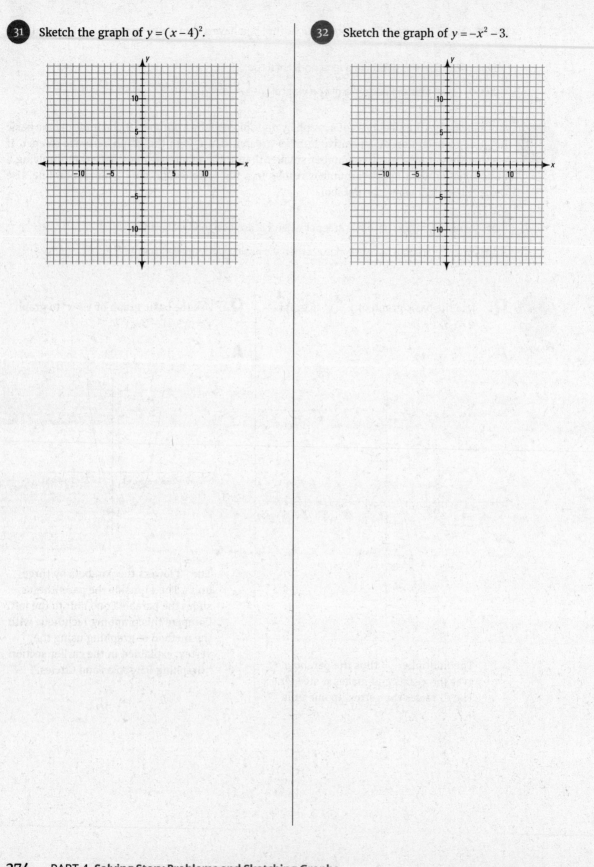

32 Sketch the graph of $y = -x^2 - 3$.

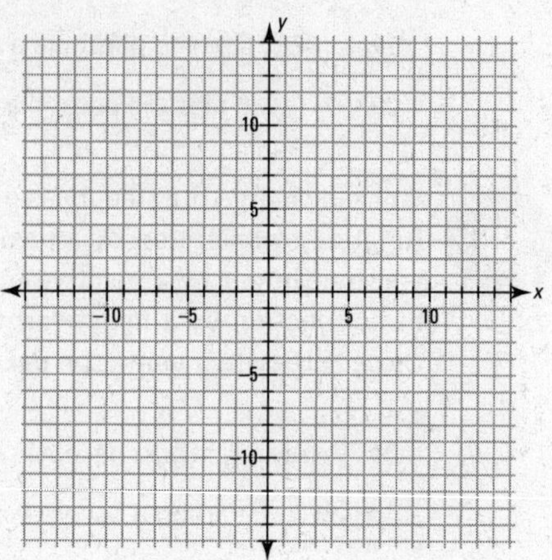

Answers to Problems on Graphing

The following are the answers (in bold) to the practice problems presented in this chapter.

1. Graph the points $(1, 2)$, $(-3, 4)$, $(2, -3)$, and $(-4, -1)$.

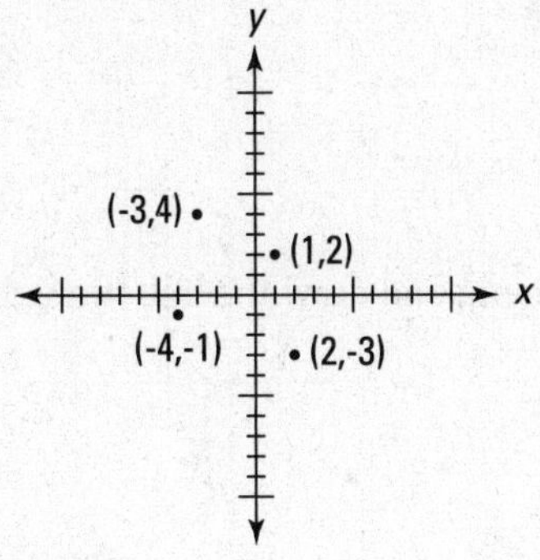

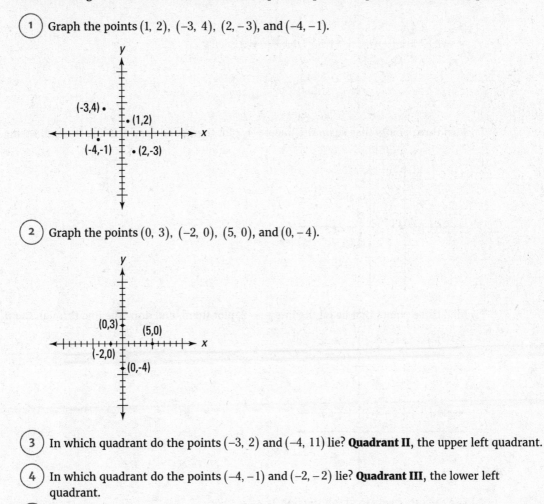

2. Graph the points $(0, 3)$, $(-2, 0)$, $(5, 0)$, and $(0, -4)$.

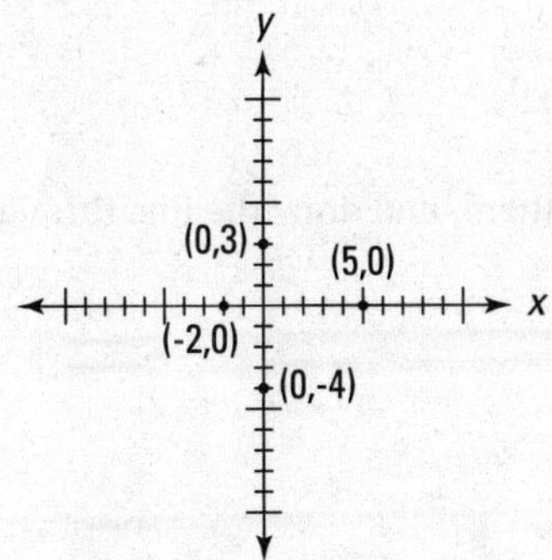

3. In which quadrant do the points $(-3, 2)$ and $(-4, 11)$ lie? **Quadrant II**, the upper left quadrant.

4. In which quadrant do the points $(-4, -1)$ and $(-2, -2)$ lie? **Quadrant III**, the lower left quadrant.

5. Find three points that lie on the line $2x - y = 3$, plot them, and draw the line through them.

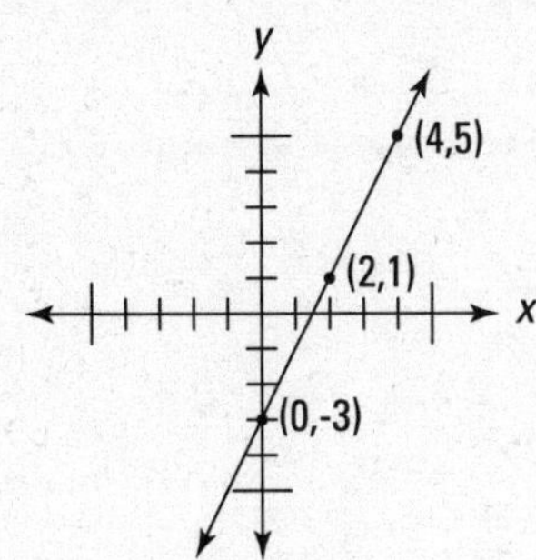

6. Find three points that lie on the line $x+3y+6=0$, plot them, and draw the line through them.

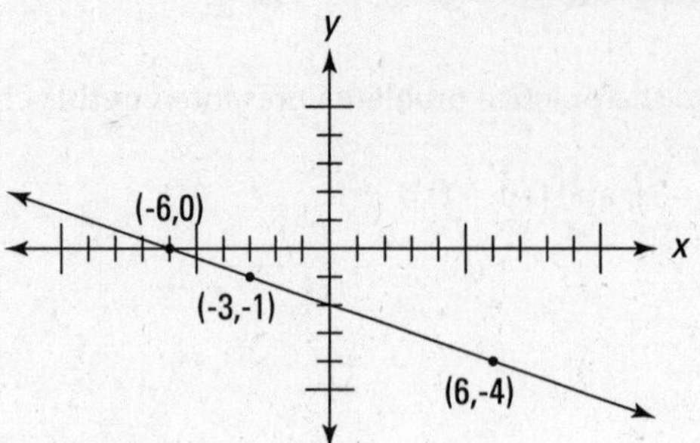

7. Find three points that lie on the line $x=4$, plot them, and draw the line through them.

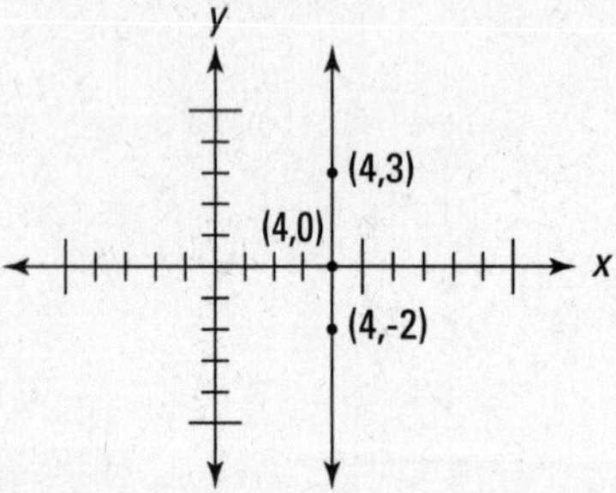

8. Find three points that lie on the line $y=-2$, plot them, and draw the line through them.

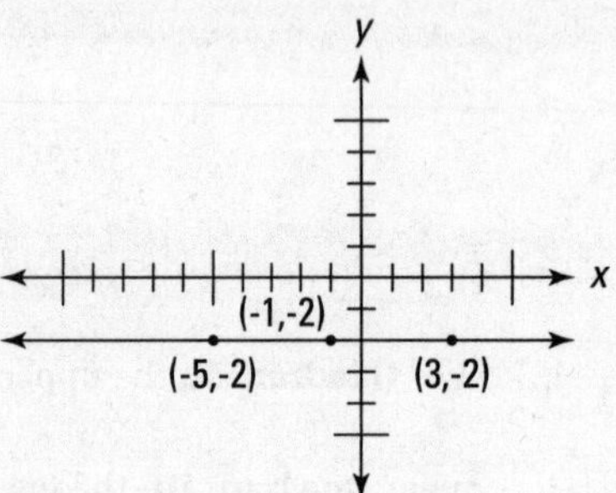

9. Use the intercepts to graph the line $3x+4y=12$.

Let $y=0$ to get $3x+0=12$, $x=4$. The intercept is (4, 0).

Let $x=0$ to get $0+4y=12$, $y=3$. The intercept is (0, 3).

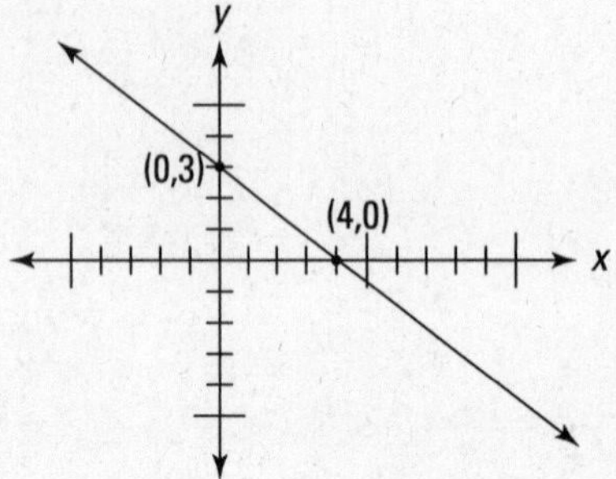

10. Use the intercepts to graph the line $x - 2y = 4$.

Let $y = 0$ to get $x - 0 = 4$, $x = 4$. The intercept is $(4, 0)$.

Let $x = 0$ to get $0 - 2y = 4$, $y = -2$. The intercept is $(0, -2)$.

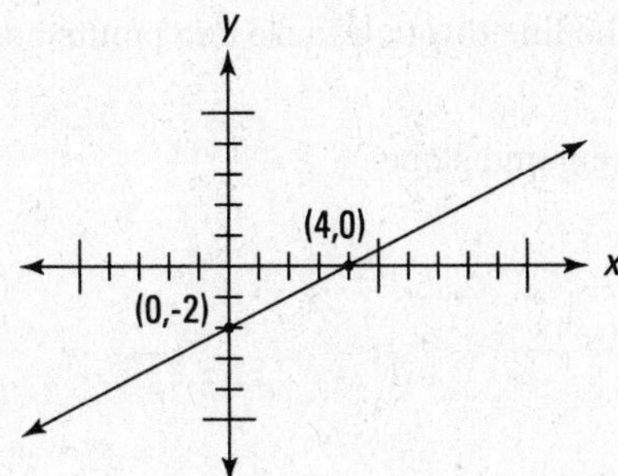

11. Find the slope of the line through the points $(3, 2)$ and $(-4, -5)$ and graph the line.

Using the slope formula, $m = \frac{2-(-5)}{3-(-4)} = \frac{7}{7} = 1$.

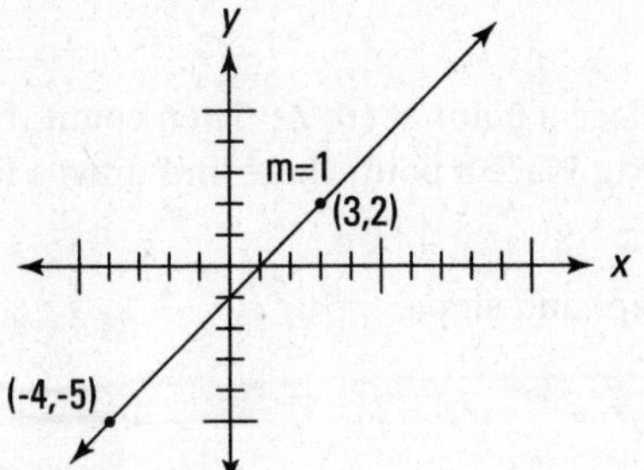

12. Find the slope of the line through the points $(-1, 7)$ and $(1, 3)$ and graph the line.

Using the slope formula, $m = \frac{7-3}{-1-1} = \frac{4}{-2} = -2$.

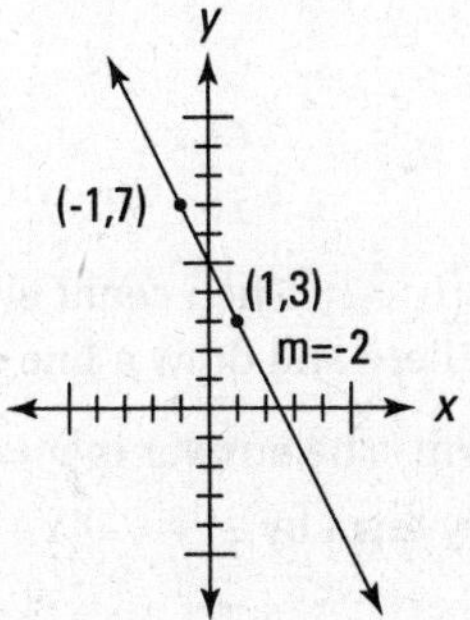

13. Find the slope of the line through $(3, -4)$ and $(5, -4)$. **Slope = 0.**

$$m = \frac{-4-(-4)}{3-5} = \frac{0}{-2} = 0$$

This fraction is equal to 0, meaning that the line through the points is a horizontal line with the equation $y = -4$.

(14) Find the slope of the line through (2, 3) and (2, −8). **No slope.**

$$m=\frac{3-(-8)}{2-2}=\frac{11}{0}$$

This fraction has no value; it's undefined. The line through these two points has no slope. It's a vertical line with the equation $x=2$.

(15) Graph the line $y=\frac{2}{3}x+4$, using the y-intercept and slope.

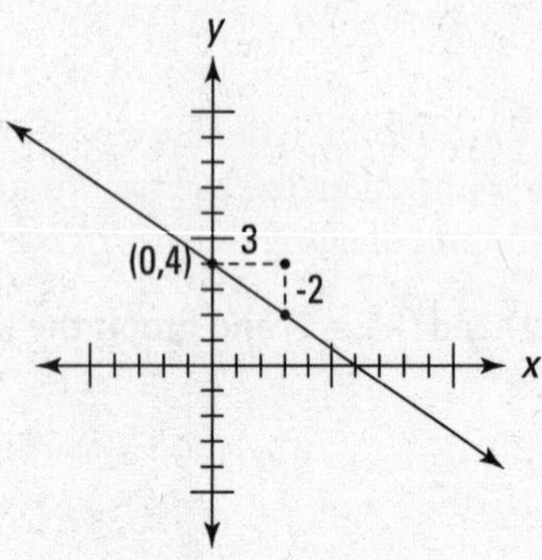

The slope is $-\frac{2}{3}$ and the y-intercept is 4. Place a point at (0, 4). Then count three units to the right of that intercept and two units down. Place a point there and draw a line through the intercept and the new point.

(16) Graph the line $y=5x-2$, using the y-intercept and slope.

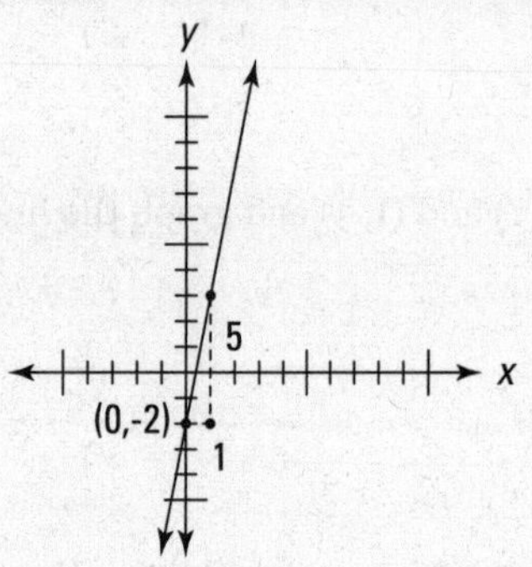

The y-intercept is −2, and the slope is 5. Place a point at $(0,-2)$. Then count one unit to the right and five units up from that intercept. Place a point there and draw a line.

(17) Change the equation $8x+2y=3$ to the slope-intercept form. The answer is $\boldsymbol{y=-4x+\frac{3}{2}}$. Subtract $8x$ from each side: $2y=-8x+3$. Then divide every term by 2: $y=-4x+\frac{3}{2}$. The slope is −4, and the y-intercept is $\frac{3}{2}$.

(18) Change the equation $4x-y-3=0$ to the slope-intercept form. The answer is $\boldsymbol{y=4x-3}$. Add y to each side to get $4x-3=y$. Then use the symmetric property to turn the equation around: $y=4x-3$. (This is easier than subtracting $4x$ from each side, adding 3 to each side, and then dividing by −1.)

(19) Find the equation of the line with a slope of $\frac{1}{3}$ that goes through the point (0, 7). The answer is $\boldsymbol{y = \frac{1}{3}x + 7}$.

You're given the slope and the *y*-intercept, so you can just put in the 7 for the value of *b*.

(20) Find the equation of the line that goes through the points $(-3, -1)$ and $(-2, 5)$. The answer is $\boldsymbol{y = 6x + 17}$.

First find the slope by using the two points: $m = \frac{5-(-1)}{-2-(-3)} = \frac{6}{1} = 6$. Using the point-slope form and the coordinates of the point $(-3, -1)$, you get $y-(-1) = 6(x-(-3))$ or $y+1 = 6(x+3)$. Distributing and subtracting 1 from each side gives you $y = 6x + 17$.

(21) What is the slope of a line that's parallel to the line $2x - 3y = 4$? **The slope is** $\boldsymbol{\frac{2}{3}}$. You can find the slope of a line that's parallel to the line $2x - 3y = 4$ by changing the equation to the slope-intercept form and the subtracting 2*x* from each side and dividing each term by -3. The equation is then $-3y = -2x + 4$, $y = \frac{-2}{-3}x + \frac{4}{-3}$, $y = \frac{2}{3}x - \frac{4}{3}$. The slope is $\frac{2}{3}$, and the *y*-intercept is $-\frac{4}{3}$.

(22) What is the slope of a line that's perpendicular to the line $4x + 2y + 7 = 0$? **The slope is** $\boldsymbol{\frac{1}{2}}$.

Change this equation to the slope-intercept form to find the slope of the line: $4x + 2y + 7 = 0$, $2y = -4x - 7$, $y = -2x - \frac{7}{2}$. The negative reciprocal of -2 is $\frac{1}{2}$, so that's the slope of a line perpendicular to this one.

(23) Find the distance between $(3, -9)$ and $(-9, 7)$. **20 units**. Using the distance formula, $d = \sqrt{[3-(-9)]^2 + (-9-7)^2} = \sqrt{12^2 + (-16)^2} = \sqrt{144 + 256} = \sqrt{400} = 20$.

(24) Find the distance between (4, 1) and $(-2, 2)$. Round the decimal equivalent of the answer to two decimal places. The answer is **6.08 units**.

$d = \sqrt{[4-(-2)]^2 + (1-2)^2} = \sqrt{6^2 + (-1)^2} = \sqrt{36+1} = \sqrt{37}$. Use a calculator and round to two decimal places.

(25) Find the intersection of the lines $y = -4x + 7$ and $y = 5x - 2$. The answer is **(1, 3)**. Set $-4x + 7 = 5x - 2$. Solving for *x*, you get $-9x = -9$ or $x = 1$. Substituting back into either equation, $y = 3$.

(26) Find the intersection of the lines $3x - y = 1$ and $x + 2y + 9 = 0$. The answer is $\boldsymbol{(-1, -4)}$. First write the equations in slope-intercept form. $3x - y = 1$ becomes $y = 3x - 1$ and $x + 2y + 9 = 0$ becomes $y = -\frac{1}{2}x - \frac{9}{2}$. Setting $3x - 1 = -\frac{1}{2}x - \frac{9}{2}$, you solve for *x* and get $\frac{7}{2}x = -\frac{7}{2}$ or $x = -1$. Substitute back into either equation to get $y = -4$.

27. Find the vertex and sketch the graph of $y = \frac{1}{2}(x-3)^2 - 2$. **Vertex: $(3, -2)$.**

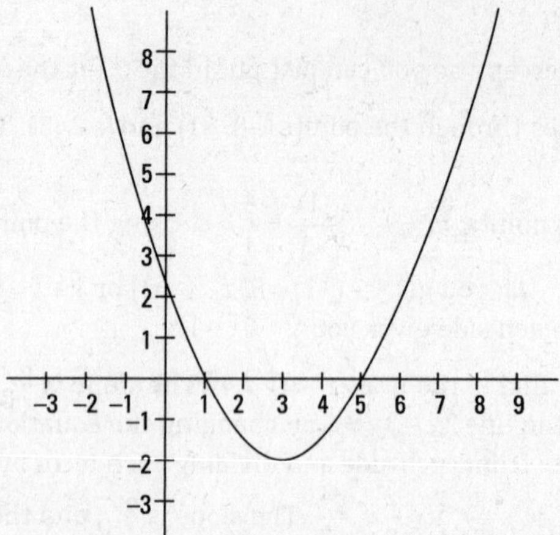

The multiplier of $\frac{1}{2}$ in front of the parentheses makes the graph open wider (more flat).

28. Find the vertex and sketch the graph of $y = 2(x+2)^2$. **Vertex: $(-2, 0)$.**

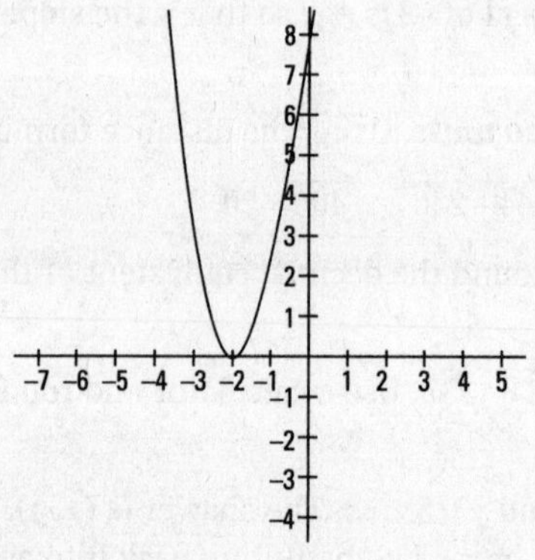

The vertex is on the x-axis. The multiplier of 2 makes the parabola steeper.

29. Find the center and radius and sketch the graph of $(x+3)^2+(y-4)^2=25$. **Center: $(-3,\ 4)$; radius: 5.**

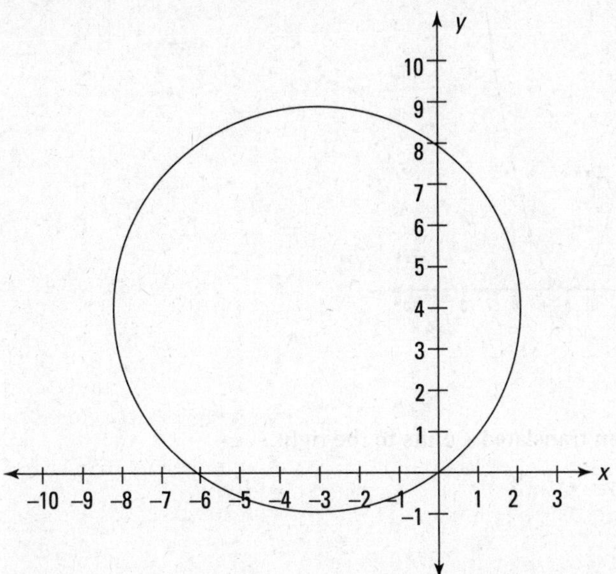

30. Find the center and radius and sketch the graph of $(x-5)^2+(y-2)^2=9$. **Center: (5, 2); radius: 3.**

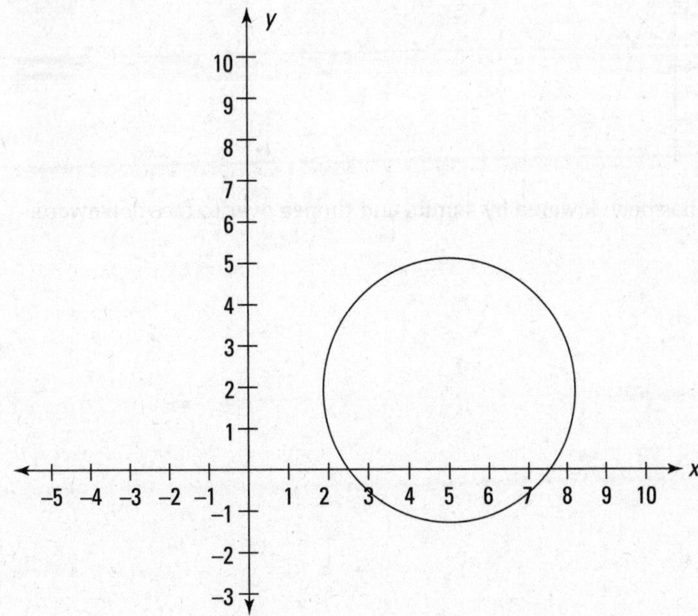

31. Sketch the graph of $y = (x-4)^2$.

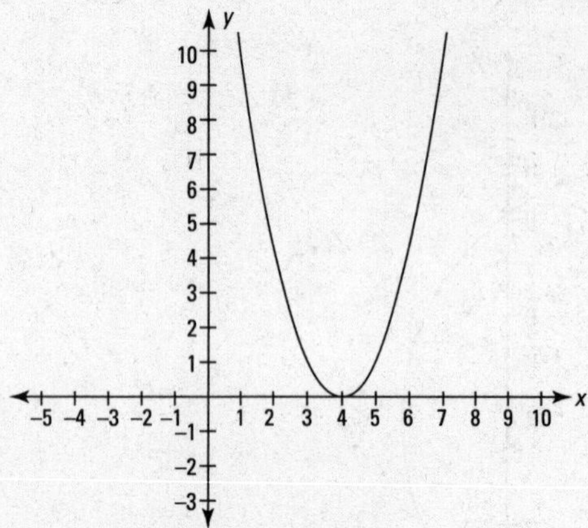

The parabola has been translated 4 units to the right.

32. Sketch the graph of $y = -x^2 - 3$.

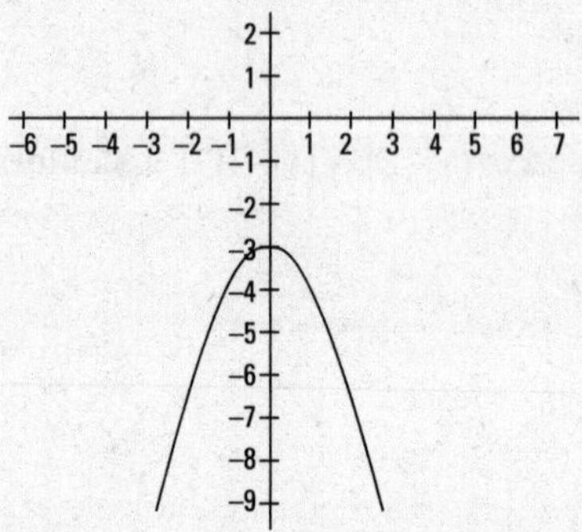

The parabola has been lowered by 3 units and flipped over to face downward.

5 The Part of Tens

IN THIS PART . . .

Discover ten common pitfalls or errors to avoid.

Gain ten quick tips to make your algebra problem solving a little easier.

Chapter **22**

Ten Common Errors That Get Noticed

Most of this book involves methods for correctly doing algebra procedures. When working in algebra, you want to take the positive approach. But sometimes it helps to point out the common errors or pitfalls that occur. Many of these slip-ups involve the negative sign, fractions, and/or exponents. Mistakes happen in algebra because people often think what they're doing works — or that two wrongs make it right! This chapter gives you a chance to spot some of those errors and sets you straight if you're making them yourself.

Squaring a Negative or Negative of a Square

The two expressions $-x^2$ and $(-x)^2$ are not the same (except in that single case where $x = 0$). For instance, let $x = -3$ and indicate which two of the following are *correct*.

A) If $x = -3$, then $-x^2 = 9$.

B) If $x = -3$, then $-x^2 = -9$.

C) If $x = -3$, then $(-x)^2 = 9$.

D) If $x = -3$, then $(-x)^2 = -9$.

Are your choices B and C? Then good for you! You remember the rules for *order of operations* (found in Chapter 6) where you perform all powers first, then multiplication or division, and then addition or subtraction. The parentheses always interrupt the order and tell you to perform whatever is inside first. So in the expression $-x^2$, if you let $x = -3$, you square the -3 first to get 9 and then find the opposite, making the final answer -9. In the expression $(-x)^2$, you would find the opposite of -3 first, giving you $+3$ in the parentheses, and then you'd square the 3 to get 9.

Squaring a Binomial

A *binomial* is two terms separated by addition or subtraction. Squaring a binomial involves more than just squaring each term; the terms also have to interact with one another.

Can you spot which expansion is correct below?

A) $(3x-4)^2 = 9x^2 - 24x + 16$ B) $(3x-4)^2 = 9x^2 - 16$

Of course, you chose A as the correct expansion. The most common error when doing these expansions is squaring the first and last term of the binomial and forgetting about the middle term.

The pattern for squaring a binomial is $(a+b)^2 = a^2 + 2ab + b^2$. When you square a binomial, remember that you're multiplying it times itself: $(a+b)^2 = (a+b)(a+b)$. You find the products of the first terms, the outer terms, the inner terms, and the last terms, and then add them up. The right way to expand is $(x+5)^2 = x^2 + 10x + 25$ or $(3y-2z)^2 = 9y^2 - 12yz + 4z^2$.

You can find more on squaring binomials in Chapter 7.

Operating on Radicals

The square root of a product is the product of the roots, and the square root of a quotient is the quotient of the roots, but this "reversal" doesn't apply when you have a sum or difference.

It's very helpful when you can simplify radicals — using the correct rules, of course. Which two of the following are correct?

A) $\dfrac{\sqrt{400}}{\sqrt{100}} = \sqrt{4}$ B) $\sqrt{2}\sqrt{18} = \sqrt{36}$

C) $\sqrt{3^2 + 4^2} = \sqrt{3^2} + \sqrt{4^2}$ D) $\sqrt{25} - \sqrt{16} = \sqrt{9}$

Had you going there, didn't I? But you spotted the fact that only A and B can be true. The rules that apply are $\sqrt{a}\sqrt{b}=\sqrt{ab}$ and $\frac{\sqrt{a}}{\sqrt{b}}=\sqrt{\frac{a}{b}}$. Finishing the simplifications of the four expressions:

A) $\frac{\sqrt{400}}{\sqrt{100}}=\sqrt{4}=2$

B) $\sqrt{2}\sqrt{18}=\sqrt{36}=6$

C)
$$\begin{aligned}\sqrt{3^2+4^2} &\neq \sqrt{3^2}+\sqrt{4^2}\\ \sqrt{9+16} &\neq \sqrt{9}+\sqrt{16}\\ \sqrt{25} &\neq 3+4\\ 5 &\neq 7\end{aligned}$$

D)
$$\begin{aligned}\sqrt{25}-\sqrt{16} &\neq \sqrt{9}\\ 5-4 &\neq 3\\ 1 &\neq 3\end{aligned}$$

Refer to Chapter 5 for more on working with radicals.

Distributing a Negative Throughout

Distributing a number by multiplying it times every term within parentheses is a fairly straightforward process. However, some people can't seem to finish the job. Can you spot the good algebra?

A) $-1(4-3x+2y)=-4-3x+2y$

B) $-1(4-3x+2y)=-4+3x-2y$

Of course, you chose B! The distributive property of multiplication over addition is $a(b+c)=ab+ac$. The pitfall or problem comes in when distributing a negative (the same as multiplying by -1) over terms. Often, people distribute -1 over the first term and not the rest. Remember to distribute the negative over every term. Basically, all the signs change. Chapter 2 has even more on the distribution rule.

Fracturing Fractions

A fraction line is like a grouping symbol. Everything in the *denominator* (bottom) divides into everything in the *numerator* (top). You need to remember that $\frac{a+b}{c}=\frac{a}{c}+\frac{b}{c}$. But this setup is too obvious. Why do people mess up with the fractions? Let me show you. Which of the following is correct?

A) $\frac{-8\pm\sqrt{3}}{4}=-2\pm\frac{\sqrt{3}}{4}$

B) $\frac{-8\pm\sqrt{3}}{4}=\frac{-\cancel{8}^{2}+\sqrt{3}}{\cancel{4}}=-2\pm\sqrt{3}$

Yes, I know that B looks much nicer, but it's wrong, wrong, wrong. The error in B is that the person broke up the fraction, putting the 4 under the –8 only.

Chapter 3 covers fractions completely.

Raising a Power to a Power

The rule for raising a power to a power is that you multiply the exponents. Sounds simple enough, but can you spot which of the following are correct?

A) $(3^2)^4 = 3^8$ B) $(4^{-3})^{-3} = 4^9$

C) $(3^x)^3 = 3^{3x}$ D) $(2^x)^{2x} = 2^{2x^2}$

You were looking for something wrong, weren't you? This time they're all correct. Applying the rule sounds easy, but putting variables or negative numbers in for the exponents can make things more complicated. In the end, you just multiply the exponents together.

Refer to Chapter 4 if you want to see more on exponents.

Making Negative Exponents Flip

The general rule for negative exponents is $a^{-n} = \frac{1}{a^n}$. Negative exponents are very handy when combining terms with the same base. A common pitfall is to forget about number multipliers when applying this rule. Which of the following is correct?

A) $3x^{-4} = \frac{3}{x^4}$ B) $\frac{1}{4x^3} = 4x^{-3}$

Okay. I made it too easy for you. Choice A is just fine, but choice B isn't correct. A common error is to mishandle the constant multiplier in the denominator. The correct way to write choice B is $\frac{1}{4}x^{-3}$ or $4^{-1}x^{-3}$.

Chapter 4 has more information on negative exponents.

Making Sense of Reversing the Sense

Because reversing the sense in an inequality doesn't come up as often as other maneuvers, people frequently overlook the process. The inequality $3 < 4$ is a true statement. When do you *reverse the sense* (switch the direction of the inequality sign)? When you multiply or divide each side by a negative number. Which of the two following manipulations is correct for multiplying each side of the inequality by –2?

A) Multiplying by –2, $-5 < 7 \rightarrow 10 > -14$

B) Multiplying by –2, $5 < 12 \rightarrow -10 > -24$

Choice A is correct. Remember that the smaller number is always to the left of a larger number on a number line.

Chapter 16 describes how to deal with inequalities.

Using the Slope Formula Correctly

You use the slope formula to determine the number that describes how steep a line is and whether it rises or falls. If you have two points, (x_1, y_1) and (x_2, y_2), then you find the slope of the line by using $m = \frac{y_2 - y_1}{x_2 - x_1}$. In Chapter 21, you find several cautions about using the formula correctly. See if you can spot the correct uses of the formula from the following choices. You're finding the slope of the line that goes through (3, 4) and (5, 6).

A) $m = \frac{6-4}{5-3}$

B) $m = \frac{5-3}{6-4}$

C) $m = \frac{6-4}{3-5}$

D) $m = \frac{4-6}{3-5}$

The line through those two points has a slope of 1, so the two correct uses are A and D. The error in choice B is that the *x* values are on top — a common mistake is reversing the *x*'s and *y*'s. The error in choice C is *mixing and matching*. You have to use the two coordinates of a single point in the same position — either both first or both last.

Writing Several Fractions as One

Fractions always cause groans and moans. They're one of the most unappreciated types of numbers. But handling them correctly helps them behave. When adding fractions, you find a common denominator and then add the numerators. See whether you can spot the correct additions.

A) $\frac{1}{2} + \frac{1}{3} + \frac{1}{5} = \frac{3}{10}$

B) $\frac{1}{x} + \frac{1}{y} + \frac{1}{z} = \frac{x+y+z}{xyz}$

C) $\frac{1}{8} + \frac{1}{9} = \frac{9+8}{72}$

D) $\frac{x}{y} + \frac{y}{x} = \frac{x^2 + y^2}{xy}$

This was probably too easy. You could see that A and B were terrible. In choice A, the common denominator is 30, not 10. And when you add the new numerators, you get $15 + 10 + 6 = 31$. Another hint that A is wrong is the fact that the answer $3/10$ is smaller than either of the first two fractions in the problem — not larger. Choice B is almost as bad. Just put in some numbers for *x*, *y*, and *z* if you want to just demonstrate that this is wrong, wrong, wrong.

Chapter **23**

Ten Quick Tips to Make Algebra a Breeze

Working in algebra is a lot like taking a driver's test. No matter what else you do, you need to know and follow all the rules. And just as you were given some hints about driving from your instructor, you find lots of helps here with your algebra. Buried in those lists of algebra rules are some maneuvers, procedures, and quick tricks that help ease the way. The helps may include eliminating fractions or decimals, or simplifying the setup or changing the form of an equation to make it ready to combine with other expressions.

This chapter offers you ten quick tips to make your experience with algebra a little easier and a little more efficient, and to improve your opportunities for success.

Flipping Proportions

A *proportion* is a true statement in which one fraction is set equal to another fraction. One property of a proportion is that *flipping* it doesn't change its truth. The rule is if $\frac{a}{b}=\frac{c}{d}$, then $\frac{b}{a}=\frac{d}{c}$. You find more on proportions in Chapter 12.

REMEMBER

Flip the proportion to put the variable in the numerator. Here's a situation where flipping makes the statement easier to solve. $\frac{8}{x+1}=\frac{1}{3}$ is a proportion. Now flip it to get the variable in the numerator: $\frac{x+1}{8}=\frac{3}{1}$. Multiplying each side by 8, you get $x+1=24$, or $x=23$. You'd get the same result by just cross-multiplying, but it's often handier to have the variable in the numerator of the fraction.

Multiplying Through to Get Rid of Fractions

As much fun as fractions are — we couldn't do without them — they're sometimes a nuisance when you're trying to solve for the value of a variable. A quick trick to make things easier is to multiply both sides of the equation by the same number. The choice of multiplier is the least common multiple — all the denominators divide it evenly. In the following example where I multiply each fraction by 12, see how easy it becomes.

REMEMBER

Multiply an equation by the least common factor to eliminate fractions.

$$\frac{x}{6}+\frac{2x-1}{3}=\frac{1}{4}\rightarrow 12\left(\frac{x}{6}\right)+12\left(\frac{2x-1}{3}\right)=12\left(\frac{1}{4}\right)$$

$$^{2}\cancel{12}\left(\frac{x}{6}\right)+{}^{4}\cancel{12}\left(\frac{2x-1}{3}\right)={}^{3}\cancel{12}\left(\frac{1}{4}\right)$$

$$2(x)+4(2x-1)=3(1)$$

$$2x+8x-4=3$$

$$10x=7, x=\frac{7}{10}$$

Zeroing In on Fractions

When you're solving an equation that involves a fraction set equal to 0, you only need to consider the fraction's numerator for a solution.

REMEMBER

When a fraction is equal to zero, only the numerator can be 0. For instance, $\frac{(x-2)(x+11)}{x^4(x+7)(x-9)(x+5)}=0$ has a solution only when the numerator equals 0. Solving $(x-2)(x+11)=0$, you find that the equation is true when $x=2$ or $x=-11$. These are the only two solutions. You can forget about the denominator for this type problem (as long as you don't choose a solution that makes the denominator equal to 0). Chapter 12 has more on rational equations.

Finding a Common Denominator

When adding or subtracting fractions, you always write the fractions with the same common denominator so you can add (or subtract) the numerators. (See Chapter 3 for more on fractions.)

REMEMBER

One way to find a common denominator is to divide the product of the denominators by their greatest common factor.

In the earlier section "Multiplying Through to Get Rid of Fractions," I provide a quick tip for multiplying through by a common denominator. Many times you can easily spot the common multiple. For example, when the denominators are 2, 3, and 6, you can see that they all divide 6 evenly — 6 is the common denominator. But what if you want to add $\frac{x}{24}+\frac{3x-5}{60}$? You'd like a common denominator that isn't any bigger than necessary. Just multiply the 24×60 to get 1,440, which is pretty large. Both 24 and 60 are divisible by 12, so divide the 1,440 by 12 to get 120, which is the least common denominator.

Dividing by 3 or 9

Reducing fractions makes them easier to work with. And the key to reducing fractions is recognizing common divisors of the numerator and denominator. For instance, do you know the common factor for the numerator and denominator in $\frac{171}{306}$? It's 9!

Now looking at $\frac{171}{306}$, you can divide both numerator and denominator by 9 to reduce the fraction and get $\frac{19}{34}$. There aren't any more common factors, so the fraction is reduced.

Dividing by 2, 4, or 8

The rules for determining whether a number is divisible by 2, 4, or 8 are quite different from the rules for divisibility by 3 and 9.

If a number ends in 0, 2, 4, 6, or 8 (it's an even number), the entire number is divisible by 2. The number 113,579,714 is divisible by 2, even though all the digits except the last are odd.

If the number formed by the last *two* digits of a number is divisible by 4, then the entire number is divisible by 4. The number 5,783,916 is divisible by 4 because the number formed by the last two digits, 16, is divisible by 4.

If the number formed by the last *three* digits of a number is divisible by 8, then the whole number is divisible by 8. The number 43,512,619,848 is divisible by 8, because the number formed by the last three digits, 848, is divisible by 8. You may run into some three-digit numbers that aren't so obviously divisible by 8. In that case, just do the long division on the last three digits. Dividing the three-digit number is still quicker than dividing the entire number.

Commuting Back and Forth

The *commutative law of addition and multiplication* says that you can add or multiply numbers in any order, and you'll get the same answer. This rule is especially useful when you couple it with the associative rule that allows you to regroup or reassociate numbers to make computations easier.

For instance, look at how I can rearrange the numbers to my advantage for doing computations:

$$9+27+11+3=9+11+27+3=(9+11)+(27+3)=20+30=50$$

$$9(8)(25)\left(\frac{5}{8}\right)\left(\frac{7}{9}\right)\left(\frac{1}{25}\right)=\left[8\left(\frac{5}{8}\right)\right]\left[9\left(\frac{7}{9}\right)\right]\left[25\left(\frac{1}{25}\right)\right]=(5)(7)(1)=35$$

Factoring Quadratics

A quadratic expression has a general format of ax^2+bx+c, and you frequently find it more useful to change that format and factor the quadratic into the product of two binomials. For example, the quadratic $12x^2+11x-15$ factors into $(4x-3)(3x+5)$. In the factored form, you can solve for what makes the expression equal to zero or you can factor if the expression is in a fraction.

REMEMBER

To factor a quadratic expression efficiently, list the possible factors and cross them out as you eliminate the combinations that don't work.

Make a list (and check it twice) of the multipliers of the lead coefficient (the a) and the constant (the c); you combine the factors to produce the middle coefficient (the b).

In the quadratic $12x^2+11x-15$, you list the multipliers of 12, which are 12×1, 6×2, 4×3, and list the multipliers of 15, which are 15×1, 5×3. You then choose a pair from the multipliers of 12 and a pair from the multipliers of 15 that give you a difference of 11 when you multiply them together.

Making Radicals Less Rad, Baby

Radicals are symbols that indicate an operation. Whatever is inside the radical has the root operation performed on it. Many times, though, writing the radical expressions with exponents instead of radicals is more convenient — especially when you want to combine several terms or factors with the same variable under different radicals.

REMEMBER

The general rule for changing from radical form to exponential form is $\sqrt[b]{x^a}=x^{a/b}$.

For instance, to multiply $\left(\sqrt{y}\right)\left(\sqrt[3]{y}\right)\left(\sqrt[5]{y^2}\right)$, you change it to $y^{1/2}y^{1/3}y^{2/5}$. Now you can multiply the factors together by adding the exponents. Of course, you need to change the fractions so they have a common denominator, but the result is worth the trouble: $y^{1/2}y^{1/3}y^{2/5}=y^{15/30}y^{10/30}y^{12/30}=y^{37/30}$.

Applying Acronyms

Some of the easiest ways of remembering mathematical processes is to attach cutesy acronyms to them to help ease the way. For example:

- **FOIL (First, Outer, Inner, Last):** FOIL is used to help you remember the different combinations of products that are necessary when multiplying two binomials together.
- **NOPE (Negative, Odd, Positive, Even):** NOPE tells you that a product is negative when you have an odd number of negative signs and it's positive when the number of negative signs is even.
- **PEMDAS (Please Excuse My Dear Aunt Sally):** When simplifying expressions that have various operations and grouping symbols, you first simplify in Parentheses, then Exponents, then Multiplication or Division, and then Addition or Subtraction.

Index

A

B

C

D

E

F

G

H

I

L

M

N

O

P

Q

R

S

T

U

V

W

About the Author

Mary Jane Sterling is the author of *Algebra I For Dummies*, 2nd Edition, *Trigonometry For Dummies*, *Algebra II For Dummies*, *Math Word Problems For Dummies*, *Business Math For Dummies*, and *Linear Algebra For Dummies* (all published by Wiley). She taught junior high and high school math for many years before beginning her current 30-years-and-counting tenure at Bradley University in Peoria, Illinois. Mary Jane especially enjoys working with future teachers and trying out new technology.

Dedication

This book is dedicated to my parents. My father, Tom Mackie, always encouraged me to pursue my interests in mathematics and science — at a time when girls were encouraged to study home economics. My mother, Jane Mackie, was a woman before her time — stepping out into the world when it wasn't all that fashionable for women to do so. And at 84 years old, she proudly announced that she had read *Algebra For Dummies* from beginning to end and understood it!

Author's Acknowledgments

I'd like to thank Chrissy Guthrie for taking care of all those nitty-gritty details, as well as the big issues. A big thanks also goes to the technical editor Amy Nicklin, who didn't let me get away with any slips or missteps. Also, thanks to Lindsay Lefevere for providing another project — lest I sit around, twiddling my thumbs.

Publisher's Acknowledgments

Executive Editor: Lindsay Sandman Lefevere
Editorial Project Manager: Christina Guthrie
Copy Editor: Christina Guthrie
Technical Editor: Amy Nicklin
Production Editor: Siddique Shaik
Cover Photo: ©Jason Edwards/Getty Images